Eliza Lucas Pinckney

Eliza Lucas Pinckney

AN INDEPENDENT WOMAN IN THE AGE OF REVOLUTION

Lorri Glover

Yale UNIVERSITY PRESS
New Haven & London

Published with assistance from the Annie Burr Lewis Fund.

Yale University Press books may be purchased in quantity for educational, business, or promotional use. For information, please e-mail sales.press@yale.edu (U.S. office) or sales@yaleup.co.uk (U.K. office).

Set in Adobe Garamond type by IDS Infotech Ltd., Chandigarh, India.
Printed in the United States of America.

Library of Congress Control Number: 2019953009
ISBN 978-0-300-23611-8 (hardcover : alk. paper)

A catalogue record for this book is available from the British Library.

This paper meets the requirements of ANSI/NISO Z39.48-1992 (Permanence of Paper).

10 9 8 7 6 5 4 3 2 1

Contents

Acknowledgments

I've been so lucky with this project from start to finish. In 2013 Sarah Case, managing editor at the *Public Historian*, asked me to review a new digital project, *The Papers of Eliza Lucas Pinckney and Harriott Pinckney Horry*. I found it outstanding in every regard, and at the close of the review wrote that Constance B. Schulz and her team had created a superb resource to inspire future biographers. I was deep into another project then, with no thoughts of writing about Eliza Lucas Pinckney, but life takes its turns. In spring 2019, Adina Popescu Berk, senior editor at Yale University Press, read an earlier draft of this book with unsurpassed care and precision and guided me toward completion. Between the first idea and the last pass, I've enjoyed countless adventures and been encouraged, advised, corrected, and inspired by a host of fellow travelers. Dan Smith shared and celebrated it all. We walked and talked about Eliza for hundreds of miles, he read endless pages, sometimes while I stood over him, and he even secured the art permissions. Lucky.

Ami Pflugrad-Jackisch and Craig Thompson Friend read each chapter draft and over several years of deep conversations offered more encouragement and wisdom than I can recount. I have learned so much, about writing, history, and kindness, from these, my treasured friends. Ami even trekked with me across London one December to visit the sites of Eliza's homes. Connie Schulz was unfailingly supportive and generously shared her boundless insights into the Pinckney family. I cannot capture my gratitude for her work, her encouragement, and her inspiration. She and Mary Sherrer both read a draft of the biography, sharpening my ideas and correcting my mistakes. The Women's and Gender Studies Research Group at Saint Louis University read and discussed all the chapters, too, keeping me on track. Matt Schoenbachler urged me along when I was doubtful, read excerpts, and fixed a wobbly introduction. My history colleagues and wonderful friends Jen Popiel and Torrie Hester read drafts, shared their own work, and generally inspired me with their examples of excellence. I benefited greatly from a fellowship with the Fred W. Smith National Library for the Study of George Washington at Mount Vernon, which offered the most precious commodity—time—in a glorious setting with first-rate staff and an incomparable intellectual community.

I continue to be amazed by how many smart and busy people will take time to talk about research, answer arcane questions, discuss museum treasures and archival holdings, read book chapters, and generously share their time and expertise with a stranger. As I result, I've encountered many wonderful people and enjoyed many happy days while working on this book. I met Christine Klepper at the Batmobile before she took me through the fourth floor of the National Museum of American History to see Eliza's yellow dress. When I arrived at the Charleston Museum, Jan Hiester had laid out artifacts of Eliza's life: her bed canopy, her salmon-colored dress, and her blue shoes. Douglas Luery drove me across (very) rough farm roads into the interior of Antigua to point out the locations of Lucas properties. Anne and Bill Williams showed me around the grounds of Ripley House, in Ripley, England, where Eliza lived in the 1750s. Emma Hart met me at a coffee shop in Edinburgh to talk about eighteenth-century Charleston. Agnes Meeker shared her knowledge about Antiguan history over lunch outside St. John's and then took me on an impromptu tour of sugar mills. Chris Phillips took time from his own research to track down information about Eliza's possible burial site in Philadelphia. Mary Jo Fairchild and Virginia Ellison welcomed me to the Special Collections and Archives at the College of Charleston Addlestone Library and Mary Jo Fairchild answered questions long after I'd gone. Rachel Monroy, with *The Papers of the Revolutionary Era Pinckney Statesmen*, read a draft chapter and offered perceptive advice. Karen Anadol corresponded about indigo dye. Anne Boylan allowed me to read her work in progress about radio shows, including two featuring Eliza. Nicholas Butler and Carter Hudgins shared their deep expertise regarding early South Carolina. The anonymous readers at Yale

University Press provided excellent recommendations for which I am exceedingly grateful.

Friends and colleagues have been incredibly generous. Geri Thoma found Eliza an ideal home with Yale, and I am deeply appreciative of her connecting me with Adina Berk, editor extraordinaire. Ivy Farr McIntyre and Sandy Slater opened doors in Charleston that aided my research and then talked about Eliza over delightful dinners. Steven Smith diagnosed ailments across three centuries. Samantha Snyder shared her expertise on Philadelphia and read excerpts. Jeff Smith introduced me to Carol Yaster, who in turn connected me to the staff of the St. Peter's Church archives in Philadelphia; then Jen Popiel introduced me to Chris Phillips, who visited the archives on my behalf: an example of how lucky I've been. I benefited from conversations and received encouragement from Gretchen Arnold, Arline Cravens, Christy Fry, David Hildebrand, Georgia Johnston, Evelyn Meyer, Rowena McClinton, Collen McClusky, Cookie and John Muntges, Chris and Tim O'Neil, Robert Paulett, Pascale Perraudin, Elisabeth Perry, Annie Smart, Jeff Smith, Kris Smith, Lucy Smith, and Eleonore Stump. Charlene Boyer-Lewis, Catherine Clinton, Anya Jabour, Cindy Kierner, Martha King, Becca Sharpless, and Megan Taylor-Shockley provided encouragement and inspiration. I work in a department filled with superb scholars who make me better by example, including Doug Boin, Flannery Burke, Phil Gavitt, Torrie Hester, Katrina Moore, George Ndege, Hal Parker, Jen Popiel, Mark Ruff, and Silvana Siddali. Saint Louis University foolishly let one of the best go: Stefan Bradley inspires from afar these days. Support from the College of Arts and Sciences at SLU and especially Dean Chris Duncan enabled me to complete this book. Idolina Hernandez, Sam Klee, Molly Lackey, Nicholas DiPucchio, and Bryan Winston provided invaluable research assistance: checking citations, running down obscure references, and proofreading. Dan Heaton, senior manuscript editor at Yale University Press, is the kind of copyeditor every writer wants: meticulous, encouraging, and deeply engaged with the book. I'm sure I've managed to retain errors, despite all their valiant efforts.

I shared parts of this project at the Southern Historical Association, the European Early American Studies Association, the Sons of the American Revolution Conference, and the Southern Association for Women Historians, and benefited from insightful commentary from Cindy Kierner, Maurizio Valsania, Holly Mayer, Christine Sears, and Ben Marsh. I tried out ideas in talks at the University of Toledo and Mount Vernon, and I was lucky enough to discuss early findings at the Newberry Library Seminar on Gender and

Sexuality, the Zuckerman Seminar in Philadelphia, and the Providence College Seminar on the History of Early America. Michael Zuckerman, Zara Anishanslin, Thomas Balcerski, Adrian Weimer, and Ted Andrews provided advice that shaped how this book unfolded. As Lawrence Nelson taught me thirty years ago, I have tried to be a good steward of my time and talents and to faithfully, intellectually write the life of Eliza Lucas Pinckney.

Eliza Lucas Pinckney

Introduction

In the early spring of 1742, a comet blazed across the South Carolina night sky. The ever-inquisitive nineteen-year-old Eliza Lucas knew it was coming—for weeks, newspapers had tracked its path—and she got up in the middle of the night to watch for it. Eliza was adventurous by nature and boundlessly curious about the world, not one to let such a unique opportunity pass her by. Remarkably cosmopolitan for her age, she had already crisscrossed the Atlantic Ocean and studied the heavens from her family's homes in the southern Caribbean, Europe, and North America. But Eliza had never seen anything like the comet. Her good friend Mary Bartlett lived nearby, but she did not share Eliza's zeal for wee-hours stargazing. Unable to rouse herself from sleep, Mary asked Eliza for a report. Eliza tried to explain the spectacular event, but the comet defied description. It was too bad, Eliza teased Mary, that "your curiosity has not been strong enough to raise you out of your bed." The two friends also laughed about superstitious people who feared that comets carried souls. Mary jokingly asked whether Eliza thought the comet a man or woman, and Eliza offered a witty reply. The comet made a "modest appearance" in the predawn hours, which prevented "every Idle gazer" from seeing "its splendour." Eliza could only conclude that the comet must be female. "Besides," she added, dropping the humor, "if it is any mortal transformd to this glorious luminary why not a woman."[1]

"Why not a woman?" was an audacious thing to ask in 1742. Everything in Eliza Lucas's world centered on hierarchy. Women were always supposed to be subordinate to men, just as children were to parents, and the enslaved to the enslavers. Laws decreed it, families modeled it, communities monitored it, and ministers preached that God ordained it. But Eliza was leading a life that invited just that question. "I hardly allow my self time to Eat or sleep," she explained, because "I am so busey in providing for Posterity."[2]

By the spring of 1742, Eliza Lucas had been "providing for Posterity" for nearly three years. In 1739, her family relocated from Antigua to South Carolina. But within weeks of the move, the British army recalled her father to military service in the Caribbean, into yet another war between European powers competing to carve up the Americas. Eliza's mother was in poor health and sometimes bedfast. There was only one choice: Eliza had to take charge of the Lucas family's three Lowcountry plantations. She was tentative at first, but also resolved. She sent her absent, anxious father careful reports on all her activities, reassuring him—and no doubt herself—that she was up to the considerable task before her.

Weeks turned into months and then years. Eliza proved herself an exceptionally skillful planter and a savvy businesswoman. The plantations prospered under her management, and she marketed to Great Britain and the Caribbean the commodities enslaved people produced on those estates. Eliza also ran the Lucas household, tutored her younger sister, tended to her ailing mother, kept up the family reputation through an active social life, and experimented with crops to diversify her commercial interests and to ensure her family's long-term wealth. She even started serving as a lay lawyer for several of her neighbors, who respected and trusted her. She became, in short, a model eighteenth-century planter-patriarch. Though a woman, Eliza acted well the part: she took care of her family, exercised racial power, enjoyed community respect, supervised a thriving plantation enterprise, and safeguarded the Lucas patrimony. Cast in that unlikely role when hardly more than a girl, Eliza Lucas reflected on her life with a mix of pride and fatigue: "I shall begin to think myself an old woman before I am well a young one having these weighty affairs upon my hands."[3]

She decided she liked the weighty affairs, commercial planting in particular. She was drawn to botany and entrepreneurial experiments—she called them her "schemes." Her work in indigo production while in her early twenties transformed her adopted home of South Carolina. No one today uses indigo, but in the colonial world the dye created from the plants was in high demand and very profitable. Eliza helped indigo to thrive in the Carolina Lowcountry, turning huge profits for the colony and paying high dividends for England. Thanks to the (often-distorted) story of her indigo experiments, Eliza became—and remained—famous. Family members wrote hagiographic accounts of her in the nineteenth century, and in the twentieth and twenty-first centuries she inspired novels and plays and children's books, and toy designers turned her into a doll. Eliza Lucas was even featured in a mid-twentieth-century radio drama, played by Gene Tierney.[4]

Across nearly three centuries, we know of Eliza's wonder as she searched the heavens for a comet in the spring of 1742, her indigo experiments, the burdens she endured, and the adventures she relished, because starting in 1739 she began a decades-long project of writing about her life. She liked the idea of keeping a record for posterity, and she often wrote late into the night. She cut short one letter to a friend, explaining, "The morn approaches and my drowsiness calls me to rest."[5] It was an unusual thing for a young woman to do. Copying and preserving letters was primarily the business of men in the eighteenth century: planters, slave traders, merchants, and political leaders immersed in Atlantic-wide networks. They needed copies of their letters in case they were lost at sea or disputed in courts of law. Eliza, the young female planter-patriarch, followed suit. Over time, her writings, like her life, took varied twists and turns. Deeply religious though independent-minded about her faith, she crafted personal prayers, a litany to start each day, to set herself on the right track. As she aged, she marked the passage of years by anniversaries she chose to commemorate: not just predictable ones such as her wedding and the births of her children, but also days that were meaningful to her alone, including the day she survived a hurricane that nearly swept away her whole family. Eliza spent those days "in devotion and meditation on the goodness of God to me and mine." Her introspection sometimes gave way to self-criticism. Strong enough to admit her weaknesses, she didn't edit her shortcomings out of the record of her life. The result: the most expansive and revealing record of any woman in the colonial South, allowing Eliza to step out of obscurity and into history.[6]

What a life she led. Eliza pursued the kind of extensive and wide-ranging formal education denied to most girls of her time. Her parents sent her to London when she was barely ten years old, and she spent five years in school there. The men in her family, first her father and then her husband and later her grown sons, respected her abilities and her judgment. None of them stood in the way of her accomplishments. She lived most of her life as an independent woman. Sometimes she sought out that independence, and sometimes it was foisted upon her by family crises, wars, and death. By the time of the American Revolution—which she found a terrifying ordeal—Eliza had been independent and pursuing her definition of happiness for decades.

Providing for posterity was the one constant in her life. As the years carried Eliza Lucas (later Pinckney) from daughter to wife to mother to grandmother, she kept her focus fixed on her family, determined to create a legacy to endure across generations. She spent decades searching for, building, and too often reluctantly leaving a place to call home. Her family both drove her quest and complicated it as she traveled around the Atlantic. Violence and conflict shadowed her: slavery and resultant uprisings, social turmoil, and war after war after war, including the often celebrated but decidedly brutal War for American Independence. Sometimes Eliza perpetrated the violence, sometimes she witnessed it, sometimes she fled.

Hers was a life, like most, of fits and starts, of inconsistencies and ironies. A devout Christian and given to contemplation, Eliza habitually scrutinized her ethics and her piety. Was she spending her time wisely? Honorably meeting her obligations? Living a Christian life? But she could not seem to see and certainly never pondered the sinfulness of slaveholding. Eliza exploited hundreds of black women and men who struggled to protect their own families under unspeakable cruelties and relentless violence unleashed by and to benefit the Lucases and the Pinckneys. Eliza ignored every moral outcry she heard: from individuals she enslaved, from radicalized evangelicals in the 1740s, from a growing chorus of revolutionaries in the 1770s, from vigorous political debates about the character of the American Republic in the 1780s and 1790s.

Eliza's long, fascinating, messy life was both bound by convention and thoroughly remarkable. She was a devoted mother to her three children. She built her life around them, insisting that they represented "all the happiness I have or desire upon Earth." But her youngest child, Thomas, grew up an ocean away from her. She left him in England shortly before he turned eight, and they did not reunite until he was twenty-one. Eliza married the love of her life and they shared an unusually happy union, but only for fourteen years. Once widowed, she never considered remarrying. She spent the first half of her life crisscrossing the Atlantic and then didn't leave South Carolina for thirty-five years. Studiously, self-consciously English until middle age, she became, under the impetus of the Revolutionary War, an American patriot. When Eliza Lucas Pinckney died, she had been a consummate planter-patriarch for nearly fifty years. Her contemporaries eulogized her as an "all accomplished lady."[7]

Readers drawn to historical biographies and studies of the Age of Revolution can be forgiven for assuming that the eighteenth century was a man's world. The ostensibly important stories, of empires expanded and thwarted, of wars waged and republics created, usually center on the ambitions and the audacity of powerful men: George III, Louis XVI, George Washington, Toussaint Louverture, the Marquis de Lafayette, Thomas Jefferson. American Revolutionaries made sure that future generations knew all about their exploits. Men such as Washington, Jefferson, and James Madison carefully preserved their writings, as an intentional legacy for themselves and for posterity. They wanted their editorial projects, begun in their own lifetimes and later supervised by their relatives, to create a national narrative: a story of the birth—and the birthright—of the United States. Early-nineteenth-century writers embraced these men, inventing a new American tradition of didactic biography by embellishing their life stories with apocryphal tales invented to instruct citizens in the young country.[8] When professional, academic historical scholarship emerged in the late nineteenth century, it prioritized the nation-state. The thousands upon thousands of letters alongside essays, travel journals, treatises, account books, and so on left by the "Founding Fathers" offered exquisite and abundant source material. The silences in these records, including the near absence of any personal introspection in the cases of many men, did not deter generations of historians and biographers. It was experiences on battlefields and in legislative halls that mattered, anyway.

Or was it? Men might have controlled political officeholding in the eighteenth century, but women managed families, and family—not politics—was the center of society. "No pleasure," Eliza Lucas Pinckney decided in her sixtieth year, "can equal that which a mother feels when she knows her children have acted their part well through life." She raised extraordinary children. Her daughter, Harriott Pinckney Horry, ran the family's vast and lucrative estates every bit as well as her mother and by the 1790s was perhaps the richest planter in the state of South Carolina. Eliza's two sons served as the young country's top diplomats in the two most important foreign capitals: Charles Cotesworth Pinckney in Paris and Thomas Pinckney in London. Women like

Eliza also played a central role in defining their family's social rank. Elites looked to women more than men to determine which families were elegant, educated, cosmopolitan, and worthy of inclusion in gentry ranks. And more often than we have appreciated, women ran complex estates and businesses—as Eliza did—adeptly, proudly, independently.[9]

This biography is the story of a woman's life—a rare thing for the eighteenth century. Books about Eliza Lucas Pinckney's contemporaries, women such as Abigail Adams, Mercy Otis Warren, Martha Washington, Jane Franklin Mecom, and Martha Jefferson Randolph, frequently turn into dual biographies of the women and the more powerful and more prolific men in their lives. Relationships with her father, her husband, and her sons mattered to Eliza, too. But she led her family and ran her estate almost entirely on her own, outside the shadow and beyond the direction of any man. When she turned forty, she said something few women at the time—or men, for that matter—could say: "I live agreeable enough to my own taste." Quite apart from the political and philosophical transformations of the late eighteenth century, she had become her own woman: independent. Still, her life unfolded across the eighteenth century, with social, political, and cultural values that she did not, perhaps could not escape. Eliza reflected the eighteenth century even when she refracted it.[10]

Through Eliza's eyes, we can see the tumultuous unfolding of the Age of Revolution: the imperial competition, the Enlightenment, the wars waged to create republics in a monarchical world. We can see, too, that world from a point of view that privileges a woman's values and priorities and experiences, which did not track with the traditional male-centered story of the Revolutionary era. Eliza's ordinary, extraordinary story calls into question fundamental assumptions about the eighteenth century, especially regarding the place and power of women and the possibility of a woman blazing her own trail.

The girl, studying the night sky, asked the question, "Why not a woman?" Her life offered the answer.

PART ONE

Antiguan Beginnings

CHAPTER I

Born to Privilege

Fortune favored her entry into the world. She was born white, in an English colony in the Caribbean Sea, where the great majority of babies were black and condemned to a life of enslavement before they drew their first breath. Her relatives were rich and powerful, perched at the top of colonial society, where rank was rigid and respect inheritable. Even the season of her birth was lucky: born in December 1722, she avoided the summertime sicknesses that claimed many infants, and she thrived.

The baby's father, George Lucas, gave her a favorite family name: Elizabeth. He liked to call her Betsey, but the name that stuck, the one she came to prefer, was Eliza.

Eliza Lucas grew up exploring the central valley of Antigua, where her affluent family relished the comforts of life on their verdant, expansive estate. George Lucas had inherited the 380-acre property that sat in the beautiful, windswept countryside, northwest of Willoughby Bay. The Lucas home looked out on the Shekerley Mountains—tall hills, really—and a stunning vista of lush greens as far as the eye could see, dotted here and there with gray stone windmills, bleached in the sun, that powered the island's lucrative sugar works. Through a cut in the hills, they could see all the way to the Atlantic Ocean, turquoise surf giving way to a deep blue sea, meeting the sky on the distant horizon. George Lucas devoted his young adulthood to expanding this estate, eventually amassing more than five hundred acres of farmland on the small Caribbean island. He bought lots and a house in the capital city of St. John's, too, and investment property on the North American mainland—a fortune surpassed by no more than two dozen Antiguans.[1] Rich families like the Lucases lived in two-story houses, designed to capture both Caribbean breezes and the style of English gentry. Antigua had no craftsmen capable of duplicating English wares, so the Lucases would have appointed their homes—the town house and the country estate—with imported furniture, rugs, dishes, and bedding. George Lucas's wealth and family name set him on the fast track for political power. By the time Eliza was born, he had already been elected speaker of the Antigua Assembly. He was well known and widely respected, both on Antigua and among influential men in England, as "a very worthy character and heir to one of the best estates in Antegoa."[2]

When Eliza's father walked her through the streets of St. John's, gentlemen doffed their caps, laborers stepped aside, enslaved people averted their eyes. She could have retained no memories from her childhood absent such displays of her family's prominence.

She must have been very young, too, when she noticed how much paler her skin was than most children's. Enslaved Antiguans outnumbered white Antiguans almost five to one when Eliza was a little girl, and the ratio skewed more over time. Even within the white minority, she stood out. Her clothes, imported from London, were more expensive than those of most other white girls and boys. Children notice such things, and they act on their noticing.

Skin color granted Eliza extraordinary authority, even as a child. Her father enslaved more than two hundred laborers. Her family's reliance on slavery was intimate and ubiquitous. Enslaved women almost certainly helped deliver Eliza, theirs among the first faces she saw. They got up with her when she cried in the night, bathed and swaddled her, and probably nursed her. As she grew, they prepared her meals, laid out her clothes, cleaned up her messes. While she played, black girls her age worked in shabby clothes and no shoes. They knew to respond if she wanted an errand or a playmate, to obey her whims, to interact only and always on Eliza's terms.[3]

Before she knew the words to express it, Eliza Lucas would have felt the racial power fixed on her at birth. She would not have been shielded from the systemic brutalization inflicted on enslaved people in Antigua's sugar fields and plantation households. Violence was elemental to slaveholding, and colonial-era planters were unashamed. The surviving records of planters lay bare their cavalier cruelty: they recorded whipping and branding, starving and mutilating enslaved black people with no more emotion than when they compiled farm inventories. Leaders in colonial governments gradually codified racial hierarchy and violence, granting white people dominion over the bodies and fates of black people. And planters instilled that mastery in their children. There was, Eliza came to see, no tension between violence and ladylike behavior.[4]

In the intimacy of her family, Eliza held another sort of authority, for she was the eldest of four siblings. The older of her brothers was given their father's name. The next child was named in honor of George's late brother, Thomas. The youngest, the family called Polly. In the universal rules of siblings, big sister Eliza was the self-appointed leader of George, Tommy, and Polly, their role model, sometimes their caregiver, and occasionally their tyrant.

Ann Mildrum was the mother of the three youngest Lucas children, but it is unclear whether she was Eliza's biological mother. Eliza referred to Ann as her "Mama," but there are no records confirming the identity of Eliza's mother. Ann's relationship with George was complicated, too. When George Lucas Jr. was baptized in St. John's Church in 1725, the parish records described him as "the son of George Lucas and Ann Mildrum his Curtizan [courtesan]." Thomas, born in 1727, was listed as "the Son of George Lucas by Ann Mildrom." The vague phrasing was unusual: normally parish records explicitly listed children as descended from a man and his wife. In the Lucas/Mildrum case, the sources are frustratingly silent about what exactly it meant that Ann Mildrum was George Lucas's courtesan and that she did not share his last name. They clearly were not married in the 1720s, at least not to the satisfaction of local officials. But they were in a long-term, committed relationship. Sometimes men abandoned their wives in the Caribbean, moving on to the next island and the next family. And some husbands were abusive. If Ann had married such a man and been unable to divorce him, she could not have lawfully married George. Perhaps Ann was not an Anglican and so denied a church-recognized marriage. Or parish officials might have doubted her whiteness; they would not have knowingly affirmed an interracial union. Whatever the circumstance, the larger community did not seem to hold the nature of their match against George and Ann; it didn't hurt their social standing or his political career. And regardless of the genetics, Eliza loved Ann and thought of her as her mother. She never mentioned anything about Ann's place in the family tree. Perhaps she never knew. What cause would a child, raised in a loving household, have to examine a parish record?[5]

Eliza's parents made sure she and her younger brothers and sister led privileged and genteel lives. The family's values blended the traditions of England's landed gentry with those of colonial planter elites. Eliza was adored and indulged, by her father in particular. She grew up, she said, always enjoying "paternal tenderness" from "the most Indulgent of Parents." George told Eliza she was special, because she was smart and because she was a Lucas. Family, Eliza learned, should be the center of life: the source of identity and the motivation for achievement. "I hope heaven will always direct me," she proclaimed, "that I may never disappoint" her family's high expectations.[6]

The Lucas family's history in Antigua was almost as old as the colony itself. Antigua is part of the Lesser Antilles, which the English called the Leeward Islands. Along with Nevis, St. Christopher (sometimes called St. Kitts), Montserrat, and Barbuda, Antigua formed from a chain of underwater mountains rising out of the ocean at twenty- to thirty-mile intervals. Antigua is small, just 108 square miles. The Shekerley Mountains rise along the southwest, giving way to rolling hills around the coastline. Antigua lacked natural rivers or streams, and it received less rainfall that its more mountainous neighbors. But the island had a wide and fertile central plain. Three generations of Lucases made their principal home there, on the plantation they called Cabbage Tree.[7]

Antigua was claimed by the English in the early seventeenth century. The first settlers, who arrived in 1632, were unwelcome, and Native Americans fiercely contested the intrusion. But as repeatedly happened in the New World, colonizers, abetted by germs and guns and often ruthless disregard for Indigenous lives, eventually prevailed. The decimation of the Caribs did not, however, give the English colonists firm control over the island. Sailors and soldiers, commanded by rival European powers, and privateers and pirates, working for their own advantages while loosely allied with these competing governments, fought across the Caribbean in the seventeenth century. It must have felt to the few hundred souls living in seventeenth-century Antigua that sovereignty shifted as unpredictably as the Caribbean winds. On the other hand, two highly addictive crops thrived in the tropical climate: tobacco and sugar. Despite the shaky hold that England asserted over Antigua, daring and ambitious (and sometimes desperate) people wagered their lives against the chance for landownership and wealth.[8]

The Lucas family story began in this dangerous and alluring Caribbean gamble. John Lucas, Eliza's grandfather, started accumulating his Antiguan estate in the 1660s. The outpost was still relatively new then and still decidedly

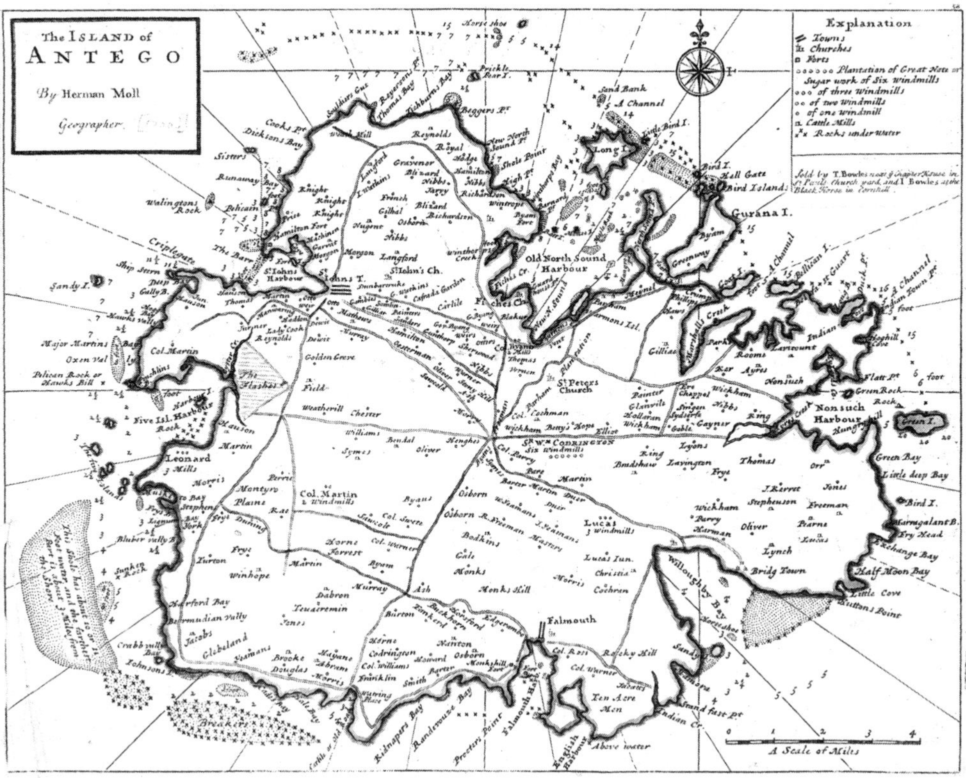

Figure 1. Herman Moll, "The Island of Antego," c. 1732. The map marks three windmills on the Lucas property north of Willoughby Bay. Harvard Map Collection, Harvard Library.

unstable. One of John Lucas's contemporaries told a friend that he had left Suriname for Antigua, "where I am hewing a new fortune out of the wild woods." John managed to survive those "wild woods" despite the diseases, natural disasters, and political violence that afflicted seventeenth-century Antigua. He persevered, amassing land in the countryside and St. John's.[9]

St. John's is perched on a northwest bay of the island, with ready access to the sea, the lifeblood of Antigua's economy. Settlers built a small wooden church in 1681, which they also named St. John's. Antigua's colonial legislature began meeting in town, and by the 1680s, St. John's emerged as the political center for all the Leeward Islands. Each of the Leeward Islands controlled its own assembly, but a royally appointed governor headed the central government. Antigua became the seat of that government and most governors kept a residence in St. John's. By the end of the seventeenth century, English colonizers had laid out the town's streets on the tidy grid pattern they always favored, with government offices in the center, a burial ground on the northwest boundary, and publicly maintained ponds to the south, for when water supplies ran low. The fortified harbor bustled with commerce tying Antiguans to Africa, Europe, and North America.[10]

As a little girl, Eliza would have listened to stories of her grandfather's adventures and his role in building Antigua, stories meant to inspire pride and emulation. How often did she and her siblings hear about their Grandfather John's exploits as speaker of the Antigua Assembly, when he stood up to the most powerful man in the Leeward Islands? Royally appointed governors often tussled with locally elected colonial legislators, but John Lucas's feud with Governor Christopher Codrington got especially nasty. Frustrated with the high-handed dealings of the governor, John wrote the Council of Trade and Plantations in London (sometimes called the Board of Trade) in the summer of 1697 to inform members "of several great mismanagements, abuses, violences, oppressions and obstructions of justice" Codrington had committed. As soon as Governor Codrington learned of John's action, he made John his sworn enemy and "contrived all ways of revenge." Allies of the governor assaulted Lucas in St. John's. And the governor himself threatened—in front of the legislature, no less—"to break my head, calling me villain and rascal." John refused to back down, and the governor ordered him imprisoned. "I am a loyal man," he insisted from jail, "and never was guilty of anything but assertion of the liberty of the subject." Codrington threatened everything Lucas valued: his reputation, his wealth, and his family's well-being. In the middle of the prison ordeal, one of John's two sons died. Governor Codrington refused to let him attend the burial. Nothing, not the imprisonment, the losses to his estate, even his son's death, broke John Lucas's will. From a jail cell in St. John's he sought—and won—reelection to the Antigua Assembly. As he proudly reported, "I am now chosen . . . by almost unanimous vote." A man of fierce conviction and determination—and not a little audacity—he insisted on going to London to make his case before the Board of Trade. John then returned to Antigua to rebuild his fortune, which along with his fortitude, he passed on to his son George.[11]

Eliza's father told his own courageous story of standing up to an imperious governor. Laws and ethics meant nothing to Daniel Parke. He abandoned his wife and young children in Virginia to chase fame in England and then manipulated his way into an appointment as governor of the Leeward Islands. As a sign of his enormous ego, not long into his tenure, he complained: "If I have my brains knokt out, the Queen must send some other unfortunate Divel [devil] here to be roasted in the sun, without the prospect of getting anything." He also publicly proclaimed that "there was no Law in Antegoa worth a farthing, that he would have regard to none of them, but would determine every thing according to his own Opinion." Governor Parke turned the local militia into his personal enforcers "to the great Terror and grievous Oppression of the Inhabitants." He preyed on women, harassing the wives and daughters of several prominent planters. When one woman rebuffed him, he tried to rape her. George Lucas and other members of the Antigua legislature, inflamed by this offensive conduct, drew up articles of impeachment, as the island's politics degenerated into chaos. Members of the Board of Trade soon removed Daniel from the governorship and recalled him to England; he exploited the distance between London and St. John's to ignore the directive. Increasingly erratic and paranoid, he ordered soldiers armed with bayonets to break up a meeting of the assembly, and, in response, assemblymen gave a call to arms. On December 7, 1710, a melee erupted between the armed factions, which numbered in the hundreds. Daniel barricaded himself in his house. As shots rang out across St. John's, men breached the governor's house. Daniel killed one man in an exchange of gunfire before he was shot in the thigh. Some Antiguans said that the mob dragged the injured governor out of his home, his head thudding down heavy stone steps, and threw him into the street, where he bled to death. Whatever the details, it was the only instance of colonists murdering a governor in the long history of the English Atlantic. Shocked members of the Council of Trade and Plantations attempted an investigation, but not a single Antiguan would testify. No one was ever punished for the killing of Daniel Parke. George Lucas and his friends were reelected to the assembly, honored for their hard-nosed resolve in defense of colonial rights.[12]

Though a child, Eliza Lucas absorbed these object lessons of her father's and grandfather's rectitude and forthrightness. She liked gossip, so it is easy to imagine her eavesdropping outside the parlor as her parents entertained guests with such family stories. But most of her girlhood she spent with books and at study. She marveled at the natural world, too, and found endless adventures on her family's sprawling plantation. The childhood interests, like the family lessons, stayed with her. "I own I love the vegitable world extremely," she said as a girl. And later in life: "I love a Garden and a book."[13]

The gardens of Eliza's girlhood were massive commercial enterprises. The Lucases, like rich colonists across the Leeward Islands, made their money from sugar.[14] As young Eliza rambled around the family's estate, she saw what it took to deliver sugar to the waiting ships docked at St. John's. She watched as enslaved men and women and children, too, suffered through a punishing work regimen. The temperature varies little throughout the year in Antigua: it rarely falls below 70 degrees Fahrenheit or rises above 90. But thick humidity coupled with unremitting sun can make it seem hotter, even with steady breezes coming off the ocean. This climate, coupled with the nature of the crop, made sugar cultivation a treacherous ordeal. It took eighteen long months to get one planting to market. Enslaved workers started by digging holes five to six inches deep and five feet square out of sunbaked clay soil. Then they laid cane tops in the middle and lightly covered them with soil. As the plants sprouted, they filled in the holes with manure until the field was level. Hour after hour, they lugged heaping baskets of manure into the fields and spread it by hand. They weeded for five or six weeks, until the canes were large enough to keep down the weeds. During these phases enslaved men and women often suffered from heat exhaustion and dehydration. They were bitten by mosquitoes carrying deadly diseases and exposed to parasites breeding in the manure.

When the canes grew tall enough to cut, enslaved men and women chopped the cane close to the ground with machetes. Then, with sweat-covered hands grasping sharp tools, they hacked the cane into four-foot-long pieces. Cuts to their hands became infected and turned deadly. Cut canes began to lose their sucrose content within twenty-four hours, so workers had to move fast. Heavy loads had to be rushed from the fields to the sugar works. Draft animals were difficult to come by on Antigua, so most planters used enslaved people rather than mules or cows. The milling process of crushing the cane to remove the liquid introduced yet more hazards.

The winds that swept across Antigua drove more than three hundred mills; the stone structures freckled the small island's verdant landscape. George Lucas ran three windmills at Cabbage Tree, making it one of the most productive enterprises in Antigua.[15] At his and the other sugar works, enslaved people fed the cane through ringers, and the liquid drained into vats for boiling. The side product of the boiled liquid, molasses, was sold or distilled into rum. The first stage of boiling produced "muscovado"—a semi-refined brown form of sugar, also known as clayed sugar, that was put into cone molds and shipped. Other sugar was refined, using added products such as egg whites or vinegar.

This manufacturing process required a high level of skill and posed terrible dangers: burns, dehydration, heatstroke, cuts, bone fractures, and crushing wounds. The boiling liquid caused excruciating and sometimes fatal blisters. While the temperatures in the sugar fields averaged a bearable 85 degrees, the constant fires inside the works pushed the heat above 120 degrees, and walls cut off the ocean breezes.

Under these horrific conditions, enslaved laborers generated prodigious profits for a seemingly insatiable global market. Sugar, after all, was not only tasty and increasingly fashionable: it was addictive. Consumption in England ballooned from two pounds per person per year in the 1660s to four pounds in the 1690s to twenty-three pounds in the 1770s.[16] Yet for enslaved men and women who produced Antiguan sugar, there was seldom enough clean water to drink, and food supplies were limited, of low quality, and inadequately nutritious. Planters devoted all the land they possibly could to growing sugarcane, neglecting to leave enough even for their own subsistence—and certainly not for their enslaved workers. Slaveholders also expected those women and men to grow their own food in the few hours they had away from the cane fields and sugar mills. Malnutrition was pervasive among black Antiguans, worsening the already bleak mortality rates afflicting them. Planters did not intentionally starve enslaved people, but they provided the bare minimum of food and shelter. Any unexpected event—hurricane, drought, war—fell much harder on them.

People who resisted were viciously beaten and, in some cases, "hung out"—locked in cages suspended from trees, without food or water, to slowly die of thirst, their cadavers left for birds and rodents and as cautionary tales for other enslaved people. Even minor infractions—a lost tool or a too-slow response—could evoke cruelty and violence. People who talked back to their enslavers could be forced to drink urine or might even have their tongues cut out. The law took care of runaways and rebels. When enslavers recaptured people who had fled, they branded the runaways, sometimes on the face, clipped their ears, sliced their Achilles tendons. The most macabre punishments were inflicted on individuals who planned revolts—or were even suspected of doing so. Magistrates used torture to elicit (often dubious) confessions and coerce alleged conspirators to name names. Courts summarily meted out torturous, often slow, always public deaths. Like all the sugar works across Antigua, the Lucas family plantations were sites of remarkable productivity, driven by routinized violence and suffering.[17]

This world, in the eyes of a child, came to seem normal, acceptable, even necessary. Eliza's youthful immersion in slavery and the lifestyle it afforded her family left a deep and lasting imprint. She learned in her girlhood to appropriate other people's labor, to take for granted the ability of whites to inflict violence on blacks at will with impunity. She learned to command. Decades passed, the girl grew up and then grew old. Her dependence on slaveholding as the foundation of her wealth and respectability became reflexive and then impervious to any criticism. Across a lifetime, Eliza's unrepentant commitment to racial power remained so unshakable that she seldom bothered even to mention it.

When she was ten years old, Eliza Lucas's entire life changed. Her father, convinced that she possessed a rare intelligence, decided to send her to England for a proper education. Antigua offered meager choices for boys, much less girls. As one critic observed, "There is nothing of Education for their Children here above Reading and Writing."[18]

Caribbean planter elites routinely sent sons to the metropole for formal education. Leaving their colonial homes as young as eight years old, gentry boys often stayed in England into their early twenties. After their instruction in Latin and Greek, history and philosophy, they learned hands-on about the sugar trade from their relatives' business associates. An English education, from boarding school to businesses, allowed male members of the rising generation of Antigua's planter class to cement the personal ties that advanced family wealth.[19]

Formally educating daughters abroad was less common. Most parents thought reading and writing—learned in families, with tutors, or at day schools—enough for girls. When well-to-do planters did send daughters abroad, they pursued refined skills: dancing, embroidery, French, and music. A more capacious education for a girl was highly unusual.[20]

Eliza Lucas was no typical girl. Neither George nor Ann could accompany her on her trip to England—the first of several life-changing transatlantic adventures. She sailed to the center of the English-speaking world knowing nothing but life on a rural Caribbean island. The population of Antigua was 24,000 enslaved people and 3,000 whites. London was home to around 700,000—over twenty-five times the population of Antigua—all in a single walkable city, and overwhelmingly white. The world ran through London: commerce, literature, science, theater. Night and day, it fairly vibrated with activity. Many people in the imperial center had never even heard of the tiny outpost four thousand miles from England that had been Eliza's whole world. She saw for the first time the contrivance of her girlhood home: a facsimile of an English gentry life plopped down on a remote tropical island.[21]

When Eliza arrived in London, Lucas family friends Richard and Mary Boddicott welcomed her into their home. Richard Boddicott was a sugar merchant, and from him Eliza learned about that side of her father's business. Having grown up around sugar production, she now witnessed commerce and distribution. It took a long time for hogsheads to cross the Atlantic, but markets shifted fast. She walked along the Thames and saw docks laden with colonial commodities, ships crisscrossing the globe. Mary Boddicott acted the part of surrogate mother to Eliza, and they formed a tight bond that lasted for years. Eliza, grateful for Mary's "tenderness," vowed to give her "all the regard I owe an affectionate parent."[22]

But Eliza spent most of her time at a boarding school run by a headmistress named Mrs. Pearson—a wholly female-centered environment. Eliza was one of about a dozen girls living there, studying dance, needlework, and French as well as history and geography. She took the initiative to broaden her education, pursuing two subjects of great significance to her future, bookkeeping and botany, and even reading a bit of law. Botany was becoming a popular field of study for women in the eighteenth century. It fit with Enlightenment ideals of scientific pursuits and self-improvement, the natural world a laboratory for reasoned inquiry, while complementing perceptions of proper femininity. Botany was also a perfect field for the nature-loving daughter of a Caribbean planter. Eliza stayed at her studies for the better part of five years. In time, she decided that the English education her parents gave her was "a more valuable fortune" than any financial inheritance ever could be.[23]

At first, of course, she must have felt terribly disoriented. She was no longer one of the best-dressed girls. Her family name and her skin color were suddenly unexceptional. She had never seen snow, never even felt 60-degree temperatures. She had to get a winter hat and coat, to learn to dodge carriages rattling down cobblestone streets, to sleep through the city's endless cacophony. The food she ate, the people she lived with, the clothes she wore, it all felt foreign to her.

At a young age, Eliza came to see that "happiness must be very precarious while we lie at the mercy of every accident to interrupt our tranquility." The secret to being happy, she concluded, was to "consult reason and follow where it dictates."[24] She would bloom where she was planted. So young Eliza found things to love in England: books, friends, the theater. For five years, her only connection to her family in Antigua came through letters that took weeks to cross the Atlantic, if they ever arrived. At Mrs. Pearson's school, Eliza started a lifelong practice of writing letters, penned in the early hours of the morning or perhaps by candlelight in the evenings and sent with hope to her family a world away. No one thought to save the girl's scribblings. But the imprint of Eliza Lucas's years in London—the education she acquired, the friends she made, the interests she cultivated, and the independence she learned to exercise—would be written all over her long, remarkable life.

CHAPTER 2

Trouble Back Home

Five years and four thousand miles from home, the girl became a young woman: confident but careful, knowledgeable, refined, resilient. Eliza Lucas learned during her London schooldays to take care of herself, in small ways at first. Small things became bigger over time. Her parents could not monitor the books she read, the friends she made, the plays she attended. She chose for herself and in choosing came to know herself. Still, she remained her parents' child, and, despite the independence she practiced, reliant on them, so that events unfolding across the Atlantic Ocean redirected the course of her young life.

It is unclear how much Eliza knew about the goings-on in Antigua during her years abroad. There was so much to tell, and so much of it was bad. Ann fell ill, the start of recurring health problems. Did Eliza's father alert her? Or did he protect her from worry?

Volatility was part of life in the Caribbean: water scarcity, hurricanes, droughts, and earthquakes. Summer months routinely brought violent tropical storms and hurricanes to Antigua. "The lightning in this part of the globe," one writer explained, "is very vivid; and the thunder bellows through the air in terrific peals, every hill and mountain reverberating the sound." The rains in England, another noted, "are but summer dews" compared to "the torrents which the overcharged clouds pour down" on the Leewards.[1] Every year Antiguans endured at least one or two severe storms that damaged the sugarcane fields. Losing a third of a crop was not unusual. Some years it could be half. Droughts were worse than storms: bereft of natural springs and rivers, Antiguans always struggled to maintain a steady supply of drinking water, and sporadic rainfall made things worse. In times of crisis, colonists shipped water in from other islands, but that was expensive and unreliable. Deprivation could quickly turn deadly. In the macabre human calculus of slaveholders, droughts brought "a most dreadful Mortality among the Negroes and Live-Stock." The damage to crops did not stop when the rains fell: "The Drought is generally followed by an Army of Worms, Flies, and other Insects," one man complained, which "eat up what little green things are left." Earthquakes convulsed the island from time to time, and even in years of relative calm, Antiguans suffered through waves of epidemic and environmental diseases. Smallpox, yellow fever, dysentery, and malaria heightened the daily dangers Antiguans needed to navigate.[2]

No one, however, was prepared for the cascade of disasters that befell Antiguans in the 1730s. Blight and infestations leveled many sugar fields in the early 1730s, and droughts finished off what the insects and disease didn't destroy. In 1731–1732, water supplies ran perilously low and sugarcane burned up in the fields under the baking sun. In 1733, the most violent hurricane in twenty-five years engulfed the Leeward Islands. As one resident of nearby Nevis described it, the "prodigious Force" struck around dawn on Saturday morning, June 30. The hurricane raged until noon, when the eye of the storm passed over, offering two hours of respite before the eyewall reappeared, unleashing several more hours of chaos. Just as residents thought the worst wind and rain passed, "it would come on again with redoubled Fury; and the longer the Calm, the greater the Fury." The 1733 hurricane leveled homes and windmills across Antigua. Ships sank or ran aground, the cargoes lost and sailors drowned.[3]

Two years later, Antiguans were still rebuilding when a powerful earthquake rocked the island. Damage to homes, bridges, and sugar works deepened the colony's troubles. Then, the summer of 1736 brought scorching, relentless heat. The drought that year was, one Antiguan observed, worse than "known in the memory of the oldest Men here."[4]

These natural disasters ravaged Antigua's economy. In the mid-1730s, fifty thousand of the island's seventy-two thousand acres—virtually all the productive land—was given over to sugarcane fields. But year after year of water scarcity and pestilence, followed by the 1733 hurricane, the 1735 earthquake, and the 1736 drought, devastated the sugar crops. Antiguan planters produced 10,276 tons of sugar in 1729, but by 1737 production plummeted to just

1,732 tons. With no diversification and no way of buying essential goods except from the sugar trade, residents endured staggering inflation on top of crippling losses. Political leaders complained to imperial officials about the "miseries we now lie under by the prices of our commodities."[5]

Like most of his neighbors, George Lucas lived on foreign credit. On the surface, Antiguan sugar planters appeared wealthy. Their families enjoyed all the trappings of a genteel lifestyle: lovely homes, fashionable clothes, lavish social lives. But most were perpetually indebted to English factors like Richard Boddicott. Since the value of sugarcane byproducts seemed to rise with only occasional interruptions, Caribbean planters did not particularly worry about those debts. Savvy planters like George Lucas were prepared to weather short-term setbacks in the Antiguan economy. The next crop would pay the bills. But what if there was no next crop?[6]

Although he continued to fund his eldest daughter's English education, George Lucas faced insolvency in the mid-1730s, and he found himself forced to mortgage more and more of his land—and then his enslaved workers—to satisfy English creditors. By 1735 he was more than £30,000 in debt. The multiple loans he had taken out on his properties exceeded the overall value of his estate. But George was not forced into bankruptcy. He sold one plantation for £13,000 and turned over the titles to most of the remainder of his assets to his creditors, to be held in trust until he produced enough sugar to pay his debts. It must have seemed to George Lucas that the situation in Antigua could not possibly get worse.[7]

Every year on October 11 the gentry families of Antigua dressed in their finest attire for a spectacular ball hosted by the governor of the Leeward Islands to commemorate the anniversary of the coronation of King George II. The island's most powerful people danced and feasted late into the night, enjoying massive bonfires and fireworks. Christopher Dunbar, a prominent resident of St. John's, offered to host the 1736 ball at his new home. No doubt George Lucas and Ann Mildrum looked forward to the evening as a respite from their financial worries and hoped Ann's health problems wouldn't keep them at home.

As the Lucases and other white couples prepared for the governor's ball, enslaved Antiguans set to work on their own plans for October 11, 1736. Antigua's ruling elite, George and John Lucas among them, had worked for decades to stabilize the colony's inherently volatile labor system. Efforts to control the island's enslaved laborers filled the records of the colonial government.

Antiguan laws forbade enslaved men and women to travel without passes, assemble in large numbers, or possess deadly weapons. Politicians levied taxes for public defense, campaigned for more white immigrants, and fined white men for refusing to serve on slave patrols. Legislators even empowered the entire white population of Antigua to police the black population with the free use of deadly force. If a white person killed an enslaved person running away or refusing to submit, the killer would not be prosecuted. Laws controlled how much free time enslavers could allow their captives and restricted the kinds of goods enslaved people could trade and the musical instruments they could play. Otto's Pasture, a market enslaved Antiguans collectively ran just outside the town of St. John's, was singled out for strict policing. Nonetheless, resistance remained pervasive.[8]

Enslaved people constituted almost 90 percent of the population of the English Caribbean in the 1730s. Never in history had so high a percentage of a population been enslaved. Demographics forced white Antiguans to begrudgingly accept everyday transgressions among their enslaved workforce: staying out late, socializing in Otto's Pasture, traveling without approval. Such acts of defiance pervaded all the slave societies that emerged in the colonial Americas. Some people ran away, many others intentionally lost tools, forgot instructions, broke dishes, and feigned illnesses. But when enslaved people directly challenged bondage—or when enslavers feared a rebellion—white colonists lashed out with macabre, public punishments designed to scare others into submission. They probably wanted to reassure themselves of their own tenuous power, too. Still, colonists understood that white laws could control black actions only so much.[9]

The twenty-four thousand enslaved people who lived in Antigua in 1736 felt the crop failures, natural disasters, and droughts far more deeply than the white minority. They rebuilt homes, replanted fields, and cleaned up debris while suffering through famine-like conditions, their diet of too few calories and too little nutritional value shrinking as their workloads swelled. Growing numbers of people fled. Some decided to take a more direct approach.[10]

In 1711, when he was ten years old—the same age as Eliza when she sailed to England for her education—a boy who came to be known as Court was stolen by slave raiders from his West African home. This son of a "considerable Family in his own Country" survived the Middle Passage to grow up in the brutal slave regime of Antigua and become an exceptionally talented and imposing man. Because of his skills, Court's enslaver, Thomas Kerby, let him work side jobs and keep part of the earnings. Court garnered the respect of black men and women across Antigua. White Antiguans found him "ambitious, very proud," and "a person of undaunted courage and strong resolve"—not, to their minds, admirable qualities in a black man. Sometime in the early 1730s, Court befriended a man called Tomboy, an enslaved carpenter who ran his own shop. He paid his enslaver a monthly sum and kept the rest of his profits. Tomboy was "a Fellow of a robust strong Body, and resolute Temper," and, like Court, commanded "a great Awe and Influence" among enslaved Antiguans.[11]

In the middle of the cascading crises besetting Antigua in the 1730s, Court and Tomboy decided to strike back at their enslavers. In 1735–1736, they conceived a meticulous plan to lead an islandwide rebellion. Across the Caribbean and throughout the seventeenth and eighteenth centuries, scores of such revolts, involving hundreds and sometimes thousands of enslaved people, unfolded: in Cuba, Barbados, Montserrat, Nevis—every Caribbean colony under every European power. For most of the decade of the 1730s Jamaican colonists were at war with people of African descent who had permanently fled enslavement to create self-sufficient "maroon" communities in the mountainous regions of Jamaica.[12]

At first, Court and Tomboy dared to share their plan only with a few trusted friends. But by the end of the summer of 1736, hundreds of enslaved Antiguans pledged loyalty to Court and Tomboy and to a bold plan: "to stand by and be true to each other, and to kill the Whites, Man, Woman, and Child . . . and to suffer Death rather than discovery." The growing ranks kept the secret from white Antiguans. Perhaps the white people did not want to see or, seeing, did not want to believe. Incredibly, on the afternoon of October 3, 1736, Court and Tomboy even organized an elaborate "Dance and Shew" to publicly signify solidarity within the black community. According to one eyewitness, it involved "the greatest Number of Negroes that were Ever known to be Assembled together, Near Two Thousand." The massive crowd included many white spectators who watched the dance and thought it all innocent fun. Some even mistook it as an attempt to imitate the king's coronation anniversary, scheduled for the following week.[13]

Knowing that the October 11 gala required all kinds of workers, including a master carpenter, Tomboy offered his services: he could build the ballroom seating at Christopher Dunbar's house. Tomboy planned to secrete gunpowder into the house with his carpentry supplies. Once "All the People of Distinction in the Island" reached "the height of their mirth," he would detonate the gunpower, killing as many white people as possible. To avoid injuring the black musicians and waiters, Tomboy would signal them just before the blast to abandon their posts.[14]

Meanwhile, rebels would take up position as lookouts across Antigua. As soon as they saw or heard the blast in St. John's, they would signal to others across the countryside, who would immediately rise up and kill their owners. From the outskirts of St. John's, four parties of several hundred people each would march on the town, entering from different directions, and "put all the white People there, to the sword." Some rebels would seize the city's harbor, while others attacked the main arsenal and distributed weapons to the gathering forces. The vastly outnumbered white Antiguans who managed to survive the night of October 11 would, Court and Tomboy explained, never manage to mount effective resistance. Court and Tomboy would then institute "a new form of Government . . . established by the Slaves among themselves, and they intirely to possess the Island." For the men and women who took up arms against colonial rule, "Freedom and the Possession of their Masters Estates were to be the Rewards."[15]

At the last minute, the son of the governor of the Leeward Islands died, and the ball was postponed until October 30, 1736, George II's birthday. Tomboy argued that the revolt should go forward on October 11. He thought the ball a dramatic but entirely dispensable pretext. Court lobbied for patience; he wanted to wait until October 30. Disagreements escalated, and whites overheard. At first, it sounded too incredible to believe. Court and Tomboy "were so entirely trusted by their Masters, that it was with very great difficulty, any Crime was believ'd against them." Then, the truth sank in.[16]

"Justice" meted out by slaveholding magistrates was swift and sadistic. Court and Tomboy were the first to stand trial. The panel of judges who presided over the conspiracy cases sentenced both men to be "broken on a wheel." This slow-motion execution started with a convicted prisoner tied, spread-eagle, to a wagon wheel, which was laid on its axle on the ground. The wheel could be rotated while the executioner clubbed the man, shattering his bones starting with his hands and feet and slowly working inward on the body. For victims who were not beaten to death, the wheel was turned upright and the condemned left to slowly die. Even under this torture, an early historian of Antigua noted, Court's and Tomboy's "fortitude did not forsake them; and their last words expressed their hatred to the whites." Slaveholders saw it differently: the two leaders "died with amazing Obstinancy."[17]

Dozens more arrests following in the ensuing months. The jail in St. John's overflowed with prisoners; some awaiting trial were confined on ships in the harbor. Short trials and swift convictions fed colonists' blood lust. In January 1737, one white Antiguan reported that "the Burning of Negroes, hanging them on Gibbets alive, Racking them upon the Wheel, &c, take up almost all our Time." By the first week of March 1737, eighty-eight people were executed: five broken at the wheel, six caged and left to die of thirst or starvation, and seventy-seven burned alive.[18] No one was simply hanged: the punishments were all vicious spectacles. Several men were executed in Otto's Pasture, doubtless to terrify others in a space where they felt a strong sense of community and autonomy. In case anyone missed the grisly executions, officials ordered the decapitated heads of several leaders to be impaled on poles "of some considerable Height."[19]

Eliza's parents learned during this bloodbath that they numbered among the intended targets. One of the men they enslaved, whom they called Caesar, had planned to kill the Lucases. Caesar was executed in February 1737, and George collected £70 for the public seizure of his "property."[20]

George and Ann must have wondered: Who else had allied with Caesar? How close had their family come to being slain in the night? Every day seemed to bring new revelations and more anxiety. Many white Antiguans concluded that it was naïve to think that every person who joined Court and Tomboy's movement had been—or ever would be—found out. Even the official report on the trials concluded "how weak and vain it would be in us to say the Country is in Safety." "How far we may be in danger still," the judges reasoned, "we cannot determine, since undoubtedly there are Hundreds by us undiscovered."[21]

Four thousand miles away from the decapitated heads mounted around St. John's, Eliza Lucas knew nothing about this threat to her parents' lives. She serenely concluded her studies. As her days in London grew short, she had to say goodbye to the gardens and the theater scene she'd come to love, and to Mary Boddicott, whom Eliza adored. Mary started out as Eliza's surrogate mother and became her close friend. Parting with schoolmates was hard, too, especially Katherine Martin, the daughter of a member of Parliament with whom Eliza shared an especially "tender regard." Eliza hoped neither "length of time or distance of place" would erase their connection, and she wished her treasured friend "all the felicity this world affords."[22]

Felicity was in short supply in Antigua. Eliza's parents' fields were decimated, their properties heavily mortgaged, and sugar prices still plummeting. The enslaved people on whose labor they had built their lifestyle had nearly murdered them. Perhaps it was time to start over again, in a new place, one safer for the family.

When the Lucas family decided to abandon Antigua, they were not alone. A New England newspaper—one of many in North America reporting on the Antigua conspiracy—informed readers that "Some of the principle Gentlemen there with their Families are making Provision to leave the Island, believing the Negros will accomplish their Designs sooner or later." Some rich families quitting Antigua returned to England, others migrated to neighboring islands, and others still set out for the mainland of North America.[23]

From the desolation of Willoughby Bay, George Lucas decided that a tract of land he had inherited from his father and kept from his creditors, located in the South Carolina Lowcountry, seemed the right place for the rising generation of Lucases to call home. The culture and environment were familiar, but the economy was more diversified and society more stable. First, though, he would have to set his affairs in order. And for that he would need his nearly grown daughter's help.

Eliza Lucas set sail for Antigua in late 1737. About to turn fifteen, she was utterly transformed from the girl her parents had sent abroad five years before. At Mrs. Pearson's school she had become a skilled musician and fluent in French, even singing French songs at social gatherings the Boddicotts hosted. She learned to dance, to craft eloquent letters in a proper feminine hand, to engage in sparkling conversation. Besides performing that gentility, she learned to detect it in others. She could recognize the clothing, the leisure pursuits, the manners that signaled one's worthiness to enter polite society. She knew a tasteful tea service and a graceful dance step when she saw it, and she could tell a sophisticate from a fop. In sum, she returned to Antigua a refined young lady, the ideal for colonial planters' daughters. But Eliza's cosmopolitan education transcended those traditionally female accomplishments. Her studies made her a clear and graceful writer. She read Plutarch, Virgil, and Milton. She understood finance, agriculture, business, and law. Eliza felt extremely grateful for the care Mrs. Pearson had taken in her extended education: "It will," she told Pearson, "be ever a pleasure to me to acknowledge it." Eliza felt, too, a keen obligation to her parents, having come to understand during her years in London, she said, "the pains and money you laid out on my Education."[24]

How small St. John's must have seemed from the bow of the ship. But if Eliza missed London or felt constrained about returning to such a remote island, her elation at the prospect of a family reunion would have carried the day. She was almost back with her siblings, her mother, and especially her father. He was always her favorite and she his.

What a thing to send away a child and welcome home a young woman. Eliza looked different and sounded different because she was different. Beyond her academic pursuits, Eliza had learned in England to be self-motivated and self-confident, and she knew how to manage on her own. But she also remained her father's "dear Betsey." George doubtless took comfort in Eliza's maturity and levelheadedness. And he must have felt relieved, too, for his plans depended on her. Eliza was ready.

PART TWO

Home to Carolina

CHAPTER 3

"in a strange country"

Eliza Lucas arrived back in Antigua in late 1737 to hear the shocking news that her days on the family's island estate were numbered. Soon, her parents told her, they would all move to a new home, on the mainland of North America. George Lucas had everything organized. He had been weighing the idea of relocating for several years. As economic crises roiled Antigua in the mid-1730s, George had kept from his increasingly impatient creditors a plot of land in the South Carolina Lowcountry. After the aborted slave uprising of 1736, he and Ann supposed that backup plan might be their main chance. In the winter of 1736–1737, while Eliza studied in London, George explored Carolina. As he walked through Charles Town, George Lucas could envision a bright future for his family. South Carolina was flourishing. The innovations and economic growth of the Lowcountry contrasted so sharply with the tumult Antiguans were enduring. His visit settled the matter: the Lucases would become Carolinians.[1]

Whatever Eliza thought about her parents' plan, she acted the part of a dutiful daughter. They needed her help, and she relished the chance to affirm her love and gratitude by rising to the occasion. Eliza's first obligation: putting her expansive education to practical use. After a too-brief reunion, the family again fractured across the Atlantic. In mid-1738 George departed Antigua, carrying Eliza's younger brothers, George Jr. and Tommy, to boarding school in England. Ann, Eliza, and little Polly stayed behind. Ann remained in poor health, so Eliza helped manage her father's estate during his nearly yearlong absence. Along with the normal rituals of a gentry girl, including socializing with the scions of Antigua's planter elite, she had a family business to run.[2]

George Lucas returned to Antigua in the summer of 1739, but he stayed only long enough to collect the women for the voyage north. The Lucases arrived in Charles Town sometime in late July or early August 1739. George retained his military appointment in Antigua, but he planned on the move being permanent. He signed a land deed on August 29, 1739, identifying himself as "George Lucas late of the Island of Antigua Now of South Carolina." Eliza confirmed the permanence: her father "removed his family . . . with an intent to settle them here."[3]

Everything about South Carolina that seemed foreign to most visitors from England and other North American colonies felt familiar to the Lucases: the heavy reliance on a single crop (rice) produced by slave labor, the black majority population, the small planter-merchant elite that dominated government and businesses, the lush environment. Certainly, Carolina was no paradise. Colonized in 1670, it almost immediately earned the reputation of a slaughterhouse. Seasoned mariners adopted gallows humor to deride the settlement: "They who want to die quickly, go to Carolina." In the 1730s the colony, though thriving economically as never before, still held the ignominious distinction of the highest mortality rates and lowest life expectancies anywhere in British North America—demographic patterns akin to the Caribbean. A smallpox outbreak killed hundreds of South Carolinians in 1738. In the summer of 1739 yellow fever claimed so many lives in Charles Town that trade stalled and the newspaper, the *South Carolina Gazette*, temporarily halted publication. But to George and Ann, South Carolina seemed far safer than Antigua. Carolinians enjoyed natural springs and flowing creeks, so they didn't need to ration drinking water. There was infinitely more land. Perhaps most important, in its nearly sixty-year history, the colony had never experienced the kind of slave revolts that roiled the Caribbean on a steady basis, the kind that pushed the Lucases from their home in Antigua.[4]

Sixteen-year-old Eliza had mixed feelings about South Carolina. "I prefer England to it," she confided to Mary Boddicott, but "think Carolina greatly preferable to the West Indias." Mary could not have heard a ringing endorsement in Eliza's conclusion: "I like this part of the world as my lott has fallen here." Slow to call South Carolina home, Eliza continued for two more years to refer to the colony as "the part of the world I now inhabit."[5]

Despite her reservations, Eliza was captivated by the Lowcountry environment. The Lucases made their home at a plantation they called Wappoo, in St. Andrew's Parish, where Wappoo Creek met the Stono River, around six miles from Charles Town by water, which was the quickest means of travel. The property encompassed nearly six hundred acres and contained "a very good Dwelling house, Barn, and Out houses, a good Garden, and many Conveniences."[6] In early reports to friends and family, Eliza admiringly described the countryside, savoring what she saw and heard and smelled when she took long walks across the estate. "The scent of the young mirtle and Yellow Jesamin with which the woods abound is delightful," she wrote. She relished the forests, filled with deer and wild turkey. Carolina nectarines, peaches, and melons tasted delicious. The already cosmopolitan Eliza Lucas could judge oranges grown in South Carolina superior to "any I ever tasted in the West Indies or from Spain or Portugal." She offered detailed reports of the landscape, from the sandy soil in Charles Town to the clay and swamplands in the countryside and the hilly backcountry 150 miles from the coast. Rivers and creeks, nonexistent on Antigua, streamed across the Lowcountry. Wealth flowed along those waterways, as enslaved people turned swampy lowlands into fertile fields, ideally suited for commercial rice production. Planters spent the profits of their slaves' labor to build majestic homes in the style of English landed gentry, shaded by towering oaks and fronting the major rivers: the Ashley, Cooper, Wando, and Stono flowing around Charles Town, and farther to the southwest and northeast, the Edisto and Santee. Most plantations had docks, for quick transport of goods to market and so that white residents could easily visit their neighbors. Eliza understood the significance of the sprawling Carolina interior, so different from tiny Antigua. She noticed untapped commercial opportunities. "The staple commodity here is rice," she observed, "and the only thing they export to Europe. Beef, pork, and lumber they send to the West Indias."[7]

Though Eliza lived on a black majority estate, she made no mention of the enslaved people who kept Wappoo Plantation—and all of South Carolina—running. At least twenty enslaved people resided at Wappoo in 1739, together with the five members of the Lucas household (cousin Fanny Fayerweather joined George, Ann, Eliza, and Polly), a ratio in line with the rest of the Lowcountry. It is unclear whether these enslaved people moved from Antigua with the Lucases, lived at Wappoo already, or were purchased by George at the Charles Town market. Carolina's labor system duplicated what Eliza had known in Antigua, so perhaps she saw nothing particularly new or notable to report. South Carolina's slave laws also mirrored those of the Caribbean colonies. The colony's first comprehensive slave code, passed in the late seventeenth century, was a near copy of Jamaica's code, which Jamaican legislators borrowed from Barbados. The Carolinians made one macabre legal innovation: courts could geld two-time male runaways. A Lowcountry judge imposed that sentence on three men in 1697. By the time Eliza's family arrived in South Carolina, the legislature had revised the colony's laws to prohibit such mutilations as penalties in criminal cases. But owners exercised nearly unchecked discretion when it came to punishing people on their estates. Black women and men bore visible scars of bondage, inflicted by courts and owners. Disfigurements included clipped ears and branded cheeks. Some people hobbled about because their owners intentionally crippled them by severing their Achilles tendons to impede further flights to freedom. Eliza took the violence for granted.[8]

Later generations of slaveholders, under a groundswell of critiques of slavery, felt self-conscious and defensive about their brutal labor system and culture. By the early nineteenth century, they fabricated stories about their benevolence and shared affections with enslaved people. But in the colonial era, few whites doubted the efficacy and morality of slaveholding, and fewer still said anything about the institution or the people trapped in it. Rich families like the Lucases, seeing no need to defend slavery, remained silent, uncritical, entitled. The Lucases never publicly discussed abandoning slavery. Despite what had gone on in Antigua, they doubled down in South Carolina.

The Lucases' new neighbors knew all about the aborted slave uprising that persuaded Eliza's parents to relocate to the mainland. The Antiguan plot had been big news throughout the Atlantic World, with the first reports arriving in Charles Town within weeks. Then, in early December 1736, the *South Carolina Gazette* published accounts from Antigua's white minority—the reportage a cautionary tale for elite Carolinians. Only "divine Providence" had saved the white Antiguans. God himself, the writers proclaimed, "awakened us from our long and deep Lethargy" and disclosed the rebels' "most hidden Secrets, and graciously enabled us to take proper Measures for our Safety and the Destruction designed for us." And this ominous conclusion: "No people were ever rescued from a Danger more imminent." Official reports from Antigua, published in the *South Carolina Gazette* in February 1737, echoed those early assessments and offered specific advice for slaveholders in other locales: Get vigilant. Antiguan officials expressly blamed the plot on the island's black-white ratio: "Next to hopes of Freedom, the greatest [cause] was the inequality of Numbers of white and black." They urged their counterparts throughout British America to aggressively recruit more white migrants. They also recommended that colonial authorities sharply curtail economic opportunities by forbidding enslaved people to work as "Handicraft Tradesmen, Overseers, Drivers or Distillers, Shop-keepers or Hawkers and Pedlars or Sailors, nor suffered to keep Horses, nor to work for themselves."[9]

At the time of the Antiguan uprising, the speaker of the South Carolina Commons House of Assembly—the highest elective office in the colony—was a rich and highly respected planter named Charles Pinckney. In the late 1730s, Speaker Pinckney tried to persuade legislators to shore up the colony's slave code. A myriad of parallels linked South Carolina and Antigua. South Carolinians lived in the only black-majority colony in North America. African Americans traded their crafts and produce in Charles Town's markets, and enslaved and free black sailors worked together in the city's harbor. Lowcountry plantations depended on black drivers and skilled craftsmen. The region had experienced a recent spike in runaways, too. Charles warned the assemblymen about the runaway problem in particular. Left unchecked, he argued, the escalating pattern would be "of very ill Consequence to the Estates and Properties of the People of this Province." "If some speedy and effectual Care is not taken to prevent it before it becomes more general," he continued, "it may in time prove of the utmost Disadvantage." Charles Pinckney couldn't persuade enough assemblymen to pass any major new laws. Perhaps it was self-delusion or the arrogance of power. Maybe they engaged in short-term thinking: why spend time and money now for something that had not happened in the past and only might happen in the future?[10]

By the time the Lucas family arrived in the Lowcountry, whatever apprehension white Carolinians felt about the connections between Antigua and South Carolina had faded from the newspaper and public conversations. As Eliza explored her family's new estate, she and her parents had good cause to believe that South Carolina was far safer than Antigua. They were wrong.

Within weeks of the Lucas family's emigration, black South Carolinians launched the most successful slave rebellion in the history of mainland British America. The 1739 Stono uprising took its name from the river that ran along the Lucas property. A core group of around twenty African American men and women, led by a man named Jemmy, set the plan in motion. Sometime early Sunday morning, September 9, 1739, Jemmy and his allies met near Wallace Creek, along the Stono, in St. Paul's Parish, twenty miles outside of

Charles Town. Nearby, two white men named Bathurst and Gibbes ran a store, called Hutchinson's. Jemmy and his followers robbed the store for necessary supplies, including guns and gunpowder, and decapitated Bathurst and Gibbes. As they left, they set the two heads on the stairs leading into Hutchinson's store. Moving through the neighborhood, the rebels continued killing colonists.[11]

Eliza and her family lived about ten miles away overland, a long distance to travel on foot or horseback. But waterways were the routes of choice in the Lowcountry. The distance, then, between Hutchinson's store and the Lucases' new home on the Wappoo River was quite close. Jemmy and his followers never came to Wappoo Plantation, however. Instead, they headed south. And they were not looking for people to kill, only for a way out of South Carolina.

The rebels had no intention of overthrowing the colonial government. Instead, they set out for St. Augustine, in Spanish Florida, where the King of Spain, to the mortification of English colonists, "promised Protection and Freedom to all Negroe Slaves that would resort thither."[12] As the self-emancipated made their way across the countryside, they ransacked and burned homes and killed white people who resisted them. They gained support among black Carolinians as they marched along, singing and dancing and shouting "liberty." The revolt kept growing and soon included a hundred self-emancipating men and women. By complete chance, Lieutenant Governor William Bull and four companions stumbled upon the rebels as they celebrated in a field just before noon on Sunday morning. Bull, the acting head of the colony, was on horseback, the enslaved people on foot, but he only narrowly escaped with his life. Quickly mustering armed white colonists, he raced back with reinforcements. As colonial officials later phrased it, "an Engagement ensued" between the two sides, "wherein one fought for Liberty and Life, the other for their Country and every Thing that was dear to them."[13]

When the white colonists eventually prevailed, vengeance—swift and bloody—was meted out to the black rebels. They killed most of the people on the spot and hunted down those who fled. The colonists disemboweled some people and staked their decapitated heads on the mileposts that marked the route back to Charles Town. In the end, the colonial government executed nearly all Jemmy's followers.

The Lucases' new white neighbors were shocked and terrified by the rebellion. Families fled to the relative safety of Charles Town, fearing "those Negroes which were concerned in that Insurrection who were not yet taken." In January 1740 so many planter families remained in the city that the minister of one rural parish complained there was hardly anyone left to come to Sunday services. As colonists weighed abandoning South Carolina entirely, members of the legislature feared "the Country seemed to be at Stake." The 1739 Stono Revolt soon spiraled into an international incident. Officials blasted their Spanish neighbors for willfully provoking the uprising. The report from the colonial legislature laid the blame squarely on Spain: "With Indignation we looked at St. Augustine . . . that Den of Thieves and Ruffians!"[14]

Legislators rushed into action. Under Charles Pinckney's leadership, the assembly set about revising the colony's slave code. The work he shepherded through the colonial government formed the foundation of slave laws that lasted more than a century in South Carolina. The colony expanded slave patrols, making service mandatory for all white men, and they rigidly restricted blacks' travel and trading opportunities. New laws also forbade enslaved people from learning how to write—too many black people had figured out how to forge passes. (Learning to read was not prohibited.) New fines were levied on enslavers who exercised too much latitude, such as allowing enslaved people to own canoes, breed horses, or hunt with guns. And legislators tried, without much luck, to recruit more white immigrants.[15] The most influential part of the code, finalized in early May 1740, was a new tax. Colonial officials blamed volatility within South Carolina's slave communities on the "barbarous and savage disposition" of people who lived on the coast of Africa. So they passed a duty of £100 for every person purchased on the international slave market. Domestic slave trading continued apace, but the international market evaporated—only five slave ships arrived in Charles Town between 1740 and 1744—and did not return to the levels of the 1730s until the late 1750s.[16]

The Lucases probably felt less panicked by Stono than their neighbors. Nothing about the revolt appears in the surviving family records, but Eliza and her parents were living together, with no cause to write to one another, and her brothers were studying in England and too young to hear the story. Certainly, Eliza and her parents would have found it chilling to contemplate white people being murdered in their businesses and homes. At the same time, the motives of the Stono rebels seemed fundamentally different from what Court and Tomboy had planned in Antigua. Enslaved Antiguans had intended to overthrow colonial rule by killing their white oppressors. Jemmy and his followers were fleeing to St. Augustine and only incidentally killing along the way. The Lucases' experience in Antigua probably taught them that a few dozen people fighting to escape to freedom was a wholly different kind of uprising than hundreds committed to creating an independent black-controlled country.

Besides, the Lucas family faced a far more immediate concern. In October 1739, after months of escalating tensions in the Caribbean, England declared war against Spain. Most white South Carolinians thought the troubles abroad paled in comparison to the "more dangerous Enemy in the Heart of their Country"—that was, the Stono Revolt. That was not the sentiment at Wappoo. George Lucas was a major in the 38th Regiment of the British army and charged with defending the Caribbean colonies. As the crisis deepened, he and his family held out hope that he could somehow stay in South Carolina. Those hopes were dashed in late 1739 when the imperial center notified all British officers to report in person and without delay to their regiments. Anyone refusing would be removed from command. If George Lucas stayed in South Carolina, he would lose all the money he had invested in his commission and be publicly, irreparably disgraced. He would not risk taking the women into a war zone. So, Eliza said, her father saw no choice but "to leave us, & return to his post in Antigua."[17]

Eliza Lucas turned seventeen on December 28, 1739, but found little cause for celebrating. Her father was back in Antigua, facing the perils of fighting in a war against Spain. Her mother suffered from an off-and-on illness that left her unable to manage the household or even the oversight of young Polly. "My Mama's bad state of health," Eliza explained in the spring of 1740, "prevents her going through any fatigue."[18]

Eliza—no longer a child and not quite an adult—took charge. "'Twas inavoidable," she said, as she assumed responsibility for her mother and five-year-old sister and the entire Lucas estate. George left it to Eliza to decide whether the family of women would remain at Wappoo or move to town. Eliza thought it was "more prudent" to live on the country property than in Charles Town, better for her mother's health. And living at Wappoo was "most agreeable" to Eliza. At first, Fanny Fayerweather helped Eliza. But in 1740 an ailing Fanny left for Boston, to seek an inheritance and escape South Carolina's environment.[19]

Seventeen was early to become a head of household, but young people often needed to grow up fast in the Lowcountry. Short life expectancy and high mortality rates meant that many children lost one or even both parents early in life and assumed adult duties in their teenage years. Children went away to boarding school at age nine or ten. Boys started college around fourteen. Girls got married in their teens. It wasn't unusual, either, to live in a family of women. A 1753 census revealed that almost one-quarter of Antiguan households consisted of adult women and minor children, and South Carolina differed little. In one Lowcountry parish, widows made up 51 percent of the white female population, and half of the widows never remarried. Eliza had spent many years in female-centered homes, from her boarding school days and while remaining at Cabbage Tree during her father's travels in 1738–1739.[20]

Now, however, Eliza had virtually no one to help her—she was independent in a most unwelcome, daunting way. South Carolina's gentry class and the colony's main businesses were built on interconnected kinship networks, forged by siblings, cousins, in-laws, and even fictive kin. Besides her five-year-old sister, ailing mother, and (temporarily) Fanny Fayerweather, Eliza was alone, with no relatives to rely upon. Years later Eliza remembered how hard she found it to part with her father and be left "to continue in a strange country."[21]

On her seventeenth birthday, then, Eliza Lucas found herself in charge of a large and complicated family fortune, or, as she put it, "imployed in business of which my father has left me a pretty good share." Besides Wappoo, George Lucas had acquired a fifteen-hundred-acre plantation on the Combahee River near Beaufort, southwest of Charles Town, called Garden Hill, and three thousand acres along the Waccamaw River, mostly dedicated to rice cultivation. Overseers managed the day-to-day operations at both Waccamaw and Garden Hill, but they served at the will and under the guidance of the planter-patriarch: first George, and then his surrogate, Eliza.[22]

Necessity forced Eliza's management of the Lucas estate, but something else drove her as well. Eliza loved her father deeply, and she wanted to excel as a plantation manager to preserve the Lucas family's wealth and to honor her attachment to him. "I shall always," Eliza promised George, "endeavour to deserve your favour by the strickest filial duty and obedience."[23]

Eliza and George's relationship was marked by candor, mutuality, and warmth. She was devoted to him and trusted by him. She thought of him as "my best friend." In the eighteenth-century understanding of friendship, that meant her most trusted counselor, the person she turned to for advice, who watched out for her and smoothed the path of life. For his part, George not only loved his eldest daughter—he often called her his "dear Betsey"—but also thought her wise beyond her years. He had confidence in Eliza's judgment and competence.[24]

Why wouldn't he? Eliza's upbringing prepared her for this unusual role, and her character predicted success. In both Antigua and South Carolina, adults routinely complained about gentry sons who squandered their time studying abroad and returned home entitled and self-indulgent. As one Antigua critic complained, "Too many of them returning here at the Age of 16, 17, or 18, full of Conceit of their Father's large Possessions, and the Herd of Slaves they are to be Lords over, and not being provided with any tolerable Stock of substantial Knowledge, seldom or never grow capable of serving their Country or themselves to purpose." Not Eliza. She felt supremely grateful for her English education and was firmly committed to using it to her family's advantage. Her girlhood in Antigua and adolescence at Mrs. Pearson's boarding school also instilled in Eliza the necessity of self-improvement. She loved learning, was capaciously curious about the world, indefatigably hardworking, and doggedly persistent in achieving her goals. Her energy and resolve matched her ambition. Though a young woman in a strange country, she set about becoming the most proficient planter possible.[25]

CHAPTER 4

Putting Down Roots

As she said goodbye to her father, Eliza Lucas set her mind on succeeding in South Carolina. She prided herself on "the eagerness of my temper to lern whatever I take in my head." Well-versed in commodities markets from her time in London with the Boddicotts and with slave-based agriculture through her family's Antiguan sugar plantations, Eliza dove into managing the family's transatlantic business with a stunning level of fervor and capacity. Sometimes she found her life at Wappoo "gloomy and lonesom." Occasional visits to Charles Town brought breaks of "giddy gayety." But once back at Wappoo, she willed herself to prioritize her family's long-term interests over any short-term pleasures.[1]

"I have the business of 3 plantations to transact," Eliza wrote Mary Boddicott in the spring of 1740, just a few months after George Lucas returned to Antigua. The work, she explained, "requires much writing and more business and fatigue of other sorts than you can imagine." "But least you should imagine it too burthensom to a girl at my early time of life," she quickly added, "I assure you I think myself happy that I can be useful to so good a father and by rising very early I find I can go through much business."[2]

At first, Eliza tried to act as a strict surrogate for George, vetting her decisions through him. But the War of Jenkins' Ear continued to spiral in the Caribbean and often waylaid their letters. (The conflict was named after Robert Jenkins, captain of a British merchant ship who was assaulted—and lost his ear—when Spanish forces boarded his vessel. The episode sparked outrage in England and, eventually, retribution by the British military.) George's sporadic contact during the war meant that Eliza soon found it necessary to exercise her own judgment.

The distance from her father and the long silences grieved Eliza. When she woke each morning, she didn't know if he was dead or alive. She kept writing. "The dangerous situation you are in terrifies us beyond expression," she confessed in one letter. She tried "to pretend to more Heroism than I deserve," but struggled with "the perpetual fears and apprehensions I am in at this time concerning you."[3] She prayed for peace. Her mother's recurrent health problems weighed on Eliza, too. Sometimes Ann felt strong enough to aid Eliza, even to socialize with her, but mostly Eliza took care of Ann. George being endangered by the far-off war provoked one kind of anxiety, the monotony of Ann's unhealthiness another. There she was, worrying about one parent in harm's way and another chronically ill. Through it all, Eliza tried to remain optimistic or at least realistic. "Wishing for what is not in our power," she believed, "is Idle." She persevered.[4]

Months of familial responsibilities turned into years, and Eliza grew more confident. No longer just her father's surrogate, she acted more and more on her own. She wrote to businessmen, lawyers, and government officials in Charles Town and in London, secure in her knowledge of agriculture and finance. Her competence and initiative earned the respect of her correspondents, who sold her supplies on credit; she signed and received bills of exchange. Eliza paid her accounts on time and shipped quality commodities to her English factors. None of her business contacts appeared to question her legal standing to operate first as her father's proxy and then on her own.[5]

At the Lucas properties, Eliza sat atop a hierarchy replicated on plantations throughout the colonial Southeast and the Caribbean. Enslaved men and women labored at felling trees and milling logs, rendering lard and churning butter, managing livestock, cooking, gardening, washing and sewing clothes, fishing, and raising crops. Resident overseers managed the enslaved laborers at Eliza's Garden Hill and Waccamaw properties. William Murray worked for the family for many years, mostly at Garden Hill, and a Mr. Starrat oversaw Waccamaw. Eliza was the absentee planter of those estates, so the people she enslaved at Garden Hill and Waccamaw likely did not know her—they probably rarely saw her. People of African descent outnumbered whites by ratios as high as nine to one in Lowcountry parishes, so most enslaved people interacted with few white people besides resident planters and overseers. By the 1740s, three of every four black Carolinians lived on plantations with more than twenty enslaved people, and half with more than thirty. Shockingly, one-third of Africans forcibly trafficked to the Lowcountry died within the first year of their enslavement in the colony. Disease claimed most of their lives—yellow fever, dysentery, malaria. The marshlands in which they worked were deadly. Snakes and alligators killed some people, infections from cuts and heatstroke others, and poor food supplies, brackish water, and exhausting labor many more. Enslaved women endured the added perils of pregnancy and childbirth. Planters coveted children born by the women they held in bondage, because those children followed the legal status of their mothers. But planters balanced those long-term reproductive ambitions against the short-term gains of black women's productivity in the fields. One result: enslaved women in eighteenth-century America lost more than half their children to stillbirth or infant mortality.[6]

Reliant on overseers at Waccamaw and Garden Hill, Eliza still commanded from afar the enslaved people who worked on those plantations. She directed Murray and Starrat regarding the movement of supplies from her properties to Charles Town, to Antigua, and to European markets. At her behest, Murray coordinated shipments of lumber and salted beef and bacon to George in Antigua, and Starrat sent barrels of butter and pitch and tar—all produced by enslaved laborers under Eliza's indirect but unrelenting control.[7]

Eliza ran day-to-day operations at Wappoo. Planting at the level she pursued there and at her other two properties was a major business, requiring elaborate management processes, savvy accounting, and exacting labor. Eliza visited the fields at Wappoo regularly but, like most commercial planters, she probably did not linger long in that dangerous environment. Most large-scale resident planters left the hands-on work to drivers: men who supervised day-to-day field operations and beat people who fell behind.[8]

Typical of Lowcountry planters, Eliza's work mostly centered on organization and bookkeeping. Her principal commercial crop at all three plantations in the early 1740s was rice. By the time Eliza arrived in South Carolina, rice was a booming business: like sugar and tobacco and coffee, it was a lucrative commodity that remade the countryside of the colonial Americas into what historians often call "factories in fields." Knowledge of how to grow rice probably came to South Carolina from countries on the west coast of Africa, especially from women from Senegambia and Sierra Leone who milled rice to feed their families. Producing rice for sale on the transatlantic market entailed elaborate construction projects—embankments and canals and gates to control flooding of the rice fields. Those were designed by ambitious planters and built by enslaved people. Commercial production of rice also required a higher concentration of labor than other crops grown by enslaved people in North America. Enslavers adopted on rice plantations what came to be called the "task" system, assigning to each person a specific daily or weekly task: a space for planting, a weight for pounding. This differed from the "gang" system used in cultivating tobacco in the Chesapeake and sugar in the Caribbean, where people labored in groups, usually from sunrise to sunset.[9]

For Eliza, as the master of her family's plantation estates, her most important responsibilities included assigning tasks for rice production. That varied by season: planting, fertilizing, reaping, pounding. How many baskets of manure could a man carry into the rice fields in a day? How many weeks would people need to wade into knee-deep, snake-infested water to scare birds away from the growing plants? How many hours could a woman lift a ten-pound pestle over her head to separate the hull from the rice? Time was money. Eliza and her overseers and drivers needed to push enslaved men and women to their limits. Eliza, skilled at bookkeeping, dutiful, and meticulous by nature, must have been a ruthless taskmaster, bleeding the most work out of each person she enslaved in order to produce superior rice crops and turn steady profits.[10]

Enslavers brutalized the people they held in bondage, and, in that regard, too, Eliza was probably no different from any man running a Lowcountry plantation. Enslaved people were extensions of and conduits for her ambitions. As Spanish ships sailed toward Charles Town in the summer of 1742, for instance, Eliza quickly apprised William Murray of the potential peril and directed him "upon the least alarm or apprehension of danger" to evacuate the enslaved people from Garden Hill. Her concern lay not with the safety of the men and women. Instead, she feared for her own financial risk: Spanish sailors might set those people free.[11]

Eliza knew about the Spanish approach because, as a responsible large-scale planter, she kept up with political and diplomatic matters likely to affect her estates. She corresponded with an Atlantic-wide network of friends and professional contacts who linked South Carolina to the Caribbean and Europe. She watched with growing concern as the widening war stalled rice exports and threatened the value of her yields. She understood diplomacy and trade in France, in Russia, and throughout various colonies. George Lucas's military service intensified Eliza's interest. She tracked the political intrigues surrounding Georgia's founder, the British military officer James Oglethorpe, and hoped that her father might somehow replace Oglethorpe and be "settled with us once again." But each passing year seemed to move Eliza farther and farther from that goal.[12]

As she launched into her new role as the female planter-patriarch of Wappoo Plantation, Eliza Lucas created a revealing and rare record of her life, in the form of a letterbook. In one sense, her letterbook—copies of letters she mailed—marked the continuation of a long-standing family tradition of careful record keeping. Under the leadership of her grandfather, John Lucas, the Antigua Assembly made sure to keep accurate records and preserve them for posterity.[13] Eliza appeared to inherit her grandfather's commitment to written records of accomplishments. More immediately, young Eliza Lucas started her letterbook as evidence of her dutifulness to her father, whom she missed terribly. Only through her letters could Eliza bridge the fifteen hundred miles that separated her from her father. She had written letters from London, of course, but no one in the family preserved those; they had little value beyond sentimentality. Now Eliza was a plantation manager, and she could not afford to be cavalier about her writings. Keeping copies made practical sense given her duties and, she must have thought, the letterbook would make it easier for George to check her work when he returned to South Carolina.

Eliza soon adopted the practice of transcribing copies of her letters with all her correspondents, friends in London as well as nearby neighbors. She was equally adept at crafting business letters and social missives, though time often worked against her. Her days were so full that she routinely wrote late into the night. Sometimes she could manage only shorthand descriptions of letters before other duties or fatigue interrupted her efforts. "Not time to coppy the rest," she jotted at the abrupt ending to one transcription.[14]

Eighteenth-century businessmen and politicians—slave traders, merchants, and colonial officials—routinely kept letterbooks. And for good cause: they conducted their affairs across the Atlantic Ocean. Crossings could be perilous, and letters were routinely lost to storms, wrecks, piracy, and warfare. Even sending letters to other mainland colonies or nearby locales could be problematic. So smart businessmen kept copies of everything; many even hired secretaries to duplicate their letters.

It was unusual for a young woman to keep a letterbook in the eighteenth century, but then Eliza Lucas was in an unusual situation. A young woman charged with tremendous responsibilities and left in an unfamiliar new home to manage a complicated business and vast estate, Eliza was keen to put her treasured education to practical use, and singularly loyal to a father she desperately missed and yearned to please.[15]

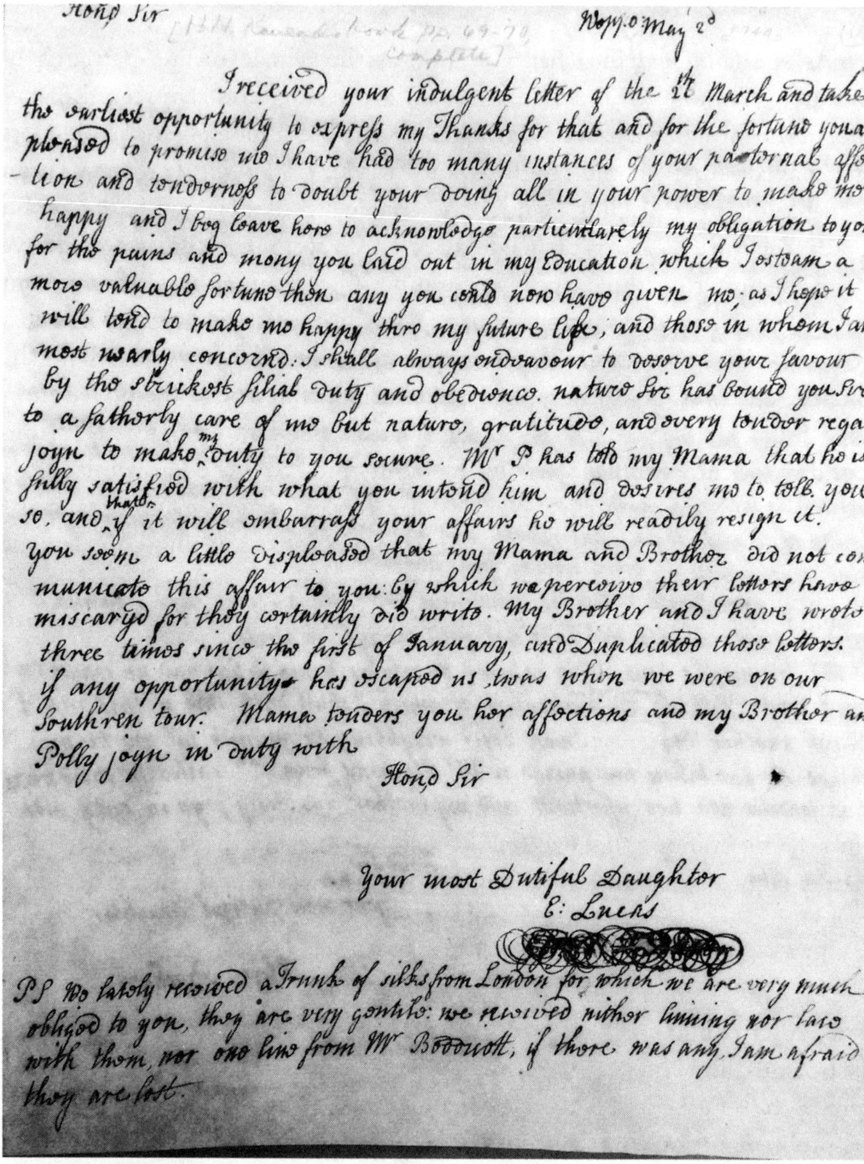

Hon'd Sir

Wappo May 2d

I received your indulgent letter of the 2[illegible] March and take the earliest opportunity to express my Thanks for that and for the fortune you are pleased to promise me I have had too many instances of your paternal affection and tenderness to doubt your doing all in your power to make me happy and I beg leave here to acknowledge particularely my obligation to you for the pains and mony you laid out in my Education which I esteem a more valuable fortune than any you could now have given me; as I hope it will tend to make me happy thro my future life; and those in whom I am most nearly concerned. I shall always endeavour to deserve your favour by the strictest filial duty and obedience. nature Sir has bound you Sir to a fatherly care of me but nature, gratitude, and every tender regar[d] joyn to make my duty to you secure. Mr P has told my Mama that he is fully satisfied with what you intend him and desires me to tell you so. and that if it will embarrass your affairs he will readily resign it. You seem a little displeased that my Mama and Brother did not communicate this affair to you: by which we perceive their letters have miscaryd for they certainly did write. My Brother and I have wrote three times since the first of January, and Duplicated those letters. if any opportunity has escaped us, twas when we were on our Southren tour. Mama tenders you her affections and my Brother and Polly joyn in duty with

Hond Sir

Your most Dutiful Daughter
E: Lucas

PS We lately received a Trunk of silks from London for which we are very much obliged to you, they are very genteel: we received nither linning nor lace with them, nor one line from Mr Boddicott, if there was any I am afraid they are lost.

Figure 2. Eliza Lucas to George Lucas, May 2, 1744. Eliza Lucas Pinckney Papers, David M. Rubenstein Rare Book and Manuscript Library, Duke University. Photo by author.

Eliza's early letters to her father reflected great care, in not only the contents but every part of the letter down to the penmanship. As she had learned in London, refined ladies meticulously attended to their letters. So she centered the paragraphs, kept the lines straight, filled the entire page. Her script was precise and elegantly crafted. It was all just as the popular conduct books at the time prescribed. Eighteenth-century elites bought those guides for their children and hounded them about precisely following the elaborate rules of writing letters. The matter was not simply of style or pretention, though there was some of that. The far-flung Atlantic World meant that people often met through letters—and formed crucial impressions based on what they read. Years, even lifetimes could pass without in-person contact between correspondents. Letters offered material evidence of a writer's character and so were scrutinized for signs of refinement (or rudeness). Eliza wanted her father to know she was responsibly supervising all the family's interests, and her letters offered easily recognizable evidence of her conscientiousness.[16]

A quick study, Eliza saw that Lowcountry society was, to a large degree, a woman's world. If she had any hopes of succeeding, she needed friends among the elites who ran South Carolina, especially the well-to-do women who held sway over who was and was not included in gentry circles. As South Carolina's first historian, David Ramsay, observed, Lowcountry elites depended more on daughters than on sons to ensure family respectability. Women decided who was welcomed and who was held at arm's length. They shared economic strategies, too, for managing households and, when men were absent or deceased, running family plantations and businesses.[17]

Eliza, with her carefully cultivated English-style gentility, made a good first impression on the gatekeepers in her neighborhood. Lowcountry elites practiced their Englishness with a zeal unsurpassed in North America. They used their deep commercial ties to the metropole and their large disposable incomes—South Carolina was the richest colony on the mainland—to buy a lot of English goods. Eliza, up to date and confident from her coming of age in London, fit right in. She was well read and well traveled, with interests ranging from music to botany. She carried herself the right way, she had read the right books, and she led the right lifestyle: all essential to gaining entry to South Carolina's elite circles.[18]

By the spring of 1740, Eliza had befriended her nearby neighbors and charmed members of some of the colony's most prominent families. "We have about 6 agreeable families around us with whom we live in great harmony,"

Eliza told Mary Boddicott.[19] She made fast friends with Mary Perry Cleland, herself a wayfarer of sorts. Mary's English father had lived for a time in Antigua, and he owned land in South Carolina. Mary's husband, John Cleland, was a native of Scotland, and the couple married in London in 1728. Mary and John moved to Carolina just a few years before the Lucases arrived, to claim possession of an estate Mary's father had bequeathed her.[20]

Elizabeth Lamb Pinckney became another intimate friend, though she was twenty years older than Eliza. Like Mary Perry Cleland, Elizabeth left her native London after marrying, in 1726. Her husband, Charles Pinckney, was a South Carolina native; he met Elizabeth while finishing his legal education in London. By the time Eliza Lucas moved to South Carolina, Charles Pinckney was serving as speaker of the Commons House of Assembly. Elizabeth and Charles had no children of their own, though Charles's nephew and namesake lived with the couple. Elizabeth was glad to have a new, young friend, and she doted on Eliza. Eliza told Mary Boddicott that both Elizabeth Lamb Pinckney and Mary Perry Cleland "insist upon my making their houses my home" whenever she visited Charles Town.[21]

Eliza also made friends with Mary Woodward Chardon, a young widow who lived three miles from Wappoo, and with Mary's mother, Sarah Stanyarne Woodward. Sarah was widowed in 1725. She never remarried and raised Mary as a single mother. Mary's husband died only a year after they married, and she was raising a young daughter on her own. Mary and Eliza grew close: they visited each other weekly, and, as Eliza put it, "are constantly engaged to each other." The two women carried their work with them on visits, spending whole days at each other's homes, doing easily transportable chores like needlework or writing letters. " 'Tis the fashion here to carry our work abroad with us," Eliza explained, so that visiting did not interfere with other responsibilities.[22]

On these visits, Eliza kept up with two sets of duties, one commonplace among Lowcountry women and the other more typical for men. Visiting allowed Eliza to build social connections to other elite women, to remain in the vital female-centered network of genteel families. Simultaneously, the work Eliza carried with her on these visits included not only needlework but also bookkeeping for her plantations, as well as such paperwork as allotting tasks to enslaved laborers and calculating her exports. Male planters spent days away from their estates, too, but they usually attended court days, visited coffeehouses, or watched horse races. Some planters were also practicing attorneys, so they worked in their offices in Charles Town or rode the legal circuit.

These were male-dominated spaces, while homes—and social visits—were female-centered.

Time deepened Eliza's connections to her female friends. Eliza especially treasured the time she got to spend with Mary Woodward Chardon. She considered her "an intimate friend." Eliza, then, felt "shocked beyound what I am able to express" when she arrived at Mary's house for one of their visits in the summer of 1742 and found Mary "quite out of her Sences." Unable to help Mary, Eliza tried to comfort Sarah, who was despondent over her daughter. From her caregiving of Ann, Eliza understood the heartbreak of attending to an ailing relative you could not cure.[23]

Eliza Lucas knew how to be a friend. She was easy to like: optimistic, eager to learn about others, witty, and winsome. She was also, as Mary Woodward Chardon's breakdown revealed, compassionate, the kind of woman other women could rely on to hold their confidence and to provide steady comfort in times of need. The women in Eliza's circle also saw that she needed their friendship. She was, they understood, doing the work of both her absent father and her ailing mother, with no kin around to help. And she was so young to bear all that responsibility.

Eliza's family duties made her more mature than her years, and she was younger than nearly all her friends, sometimes by decades. She was understandably thrilled when Mary Bartlett, the niece of Elizabeth Lamb Pinckney, moved into the neighborhood in January 1742. Mary came to South Carolina from England for a visit and stayed for more than a year. Eliza was only a couple of years older than Mary. The two had much in common, and they fell into an easy friendship. Mary and Eliza loved spending time together, at Wappoo, at Charles and Elizabeth Lamb Pinckney's country estate, Belmont, and at their home in Charles Town. The two young women wrote frank letters when they couldn't visit. Eliza was at her most open in her correspondence with Mary Bartlett, sharing doubts and vulnerabilities she usually hid with other, older correspondents. Eliza and Mary were also drawn to each other by their differences. Mary liked "amusements suitable to her time of life"—music, socializing, and balls. Eliza was bookish, always seeking out new knowledge and the next experiment—what she called her "schemes." Eliza joked about Mary's habit of sleeping late, and Mary teased Eliza about working too hard.[24]

Eliza Lucas and all the women whose friendship she cultivated visited in the style befitting eighteenth-century gentry while conforming to the physical realities of the colony. Planter families owned estates along South Carolina's waterways, and they maintained both a land and a water entry. For travel on land, Eliza Lucas kept an expensive four-wheeled carriage, imported from England. Most people found it easier (if less refined) to travel by cypress canoe. Rivers were the main highways in South Carolina—it was a river society—and the vessels were safe and reliable. Half a dozen people could sit in Eliza's thirty-foot-long canoe, as six more, all enslaved, rowed. A well-maintained road—a rarity in that age—ran from where Wappoo Creek and the Ashley River met, near Eliza's residence, and it traced the Ashley north to Dorchester. Along that road stood the majestic country homes of some of South Carolina's wealthiest planters, including Drayton Hall and Middleton Place.[25]

Eliza Lucas's immersion in a female network and her frequent visits with wealthy friends and neighbors signaled her earliest desire—and ability—to put down roots in her new community. Those connections helped Eliza to start to think of South Carolina as her home.

As she deepened those new ties, her oldest and dearest ones, with her brothers George Jr. and Tommy, never faded from her mind. Being separated from her brothers grieved Eliza. She tried to compensate for the distance between them with affectionate letters, offering advice and love. When George Jr. entered the military, she urged him "to beware of false notions of honour" and to make "proper distinctions between Courage and rashness, Justice and revenge." She worried about his character and his Christian faith. "Consider," she lectured George Jr., "to how many dangers you are exposed, (I don't now mean those of the field) but those that proceed from youth, and youthful company, pleasure, and disipation." Reflecting Enlightenment sensibilities, she insisted: "The greatest conquest is a Victory over your own irregular passions." She sought out shared interests with her brothers, too, urging Tommy to write to her about anything, any chance he got. To stay connected—and, no doubt, set a good example—she sent her brothers long letters describing the Lucas estate and the local people. Sometimes the siblings practiced French in their letters.[26]

Eliza sensed the unconventionality of "a girl at my early time of life presuming to advise" her brothers. But advise she did, and confidently so. She had gained wisdom from her wide experiences and seldom held back on telling her brothers what she thought. "I am a little older than you," Eliza reminded George Jr., and she counseled him from "the tenderest regard for your happiness." When George Jr. or Tommy neglected to write as often as she expected, Eliza upbraided them. It vexed her when those schoolboys failed to send letters. She always kept up her side of the correspondence. Alongside caring for her mother and managing the Lucas estate, Eliza saw maintaining connections with her brothers as an inviolable responsibility.[27]

"I have so much business on my hands at present," Eliza explained in a 1742 letter, "I hardly know which to turn my self to first and most of it such as cant be defered." When casually asked about her activities, Eliza replied with an exhaustive (and exhausting) accounting of how she balanced her myriad responsibilities. Her schedule reflected Eliza's bridging of two roles: planter-patriarch, a role typically held by male heads of households, and genteel young mistress. She did not leave behind the latter to pursue the former. "I rise at five o'Clock in the morning," she began, and "read till Seven." George Lucas left behind his library, which Eliza put to steady use, expanding her already capacious education. She read, too, her accounts and correspondences with London factors and the overseers at her other properties. After that, she would "take a walk in the Garden or field [to] see that the Servants are at their respective business." Only then did she eat breakfast, prepared for her by enslaved women. After breakfast, she studied music and French, to keep up her feminine respectability, and practiced shorthand, the better to manage her business interests. In the afternoon, she turned to educating her sister Polly.[28]

Eliza also taught two enslaved girls to read. Here she seemed to follow the example set by her parish priest, Reverend Alexander Garden, who started a school for enslaved children in Charles Town around this time. As Eliza explained to Mary Bartlett, "I intend [them] for school mistres's for the rest of the Negroe children—another scheme you see." Clearly, Eliza was imagining a long-term future in South Carolina as a slave owner, which included controlling literacy on her estate. These two girls, in her "scheme," would teach other children to read—mostly the Bible, emphasizing lessons of obedience, and the Book of Common Prayer. Passively literate children (reading and not writing) might grow up to serve Eliza's business interests, too: they could read directions, convey messages, assist her in keeping up with correspondence. Eliza did not violate the 1740 law prohibiting enslaved people from learning to write. While that specific law was driven by white fears of black flight, the separation of reading from writing was commonplace in the eighteenth century. White children usually learned to read before learning to write, and some white girls never became actively literate. Whether the two girls Eliza trained made that transition is unknown. But they doubtless put their education to ends other than those imagined by Eliza. She soon dropped the scheme.[29]

In the evenings, Eliza returned to her music, for at least an hour when possible. Eliza loved music. She was convinced it would be "one of the imployments of Eternity." She took harpsichord lessons from Charles Pachelbel, one of the most renowned musicians in Charles Town, and tried, without much success, to play the flute.[30]

Such gratifying pursuits often got sidelined by the demands of running an estate. Dealing with overseers interrupted her music lessons, French studies got delayed by her responsibility for supervising rice cultivation. Changing seasons shifted her management of enslaved laborers: she adjusted for storms and droughts, epidemic diseases, wartime seizures of her shipments, fluctuating markets. At night Eliza attended to her ever-growing correspondence. She wrote to friends and relatives, business contacts, foreign creditors, and overseers. She read by candlelight before going to bed, to rise the next day and start again. Eliza reserved Thursdays for catching up on business matters. Fridays she usually visited friends or entertained guests. Her work kept those social calls to once a week.[31]

During the times Ann fell ill, Eliza must have devoted considerable parts of her days to caregiving, to supervising the enslaved women who tended to Ann, or just to sitting by Ann's bed. Though she occasionally mentioned her mother's health setbacks in her letters, Eliza seldom gave details. Perhaps her practiced optimism kept her from saying too much. Ann's exact condition was never diagnosed, and the family did not discuss her symptoms. She had stretches of good health, but often receded into the family background because of what Eliza called her "bad state of health." Reticence aside, caregiving was an important and energy-consuming part of Eliza's days.[32]

Eliza's packed schedule worried her friends, who chided her for working such long days. One neighbor cautioned that losing sleep would "make me look old long before I am so." Eliza disagreed: "I believe she is mistaking for what ever contributes to health and pleasure of mind must also contribute to good looks." Eager to avoid overtly contradicting her friend, Eliza explained, "I reason with her thus: If I should look older by this practise I really am so; for the longer time we are awake the longer we live." So, she concluded, "I have the advantage of the sleepers in point of long life."[33]

One thing occasionally forced breaks: Eliza suffered from migraine headaches. Women in the neighborhood joined Mary Boddicott in offering suggestions and fretting. At their urging, Eliza tried all kinds of home remedies. She also took medicine shipped from London at the direction of Richard Mead, an eminent physician in England. In her careful way, she even charted the migraines to search for patterns in weather, season, and frequency. But Eliza found no permanent relief, and sometimes the headaches grew so intense she became nauseated. Strains caused by her father's absence and her mother's health didn't help.[34]

At times, long stretches passed without a letter from her father. During the first six months of 1741, Eliza heard not a word from Antigua and feared the worst. Her relief at getting a packet in June was almost overwhelming: "Never were letters more welcome than yours," she declared.[35]

Eliza turned to her strong faith in God to try to counter the anxiety she felt over her father—and, no doubt, her mother, too. "I indulge no melancholy apprehensions," she pronounced, "but endeavour cheerfully to resign to the Devine appointments." "I make this a rule," she vowed three years into her management of the family's estate and reputation. She then added, more hopeful than truthful: "It enables me to keep up an habitual cheerfulness of temper." As months turned into years and the reunion with her father kept getting postponed, Eliza rose early and worked late, determined to be a good steward of her family's fortune and future—a good planter-patriarch.[36]

By the summer of 1742, Eliza had taken on yet another responsibility common to Lowcountry planter-patriarchs but highly unusual for nineteen-year-old women: lay lawyer. She began studying law by reading Thomas Wood's *An Institute of the Laws of England*, the standard book for students at the Inns of Court in the early eighteenth century. Eliza struggled to understand the text, but armed with both her English and French dictionaries she refused to give up. "Nor," she added, "shall I grudge a little pains and application if that will make me useful to any of my poor Neighbours." Eliza's neighbors knew she was well educated, compassionate, and reliable. They turned to her in their times of greatest need. "What can I do if a poor creature lies a dying and their family takes it in to their head that I can serve them?" Eliza asked. "I'll Trust you with a secret," she confessed to Mary Bartlett in 1742: "I have made two wills already." As with her early business dealings, no one publicly challenged Eliza's ability to undertake legal work. She had studied enough to write a workable will.[37]

Another of Eliza's neighbors, a widow about to remarry, begged Eliza to draw up a marriage settlement for her. This Eliza refused. As she understood from close study, English law gave greater latitude for the writing of wills than most other legal documents. Eliza always made sure to get the signatures of three witnesses for the wills she wrote. She felt confident her work would hold up in court if contested. But marriage settlements were another matter:

time was less pressing, the courts more scrupulous in lawsuits, and the stakes more fraught. She didn't risk the chance that her (extra)legal work might get challenged in court and damage her reputation. Eliza did, however, agree to serve as one of the two trustees of the 1742 marriage settlement—yet another role usually filled by men.[38]

As Eliza's interests and duties multiplied, she remained ever enthralled by the natural world and fascinated by the discoveries she made at Wappoo. Writing Mary Bartlett after one springtime walk, Eliza longed to find the words to capture "the beauties of pure nature." "The majestick pine imperceptably puts on a fresher green," she ventured, "the young mirtle joyning its fragrance to that of the Jesamin of golden hue perfumes all the woods." As she had done as a little girl in Antigua, Eliza loved roaming the Carolina countryside, strolling through fields of daisies and breathing in honeysuckle. Eliza recounted in another letter to Mary her joy at hearing a mockingbird early one morning. Inspired by the sounds, she dashed off a short poem while lacing her stays. Eliza's affinity for the natural world pleased her father. He had, since her girlhood, encouraged it. George told Eliza that someday her love of plants "might produce something of real and public utility."[39]

Eliza would prove him right.

CHAPTER 5

A Brilliant Scheme

Soon after she took over Wappoo Plantation, Eliza began experimenting with ginger, cotton, alfalfa, and cassava, dutifully describing to her father "the pains I had taken" to diversify crops. The experiments blended her affinity for botany with her eagerness to protect the Lucas family's assets. As England's war with Spain stalled her rice exports, Eliza got imaginative. She even tried her hand at preserving and shipping eggs. "My scheme," she explained, "is to supply my fathers refineing house in Antigua with Eggs from Carolina." Eliza knew that sugar could be refined using egg whites. Most of the refining of Antiguan sugar took place in North America or Europe, which cut into island planters' profits. Supplying George with Carolina eggs would give him a competitive edge over other Antiguan planters and increase his profit margins. Far from dismissing these "schemes" as a young woman's flights of fancy, George Lucas and Carolinians who got to know Eliza viewed her experiments as intriguing and important. They took her and her work seriously. Ever an optimist, Eliza didn't give up on herself either, even when several of her schemes, including the egg idea, failed. "Out of many," she calculated, "surely one may hitt." And one did—bigger than she ever imagined.[1]

Blue was the most widely worn color of the eighteenth century. From ball gowns to sailors' uniforms to the fabric stingily rationed out to enslaved families, everyone in the Atlantic World dressed in blue. People found blue dye the easiest to acquire, and they dyed upholstery, blankets, and wallpaper blue, too. Using it was simple: essentially dunking cloth in a vat of water containing the dye. Varying times and techniques yielded colors ranging from faint blue-gray to cobalt, with elites preferring (and monopolizing) the deepest hues. The dye that could turn silk, wool, cotton, and paper this rich variety of blue came from the leaves of indigo plants. If sowed in the spring in the right environment, the scrubby plant bloomed in midsummer, and with minimal tending.[2]

Transforming a simple plant into a globally trafficked dye was another matter entirely. Producing indigo dye was physically arduous and highly nuanced, and it smelled terrible. Manufacturing on a commercial level was an ordeal.

Like every other commodity in the colonial Americas, large-scale indigo production depended on slave labor. Enslaved men and women produced the dye in a series of open-air vats, made of either brick or wood. Submerged in hot water, indigo plants fermented in the first vat. Workers transferred the substance that dissolved off the leaves into a second vat. They then beat that thick liquid as fast as they could, in the heat and stench, for several hours. As the mixture turned darker and darker green, a skilled supervisor (sometimes a white hired hand, sometimes an enslaved man) would order the beating stopped and add lime to set the dye. The mixture was then left to sit, until a mudlike substance settled to the bottom. Enslaved laborers drained the sediment into a third vat, scooping out the fetid residue. Because the dye was sold internationally, men and women pressed out the remaining liquid and shaped the indigo dye into transportable cakes. The cakes were then set to dry. But even that seemingly simple process was onerous: cakes had to be turned three or four times a day, could not be exposed to direct sunlight, and needed to be protected from flies and other insects. Finally, the dried blocks were packed into barrels for shipping abroad.[3]

Lacking a clear scientific understanding of the chemical processes that occurred in indigo production, eighteenth-century manufacturers treated it like distilling whiskey: they depended on sights and smells, they learned through trial and error. Success required well-honed skills, good luck with the elements, and meticulous timing. The risks of failure were high. It was not an undertaking that attracted many novices.

Until the 1740s, Spanish and French colonists controlled most of the Atlantic indigo trade. They shipped dye from the West Indies by the hundreds of thousands of pounds. French Huguenots moving to South Carolina in the late seventeenth century tried their hand at growing indigo there, and they

Figure 3. Eliza Lucas played a central role in developing indigo production in colonial South Carolina. *A map of the Parish of St. Stephen, in Craven County: exhibiting a view of the several places practicable for making a navigable canal, between Santee and Cooper Rivers. Henry Mouzon, Jr. & John Lodge. Surveyor or engraver.* London: 1773. David M. Rubenstein Rare Book and Manuscript Library, Duke University.

found the environment hospitable. But rice yielded much higher profits and consumed Lowcountry planters. Attempts at commercially producing indigo had essentially been abandoned by the turn of the eighteenth century.[4]

Just as Eliza embarked on the management of the Lucas plantations, Carolinians started to revive their interest in growing indigo. The resurgent attention was largely driven by the War of Jenkins' Ear—the conflict that forced George Lucas back into active-duty service in Antigua. That conflict (eventually subsumed by the War of the Austrian Succession), pitted Britain against Spain in a contest over trade and territory in the New World. Battles on the high seas destabilized commerce and undermined colonial profits. In South Carolina, the war damaged the rice market by cutting off access to Spanish and French importers. In the 1720s and 1730s, hogsheads of Carolina rice filled the cargo holds of hundreds of ships bound to ports across Europe and the larger Atlantic World. But after the commencement of war with Spain in 1739, that expansive international marketplace was quickly reduced to a trade with only the imperial center. Rice profits fell by half in 1740. Colonial planters and merchants soon discovered another downside to producing rice in the middle of a war. The bulkiness of shipping it abroad coupled with escalating threats of attack led ship captains to charge exorbitant fees for carrying rice to England. Insurance rates also skyrocketed.

Lowcountry planters, including Eliza, scrambled to find alternative sources of revenue. In the summer of 1740, she wrote her father that she had higher hopes for indigo "than any of the rest of the things I had tryd." She needed only good seeds to start the project. George sent seeds from the Leewards, and Eliza made her first significant attempt at planting indigo in March 1741, but a late frost destroyed the young plants. Undeterred, she salvaged what survived. The men and women she enslaved started again. Their second efforts yielded barely a hundred bushes—a disappointing number to Eliza. But she remained confident. "I make no doubt Indigo will prove a very valuable Commodity in time," she reassured her father. She was already preparing for the next season.[5]

To build the vats necessary to mass-produce the indigo Eliza felt confident she would eventually grow, she turned to a man named Quash, enslaved at Wappoo. Quash was listed in Lucas family papers as a "Mulatto," meaning that at least one of his ancestors was white. He had almost certainly lived in the Lowcountry longer than any of the Lucases, and probably he had been born there. Quash left no records by his own hand, and his story appears only fleetingly in Eliza's writings. But it is abundantly clear that he played a critical role at Wappoo. He was a highly skilled carpenter and literate—he could both read and write. He was perhaps the driver at Wappoo, the man who supervised the day-to-day work of other enslaved laborers. He and Eliza worked closely together for many years. She depended on him in her management of Wappoo in general and for her indigo scheme in particular.[6]

Quash managed the building of the Wappoo indigo vats, but neither he nor Eliza yet knew how to process the plants. So George Lucas hired an experienced dye maker to sail to South Carolina to teach Eliza how to turn her plants into profits. James Nicholas Cromwell, called Nicholas, lived on Montserrat, just thirty-odd miles southwest of Antigua. Antiguans could see Montserrat from their southern shoreline, and travel between the two colonies was frequent and quick. As men of African descent built the equipment, a French colonial arrived with knowledge acquired in the Caribbean to work on Eliza's latest Carolina scheme.

Eliza knew herself well: "I hate to undertake any thing and not go thro' with it." On her third attempt to grow indigo, the plants finally reached maturity, but Eliza was done in again, this time by outright duplicity. James Nicholas Cromwell was paid handsomely to teach Eliza how to manufacture indigo dye. But as Eliza persevered, Nicholas began to weigh the long-term consequences of the deal. Skittish about the prospects of Carolina indigo's undercutting profits on his native Montserrat, he sabotaged her. Dumping too much lime in the middle vat, he spoiled the color of the dye.[7]

If Nicholas thought he could fool this girl watching him work, he sorely underestimated Eliza. Sharp-eyed and learned, she saw through his ploy. "I observed him as carefully as I could," Eliza later recalled. Though disgusted by what she called Nicholas's "churlishness," she stuck with her experiments. As eager as his daughter to pursue indigo production, George Lucas sent her a second adviser, Nicholas's brother Patrick. At long last, with seeds from her father, guidance by Patrick, the carpentry of Quash, and labor from scores of enslaved men and women, Eliza found success with indigo. On October 14, 1741, she happily reported to her father that she had managed to make "20 w[eight] of Indigo and expected 10 more." The dye was not quite dry, so she could not send it along just yet. But she did not hide her optimism about the future: she asked George to send more seed. She also expanded her indigo works beyond Wappoo, relying on Quash's carpentry skills to build vats for Garden Hill.[8]

Though Eliza Lucas would be widely celebrated for introducing indigo to South Carolina, she was hardly alone in her efforts at Wappoo and Garden Hill or even in the idea of experimenting with indigo. Several Lowcountry planters were trying to manufacture the dye in the early 1740s. Eliza consulted with neighbors, including Andrew Deveaux, a Frenchman who knew a good deal about indigo cultivation. Andrew, Eliza told her father, proved "very kind in Instructing me in planting affairs." There was, in fact, a good deal of sharing of information in the quest to find alternatives to rice. Advice about successful indigo production methods was even published in the *South Carolina Gazette*.[9]

Eliza Lucas's efforts came especially early, though, thanks to her father and his connections on the Leeward Islands. She was also the only woman in the cohort. Other women ran plantations in South Carolina, but none seemed as keen about innovating in this era as young Eliza. And time proved her right about the tremendous payoff of experimenting with indigo.

As South Carolina slaveholders expanded indigo cultivation in the 1740s, they learned that their long summers made it possible to harvest twice a year. The South Carolina Assembly proclaimed indigo "an excellent colleague Commodity with Rice." Indigo fit smoothly with the colony's racial order and plantation values: producing it exploited the labor of men and women already enslaved and at times of the year when they were not overwhelmed with cultivating rice. Planters could maximize land and labor resources while offsetting temporary income fluctuations in the rice market. The innovation brought new and steady profits while requiring minimal adjustments for well-to-do planter families. The changes for enslaved laborers were more thoroughgoing. Planters used the "gang" system to produce indigo. Enslaved women and men worked in smaller groups and under closer white oversight harvesting the plants, tending the vats, and molding the dye cakes. The addition of indigo production all but eliminated slack periods, pushing laborers to the breaking point.[10]

During the War of Jenkins' Ear, Carolina planters saw that they could ship indigo to England in far fewer heavily guarded ships than rice, with less risk and lower insurance costs. The war also increased England's demand for the dye: the metropole needed more and more of it to make uniforms for sailors and soldiers. Eliza knew that the empire lost thousands of pounds every year by trading for indigo with foreign manufacturers. Cultivating indigo in South Carolina, then, had a patriotic as well as a financial payoff. "We please ourselves with the prospect of . . . supplying our Mother Country," Eliza announced. She and other Carolinians could benefit the empire fiscally and strategically and get richer in the process. By 1744, Eliza reported that Carolinians felt "very sanguine" about indigo. Ever a shrewd businesswoman, she focused on opportunities for increased profits. South Carolina had already placed a bounty on the crop, paying five pence per pound, and she hoped England would soon do the same.[11]

Eliza's confidence in the future of indigo turned out to be well-placed. In 1746, Carolinians exported 5,000 pounds of indigo. The next year the figure jumped to nearly 150,000 pounds. The Carolinians' growing market presence allowed merchants in Charles Town and their London factors to successfully petition Parliament to offer a bounty on South Carolina indigo in 1749. Quality remained a problem. Eliza and her fellow Carolinians could never quite match their French rivals, whose superior production yielded the richer, deeper shades of blue preferred by the wealthy. Astute consumers in London voiced skepticism about Carolina indigo, and some openly declared it inferior to French-produced dye. But Carolina indigo seemed perfectly fine for dyeing military uniforms and clothes of nonelites. And it offered a ready substitute for Lowcountry planters when imperial conflicts disrupted the rice trade. By the 1750s, Henry Laurens, the most successful merchant in Charles Town, pronounced South Carolina "an Indigo Country." Indigo remained a cornerstone of the colony's economy until the Revolutionary War.[12]

Though the project was not hers alone, the tremendous success of indigo made Eliza more independent, in terms of both her family wealth and her personal confidence. But her mastery of the people who produced that indigo remained highly contested. The men and women the Lucases held in bondage resisted enslavement as best they could and at every opportunity. Colonial laws made collective rebellions—organized challenges to the institution of slavery as opposed to personal resistance to enslavement—difficult to achieve and rare. But the people enslaved at Wappoo, Garden Hill, and Waccamaw, as in all the slave societies that emerged in the colonial Americas, routinely engaged in individual acts of defiance. Some people ran away. Many others intentionally lost tools, forgot instructions, broke dishes; some feigned illnesses and sabotaged tasks; others flouted commands. It is easy to imagine indigo intensifying both the demands of enslavers and resistance among the enslaved. Planters, impatient to succeed at the complicated business of turning indigo plants into marketable bricks of dye, brutalized laborers. Enslaved people, forced to do noxious work for interminable hours, resisted and fled for their lives.

In the winter of 1742–1743, Quash decided he'd had enough and seized a chance to escape Wappoo. He and several other men fled toward St. Augustine, but they were soon caught. In January 1743, they stood trial in Charles Town, for the capital offense of organizing their flight. Eliza attended Quash's trial. Her attitude during the proceedings echoed that of the Antiguan planters after the aborted 1736 uprising. There, accused conspirators "were so entirely trusted by their Masters, that it was with very great difficulty, any Crime was believ'd against them." Eliza didn't believe the charges against Quash, either. More likely, she couldn't entertain the idea of losing him to the colonial courts. Under the 1740 slave code, the punishment was death for any enslaved person who "shall endeavor to delude or entice any slave to run away and leave this Province," as well as any "accomplices, aiders and abettors" to the flight. If the court convicted and executed Quash, the maximum payment Eliza could receive was £200—a figure that did not reflect his skill and experience.[13]

What Quash said in his defense is unknown; the trial records did not survive. But Eliza said he "proved him self quite Innocent." Her relief at his exoneration had little to do with his well-being and everything to do with her indigo works. Eliza needed Quash. Perhaps she also felt confident in her ability to control him, or at least prevent another flight. In any event, Quash returned to Wappoo with Eliza, to resume his life under the command of a typical Lowcountry planter-patriarch who also happened to be a twenty-one-year-old never-married woman.[14]

Between 1739 and 1743, Eliza Lucas conducted herself like most other large-scale planters in the Lowcountry. She supervised agricultural experiments on her plantations and commanded enslaved people to produce commodities for transatlantic markets. She ran a complicated enterprise and understood how trade and foreign affairs intersected. There was no part of the Lucas family business she did not manage. The list of her correspondents included politicians, merchants in Charles Town and London, lawyers, ship owners, and her plantation overseers. Like other prominent planters, she even provided legal services for her poorer neighbors, based on independently reading English legal treatises.

Eliza Lucas differed in one key way. She had no interest in starting her own family, a preoccupation of many young male planters. Perhaps watching her mother suffer during her father's years-long absence disabused Eliza of romantic ideas about marriage. Or maybe she enjoyed her life just as it was, the responsibilities and growing independence. She definitely did not want a suitor. Most young male members of the planter class wanted a wife, to manage their households, as sexual partners and companions, and to expand their fortunes. As one new husband put it, "I have allied myself to a very numerous and wealthy family which enlarges my Interest more ways than one." Most women enjoyed entertaining suitors. It was a rare period in their lives when they held power over men. And, without independent means of support, most young women needed to find a husband. Of course, romances could also be awkward. One young woman explained that courtship could put both men and women "under the dread & fear of some sad Catastrophe."[15]

Shortly after his departure from South Carolina, George Lucas wrote Eliza to broach the subject of courtship. He even suggested two likely candidates: a "Mr. Walsh" and a "Mr. L." Though we have only Eliza's side of the correspondence to judge, her father seemed neither especially concerned about her safety in South Carolina nor fearful that she would jeopardize the family estate without a husband. Even at seventeen, she was a formidable woman, just fine without a male protector. Rather, George apparently worried that in his absence Eliza might fall in love with the wrong kind of man. Did he think Ann too frail, too indulgent, too disconnected from the social scene, or perhaps too dependent on Eliza to check her romantic inclinations? Colonial elites routinely monitored youthful passions, because an ill-advised match exposed young people—and their relatives—to all kinds of financial risk: squandered estates, poverty, and disgrace. A well-chosen spouse, on the other hand, deepened connections with other elites and enhanced wealth. Colonial southerners' predilection for cousin marriages and exchange marriages, in which siblings from one family married siblings from another, grew out of intentional efforts to consolidate estates and protect them from fragmentation. So for George, the right kind of man for Eliza meant a rich, well-connected one. In a gentle admonition, George assured Eliza of his confidence in her prudence. He said he felt certain she would never "entertain an indiscreet passion for any one." Ever eager to please her father, Eliza vowed, "I would indulge no passion that had not your approbation."[16] Eliza's promise followed social convention. Well-to-do young people in eighteenth-century South Carolina rarely pursued serious relationships without familial approval. Those few who did risked estrangement and disinheritance. When one concerned patriarch saw his nephew on the verge of making "a very imprudent matrimonial connexion," he gave a warning familiar to young people across the Lowcountry: either break off the engagement or "you must not expect any assistance from me whilst I live, or, to be remembered in my Will." Elopements were rare and scandalous. Eleanor Austin, daughter of one of the richest merchants in Charles Town, eloped, and tore her family apart. Her father flew into "violent outrages" at the very mention of his (unapproved) son-in-law's name. Eliza knew better than all that.[17]

Eliza would have drawn a lot of suitors. She was refined, rich, and well connected. Her physical appearance was largely irrelevant in the gentry marriage market—and a bit of a mystery. Eliza seems never to have sat for a portrait. If she allowed her image to be captured for a silhouette or a miniature painting, as was quite common among elites in the eighteenth century, it remains lost to history. Furthermore, none of her friends or relatives ever offered a physical description, which they likely would have done if she had been especially tall, for example, or red haired. This much is clear: Eliza was extraordinarily attractive in every way that mattered to South Carolina suitors.[18]

She rebuffed them all. To her father's suggestion of Mr. Walsh, Eliza replied that she knew far too little about him to judge his character. She had no interest in learning more. The mention of Mr. L. brought a blistering response: "The riches of Peru and Chile if he had them put together could not purchase a sufficient Esteem for him to make him my husband."[19]

To preempt further matchmaking, Eliza closed the subject: "A single life is my only Choice." Reminding George that she was just seventeen, she asked him to set aside any thought of her marrying for at least two or three years. George Lucas honored his daughter's desire: no more overtures were sent from Antigua. Eliza put the matter out of her mind, too, concentrating on her work. "As to the other sex," Eliza told Mary Bartlett, "I don't trouble my head about them."[20]

Her lack of interest in courting did not keep Eliza from occasionally enjoying Charles Town's vibrant social scene. Though nothing to compare with London, the city offered a welcome break from life at Wappoo. Plays, balls, dinner parties, and musical performances drew the colony's rich and powerful, women and men alike adorned in imported fineries. Eliza liked to get dressed up and attend events alongside Carolina's first families. Doing so was an important part of her reputational responsibilities, too. Sometimes Ann felt well enough to go with her, but it was Eliza who principally represented the Lucas family at social events. She needed to balance those duties with her planting responsibilities. Besides, too much frivolity ran counter to her serious-mindedness. "Playing a game at Cards or going to a ball now and then to relax the mind," Eliza concluded, was perfectly fine. "But the immoderate love of them," she believed, "is sinful." Overindulging in social life wasted time and skewed priorities. The results, she pronounced: "downright dullness."[21]

In late October 1742, Eliza attended a lavish ball in Charles Town, thrown by elite Carolinians to honor the king's birthday. Eliza described the crowd and the entertainment to her father, including how she danced a minuet with one of his friends. Then, unfortunately, she got cornered by the kind of tedious, pompous man she dreaded, and she complained about hearing "a great deal of flashy nonsense from him." Courtship conventions called for young gentry women to gratify men's exaggerated sense of self-importance with feigned interest, but Eliza fancied herself far too busy to indulge such "nonsense." She could flout what she saw as silly rituals because, unlike most young women her age, she had absolutely no interest in finding a husband, and no need for one.[22]

Instead, Eliza concentrated on her plantations and her family, both of which were threatened by the spiraling war. In 1742, Spanish forces moved the fighting to mainland North America. A coalition of Georgia and South Carolina troops mustered under the command of James Oglethorpe to defend the Georgia-Florida border—and control of the southeastern mainland. In July, Spain landed five thousand soldiers and sailors on St. Simons Island. Attempting to fight their way inland, the troops were stymied by Oglethorpe's forces and driven back to sea. This temporary victory was of cold comfort to most colonists. "We were," Eliza informed her father, "greatly alarmed in Carolina."[23]

George Lucas was starting to worry, too, about the danger confronting his wife and daughters in South Carolina. Meanwhile, his prospects in the Caribbean brightened considerably with an appointment as lieutenant governor of Antigua. Ann's health had gotten no better after several years on the mainland. She remained mostly homebound and of only intermittent help to Eliza. Polly was old enough to attend boarding school. For £140, Eliza secured her a place with Mary Hext, who ran a school for girls in Charles Town. George Jr., eighteen and finished with his studies in London, received a commission in the British military in 1742. He soon joined his father in Antigua. The thought of both her father and her brother being in mortal peril, Eliza admitted, "depresses me to the greatest degree." With a young man's idealism of war, George Jr. confided in his older sister how disappointed he felt when their father went on a military campaign without him. Eliza saw that good might come from her brother's frustration: "It may teach him to bear disappointments and curb too ambitious aspireings in his young tho' good mind." Without a note of irony, she added that she needed to "cease morrallezeng [moralizing] and attend to business."[24]

As the family members' circumstances changed, George Lucas began to reconsider where their interests might best be pursued. The answer, he gradually concluded, was Antigua.

Getting Tommy out of England posed the biggest problem. Despite Mary Boddicott's vigilant care and the efforts of the best physicians, he'd been sick for more than a year. In June 1742 Eliza got dreadful news "of my much loved brother being given over by the Phiscians." The next day she wrote directly to Tommy, commiserating with him about his long illness and struggling to convey her "inexpressible concern."[25] Fearing Tommy might die, Eliza turned to her Christian faith. She discussed with Mary Woodward Chardon her efforts to become "resigned to that Almighty Being in whose hands are life and death." "Your long and incurable illness," Eliza wrote Tommy, "is a proof that unmingled happiness is not the portion of mortals." For years, she had looked forward to being reunited with "my much loved brother, when he arrived at the state of manhood." Now those hopes turned to grief. Her faith offered some comfort, in her belief that she and Tommy would meet again, if not in this world, then "in the realms of everlasting bliss and amity."[26]

As months dragged on with no new details forthcoming about Tommy's purportedly grave illness, family members grew suspicious. Was Tommy still sick or malingering? It was not uncommon, when called from the elegance and ease of London to responsibilities in the colonies, for boys to stall. At first, George was patient with Tommy. By the winter of 1743—eighteen months into the family drama—he reached his limit. That December, Eliza wrote Mary Boddicott that George had ordered Tommy to sail for Antigua. Everyone now understood the trip posed no threat to Tommy's health. It was just "much against his inclination." The father, not the son, got the last word. In early 1744 Tommy Lucas left England.[27]

Meanwhile, Eliza prepared for her own return to Antigua. She'd wanted a family reunion for so long. Now it was upon her, and she had mixed emotions.

She had set down roots in the Lowcountry, figuratively and literally. In the spring of 1742, Eliza had announced to Mary Bartlett, "I am making a large plantation of oaks." To be precise, she had directed enslaved men to plant the trees. The grove reflected her sense of ownership of Wappoo. Lest anyone doubt her intentions, she clarified: "I look upon [it] as my own property; whether my father gives me the land or not." She imagined her trees eventually providing lumber to build fleets of ships for South Carolina. The layout of the grove included fruit trees and flowers, and Eliza conceived it as a tribute to her treasured friend Elizabeth Lamb Pinckney.[28]

Eliza hated to leave behind that grove and her agricultural experiments and the network of neighbors and friends she had carefully cultivated. South Carolina, once just a place she inhabited, had become "a country for which I shall always have the greatest regard." But in Antigua, the Lucases, for years scattered across the Atlantic, could at long last reunite. Practical and dutiful, Eliza never challenged her father's decision and instead focused on the business of leave-taking. She needed to hire overseers, settle accounts, and navigate volatile geopolitics. She made no overtures to sell the family properties; perhaps George planned to resume the absentee ownership he had practiced before 1739. In late 1743, George, still unable to leave Antigua because of his military obligations, sent George Jr. to escort Eliza, Ann, and Polly back to the island. On December 14, Eliza wrote Mary Boddicott that she expected George Jr. any time. The exact date of her departure Eliza did not yet know: perhaps after the family celebrated one last Christmas at Wappoo Plantation.[29]

Whatever reluctance Eliza Lucas felt about leaving the life she'd made for herself in South Carolina, her optimism and resolve and sense of family duty prevailed. Fretting about changes beyond one's control, Eliza had long since decided, was a waste of time and pointlessly demoralizing. So she looked on the sunny side. She had been separated from her beloved father for more than four years, her brothers even longer. Soon they would all be back together. At the close of 1743, as Tommy resigned himself to leaving London, Eliza counted the days until George Jr.'s arrival.[30]

Then, the New Year brought grievous news to the neighborhood. Eliza's close friend Elizabeth Lamb Pinckney was sick again. Like Ann, Elizabeth had struggled for years with poor health. Only this time, Elizabeth didn't get better. She died on January 23, 1744. And just that fast, everything changed again.[31]

PART THREE

Romance and Resolutions

CHAPTER 6

"I have changed my condition in life"

"I have changed my condition in life," Eliza announced to her old school friend Katherine Martin (now Carew). Despite the well-laid plans of this inveterate planner to return with her family to Antigua in early 1744, Eliza would stay in South Carolina after all. "You will be apt to ask me," she anticipated, "how I could leave a tender and affectionate Father, Mother, Brothers & Sister." Eliza assured Katherine that she would understand "if you knew the Character & merit of the gentleman I have made choice of."[1]

When Eliza shared the big news with her cousin Fanny Fayerweather, she could, she wrote, almost "see you smile and wonder, that difficult girl (that's your phrase) ever married." Eliza had never shown any interest in courtship—too consumed with her work and experiments and too careful to lose her heart to some passing fancy. Eliza knew Fanny would recall her repeatedly "preaching" about the high stakes of marriage and disparaging their friends who took courtship too lightly and fell into imprudent marriages. She had often warned Fanny that if women "happen to judge wrong and are unequally matchd there is an end of all human felicity." To avoid such perils, Eliza Lucas had always thought about marriage rationally. She had even drawn up a list of qualifications she required in a prospective husband. It ran so long, Fanny teased Eliza, that she would probably "dye an old maid." "But you are mistaken," Eliza proclaimed. "The Gentm [gentleman] I have made Choice of comes up to my plan in every title." She made

Fanny wait until the last third of the letter to learn " 'tis Mr. Pinckney I have married."[2]

Charles Pinckney, like Eliza Lucas, descended from a family of ambitious wayfarers who struck it rich in the colonial Americas. Charles's father, Thomas (1666–1705), left England to seek his fortune in the West Indies and hop-scotched across the Atlantic in the 1680s and 1690s. Along the way Thomas married twice; he wed his second wife, Mary Cotesworth, during a trip to England. They eventually moved to South Carolina. In the patchwork family tradition created by pervasive death in the early modern Atlantic World, Mary raised her new husband's young son, Thomas Jr., as her own. Family genealogies sometimes list her as his biological mother.[3] Mary and Thomas had two more sons: Charles (1699–1758) and William (1704–1766). Like John and George Lucas, Thomas Pinckney was lucky—not least for surviving the "seasoning" in the tumultuous Lowcountry environment. He used money he earned privateering in the Caribbean to start a merchant firm in Charles Town. Soon enough, he made sufficient profits to build a house in town and buy a plantation on the Ashepoo River, which he named Auckland. When Thomas Pinckney died in 1705, Mary Cotesworth Pinckney took care of the inheritances of her three sons.

The middle boy, Charles, was quite bright, and in the 1710s his mother (remarried and now Mary Cotesworth Pinckney Betson) sent him to England for a proper education. Charles studied law there and became the first native-born South Carolina attorney. While in London, he met Elizabeth Lamb. They married in mid-September 1726 and shortly thereafter moved to South Carolina. Representing both London and Charles Town merchants in the colonial courts, Charles made a small fortune and diversified into slave-based commercial planting. He and Elizabeth divided their time between a house in Charles Town and their 175-acre country estate, Belmont, located on the east side of the Cooper River, around four miles north of the city, on Charles Town Neck.[4]

Charles Pinckney was charming, even-tempered, and pious. Like Eliza Lucas, he enjoyed a first-rate English education and was well read with sophisticated interests. He also shared with Eliza extraordinary vigilance and meticulous organization in all his business endeavors. His neighbors trusted him, both with their personal legal needs and as an elected official. By the early 1730s, he was an active member of the Commons House of Assembly, the locally elected legislative wing of the colonial government. He rose to the

Figure 4. Unknown artist, Charles Pinckney (1699–1758), c. 1740. Oil on canvas; museum purchase; 2006.002. Courtesy of the Gibbes Museum of Art.

rank of speaker in 1736. As his public reputation and responsibilities grew, Charles remained focused on profiting from his expanding landholdings and explored new commercial opportunities.

Charles and Elizabeth belonged to the elite circle that controlled much of colonial South Carolina. Their life was privileged and, in comparison with most people's around them, easy. It was not without disappointments, though: they were infertile. The absence of children in the Pinckney household stood out among eighteenth-century elites, and it doubtless saddened the couple.

A setback, ironically, offered a partial solution. Charles's younger brother, William, had a house full of children with his wife, Ruth Brewton. (Their half-brother Thomas Jr. had relocated to England). In 1735 William and Charles partnered to organize the first fire insurance company in Charles Town. They turned a reliable profit until 1740, when fire engulfed the city. Unable to pay all the claims, their venture collapsed. William and Ruth, with their large family, suffered worse than Charles and Elizabeth. To help lessen William and Ruth's difficulties—and perhaps to at last welcome a child into their home, too—Charles and Elizabeth took in one of their nephews, eight-year-old Charles, who had been named after his uncle. The boy spent most of his time at their home, and his uncle oversaw his education, funding his studies in town while planning to send him eventually to England.[5]

When George Lucas and Ann Mildrum moved to South Carolina, Charles Pinckney was attending to all these family demands while also managing his law practice, civic duties, and planting interests. No one seemed to know or care about the legalities of the Antiguan couple's relationship. The Carolinians welcomed Ann as George's wife and knew her as Ann Mildrum Lucas. When George returned to Antigua, the Pinckneys took the couple's daughter, Eliza, under their wing.

Eliza Lucas, Elizabeth Lamb Pinckney, and Charles Pinckney became good friends. They visited regularly and wrote often. Soon they had grown so close that Elizabeth insisted Eliza make their Charles Town house her home when she visited the city. She traveled around the Lowcountry with them, and in the fall of 1740 she almost joined them on a trip to Philadelphia and Boston. Eliza demurred only because she could not secure her father's approval before the Pinckney's departure.[6]

Charles enjoyed being around young Eliza as much as Elizabeth did. Eliza wrote her father about "the friendly and pressing invitation they continually give me to give them as much of my company as I can." When she could break free of her plantation management responsibilities, Eliza loved visiting Belmont. "I am afraid to trust myself on that agreeable spott and the Company I meet there," she told Elizabeth Lamb Pinckney, "least it should make it too difficult for me to return at the time I ought to be at home." Impressed with Eliza's intellect and curiosity, Charles sent her a copy of Locke's "Essay Concerning Human Understanding." She read it right away. "You see," Eliza told Elizabeth, "what regard I pay to Mr. Pinckney's recommendation of Authors." Charles lent Eliza all sorts of books—poetry, religious and legal treatises, works of philosophy. He shared her early enthusiasm for indigo. He made clear he admired her "fertile brain at scheming."[7]

The admiration was mutual. Eliza delighted in the Pinckneys' company. Elizabeth's friendship smoothed her entry into Lowcountry gentry circles. Charles coached her on how to manage enslaved laborers and improve her nimble mind. She was grateful for their attention. But her fondness ran deeper than gratitude. In 1742 she said that she saw in Charles "a graceful ease and good nature peculiar to himself." Charles's letters to Eliza have disappeared, but his perceptions come through in her responses. In one 1741 letter to Charles she proclaimed herself unable to match "the profusion of Compliments you have bestowed on me." Writing to her friend and Charles and Elizabeth's niece, Mary Bartlett, Eliza imagined Charles calling her "the little Visionary."[8]

If not outright flirtatious, the 1740–1743 correspondence between Eliza Lucas and Charles Pinckney certainly reflected how close and comfortable Eliza felt with so established and powerful a (married) man. She was quite candid in their correspondence. She wrote him, for example, about missing her father and her struggles to live a moral life. Although at very different stages of life—he was twenty-three years older than she—they had a lot in common, even their basic values. "You justly observe a completion of happiness is not attainable in this life," Eliza wrote Charles in 1742, "to wch truth I readily subscribe at all times." She even repeated that aphorism in an advisory letter to her brother Tommy: "Unmingled happiness is not the portion of mortals."[9]

None of this transpired behind Elizabeth's back. She, Charles, and Mary Bartlett read Eliza's letters together. Eliza and Elizabeth adored one another, too. As their bond deepened over the years, Eliza remained ever thankful for Elizabeth's friendship. In the summer of 1743, Eliza joined Elizabeth and Charles on a tour of Goose Creek and St. John's Parish. A highlight of the trip came when they visited William Middleton's Crowfield Plantation. Named after his great-aunt's English manor, Crowfield was one of the most lavish estates in the Lowcountry, with a two-story brick mansion and elaborate gardens that included serpentine flower beds, a series of ponds, and a bowling green. Eliza captivated William Middleton. She joked with Mary Bartlett about "the Conquest I made of the old Gentleman." Charles, she added, would doubtless give Mary a full account of the encounter. He had watched the whole thing and been "much pleased" with his young traveling companion's charm.[10]

In the early winter of 1743, when Elizabeth Lamb Pinckney fell ill, Eliza visited her often, joining a circle of close female kin and friends who provided medical aid and solace. Eliza was a precociously capable caregiver. She had learned a bit about medicine from her botanical studies, and she acquired even more knowledge through her responsibilities at Wappoo. She spent years helping care for her ailing mother. And Eliza followed a pattern common among cost-conscious planter-patriarchs: providing medical care for sick and injured people she enslaved. A quick canoe ride could carry Eliza from Wappoo Creek to the Ashley River, past Charles Town, and up the Cooper River to Belmont. Eliza helped attend to Elizabeth "a great part of the time she was Ill." Charles took time off from his legal work to be at Elizabeth's side, too.[11]

As they cared for Elizabeth, Eliza and Charles gained new insights into each other's character. Caregiving brought a new intimacy to their friendship and, perhaps, a sense of urgency to their lives. Elizabeth Lamb Pinckney died on January 23, 1744. Within two months Charles proposed to Eliza. She had just turned twenty-one. He was forty-four—more than twice her age and only four years younger than her father.

Eliza quickly—and on her own accord—said yes. As she told Katherine Martin Carew and Fanny Fayerweather, Charles was the man "I have made choice of." She dropped the business of settling her father's affairs and planning her return to Antigua. Eliza explained her thinking to Mary Bartlett, who was back in England: "I was just upon the brink of departing for Antigua with my Mama, Brother, and Sister to my dear father whom I have not seen for upwards of five years," when Charles Pinckney proposed. "I found it," she confided, "a very hard task to part with the tenderest of parents and all my relations." But she also "knew how tender a husband" Charles had been to Elizabeth. So she accepted. Only then did Eliza notify her father of the stunning change of plans. "You seem a little displeased," Eliza acknowledged in a subsequent letter to George, "that my Mama and Brother did not communicate this affair to you." Eliza assured George that the Carolina family had written to tell him about her engagement. Perhaps, she suggested, the letters got miscarried.[12]

Eliza had not waited for her father's reaction before agreeing to marry Charles. What a long way she had come: once driven by filial obedience, she made the most important decision of her life independent of her father. Ann and George Jr. went along with Eliza's judgment—a fact she underscored to her father. But she made clear to him, as with her friends, that getting engaged was her choice. Eliza told George: "I thought it prudent, as well as intirely agreable to me, to accept the offer." Still, Eliza wanted her father to be pleased with the match. She hoped that George agreed with her assessment:

"I have put myself into the hands of a man of honour, whoes good sense and sweetness of disposition gives me a prospect of a happy life."[13]

While not an elopement, an engagement without her father's approval, or even his knowledge, was risky. Eliza's contemporaries ultimately chose their own spouses, but they did so after closely considering their relatives' interests. South Carolina elites didn't arrange marriages, but they certainly circumscribed the range of acceptable suitors and vetted serious courtships. Just a few years before Eliza married Charles, Thomas Smith, a prominent Carolinian, disinherited his eldest son for failing to get his consent before entering into what Thomas derided as a "most disgraceful marriage." Eleanor Austin became estranged from her powerful father, too, when she miscalculated that he would come around to her unapproved marriage. Young people learned to check their passions against their family's preferences, which habitually bent toward alliances with wealthy, refined, well-known neighbors. As a young man visiting the Lowcountry quickly saw, elite Carolinians "plume themselves on rank & fortune, in the making of matches." Charles Pinckney fit that bill: he was a rich and respected man. But marrying him would necessarily keep Eliza in South Carolina.[14]

This was a lot for George Lucas to absorb. Apart from her sudden (and unapproved) engagement to a man nearly his age, Eliza was not returning to Antigua, despite all their plans. They would remain apart indefinitely. And he would no longer be the most important person in his daughter's life. What could George do, really, but acquiesce? The decision had already been made and the wedding was imminent.

Eliza was elated—and no doubt a bit relieved—when George replied that he supported her decision to marry and stay in South Carolina. "It gives me all imaginable satisfaction," she told him, "to know that I have the approbation of the tenderest of Parents . . . of my Choice."[15]

It was still an eighteenth-century marriage, which meant that it was a business transaction as well as an affair of the heart. In elite families, prospective grooms and future fathers-in-law often negotiated marriage settlements. These legally binding prenuptial agreements typically called for the bride's family to transfer to the groom land or other assets to be used to safeguard the daughter's financial well-being. The husband held the property, but the value was intended for the wife. George Lucas adored Eliza and he respected her excellent stewardship of his estate. He wanted to protect her and to ensure that her future husband understood her family's commitment to her best interest. But there was a problem: George's Antiguan properties remained heavily mortgaged. He had not fared nearly so well in Antigua as Eliza had in South Carolina. He was, he conceded in the offer he made to Charles, "at present destitute" except for his Carolina holdings, ably managed by Eliza. George could spare no more than £500, and even that was "not in ready money." So he offered Charles a stake in Wappoo Plantation, including twenty enslaved people. But, he sheepishly explained, there was another problem. George had borrowed against Wappoo, so there were liens on the property.[16]

Charles, keen to marry Eliza as soon as possible, accepted immediately. He even added that if the offer put George in a bind, he would forgo it entirely. Eliza thanked George and assured him, "I have had too many instances of your paternal affection and tenderness to doubt your doing all in your power to make me happy." Besides, she had her education, which, she decided, was "a more valuable fortune than any you could now have given me."[17]

Eliza married Charles three weeks later. Their wedding, on May 27, 1744, took place barely four months after Elizabeth Lamb Pinckney's funeral.

The day she wed Charles Pinckney, Eliza Lucas sat down with a devotional diary she had started several years before. She usually reviewed her prayers—personally composed, not from any Anglican liturgy—every December 28. Serious-minded, she used her birthdays to reflect on God's plan for her life and weigh whether she had been a faithful Christian. Had she consistently sought God's will and not her own? Could she "measure my time by improvement"? The morning of May 27, 1744, Eliza added a new prayer: for God's guidance in her marriage. Perhaps she had a bit of last-minute cold feet, too, for she also prayed that if the marriage "is not agreable to thy Devine Will, May I never Enter into it." The marriage settlement was finalized, and news of the match had spread across the South Carolina Lowcountry and to Antigua. The ceremony was only a few hours away. Breaking off the engagement at that point would have gone far past embarrassment into full-blown scandal, and perhaps litigation. But if she felt nervous, Eliza also loved Charles. Satisfied through her prayerfulness that God approved of their marriage, she resolved, with God's help, to "lead a Life of virtue and true religion."[18]

Before she carefully put away her personal prayers, she signed her name—for the last time—"Eliza Lucas." For her whole life, she'd been Eliza, sometimes Miss Lucas, and to her father, his dear Betsey. Her marriage brought a new identity and new responsibilities as Mrs. Charles Pinckney.[19]

As her name changed, so did her priorities. From that day forward, Eliza began to think more and more of herself as a Pinckney rather than a Lucas, and to act accordingly. In more ways than one, then, Eliza's wedding day altered the trajectory of her life.

Weddings for Carolinians of their rank usually took place in private homes, with ministers officiating and a good deal of celebrating. Elites drank, feasted, and danced, sometimes for two or three days. Scores of relatives and neighbors attended, socializing late into the night. Whether Eliza and Charles indulged in such revelry is unclear. Reverend William Guy, a local Anglican priest, officiated. And though twenty-one-year-old Eliza was just two years older than the average Lowcountry bride, the man who recorded the license designated her "Spinster." The newlyweds were deeply in love. "I have the greatest esteem & affection imaginable for you," Eliza told Charles. "My heart is entirely at your disposal." She talked to her family about how much she admired his "good Sence and Judgement" and "extraordinary good nature and evenness of temper." Charles adored Eliza, too. Marriage, he believed, was "the only happy life in this world." Being Eliza's husband made Charles, he told her mother, "one of the happyest Men in the world."[20]

Making such a love match was preferable but not a prerequisite for getting married in colonial South Carolina, and happiness was not the lot of all wives. Some Lowcountry couples were companionable and affectionate. Margaret Manigault counted the days when her husband traveled and longed for his "presence & conversation." He agreed: whenever they were apart, the high point of his day came when he sat down to write to Margaret. Oliver Hart echoed Charles's sentiment: his wife Ann made him "the happiest of Men." But many other husbands were far less sentimental. "I am sure I want one to look after my House and Negroes as much as any Body in the world," concluded the newlywed Thomas Dale.[21] Once married, women lost nearly all legal power and every personal asset to their husbands. In South Carolina divorce was impossible. Women who married irresponsible, unfaithful, or violent men were stuck for life. Eliza made a good match. In some ways, she was just lucky. She wasn't pushed into marriage by dependence or poverty. She exercised a rare degree of financial autonomy, empowered by her father and by her own accomplishments to manage the family holdings, and remained single as long as she wanted. She was also savvy enough to see though foppish dandies. She studied Charles's character; she even watched him care for his wife as she lay dying. They were friends before they were lovers. She knew that he knew her, and that he respected her.

But not everyone respected their choice to marry so quickly after Elizabeth's death. At minimum, the match raised some eyebrows. Charles and

Elizabeth had, after all, opened their home to the precocious young woman, offered her guidance and support, and taken her with them on visits to their prominent friends. Then, within two months of Elizabeth's death, Eliza agreed to become the second Mrs. Pinckney.[22]

Some of Elizabeth's kin in England heard rumors out of North America regarding just how quickly Eliza and Charles moved from grief to matrimony. A Mrs. Gregory, who had been visiting South Carolina in early 1744, carried to England gossip that got passed on to Mary Bartlett. Mary felt concerned enough to write to Eliza. According to Gregory, Charles had badly neglected Elizabeth as her health faltered. At one point, he was "about his business and the negroes out of call," so that when Elizabeth needed help, she had to "call a strange negro boy up into her chamber." In eighteenth-century South Carolina, a well-to-do white woman required to seek help from a black boy—and in her own bedroom—was the ultimate inversion of the social order. Infuriated, Eliza blasted Gregory as a petty woman of "envious malicious temper" peddling a lie for no reason other than "to study and love mischief." Having been often at Belmont during Elizabeth's last illness, Eliza vouched for Charles's unfailing devotion. To be with Elizabeth as much as possible, Charles had curtailed his business demands. When he needed to be away from Belmont, he never left Elizabeth alone. "Had I not known him to have made the best of husbands," Eliza informed Mary, she never would have agreed to marry Charles.[23]

Though confident in dismissing Gregory, Eliza was brought up short by Mary's concerns. Both women reflected the era's preoccupation with reputation. Mary fretted over her beloved aunt's legacy: had she been neglected at her weakest moments, humiliated by being forced to call out for help from strangers? Was Elizabeth's legacy damaged by a scandalous death? Eliza's concerns were even more pressing, for they involved her and her new husband's reputation. Had Charles been in a hurry for a new, young bride and neglected Elizabeth? What did it say about Eliza that she married such a man?

Eliza assured the extended Lamb family that she and Charles had behaved honorably toward Elizabeth. She continued to correspond with Mary Bartlett for several years, and Charles maintained ties with women in the Lamb family for the rest of his life. "I am conscious," Eliza wrote Elizabeth's sister Sarah Lamb Bartlett, "how unworthy I am to supply the place of so good a wife as your sister." Eliza vowed to equal her late friend in one regard: by doing everything in her power to aid Elizabeth's relatives. Whatever hurt the Lamb family initially felt about the quick remarriage, no one seemed to hold a permanent grudge.[24]

While Eliza worried about her and Charles's reputation, she never doubted their decision to marry. "We should," she counseled her brother George Jr. in a 1742 letter, "remember no time is ours but the present—and that so fleeting that we can hardly be said to exist." That was her attitude: "Stand firm and unshaken then in what is right in spite of infidelity and ridicule."[25]

Eliza embraced some of the new obligations brought on by her new "condition in life," but others fit uneasily and others still she disregarded. Her life, she said, now centered on Charles, and she recorded what it meant to be a good wife to him: "To pray for him. to contribute all in my power to the good of his soul, and to the peace and satisfaction of his mind. to be careful of his Health, of his interest, of his Children; & and of his reputation; to do him all the good in my power; and next to My God to make it my study to please him."[26]

Life interceded. Eliza and Charles couldn't move in together during the first weeks of their marriage. Ann's health had taken another bad turn. As much as she loved Charles, Eliza felt a stronger duty to care for her mother. So Eliza stayed at Wappoo after the wedding. Eliza seldom wrote about Ann's troubles and her caregiving, but her actions spoke volumes. Charles was unable to join his bride because his mother's health was flagging, too. He stayed at his mother's house. Eliza admired Charles's filial devotion even as she lamented their separation. She sent him a poem that captured their situations:

> you may the tender office long engage
> to rock the cradle of reposing age,
> with lenient arts extend a parent's breath
> make languor smile, and smooth a bed of death,
> explore the thought, explain the asking eye
> and save awhile one parent from the sky.[27]

George Jr., Ann, and Polly remained in South Carolina considerably longer than they had planned: for Eliza and Charles's wedding, because of Ann's health, and when an embargo prohibited ships from leaving the harbor. The Lucases finally sailed on July 2, 1744.[28]

Eliza and Charles could be together at last that summer, to start their new life together. But she missed her old life and her family. As her mother and siblings sailed, they carried Eliza's hopes of a reunion with her father. "Leaving you at such a distance," she wrote George, "was an objection I could not easily get over." Used to making things happen by executing well-thought-out plans, Eliza was left with only vague hopes for a reunification, though when she could not predict.[29]

A flurry of activities and newlywed affections helped distract her. She and Charles moved immediately to Belmont. The couple—finally under the same roof—spent the late summer of 1744 there "without being . . . at all lonesome," she assured her mother. Charles went to town to attend to business once a week; otherwise he didn't leave Eliza's side. It was easy for Eliza to feel at home at Belmont. From her many visits with the first Mrs. Pinckney, she knew the layout of the stately brick mansion and the paths winding through the gardens. The grand vista from the riverside entry to the house, set against a bend in the Cooper River, was quite familiar, too. Eliza soon made her own mark on Belmont, starting with the grounds. She directed enslaved men to plant indigenous oak and magnolia trees, and she experimented with imported plant species.[30]

Eliza also undertook at Belmont a new agricultural project: cultivating silk. Sericulture was an old dream, dating to the colony's origins. But when rice took off, interest in the tedious work of silk eroded. At Belmont, Eliza studied the process and sought out the advice of experienced contacts across the Atlantic. She imported silkworm eggs, and enslaved men planted mulberry trees. Enslaved children gathered mulberry leaves to feed the silkworms: it was a hard job but not too complicated for little boys and girls. In time, the scheme succeeded, but never on a level that allowed Eliza to enter the commercial silk market. Eliza and Charles leased Wappoo, in accordance with the marital agreement, but they kept close watch over Eliza's ongoing—and thriving—indigo experiments.[31]

Eliza's continued engagement with commercial agriculture at Wappoo and Garden Hill did not sit well with George Lucas. He urged her to fill a narrower role than she had grown accustomed to over the prior five years. She should be a wife now, he counseled, not an independent planter. In his view, Eliza, once married, needed to stay in a woman's "proper province" and avoid "invading" Charles's realm. George worried, as a descendant put it, "lest his managing daughter should attempt to be also a managing wife."[32]

Not temperamentally inclined toward submissiveness in the first place, Eliza had grown more independent and self-confident during her oversight of the Lucas family enterprise. She assured her father that she understood his point of view and promised to respect Charles and act appropriately as his wife. Her deference would not be reflexive, however, but rational. Charles had more experience, Eliza reasoned, which left her "nothing but the easy task of obeying."[33]

Whatever Eliza told her father—or tried to tell herself—she did not set aside her planting interests and commercial schemes. She and Charles followed their own preferences about apportioning their time and talents. Though George wanted Charles to administer his holdings in South Carolina, Charles seemed to conclude that doing so meant sometimes entrusting his capable wife to manage in his stead.[34] Charles respected Eliza's abilities and he supported her varied pursuits and independent actions. Many eighteenth-century wives were not so free to exercise their talents. When her first husband died, Virginian Martha Dandridge Custis proved a supremely capably manager of several plantations, seventeen thousand acres of land, and complicated business matters with London factors. "I now have the Administration of his [Daniel Custis's] Estate & management of his Affairs," she informed one English merchant. But when Martha remarried, her new husband, George Washington, took over all her finances. Alice DeLancey Izard, a neighbor and friend to Eliza Lucas Pinckney, ably managed all sorts of family responsibilities when business or politics frequently called her husband, Ralph, from home. But Ralph controlled things from a distance and scrutinized Alice's efforts. By contrast, Mercy Otis Warren's husband supported her literary talents, and he encouraged her to venture into traditionally male realms of publishing and politics. Charles Pinckney was more like James Warren than George Washington and Ralph Izard and most other eighteenth-century men, and that made all the difference for Eliza.[35]

In the same letter in which she vowed to act only in her "proper province," Eliza detailed her predictions for the fall crops at Garden Hill, discussed Atlantic trading markets, and reported on her ongoing indigo works. In the months and years after her marriage, when her father expected Eliza to recede to the background of the Pinckney and Lucas plantation enterprises, she continued to keep abreast of land prices, international affairs, and commodities markets, advising both her father and her husband about family businesses.[36]

Eliza's efforts to balance her individual inclinations against social conventions made her at once exceptional and emblematic of the eighteenth century. According to the ideals of white womanhood, single or widowed women who ran businesses should focus on their domestic duties once married. In some instances, Eliza did act this part of a deferential wife. Charles took over much of the correspondence with English factors, for example. But her influence lingered. Charles benefited from Eliza's connections and reputation. In April

1745, apprised of the news of Eliza and Charles's marriage, her long-standing friend, English merchant Richard Boddicott, sent his congratulations. Because of his fondness for Eliza, Richard was glad to aid Charles. Gradually Charles also became the principal contact for Lowcountry overseers. In the short term, William Murray continued to report to Eliza about rice production and shipments at Garden Hill. In the summer of 1745, he started writing to Charles Pinckney instead. Meanwhile, Eliza openly professed her deference to Charles—especially in letters to her father. "I shall," she assured him, "make it the whole Study of my Life to fix that esteem and affection Mr. Pinckney has professd for me, and consequently be more worthily your daughter."[37]

Still, Eliza remained involved in managing family properties and in her agricultural experiments. Work that had started out as unavoidable because of her father's absence and her mother's illness had become a source of deep interest and personal pride.

The year 1745 was transformative for Eliza and Charles. In June, their thirteen-year-old nephew Charles sailed to England to pursue his education and ready himself to follow his uncle into a legal career. Charles's remarriage had changed nothing regarding his commitment to the boy. He remained devoted to his namesake's well-being, joined by an ever-dutiful Eliza. She was considerably closer in age to her new nephew than she was to her husband. Still, she acted the maternal part, writing Mary Bartlett to let her know what they were sending with Charles and suggesting things Mary might provide for him. They missed their nephew but had every reason to be hopeful that he would enjoy a bright future, made brighter by the best education Pinckney money could buy.[38]

Meanwhile the Lucases were growing weary of Antigua and thinking of returning to South Carolina. By 1745, George was acting governor of Antigua. He was proud of the honor but vexed by the interminable duties. The War of the Austrian Succession now involved most of the major European powers. Governor Lucas was responsible for defending Antigua from Spanish and French predations. "We have been greatly Allarm'd for about Two Months past," he wrote Charles in late May, and he feared an imminent invasion from Martinique. The weight of leadership turned his thoughts to Wappoo. George confided to his son-in-law that he had always imagined retiring in South Carolina. Eliza's brother George Jr. wanted to move, too. Charles tried to get his brother-in-law reassigned to a post in South Carolina. George Jr. wanted to move for many reasons, not least of which was to be in his "Dr. Sister's

Company." The appointment never came, and the war continued, dragging father and son deeper into their Antiguan duties and farther from a reunion with Eliza.[39]

October brought the year's worst news: Charles's mother, Mary Cotesworth Pinckney Betson, died. Charles endured the loss of his only surviving parent while taking on the duty of settling her estate.[40]

By then, Eliza knew she was pregnant. The Lucases, mired in Antigua, cheered when they learned the happy news in late 1745. They also worried. Pregnancy was dangerous, and Eliza had no female kin nearby. George missed Eliza terribly and prayed constantly for her safety. He assured Charles that "neither her Mama or I have the least room to Doubt of your utmost care and tenderness to her" and saw "great reason to Rejoyce at her Situation." Nevertheless, they remained uneasy. Charles fretted, too. He kept in steady contact with the Lucases, assuring them that he was doing everything in his power to care for Eliza. All the while he tried to hide his own anxieties for fear of escalating theirs. Ann, whose health had improved since the return to Antigua, grieved "at being at this distance from her in so dangerous a time."[41]

Everyone's fears were born out of clear-eyed understanding of the hard reality of bringing children into the world. Common illnesses, to say nothing of breech births, hemorrhages, and infections, made pregnancy perilous and often fatal. Every woman in colonial South Carolina knew personally a woman who had died during childbirth. Aware of the dangers, elite and middling-rank women gathered for days and sometimes weeks in anticipation of a birth. The labor required of black women, in fields and houses, often precluded them from gathering together for childbirths. For mothers of all ranks, childbearing was not yet a medical matter, but still managed by women. The dangers associated with pregnancy continued after a mother safely delivered her infant. South Carolinians endured a shocking level of child mortality. Case-study research shows that 20–25 percent of white children died in the first five years of life; factoring in adolescent deaths, nearly one in three young white South Carolinians died before reaching age twenty. Mortality for black children was even higher: above 50 percent. Ann and George had good cause to worry about Eliza. Ann clung to the hope that the "merciful God who has hitherto guided & assisted her [Eliza], will still continue his favour in her time of danger." But faith did not arrest her fear. "Very many, & melancholy hours have I had on this Subject," Ann confessed. The family shored up prayers with action. Ann and Charles got Eliza's friend Sarah Stanyarne Woodward to superintend the birth. Eliza had supported Sarah when her daughter, Mary

Woodward Chardon, endured a mental breakdown. Now Sarah would care for Eliza, a stand-in for her absent mother.[42]

Because the Lucases closely tracked Eliza's pregnancy, when George and Ann wrote at the end of January 1746, they hoped that by the time their letters reached South Carolina their prayers would be answered, and both mother and child would be healthy. "Nothing this side the Grave," George declared, "can be more Joyful to hear."[43]

They calculated correctly: a healthy baby boy was born on February 14, 1746. Eliza was safe, too. Charles Pinckney became a first-time father at age forty-six. Eliza gave him the family that he thought he'd never have. And it was a son, too, to carry on the Pinckney name. The thankful parents named him Charles. To honor his maternal grandmother and distinguish him from his cousin, they gave him a middle name that he used all his life: Cotesworth. Eliza hoped her son would "inherit all his father's virtues, his good sence, his sincere and generous mind with all his sweetness of disposition."[44]

"Thank God," Eliza wrote Mary Bartlett in the spring of 1746, "I have no disorder but weakness." She was lucky. When Elizabeth Wragg Manigault delivered her first child a decade later, she was bedfast for nearly a month and had to have her breasts lanced—a not uncommon procedure. Still, Eliza found becoming a mother a physical ordeal. She had been "much out of order" throughout the pregnancy and spent the first three months after Charles Cotesworth's birth trying to regain her strength. She remained starkly "reduced and weakend." "You would," Eliza told Mary, "be surprized to see me." But she was getting stronger by the day. To speed her recovery, she and Charles decided to leave Charles Town, where they'd been for the delivery, and return to Belmont.[45]

While enslaved women tended to her and her newborn, Eliza made a leisurely recovery. At Belmont, as it had been at Cabbage Tree, enslaved women got up in the middle of the night to comfort the crying baby. They cleaned and dressed and sometimes nursed him. When Eliza felt strong again, she had plenty of time to dote on her son. "As promising a child as ever parents were blessd with," she boasted.[46]

When he was just three months old, Eliza swore she could see in little Charles Cotesworth "all his papas virtues already dawning." Before he could sit up on his own, his parents were already vigorously preparing for the (brilliant) future they imagined for him. When Eliza learned of a new English toy that could teach little Charles Cotesworth "to play him self into learning," she immediately wrote to Mary Boddicott and asked her to find one and ship it to South Carolina. Eliza had carefully studied the toy and included a detailed description, lest Mary get confused. Charles, meanwhile, proved an exceptionally hands-on father. He was, Eliza told Mary, "contriving a set of toys to teach him his letters by the time he can speak." Eliza saw the humor in what they were doing for a baby who was only three months old.[47]

Parental bragging continued apace. When Charles Cotesworth was twenty months old, Eliza wrote her sister Polly in Antigua that he "prattles very intelligibly," knew all the letters in the alphabet, and was starting to spell. He was indulged in every way: toys came from England and Antigua along with beautiful clothes and shoes, books, and treats. Eliza and Charles spurned the physical correction and control that earlier generations of parents pursued. They were affectionate and encouraging as they tried to bind him to them through loving guidance. Their friends and neighbors mostly raised their children that way. William Read proclaimed his daughter "very handsome, quite a lively prattler, and in fact the delight of my eyes." Henry Laurens adored his children, too. "Their noise," he decided, "which would disturb anyone else serves to lighten my labors."[48]

Eliza taught Charles Cotesworth, as soon as she thought the toddler could comprehend, the importance of family. He played beside her as she wrote to Polly, and Eliza made sure he sent "his duty" to his aunt. Eliza also coached the not-yet two-year-old to send to Polly "a dollar out of his own mony, to buy you some fruit at school."[49]

As Eliza planned for her son's future, she worried about her father's safety. Antigua's trade suffered terribly because of the continuing war, and in 1746, apparently to appeal for aid, Governor Lucas sailed for England. A French warship intercepted his vessel, and he was taken prisoner of war. French forces carried George on toward Europe and imprisoned him in the military port city of Brest.

George Lucas never made it back home. He died in French custody in January 1747, from unknown causes. The news devastated Ann and the Lucas siblings in Antigua. How could they possibly tell Eliza? She was pregnant again. Everyone understood how much Eliza loved her father and how long she had yearned to be reunited with him. "All my happiness in this life depends on your welfair," Eliza had often told him. What would happen if she learned this shocking news in her weakened state? Losing her or her child was unthinkable. And so, with Charles's help, the Lucases designed to keep George's death a secret from Eliza until she safely delivered her second baby.[50]

That the plan was born of compassion made it no less foolhardy. Eliza, predictably, uncovered the awful truth when she came across a mislaid letter from Antigua. She might have just as easily found out any number of ways, including in a newspaper; hiding the wartime capture and death of a neighboring colonial governor was no easy feat.

The family's fears came true. The shock threw Eliza immediately into labor. She delivered a premature baby early the next morning, August 14, 1747. In his loving mother's eyes, the infant seemed "as fine a boy as ever was born." He survived two weeks. Shortly before the baby died, Alexander Garden, the rector at the Pinckneys' parish church, St. Philip's, privately baptized him George Lucas Pinckney. Eliza and Charles had chosen the name when the future looked bright and God seemed to favor their family.[51]

CHAPTER 7

Faith and Self-Government

Discovering that her father was dead and losing her newborn child in the same horrific month shook Eliza Lucas Pinckney to her core. She had pondered death from a young age, confiding to Mary Bartlett in 1742 that she thought a lot about mortality, and telling her brother Tommy the following year that dying was "a scene that has been often acted over in my imagination." It was an odd preoccupation for a young person, perhaps explained by Eliza's deep piety coupled with the dangerous circumstances she faced. In her youthful writings, Eliza had felt certain that strong faith enabled Christians to accept mortality. "To those that have a well grounded hope of a blessed immortality to come," she believed, "all beyond the grave is gay and Serene." The sooner one accepted the inevitability of death, she advised Tommy, the quicker one could get on with living an upright, meaningful life. But she was twenty then, and he just fifteen. In those musings, Eliza was thinking about dying, not about being left behind to grieve. And death was still an abstraction.[1]

Nothing in her youthful introspection had prepared Eliza for the agonizing fact that her beloved father was lying in a grave an ocean away from her. She must have considered what it would mean to lose her mother; Ann was so often sick. But George was vibrant and strong, and even when Eliza worried about his engagement in military combat, in the back of her mind she knew that it was highly unlikely that he would be killed in action. Eighteenth-century European rules of war barred targeting such high-ranking men. But then, the improbable, the unthinkable happened. Worse still was the loss of her infant son. The tragedies Eliza imagined in her girlhood never included rocking her dying baby or standing over his grave.

In the face of crippling grief, Eliza turned to her Christian faith, long a cornerstone of her identity. Throughout her life, Eliza found solace and a sense of purpose in her faith. She was a practicing Anglican and attended Sunday services, mostly at St. Philip's, in Charles Town. Located on Church Street, St. Philip's was the oldest Anglican church in South Carolina, and it was spectacular. One visiting Anglican minister pronounced it "the most elegant Religious Edifice in British America." The church was one hundred feet long and sixty feet wide, with a cupola that soared eighty feet and held a clock visible across the city. Wide porticos fronted by Tuscan columns ran along the east, west, and north sides of the building, with the churchyard to the rear. The floor of the sanctuary held eighty-eight pews, with doors, as was the style at the time, and another sixty pews filled the second-floor galleries. Sculptures adorned five arches that lined both sides of the interior. Parishioners sang along with their prized organ, imported from London. Alexander Garden arrived in 1719 and served as rector for thirty-three years. Eliza and Charles and other rich parishioners sat up front, to signify their rank and display their elegant clothes. For many members, going to Sunday services was considerably more performative than pious. Josiah Quincy, visiting from New England, was taken aback by the low turnout and lax attentiveness when he attended a service at St. Philip's: "It was very common in prayer as well as sermon-time to see gentlemen conversing together." But Eliza took her faith seriously. As a devout Anglican, she believed in the ordered services and the traditional, structured liturgy laid out in the Book of Common Prayer.[2]

Attending Anglican church services was an important part of Eliza's duty and identity as an English woman, too. The Church of England had been the established church of South Carolina since 1706. Dissenters, including Quakers and Jews, freely practiced their faiths in Charles Town, but Anglicanism was the official church, and it tethered the colony to the metropole, religiously, socially, and politically. The parishes even determined representation in the assembly, and churchwardens coordinated elections. Attending St. Philip's allowed Eliza to affirm simultaneously her piety and her Englishness.[3]

But her religious convictions ran deeper than church affiliation. She inclined toward ecumenicalism, and her beliefs blended Anglicanism with Enlightenment ideals. The Enlightenment embraced the primacy of scientific thought, prioritized reason over emotion, and promoted belief in self-improvement and social progress. Eliza weighed what she read in the Bible and heard at church against what she knew to be factual and reasonable. She was, in sum, independent-minded in her religious views. Eliza made her personal faith a studied habit. She wrote often about her quest to follow God's will. Personal prayers conceived when she was a girl, along with a list of "resolutions" written in the early years of her marriage, reveal the centrality of practiced, self-conscious piety to Eliza's life.[4]

Eliza's earliest memories involved her parents teaching her about religious faith. "My Infant Lips were taught to call upon thee," she recorded in her personal prayers. In her youth, Eliza's religious sensibilities were every bit as precociously sophisticated as her botanical pursuits. A meticulous organizer from her girlhood, Eliza urged her brother George Jr. in 1742 to join her in devising "a plan for our conduct in life in order to living not only agreeably in this early season of it, but with cheerfulness in maturity, comfort in old age, and with happiness to Eternity." There was, she counseled her brother, only one sure foundation for such a worthy life: unshakable faith in the wisdom of God and unremitting efforts to do God's will. Religiosity marked by Enlightenment sensibilities underlay Eliza's quest for constant improvement. She regularly prayed for God to daily increase her wisdom and virtue. She believed that as a good Christian she should "measure my time by improvement." And she grounded her faith in rationalism.[5]

She spurned evangelical revivalism. Eliza generally followed the Anglican tradition of latitudinarianism—that Christianity was wide enough to embrace many believers, regardless of doctrinal specifics. The evangelical message was less centered on reason and more driven by emotion, but it otherwise differed little from what Eliza heard in Anglican services in Charles Town. She probably would have viewed the theological variations with her usual ecumenicalism were it not for evangelicals' social critique. In 1741–1742 she joined most of the rest of the South Carolina ruling class in rejecting the message spread by Great Awakening ministers. The Anglican Church succeeded in South Carolina because clergy adjusted to the priorities of the local laity, expressed through powerful vestries, especially the gentry's affinity for class and racial hierarchy. Anglican ministers didn't demand much from their elite parishioners. The sermons they delivered were comfortable, obliging to social hierarchy and slaveholding. St. Philip's and other parish churches were elegant, ordered spaces, built on metropolitan models and reflecting the majesty of God and the refined sensibilities of well-to-do parishioners. Evangelicals cast all that aside. In a brief, provocative visit to Charles Town in 1741, well-known minister George Whitefield blasted rich residents for being "wholly devoted to pleasure, polite entertainments . . . dancing . . . and the sin of wearing jewels." That did not go over well in Eliza's circle.[6]

The most troubling part for people like Eliza was that some evangelicals publicly rebuked slaveholding. In the spring of 1742, Hugh Bryan, an affluent local planter enthralled by evangelicalism, denounced South Carolina's gentry culture and began to preach a liberation gospel to enslaved people. South Carolina, he charged, had devolved into a latter-day Sodom and Gomorrah. Recent history—the Stono uprising, smallpox epidemics, the 1740 fire—all signaled God's displeasure with the wicked Carolinians. Until they repented from the sin of slavery, Hugh proclaimed, white colonists would continue to suffer under God's growing wrath.[7]

Hugh Bryan struck Eliza as another overwrought evangelical "very much deluded." White people in colonial South Carolina did not discuss the sinfulness of slavery—few seemed to ever contemplate it. When, under threat of imprisonment and execution, Bryan publicly repudiated his past conduct, Eliza looked with disdain—and pity—on the whole affair: "I hope he will be a warning to all pious minds not to reject reason and revelation and set up in their stead their own wild notions."[8]

God, Eliza perceived, had endowed her "pious mind" with reason. As a good Christian, she therefore needed to submit theological interpretations, liturgical practices, even scripture to that God-given reason. Unlike Hugh Bryan, she was unwilling to scrutinize her ownership of other people, including fellow Christians. Perhaps to avoid the matter, Eliza made no sustained effort to encourage Christianity among the enslaved people on her estates. (Her early effort to teach enslaved children to read fell by the wayside.) Few of her neighbors evangelized among the enslaved community, either. Popular ministers like Alexander Garden fell in line.[9]

Eliza struggled with some biblical stories, particularly the resurrection. How could she rationally explain a supernatural occurrence? She decided that while resurrection (among other parts of the Bible) was "above reason," nothing in the Anglican tradition was "contrary to reason." "It has been acknowledged by the greatest men of our nation and many others," Eliza wrote in 1742, "that revealed religion is consonant to the most exact reason tho some things may appear at first sight contrary to it." Further study and more knowledge would, she concluded, solve any contradictions.[10]

Like most people of faith, Eliza sometimes wondered: what if she was wrong? What if there was no all-knowing God? She found a rational answer.

"If we lead a life of piety here," she reasoned, "'tis a life of all others the most pleasing and agreeable. And if there is no future state we are in as happy a situation as the irreligious." Eliza decided in her youth that Christianity offered the greatest chance for fulfillment in life. At the same time, she knew that perpetual happiness was an illusion. Instead, she believed God could help her withstand inevitable suffering. When fear clouded her thoughts, she turned to prayer.[11]

Eliza drew on all her deep-seated beliefs during the terrible summer of 1747. With time, her Christian convictions began to deliver her out of the crushing grief of losing her father and her son. "I dare not complain," she had decided by the winter, "for God knows best what is best for us, and infinite Wisdome and goodness are his indispenseable attributes." Certainty about the goodness of God and her optimistic outlook on life allowed Eliza to focus, at least after a few months and the raw heartbreak subsided, on her blessings. She thanked God for giving her Charles and Charles Cotesworth. She kept her faith.[12]

The following summer, Eliza safely delivered a healthy baby girl. Harriott Pinckney was born August 7, 1748. Another child, a boy, arrived just over two years later, on October 23, 1750. Eliza and Charles named him Thomas, the name of both Charles's father and Eliza's brother. The couple did not give this boy the name of their dead baby, though that was a common practice in the eighteenth century. Perhaps Eliza thought it would be too painful to be constantly reminded of the child she'd buried and the treasured father she'd lost. On the other hand, Eliza always looked forward in her life, so perhaps she preferred a new name for this new son.

Thomas Pinckney was Eliza's last child. Why, at twenty-eight, she stopped getting pregnant, Eliza never said. She and Charles talked a lot about how much they loved Charles Cotesworth, Harriott, and Thomas, and about the grand plans they had for these precious Pinckney children.

In 1750, the year that Thomas was born, Charles's nephew Charles Pinckney finished his English education and returned to South Carolina. He rejoined the family well on his way to a distinguished future and as a role model for his little cousins. Not yet twenty-one, he was admitted to the South Carolina bar and started a practice. He prospered in his legal career and at his plantation, Snee Farm. He rose quickly into the ranks of political power, winning election to the assembly and serving as a justice of the peace. The future looked bright again.[13]

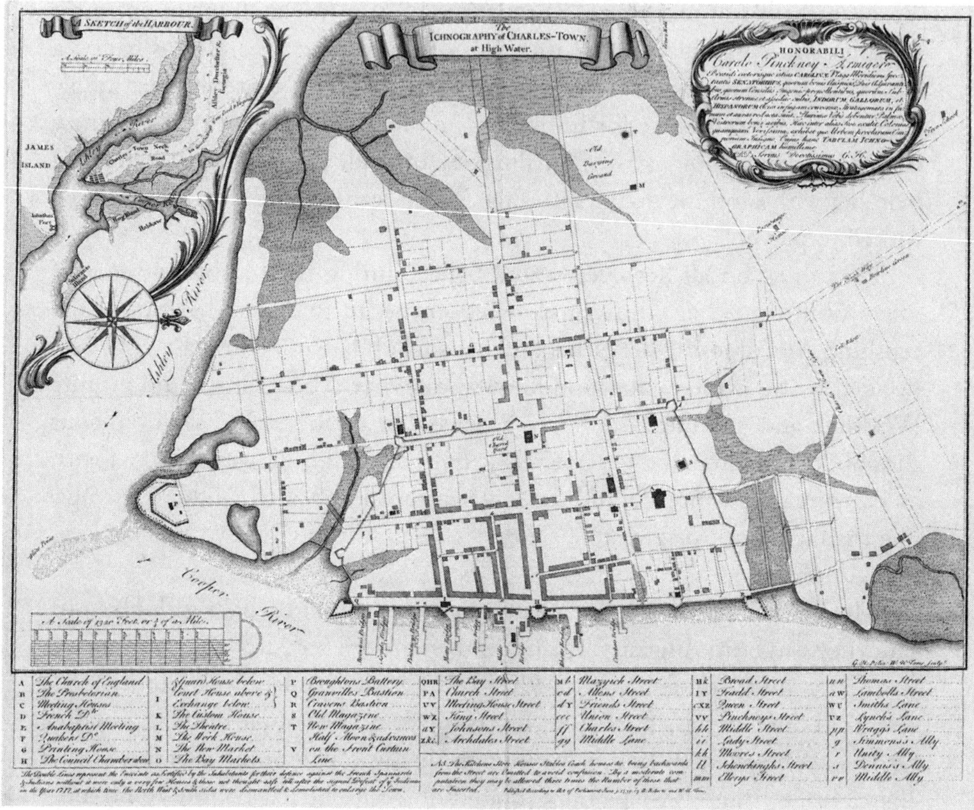

Figure 5. George Hunter, "The Ichnography of Charles-Town at High Water," 1739. Hunter dedicated the map to Charles Pinckney. The Miriam and Ira D. Wallach Division of Art, Prints and Photographs: Print Collection, The New York Public Library Digital Collections.

As their young family grew, the Pinckneys spent much of their time in Charles Town. "Ichnography of Charles-Town," a famous map completed in 1739 by George Hunter, a surveyor for the South Carolina colony, shows a well-planned city, with streets laid out on a grid, and all the major buildings noted. Hunter dedicated his work to Charles Pinckney. His map showed the easy walk connecting all the iconic buildings in town: the court house and the workhouse, where enslaved people were sold; the markets and magazines; St. Philip's, the Quaker Meeting House, and the Huguenot Church; and along Bay Street, the imposing houses of the city's leading families.[14]

Elite residents of Charles Town bragged that their city was "the most opulent and flourishing" place in all of mainland British America. The city's highly regarded theater company was founded in the 1730s, as was the St. Cecilia Society, which hosted concerts and operas. City leaders established the Library Society in 1748. Residents had their own weekly newspaper, they enjoyed traveling musicians and public lectures, and they founded numerous charitable and fraternal organizations. Charles Town boasted every cultural venue to serve the tastes of well-heeled residents, save for one: there was no institution of higher learning. Elites preferred an English education for their children.[15]

Artisans and middling-rank shopkeepers built their own communities in the city and prospered there. Silversmiths, carpenters, coopers, milliners, washerwomen, masons, tailors, and printers plied their trades in houses and workshops. Half the residents were enslaved, but some free black women and men lived in town, too, working in commercial trades, at skilled crafts, or on the docks.[16]

The harbor at Charles Town was the center of one of the most successful economies in the eighteenth-century Atlantic World. It was not uncommon for a hundred vessels to be riding anchor. Ships carried out hogsheads of rice and indigo and brought in luxury goods from around the globe: spices from the Far East, the latest fashions from London, wine from Spain and France.[17]

Not coincidentally, Charles Town also saw the greatest human trafficking on the British American mainland. Nearly one in four people held in bondage in North America came through the city. Slavery allowed the whole colony to thrive. The Atlantic-wide prominence of leading families, including the Pinckneys, grew apace with their slave-based wealth.[18]

Numerous churches dotted the cityscape. Visitors agreed that St. Philip's was the most impressive. St. Michael's, the other iconic church in the city, was constructed in the early 1750s, after St. Philip's Parish was divided to accommodate Charles Town's growing population. St. Michael's steeple rose 186 feet high. Fronted by a two-story portico, the church was made of brick and painted stark white. Boxed pews, built of cedar, filled the floor. The church sat at the corner of Broad and Meeting, opposite Charles Town's main marketplace. Completing the square was the Watch House and the building where the South Carolina Assembly and the Royal Council met. So the hubs of power—religious, political, commercial, and racial—all intersected in the heart of Charles Town.[19]

When she first visited Charles Town in 1739, Eliza Lucas had found much to admire. She told Mary Boddicott and her brother Tommy that she thought the city's architecture and layout quite lovely. "The people," she added approvingly, "live very Gentile and very much in the English taste." The poor were another matter entirely. Eliza dismissed them as "the most indolent people in the world or they could never be wretched in so plentiful a country as this."[20]

Eliza's glowing assessment of all save the poor was doubtless shaped by her quick entry into Charles Town's gentry. The bustling commercial hub felt to elites like a small, interrelated community because it was. Interrelated elites ran the city like a family business. For one telling example, there were no banks in Charles Town before the 1790s: merchants extended (or denied) credit based on personal connections. Elites enjoyed the city like a playground. On top of the concert halls, theaters, and social clubs, there was a bowling green, opened in 1748, and a racetrack, founded in 1754.[21]

Wealth from the city's commerce, particularly human trafficking, and deep family ties allowed Lowcountry elites to weather all sorts of difficulties: economic turmoil, warfare, natural disasters. On the afternoon of November 18, 1740, a fire raged through Charles Town, engulfing warehouses, stables, boats anchored in the harbor, and nearly every private residence from Broad and Church Streets south to the East Battery—the oldest, richest part of the city. By dawn November 19, all that remained of more than three hundred houses was smoldering ash. The fire led to the collapse of Charles and William Pinckney's insurance company. The city quickly rebuilt, with more elegant architecture than before. Within a year, the devastated parts of town were repaired. The multiplying buildings amazed newcomers.[22]

Outsiders entering Charles Town for the first time were often taken aback. German Pastor John Martin Boltzius, who had set about evangelizing for the Lutheran Church in Georgia, passed through town on his way to Philadelphia in October 1742. He was appalled: "One can hardly imagine how bad splendor and luxury are practiced here unless one sees it himself." Charles Town's economy was certainly flourishing, the minister conceded, but tumultuous. The planter-merchant class overspent at a rate Boltzius found staggering. To finance their opulent lifestyles, they incurred impossible debts. He walked past auctions nearly every day, which he attributed to people who had bought too many luxury goods on credit and been foreclosed on. Five days in town were enough for Boltzius: "I long to get out of this sinful city." Everywhere he looked, he saw "prejudice, wickedness, indifference, epicureanism, and atheism." As he fled the city's hedonism, Boltzius offered up a desperate prayer: "May God have mercy on this misery!"[23]

This was an outsider's point of view. Eliza and Charles—consummate insiders—perceived their hometown very differently. They felt comfortable and welcomed everywhere they went and took part in all the vibrant city offered. The luxury Reverend Boltzius derided suited the Pinckneys just fine.

For his new bride, Charles Pinckney ordered the construction of what was at the time the grandest house in all of Charles Town. Charles studied his friends' homes for inspiration—and to determine the new standard he and Eliza would set. He planned every detail, down to the shelving in the closets and the matching locks installed throughout the mansion, intent on his and Eliza's house being unsurpassed in stylishness and splendor.[24]

Eliza and Charles's city estate sat on a large lot just off Colleton Square, a block away from the court house and guard house, on East Bay Street, bounded by Market and Guignard Streets. Their house faced the Cooper River, and their property ran to the shoreline. Eliza and Charles enjoyed a beautiful view of the harbor, and a private wharf afforded immediate access to the Cooper River, for travel and trade. The lot couldn't provide the lavish grounds that Eliza loved to roam, first at Wappoo and then at Belmont, and there was little space for her agricultural experiments. When Charles shared the architectural plans with George Lucas Jr., he noticed at once the absence of a place for Eliza to continue her "schemes" while in town. "I hope you have room enough behind the house for a Small Garden," George Jr. suggested, "I know yourself & my Sister are Extremely fond of that amusement." Still, a quick canoe ride could carry them back to Belmont, and the city mansion offered many other attractions.[25]

It was quite a place for Eliza and Charles and their children to come home to, made of more than 200,000 bricks and adorned with marble and stone. A curving entrance and a high flight of stone steps carried them across an open portico and inside. Eliza and Charles slept downstairs, at the rear of the house, behind their library. Enslaved women cooked for them in the basement kitchen—fires being of less concern in this brand-new brick and stone house topped with a slate roof. Flower beds dotted the property, tended, like everything else, by the enslaved black residents at the command and for the pleasure of the white residents. Except for a few household laborers, the men and women the Pinckneys enslaved lived on the northern edge of the lot, in "a long row of buildings" with "rooms in great numbers." The polar opposite of the mansion, those rooms would have been spare and cramped and devoid of privacy. On most Lowcountry plantations, enslaved people made small

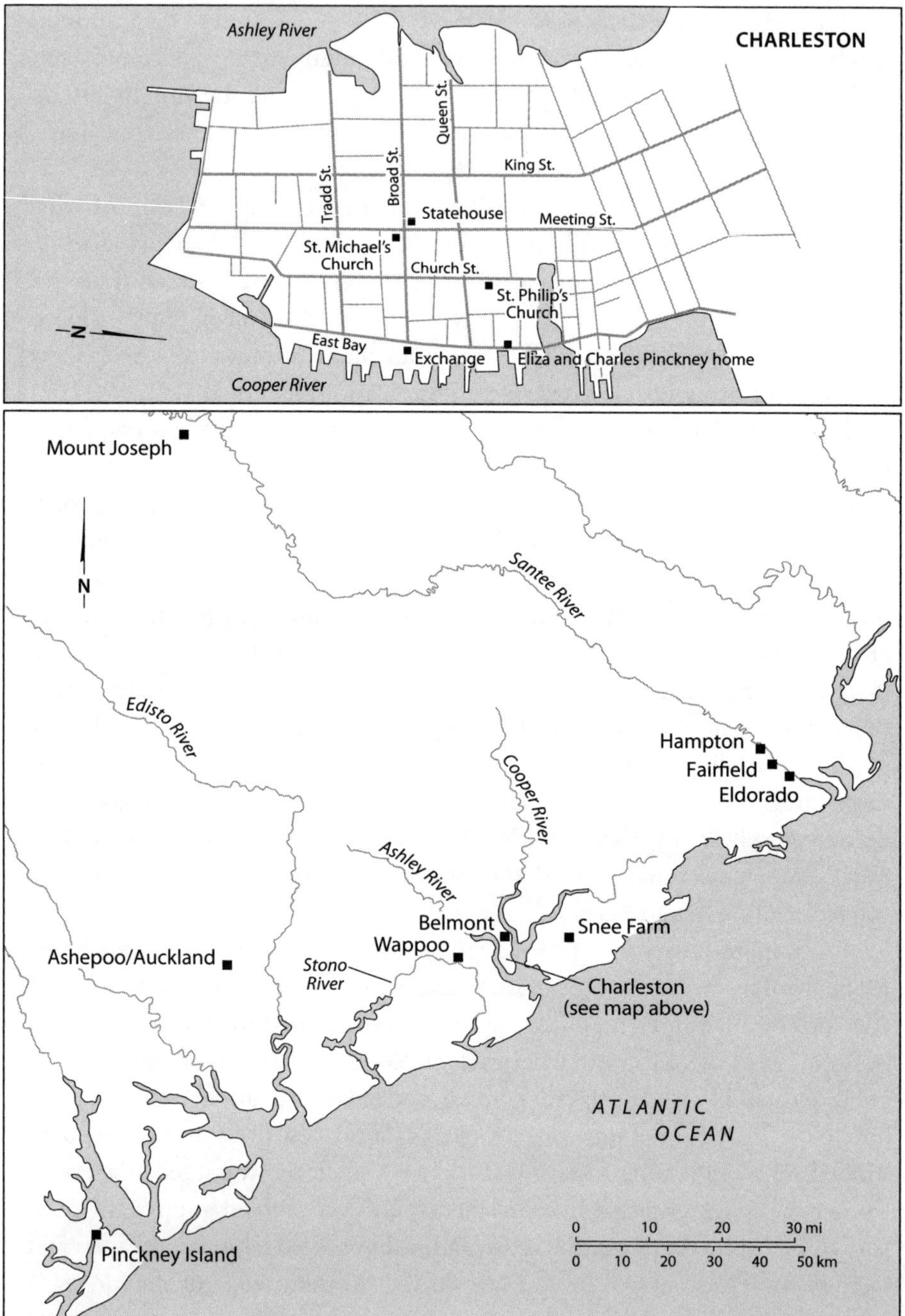

Figure 6. Map of various Pinckney plantations and Charles Town (Charleston). Map by Bill Nelson.

gardens, growing vegetables for their families or even tobacco for trading. The spatial limits of the East Bay property meant that the enslaved people in town had fewer, if any, opportunities to supplement their diets and earn income from garden plots. The Pinckneys located the slave quarters, as was customary among wealthy enslavers, close enough so that any call could be quickly answered, at any hour of the day or night.[26]

The home, by design, communicated the couple's wealth and power. The eastern front of the second story of the house was entirely occupied by a grand dining room, thirty feet long, with a fourteen-foot vaulted ceiling and elaborate crown molding. A twelve-by-eight-foot balcony opened off the room. When guests walked upstairs for socializing, they looked through an exquisite Venetian window that descendants recalled as "one of the most remarkable features of the house": three tall, arched windows in beautifully hand-carved frames. The children's rooms were on the second floor, too. So that the Pinckneys could linger over the view and read in direct sunlight, the staircase included "a deep window-seat extending the whole length of the landing-place."[27]

The woodwork in every part of the house was magnificent, from the cornice in the dining room to the wainscoting and door frames. The fireplace mantles were adorned with intricately carved "processions of shepherds and shepherdesses." Perfectly crafted frames built into the paneling above the mantles were filled with art.[28]

Women like Eliza Lucas Pinckney who lived in such houses played a central role in perpetuating South Carolina's unique, highly Anglo-centric gentry culture. Elites fairly obsessed over outward signs of wealth and Englishness: in their estates, carriages, gardens, clothing, leisure activities, and education. Women maintained many of these symbols. They hosted elaborate dinner parties in stately mansions they decorated in high style. They danced at balls wearing imported gowns and shoes.[29]

Eliza's education and personality made her quite adept at the role of a refined lady. She acted her part. But sometimes she found it all a bit boring in comparison to botanical experiments. She both liked Charles Town and wanted breaks from it. In the summer of 1745, she confided to Mary Bartlett that "our town is so dull it will not afford a subject for half a sheet."[30]

Though she resided in the most majestic house in Charles Town, Eliza's mind, as a descendant explained, "does not seem to have dwelt on furniture or bric-a-brac." She didn't write about her home: not about the decorations or the parties she hosted. Instead, her letters in the decade after she married

Charles focused on her new role as wife and mother and her long-standing interests in taking care of her larger family and its commercial plantations.[31]

The beauty of the city mansion, including the elaborate woodwork, came not from Eliza or Charles, but rather from the black man who built the home to secure his freedom. In doing so, he escaped both slavery and the historical anonymity common among people enslaved in colonial America.

Quash, the enslaved carpenter who built the indigo works at Wappoo and Garden Hill, numbered among twenty African Americans given to Charles Pinckney by George Lucas as part of Eliza and Charles's 1744 marriage settlement. Quash was listed first, signifying his financial value as a skilled carpenter. Next on the list was Dick, a cook, followed by Mary Ann, who was probably Eliza's maid. George soon regretted the transaction. In the summer of 1745, George, ignoring the marriage settlement, asked Eliza and Charles to send Quash to him. "I could," George told them, "make considerably more of his Labour here than he produces at Carolina." He also wanted Dick—another singularly skilled individual. Eliza and Charles explained that they would not part with Quash because he was working on their city house. Quash's skills were impressive. He carved many of the intricate details, calculated payments to men who built the stairs and installed the windows, and generally managed the project, bringing Charles's vision to life.[32]

George accepted that he was not getting Quash back, but he wrote again in the fall of 1745, requesting Dick. Eliza explained to her father that Dick was suffering from a sore throat and could not travel. Every time George pressed, Eliza stalled. In one letter she claimed that the only boat bound for Antigua was too small to risk Dick's passage. In another, she said she feared privateers, lying in wait off the coast of South Carolina. "I am," George insisted in the spring of 1746, "in Extream want of him." If Eliza felt so concerned about the privateers, George advised, she and Charles should take out an insurance policy and send Dick on—the worry, George assumed, centered on Dick's value, not his safety. Insurance was not purchased because Dick, like Quash, remained with the Pinckneys.[33]

After George Lucas died, Charles paid one of George's creditors £1,300 to secure clear ownership of five people: Dick, the cook; Mary Ann and her young children, a son Prince and a daughter Beck; and Quash. These five people were very important to Charles and commanded a steep price. Pinckney and Lucas financial papers listed Quash, Dick, and Mary Ann and her children as "Mulatto"—of racially mixed ancestry. Beck and Prince were born in South Carolina, on Lucas and Pinckney properties. Their father's identity is unknown. Beck and Prince were raised by their mother; Mary Ann never had to endure their being sold away from her. But they never got free. Dick, too, remained enslaved by the Pinckney family for decades.[34]

Quash's life took a different turn. He was listed on the 1750 bill of sale as "since Baptised by the name of John Williams." Slave owners and Anglican ministers allowed only a few enslaved people to be baptized because it raised a host of questions white Carolinians preferred to avoid. Could Christians be enslaved? Weren't all baptized church members spiritually equal? Would baptized Christians share communion regardless of race? Converting sometimes alienated individuals from the larger slave community, too. According to white ministers, enslaved people laughed at black women and men who chose to be baptized in white churches.[35]

John Williams, then, made a highly unusual move in converting to Anglicanism, and he adopted an English-sounding name to signal his new identity. His reinvention continued. Four months after Charles's lawyers finalized the purchase of Mary Ann, Prince, Beck, Dick, and John Williams (formerly Quash), John persuaded Charles to legally endorse his emancipation. The paperwork, signed on May 12, 1750, identified him as "John Williams (a mulatto man) . . . heretofore a Slave named Quash." At the time, free blacks constituted barely 1 percent of the black population in South Carolina. And three-quarters of adult manumissions were for women (a third of all manumissions involved children). Somehow, John Williams became the rarest of rare Carolinians: a free black man. Charles said only that he signed the manumission papers "in Consideration of the good & faithfull Service . . . heretofore done & Perform'd and for Diverse other Good and Valuable Considerations." Eliza signed the paperwork as one of the lawfully required witnesses, so she supported the decision, too.[36]

In bondage in the 1730s and 1740s, Quash had spent so much of his life controlled by others: where he worked, whether he stayed in South Carolina or moved to Antigua, whether he lived or died. In 1750, John Williams took charge of his own life. He stayed in South Carolina, though laws at the time required freed people to leave the colony or risk re-enslavement. A few weeks after securing his freedom, John Williams bought an advertisement in the *South Carolina Gazette* proclaiming himself a free man and promoting his carpentry business. He promised his work would be "well done and handsomely finished . . . with great fidelity justice and dispatch." The business thrived. In 1763, he departed the colony for parts unknown. Before leaving, he took out another ad: this time to sell his property. He had earned enough money in his business to own two lots in town, a house, and four hundred acres of land on the Santee River. When he left South Carolina, John/Quash disappeared from the historical record, carrying with him boundless mysteries about his unusual life.[37]

During the years when the slave once named Quash became the free man John Williams, Eliza Lucas Pinckney was sorting out her identity, too. To focus her energies, she created a list of "resolutions." Like her personal prayers, Eliza's resolutions offer rare insights into the interior life and priorities of an eighteenth-century woman. The resolutions reflected both Eliza's independent-mindedness and the ways the wider culture influenced her. She read the resolutions every day, first thing in the morning, before she left her bedroom. Reviewing them prepared her to plan the day's business. First on Eliza's list was her faith: her belief in God, her dedication to proclaiming her faith in word and deed. She believed she was personally responsible for improvement and evaluation: she vowed to "Govern my self in every circumstance of Life by the rules of the Gospel of Christ."[38]

Christian faith underlay her ethics, which she turned to second. Eliza resolved "to govern my passions, to endeavour constantly to subdue every vice; and improve in every virtue." "I will not," she vowed, "give way to Envy, Ill will, Evil speaking, ingratitude, or uncharitableness, in word, in thought, or in deed. or to passion or peavishness . . . to intemperance in my Eating, drinking, sleeping or pleasures and divertions, nor to Sloath and Idleness but to endeavour after all the Contrary virtues humility, gratitude; good nature, generosity charity and compassion, piety, temperance and industry." She pledged to spurn extravagance and covetousness and resolved to be personally frugal and charitable toward others, to do good and avoid evil.

The third part of Eliza's resolutions, following (and flowing from) her faith and her character, centered on her family and community obligations. She resolved to responsibly fill the "Several Stations wherein providence has placed me." First among these: being a good wife to Charles. Next, she committed herself to being a good child to her mother and a good mother to her children. As with other things that mattered deeply to her, Eliza raised Charles Cotesworth, Harriott, and Thomas with well-reasoned plans, diligence, and intentionality. Being a good mother meant fulfilling a precise set of responsibilities that reflected childrearing ideals at that time: "to pray for them, to set them good examples, to give them good advice, to be careful both of their

Souls and bodys, to watch over their tender minds, to carefully root out the first appearance and buding of vice; and to instill piety, Virtue, and true religion into them. to spair no pains or trouble to do them good. to correct them for their Errors whatever uneasiness it may give my self and never omit to encourage every Virtue I may see dawning in them."

Ever orderly, Eliza catalogued her other familial and community roles according to importance. She vowed to be devoted to her and Charles's siblings, dutiful and loving to their nieces and nephews, benevolent toward the people she enslaved. In her resolutions, slaveholding occupied the place between her family and her friends. Self-identifying as a "good Mistress," Eliza pledged "to treat them [enslaved people] with humanity, and good nature; to give them sufficient and Comfortable Clothing, and provisions, and all things necessary for them, to be careful and tender of them in their sickness, to reprove them for their faults, to encourage them when they do well, and pass over small faults. not to be tyrannical, peavish or impatient towards them but to make their Lives as Comfortable as I can." This was not the sort of self-serving hyperbole offered by pro-slavery zealots in the nineteenth century under pressure of moral condemnation. Eliza was an eighteenth-century woman. She so normalized slavery in her own mind, and the world she inhabited was so bereft of serious critiques of slavery, that she appeared to believe what she wrote was possible. Eliza then turned to her next resolutions: to be honest and steadfast with her friends, agreeable and companionable with neighbors, and a "universal Lover of all mankind."[39]

Every day, Eliza set out to adhere to this carefully laid plan, never seeming to understand, despite dearly bought experience, how quickly life could veer off course. Or perhaps she steeled herself first thing every morning because she understood it all too well.

The summer of 1752 was brutally hot, even by Charles Town standards, and the heat had not broken in mid-September. Thursday night, September 14, residents noticed the winds pick up. At dawn, they saw ominously thickening clouds. Early risers marveled at dramatic shifts in the tide. Shortly after 9:00 A.M. a deluge began and soon "the whole town became a raging sea." When Governor James Glen tried to describe the ensuing hurricane for the Board of Trade in London, words escaped him: "Its Fury was irresistible and indeed inexpressible; Words are too weak to give your Lordships a just Idea of it."[40]

Eliza and the family were at their East Bay mansion when the storm struck. Four feet of water flooded the downstairs before the Pinckneys and enslaved household workers could think to flee. Charles rushed his family into a boat and got everyone to higher ground, as the surge swelled. Though no mention was made of Mary Ann or the other African Americans, they were apparently evacuated, too. As the Pinckney household sailed to safety, the surge rose nine feet above high tide. Houses caved in, ships ran aground, and wharves broke apart, driving debris "with great violence, thro' the streets, and round about the town." Under the rushing sea, "many people being already up to their necks in their houses, began now to think of nothing but certain death."[41]

The hurricane raged for five hours, leaving staggering damage in its wake. Five hundred buildings in Charles Town were either badly damaged or destroyed. The devastation extended forty miles inland. Only one ship, HMS *Hornet*, rode out the storm. Every other vessel in the harbor either sank or wrecked. Some crash-landed against houses; others were pushed so far into the swamps that removal was hopeless. Thousands of trees covered the roads out of town, making travel by carriage nearly impossible. The city's fortifications were wrecked, the year's rice crop all but lost. As was nearly always the case with catastrophes in colonial America, enslaved African Americans bore the brunt of the suffering: their houses were most vulnerable, their opportunities for escape most circumscribed, their deprivation of clean water, food, and shelter amplified, their labor exploited to rebuild.[42]

In the scheme of things, Eliza's family was lucky that September. The house was flooded, but not structurally compromised. After the Pinckneys escaped, a towering wave sent a boat crashing into the southeast corner of their house. It caused minor damage to the brickwork, which Charles took in stride. When the waters receded and cleanup started—a new kind of punishing work for enslaved African Americans—Charles directed repairmen to "omit three or four bricks from the outer layer to show the spot where the blow had been received." The "scar" remained as long as the house stood, just under a second-story window, twenty-five feet above the ground.[43]

The hurricane made a deep imprint on Eliza, too. In addition to her personal prayers and daily resolutions, Eliza kept a list of days to be "sett apart to be rememberd with the utmost Gratitude and thankfulness to Almighty God by me for great and particular mercys received." Every year she commemorated the anniversaries of her most treasured blessings: the birthdays of her husband and children, her wedding date. September 11 became special, too: "the day of the great Hurricane in 1752 when our whole family was mercifully preserved." Eliza got the date wrong, though she can certainly be forgiven. Besides the chaos of the storm, Britons were making a transition from the

Julian to the Gregorian calendar that month. The shift eliminated September 3 to September 13 for 1752. So Carolinians went to bed on the night of September 2 and awoke the next morning to September 14.[44]

As she reviewed her private prayers and the accomplishments of her life on her birthday in December 1752, Eliza Lucas Pinckney must have been even more reflective than usual. She turned thirty that year. And though she had endured a great deal of loss in her life, she was still lucky in many ways. Most recently, everyone in her family had survived the catastrophic hurricane. She and Charles had money to rebuild, three healthy children, and much for which to thank her God.

As she studied her prayers, renovations were under way at the East Bay house and probably at Belmont, too. She would have heard carpentry sounds in the background, mixed with the everyday noise of three vivacious children. Her nephew Charles was getting married the next week. He had made a wise and welcome choice: Charles's fiancée, Frances Brewton, was his first cousin, the daughter of his mother's brother. The wedding was scheduled for January 2, 1753. It would reconnect a family fortune: a joyful (and lucrative) cause for celebration that Eliza and Charles looked forward to attending.[45]

New Year's 1753 seemed hopeful, then. The toddler Thomas was thriving. Eliza and Charles had almost lost him when he was an infant. Eliza prayed frantically over the gravely ill baby. She counted it as divine intervention when Thomas recovered. That was all behind them now. The family marked Charles Cotesworth's seventh birthday in mid-February. He was a smart, healthy child, as was his sister, Harriott. The family lived luxuriously and happily ensconced in Charles Town society. The first signs of spring promised new crops, longer days, outdoor socializing.[46]

Instead, the Pinckneys got unexpected and unwelcome news regarding Charles's career. Since September 1752, Charles had been acting as chief justice of South Carolina at the request of the royal governor. It was the most recent in a long line of impressive positions. He had already served as South Carolina's attorney general and as speaker of the assembly. His legal training was first-rate, his reputation impeccable, his experience deep. Governor James Glen assured Charles that the required imperial approval was a mere formality. Charles accepted the job and set to work while waiting for confirmation to arrive.[47]

Alas, political intrigues in London and metropolitan prerogatives resulted in the rejection of Governor Glen's recommendation. Instead, Peter Leigh, a nobleman from Cheshire, received the appointment. He arrived in Charles Town and, as Carolinians saw it, Charles Pinckney, "an able lawyer, an upright man, a native of the province, was made to give way for this stranger."[48]

For generations, Pinckney descendants remembered the public embarrassment that ensued. Indignation was not limited to the Pinckney household. Charles's friends and neighbors resented his mistreatment, too. Carolinians had taken special pride in his appointment: no native-born Carolinian had ever been named to the position.[49]

In response to the rebuff, residents offered Charles the position of agent to London, the representative of South Carolina's interests in the imperial center. The salary was modest, only £200 per year, but the appointment was prestigious in Charles Town. Eliza and Charles had long discussed taking a trip to England; she was keen to see the London friends she'd corresponded with since her departure from school. Charles had contacts in London, too, from his school days and ongoing business interests, and relatives, both his and his late wife's. Charles's older brother Thomas had recently passed away and left Charles property in England, to which he needed to attend. The children were healthy and big enough to travel. Eliza and Charles wanted Charles Cotesworth to enter into more rigorous, formal study which could be acquired only in England.[50]

That quickly, a problem offered a solution. The Pinckneys could move to England. But ocean voyages were treacherous. Should Eliza risk her children's lives on an unpredictable Atlantic crossing? What of the happy life she and Charles had made in South Carolina, of his legal business and her experiments? What about her family in Antigua? What hope would she have of a reunion if she moved to England?

As she and Charles weighed their future, Eliza must have reflected on how much of her life, despite her careful planning, had been driven by unexpected events, accidents, and death. A slave uprising in Antigua carried her to South Carolina, a war with Spain made her an independent planter, a dying friend brought a sudden proposal from an unlikely love. Always searching for order in the tumult of her life, Eliza sought guidance in her prayers and resolutions. There it was: the vow, written in her own hand and repeated every morning, "not to be anxious or doubtful, not to be fearful" but to "contentedly leave the Event to Gods providence." And so she did.[51]

PART FOUR

Provincial in the Metropole

CHAPTER 8

Becoming an American in London

In the spring of 1753, Eliza Lucas Pinckney looked forward to being back in London—to seeing Mary and Richard Boddicott, reconnecting with old friends from her schoolgirl days, and attending the theater, which she loved. But she feared sailing her entire adult life, and this voyage felt especially perilous because her whole family was traveling together. A storm, a wreck, a pirates' raid could claim all their lives, all at once. Planning for the Atlantic crossing tested Eliza's vow to always trust God and "not to be anxious or doubtful, not to be fearful." The very week the Pinckneys were to depart Charles Town, a schooner filled with rice sailed into a violent storm. Gale-force winds destroyed the mast. By luck, a boat coming from Virginia rescued the sailors. Had the vessel not been towed in, the *South Carolina Gazette* reported, "'tis probable every Soul in her must have perished." Eliza knew that such accidents happened all the time and that when trouble struck on the high seas, catastrophic losses occurred more often than lucky rescues.[1]

Even if she and her family enjoyed an easy passage, Eliza was leaving behind the life she had made for herself in South Carolina. She was widely respected as "an all-accomplished" woman—as successful and prominent as any female in any of the American colonies.[2] Eliza's inclusion in South Carolina's ruling class, her refinement and respectability, her power as a plantation mistress were above question in the province. Soon all that would be an ocean away. England was the home of real aristocrats—dukes and duchesses, barons and baronesses—born to wealth exponentially greater than even the richest of colonial elites, inheritable titles, membership in the House of Lords, and enormous country houses—family seats—that dwarfed the largest buildings in the Americas and made the finest homes in the Lowcountry look small and rustic by comparison. Eliza prided herself on her introspection, so she must have contemplated what the move would mean for her place in society. Her religion, her cultural affinities, her education—it was all English. She and Charles had spent their adult lives idealizing and emulating the metropole, from afar. She was a proud member of the British Empire, but of the provinces. What would it be like to live in London? How would she be viewed by the women and men born to power and privilege at the center of the empire?

On Tuesday, April 4, 1753, Eliza and Charles boarded the *Edinburgh* with their three little children: Charles Cotesworth, age seven; Harriott, soon to turn five; and Thomas, just two and a half. The ship's commander, Captain Russell, expected to be at sea for the better part of a month.[3]

Eliza carried an unopened letter from one of her dearest friends, Mary Wood Wragg. Mary grew up in England and moved to South Carolina after she married a Carolinian studying law at Middle Temple. The Wraggs socialized with the Pinckneys and led a similar lifestyle: William Wragg served on the Royal Council, they owned seven thousand acres of property and 250 enslaved people, and they split their time between plantations and a home in Charles Town. When Mary gave Eliza the letter, she made her promise to wait to read it until she crossed the bar in Charles Town harbor. As the ship headed out to sea, Eliza gazed back at the city she had made her home. She thought about all the friends she was leaving behind. "I gave a wistful look at your house," she later told Mary. As the cityscape faded from view, Eliza found a quiet place on the *Edinburgh* and, once alone, opened Mary's farewell letter. Both women knew they might never again see one another. Eliza studied the familiar handwriting in the letter, a comforting, lasting expression of her and Mary's affection for each other. Then, the American shoreline disappeared, and there was only the vast ocean. Eliza was on her way.[4]

Eliza couldn't have lingered long over Mary's letter; time alone onboard the ship was rare and fleeting. In addition to Charles Cotesworth, Harriott, and Thomas, Eliza took care of two other children. Ten-year-old William Henry Drayton, called Billy, and his nine-year-old brother, Charles, sailed with the Pinckneys. The Drayton brothers descended from two of Charles Town's most prominent families. Their father, John Drayton, ranked among the colony's wealthiest planters. Their mother, Charlotta Bull Drayton, was the daughter of William Bull, South Carolina's royal governor from 1737 to 1743, and another of Eliza's well-off, well-connected friends. Wealthy Carolinians routinely sent young children—boys especially—abroad for formal education, and members of the colony's gentry families watched out for one another's children. When the Drayton brothers needed a surrogate family, the Pinckneys happily obliged. But the Drayton boys also added to Eliza's trepidation: the lives of five children rested with her and Charles and a blind bargain on the Atlantic Ocean. As always, Eliza had help, as she and Charles forced some enslaved people to travel with them.[5]

Ships that traversed the Atlantic in the eighteenth century were small and passengers' quarters cramped, even for rich families traveling in relatively high style. The Pinckneys, used to elegant feasts prepared by excellent cooks, suffered through meals that were, at best, edible. Water on ships was notoriously terrible: there was never enough and what was available smelled bad and tasted worse. Seasickness and contagious diseases were rampant and anxiety high until voyagers made land.

The *Edinburgh* was twenty-five days at sea, arriving in England on April 29, 1753. Luck sailed on their side. The voyagers avoided all the gravest perils of ocean passages: they weren't overtaken by privateers or cast away in a storm. It was, Eliza wrote Mary Wood Wragg, as fine a journey as anyone could expect. Still, the sea did not agree with her: "Never poor wretch suffered more that escaped with life than I," Eliza complained. She felt so relieved to have survived the crossing that she added the date of the ship's safe arrival to her list of special days to commemorate: April 29 joined the birthdays of her children, her wedding, and the day the family escaped the 1752 hurricane as anniversaries of singular importance, "to be," Eliza vowed, "spent in devotion and meditation on the goodness of God to me and mine."[6]

The deliverance was short-lived. Captain Russell intended to land at Portsmouth, a center for commercial trade south of London, on the English Channel. Colonial planters often sent their commodities there, so it was well known to Carolinians. But Russell received word that smallpox was raging in Portsmouth. Instead of docking, he headed north toward London, in hopes of escaping a disease that terrorized people across the Atlantic World.[7]

Smallpox is ruthlessly contagious, excruciating, and often deadly. People can catch it simply by handling the bedclothes of an infected person or even by shaking out linens or sweeping floors and inhaling particles from the scabs.

The first telltale physical signs of infection are sores in the mouth or throat. Then a skin rash breaks out, starting on the face and covering a person's skin as it spreads down the body. Sufferers emit a terrible odor from the infected eruptions, and they endure agonizing pain from open sores and spiking fevers. After a week or two, the pus-filled sores become hardened pustules that break open and then, if the patient survives, form scabs. This phase makes every move torturous, as the whole skin scabs over and peels away. Smallpox also attacks internal organs: the heart, lungs, and liver. Internal sores can cause patients to hemorrhage through various orifices. Survivors are often left with disfiguring scars, and some are blinded.[8]

Eighteenth-century doctors seeking a vaccine settled on a method called variolation: infecting people with the live smallpox virus. In the most widespread technique, a doctor used a needle to draw a thread through a pus-filled sore of a smallpox patient. When it got completely wet, the physician cut the healthy patient's arm and inserted the contaminated thread into the fresh wound. Patients needed to be quarantined for two to three weeks and seen regularly by a physician. The process was complicated, risky, and expensive.

Before Eliza even stepped off the *Edinburgh*, she experienced via the smallpox outbreak the first hints of tension between her colonial past and her metropolitan future. In South Carolina, inoculating children was still controversial. But variolation was common in England. Londoners had even founded a smallpox hospital in 1746, and in 1755 the London College of Physicians officially endorsed inoculation.[9] Should Eliza inoculate the children? What about the Drayton boys? Luckily, she had herself been inoculated when a student in London in the 1730s. That experience and her familiarity with scientific studies led her to set aside her fellow Carolinians' skepticism of smallpox science. She understood that if administered carefully, variolation worked, so all five children were inoculated. The procedure succeeded. Once the children finished the quarantine, Eliza and Charles could at last enjoy their return to the magnificent and bustling seat of the British Empire.

It had been nearly twenty years since Eliza had seen London. Many of her school friends still lived there, as did Mary and Richard Boddicott. Eliza and Mary had stayed connected through letters, and now rejoiced at their reunion. Places felt familiar. But the city had changed, too. London was twenty times larger than Philadelphia, the biggest city in North America. It was constantly expanding and always busy, filled with noise and packed with people. Shops, streets, neighborhoods had been transformed from her schoolgirl days.[10]

More important, Eliza had changed. She was a grown woman now, a mother of three, and by the measure of the time, arriving at the middle part of life. She'd spent the better part of two decades building a life in South Carolina, economically contributing to and culturally identifying with England, but from a distance. Moving back to the metropole tested—and reshaped—how she saw herself.

The Pinckneys moved into a house on Southampton Street, in central London, between the Strand and Covent Garden. One of their neighbors was the famous actor and theater owner David Garrick. The theater district was just a few short blocks to the east. Eliza had a long-standing love of plays, and she must have been thrilled. Southampton Street was also convenient for Charles's work. Whitehall, where the Board of Trade met, was a fifteen-minute walk away. Craven Street, where many prominent Americans elected to reside while in London, was even closer. The Pinckneys, then, lived in the middle of the action. It could get raucous. In 1755, after the Pinckneys had moved off Southampton Street, a riot broke out at David Garrick's Drury Lane Theatre and spilled over to his house, where several windows were broken. Even when things were peaceful, the city was never quiet. Londoners lived cheek to jowl: town houses, cobblestone streets, and people everywhere. Clearly, Eliza and Charles were not in Carolina anymore.

Seeing familiar faces eased the jarring move from province to metropole. The transition proved harder for Charles, who had not been in London for nearly thirty years and was, by nature, less embracing of change than Eliza. They both felt relieved to be warmly received in London by a group of fellow South Carolinians temporarily living in the city: diplomats, students, merchants, and travelers. These provincials in the metropole provided one another support and a sense of belonging: they shared news from home, socialized, and welcomed newcomers. The Pinckneys expressed "great Satisfaction with regard to the Civility that they have been received with by every body."[11]

One of the first Carolinians the couple sought out was Peter Manigault. Twenty-two and in London to study the law, Peter was the only son of Gabriel and Anne Ashby Manigault, wealthy Lowcountry planters and friends of the Pinckneys. Gabriel was one of the richest merchants in South Carolina, and Anne a fixture in Lowcountry society. Peter and Eliza hit it off immediately. Eliza bragged about his character to his mother, assuring Anne that Peter would "make her amends for all her cares and answer all her hopes." He was gracious, refined, and winsome. Peter found Eliza confident and engaging, forthright and forthcoming. He delighted in her company and pronounced her "an excellent Woman." Eliza reminded Peter of his home, and she was an easygoing, lively conversationalist. He quizzed her about everything and everybody in Charles Town. The two fast friends shared a fondness for gossip. Eliza conceded her part. She fell behind on her correspondence, she wrote one friend, because of "having been such a Gossip." Peter listened intently and then gossiped himself: "With all her Virtues," Peter confided to his mother, Eliza seemed "a little addicted to Scandal."[12]

For London-based Carolinians, juicy gossip as well as vital news from home emanated from the Carolina Coffeehouse, at 49 Birchin Lane. A Pennsylvania Coffeehouse and a Virginia Coffeehouse were on the same street. Each served as unofficial headquarters for colonials in England. Students and travelers met up at colony-centered coffeehouses to gather news and socialize. Lowcountry-born merchants and lawyers also conducted serious business at the Carolina Coffeehouse. Writers found inspiration there, and homesick travelers waited for updates from their faraway kin. The Carolina Coffeehouse even served as a post office for newcomers to London. Colonials moving abroad often didn't know where they might wind up living—that was the case with the Pinckneys—so letters from home arrived there. The Carolina Coffeehouse was, then, both a site for provincial networking and a quintessentially London establishment. The space allowed Carolinians to feel at home while also performing their Englishness: to be Carolinian and English at once.[13]

London was a huge city, but the Carolinians formed a close-knit community. Secrets were not easily hidden. Sent abroad to acquire the education and reputation to make them worthy gentlemen back home, scions of wealthy Lowcountry families sometimes got carried away with the socializing opportunities in London. When they fell into trouble, members of the provincial community interceded. Carolinians abroad lent money to profligate students, offered advice, issued admonitions, and sent home reports.

Not long after they arrived in London, Eliza and Charles got drawn into a drama involving the wastrel son of their former parish rector, Alexander Garden. Twenty-year-old John Garden was supposed to be in London studying the law. Instead, he had taken to drinking and developed a gambling addiction. Eliza and Charles were shocked to discover that John was "prisoner at a spunging house in London." He had stiffed his tailor over £100—a steep debt for a student's wardrobe. Eliza, who usually tried to moderate her criticism in letters, blasted John as "inconsiderate and thoughtless." Eliza and Charles tried to help but found the tailor's bill only the start of young John's legal troubles. They watched hopelessly as he was carted off to Newgate

Prison, where the worst English criminals were kept. "A fine school for the reformation of youth!" Eliza complained, "To be a companion to the wickedest and vilest of wretches the very dregs of mankind." She and Charles lamented the sad fate that awaited John Garden and felt frustrated by their inability to do more for their dear friend back home.[14]

Though conscientious about preserving connections with South Carolina families, Eliza wanted to embark on new and thoroughly English experiences. Nothing seemed more English or more exciting to her than the prospect of seeing the royal family. With savvy forethought, Eliza planned long before leaving South Carolina for her chance to meet royalty. In particular, she wanted to see the Dowager Princess Augusta, the recently widowed wife of Frederick, Prince of Wales, and Augusta's son, the new Prince of Wales and future King George III.

Princess Augusta and her children spent much of their time at a royal estate at Kew, near the village of Richmond. The London suburb of Richmond was a popular destination for aristocrats—a bucolic retreat from the hubbub of London. The princess lived in a palace called White House, also known then as Kew Palace. Her sons resided opposite Augusta, in another palatial house, this one of red brick and sometimes called the Dutch House.[15]

The stunning grounds at Kew, founded by Princess Augusta and Prince Frederick, transported visitors to a fantasy world of exotic architecture and gardens, evoking Rome, China, and the Middle East. Kew Gardens, a work in progress in the 1750s, presented the world in microcosm. Buildings included a mosque and a great pagoda. In less than two miles, visitors could stroll across manicured landscapes imitating regions around the globe.[16]

Eliza intended to see it all, starting with the royal family. Before she left South Carolina, Eliza studied the princess's interests. During the Atlantic crossing, she carefully tended to three small and exquisite Carolina birds. She brought them as a present for—and an entrée to meet—Princess Augusta. The painted bunting, which Eliza called a nonpareil, is the most magnificently colorful bird of North America: an orange-red belly, bright green back, black and yellow wings, and a deep blue head. Eliza also brought a yellow bird, probably a warbler. In a clever move, she rounded out the collection of live specimens with a small bird with a turquoise body and royal blue head: an indigo bunting.[17]

Upon their arrival in London, the Pinckneys began cajoling various contacts to make overtures on their behalf to the royal family's attendants. Eliza and Charles, their friends insisted to the gatekeepers, were "persons of Character and Distinction in the Country from whence they came." At the same time, Eliza's friends warned her that colonists rarely got to meet the princess and her children.

Eliza pushed back: did the princess's attendants understand how important Charles had been in South Carolina? Eliza seemed reluctant to accept where South Carolina—and her family—ranked in the empire. Her family, she pressed, only wanted to show their affection and loyalty; they asked for nothing but a bit of the princess's time. To help her case, Eliza claimed the three Carolina birds were a gift from five-year-old Harriott. Resisting so young an adoring subject would be, she hoped, harder than declining to meet a grown woman. Eliza coached Harriott to carefully write a card: "Miss Harriott Pinckney, daughter to Charles Pinckney, Esq., one of her Majesty's Council in South Carolina pays her Duty to her highness." Weeks passed, and Eliza fretted about the birds. They were native to America and so long caged. What if they died? All that tending for nothing.

At last, sometime in the fall of 1753, the visit was approved. "It was attended," Eliza recognized, "with great difficulty" because Princess Augusta's guards were "extreamly causious who they admit to her presence."

Eliza and Charles were told to arrive at Kew at 11:00 in the morning. Three little children, three delicate birds, dressing to meet the royal family, a carriage ride—the morning sped past, and the family ran late. "We exceeded our time a little," Eliza acknowledged. The princess, they were informed, was no longer available. All dressed up, birds in hand, the family learned a hard lesson about keeping royalty waiting. The princess's attendants told the Pinckneys to come on time next time. They kept the birds. The Pinckneys returned home, with no visit and no birds, Eliza ruefully noted, "lamenting as we went."

When at last the Pinckney family met Princess Augusta—on time—Eliza found her remarkably warm and welcoming. She greeted them, Eliza reported, "with all the cheerfulness and pleasure of a friend." Though awestruck to be in the company of Princess Augusta, Eliza found in her a kindred spirit: warm, affable, and boundlessly curious. The princess kissed little Harriott—the boys did not make the trip, probably because Thomas was so little and Charles Cotesworth in school—and asked how she liked England. When, doubtless to her parents' mortification, Harriott replied "not so well as Carolina," Princess Augusta burst out laughing.

Augusta seemed to find the Pinckneys exotic curiosities from the far-off provinces, worth examining. She peppered them with questions: How was the ocean voyage? Did they fear bringing their children across the Atlantic? How did they like South Carolina? Did they approve of the royal governor? She chatted on for a half-hour, still standing.

Eliza, dressed in her finest (and least comfortable) clothes and shoes, had to stand, too, and soon found herself "in great pain." Charles, seeing Eliza's growing discomfort, was helpless to suggest she sit; so long as the princess stood, no one could take a seat. Charles tried to rescue Eliza by leaving. He deferentially apologized to Augusta for their long intrusion and attempted to depart.

The princess would hear none of it. Didn't they want to meet the Prince of Wales, she asked? She went in search of an attendant to call her children to meet the Pinckneys. The fifteen-year-old heir apparent joined the conversation.

By the time the future King George III arrived on the scene, Harriott, overstimulated from the visit and getting tired, had started to cry. She knew how important the meeting was to her parents, so she tried to hide her tears, in the hopeless way of five-year-olds. Princess Augusta was mother to a house full of children, and she knew just what to do. She got down on her knees to comfort the teary Harriott. When that didn't work, she searched out a distraction. The walls of the room were lined with cabinets filled with curios. Eliza watched in wonder as Augusta climbed up on a stool and pulled a trinket from a high shelf.

"This, you imagine," Eliza wrote to a South Carolina friend, "must seem pretty extraordinary to an American."

That moment marked the first time in her life that Eliza Lucas Pinckney referred to herself as "American." In the presence of England's royal family, she saw herself not as a Carolinian or a Briton, but an American. She was a part of the empire but intuited how the Atlantic Ocean made her apart from it. No small share of Eliza's astonishment at the scene before her was how much the princess did for herself. At her homes, Eliza did not carry stools to reach high shelves. She did not go in search of messengers. At every place she'd ever lived, enslaved African Americans waited on Eliza. But now it was Eliza who stood at attention, even after Princess Augusta sat.

Eliza resigned herself to the discomfort of standing so long and made the most of the visit. She captivated the princess with stories from America. The conversation reflected the two women's worldliness and wide interests. They talked about the government and legal systems in South Carolina, the 1752 hurricane, the architecture of colonial houses, French diplomacy with Indian nations, turtle recipes, and the territorial boundaries of the colonies. Eliza, careful to tout her latest experiment, described her silkworks.

The royal family seemed especially curious about North American slavery, quizzing the Pinckneys about their experiences, including in the intimate parts of life. Augusta asked, Eliza recalled, "if I ever suckled one of the Children," and Eliza replied, "I had attempted it but my constitution would not bear it." Eliza explained that "we had Nurses in our houses." By that, Eliza meant that in her world, enslaved women nursed white babies while denying their own children breastmilk, or after their babies died. This use of what Eliza cavalierly called "suckling blacks" surprised the princess. Perhaps Augusta thought of the advice writers who chastised women for failing to breastfeed their children and warned that wet nurses corrupted the infants in their care. Eliza did not substitute those self-appointed experts' judgment for her own. She confidently explained to Augusta her choices and the racial dynamics of childcare in colonial America. Augusta stroked Harriott's cheek and marveled that being breastfed by black women "made no alteration in the complexion." Augusta said she found Harriott "very fair and pretty."[18]

The 1753 royal visit was a very big deal, and fellow Carolinians in London were duly impressed. Some even wrote home to report, with fascination and envy, about the day the Pinckneys met the princess.[19]

The visit with Princess Augusta marked the high point of Eliza's 1753 adventures in England, but it was hardly her only one. To Charles's chagrin, his colonial appointment turned out to be a low-level letdown. On the upside, he found himself free of the time-consuming political offices he had held in South Carolina. Eliza and he indulged their interests and journeyed around the country. She calculated that they traveled more than seven hundred miles by land their first summer in England. "'Tis a very pleasant but expensive way of spending time," Eliza told Anne Ashby Manigault.[20]

Leisured and flush from their Carolina plantation profits, the couple took a long tour through the south and west of England in 1753, visiting all the interesting sites: a "Peregrination," as Eliza called it, "to see what ever was curious." They wandered through art museums and cathedrals and castles, and explored the remains of England's ancient history, including Stonehenge. Enslaved workers transported from South Carolina and servants hired in England could maintain the Pinckney household in their absence. Harriott and Thomas could be left with their tutors and the maids, and Charles Cotesworth and the Drayton brothers were at boarding school.[21]

They traveled to Bath their first winter in England. The city's famous hot springs had attracted visitors since the first century A.D. Eighteenth-century visitors flocked to Bath for health benefits and the social scene, which included several thriving theater companies. Relatives of Mary Wood Wragg welcomed the Pinckneys into their inner circles at Bath. Eliza bragged that she got to see everything that "was curious and Elegant." It was the first of several times when Eliza's social connections opened more doors in England than Charles's political ones.[22]

Between trips, Eliza relished evenings at the theater in London. She tried never to miss one of David Garrick's plays. Garrick transformed mid-eighteenth-century London theater. He adopted a decidedly more naturalist approach to acting, teaching performers to re-create the humanity of characters. He also spurned the liquor-soaked revelry that turned many performances into scrums. Garrick was at the apex of his career in the 1750s: wildly popular, wealthy, and internationally acclaimed. His artistic and ennobling plays matched Eliza's interests while hewing to the respectability she always sought to project. She was not one for drunken spectacles. But a creative innovation steeped in Enlightenment values and interrogating the human condition—that suited her perfectly. London also offered street fairs, boat trips along the Thames, and, in the winter, ice-skating. Spectators could watch cricket matches, or, if they were inclined more toward the macabre, public executions. Residents bowled and played backgammon in taverns and coffeehouses and strolled through parks. For the rest of her life, Eliza "always spoke with pleasure of the gayeties" she enjoyed in London.[23]

Back in South Carolina, black families labored to bankroll Eliza's English adventures, and they endured the consequences of the Pinckneys' becoming absentee planters. Leaving provincial holdings in the hands of overseers and kin was not unusual in colonial America, and it was particularly common in the Caribbean. Wealthy planters moved to the metropole, sometimes for an extended visit and sometimes for good, and let their colonial investments work for them. In that tradition and well in advance of their departure, Charles, who took the lead in coordinating family finances, anticipated the steep costs of the move. Like his wife, he was an avid planner, and he took meticulous care with the preparations. In early 1753 he compiled an extensive "rent roll"—a listing of all his property and the rental agreements he negotiated. Governor James Glen leased their Charles Town home. The Georgian-style mansion made a suitably elegant residence for the most politically powerful man in the colony. (Throughout the 1750s and 1760s, the house continued to serve as the residence of successive royal governors.) Charles

Pinckney owned other buildings in Charles Town, too, including warehouses and his late mother's former home. The scope of the Pinckney properties was staggering: almost 1,000 acres of rice land near Belmont; 445 acres of land on Goose Creek, with another 400 acres nearby; a 1,000-acre estate at Port Royal with 500 more acres spread across three nearby holdings; 500 acres on the Savannah River; land in parishes across the colony, including Prince George's in the north and St. Bartholomew's and Prince William's to the southwest. The list kept going.[24]

With each estate, Charles recorded the most valuable assets: the people he and Eliza held in bondage. He noted along with each person's name the age and any special skill the person possessed, which affected market value. It was a fairly typical list, although more often the naming of enslaved people appeared in planters' wills or estate inventories than in the sort of document Charles created. The effect was the same: with a stroke of the pen, black families found their lives upended. Scores of men, women, and children laboring on the Pinckneys' various properties suddenly answered to new owners. When, for example, Charles rented Belmont to his brother William, their agreement included more than fifty people. Charles named them all, down to one-year-old Mariah, daughter of Duja. The enslaved people at Belmont netted him £235 per year in rental fees. He valued them at more than ten times the worth of the 175 acres of land they worked. Another forty-six people were rented at Auckland (which the family sometimes called Ashepoo), including Mary Ann and her children Prince and Beck. Among the other people legally bound to that rental property, Nancy was two years old, Joe only one. Charles listed at least eighteen children who were under the age of six, younger than his oldest child, Charles Cotesworth. Did he think about Rose being the same age as Harriott, or that Ned and Thomas were not yet three years old? That Charles recorded in the rent roll children too young to labor reflected, first, that he thought of slavery as a long-term investment: babies in their mothers' arms would, in time, pay dividends and so needed to be counted among his assets. Second, the listing signaled that his and Eliza's trip was open-ended. They might remain in England long enough for toddlers to grow into laborers.[25]

The people tethered to the Pinckneys' various properties had their own families, a fact that Charles understood. His log listed many people as family members: for example, John and Helena and their five children, recorded in birth order, from fifteen-year-old Peter to two-month-old Lena; and Cuffee and Annabel and their sons, Berwick and John. The names continued, page after page. Charles named fathers first, then their wives and children under the notation "& his family." Some mothers raised minor children without an adult male, including Sue, who was listed with her children, Jenny, age ten, seven-year-old Lyn, and Dido, only four. And some children at Belmont were alone: Will and Bob, both eleven, Nancy, age seven, and six-year-old Abram. Perhaps they picked the mulberry leaves to feed the silkworms. Some enslaved people, then, including young children, lived apart from their kinfolk, the ties severed by death or sale or the work needs and whims of Eliza and Charles. But for the husbands and wives and parents and children who already lived together, Charles intended them to stay together in his absence.[26]

How common that impulse was among large slave owners is hard to say. The surviving evidence from colonial South Carolina is too sparse to make any firm conclusions except that enslavers kept their own interests paramount. Some Lowcountry planters ignored families altogether, making no mention of kin ties in lists of people they enslaved. Other enslavers clearly preferred to keep families together, for a variety of reasons. Henry Laurens, for example, tried "to avoid that inconvenience and I will say inhumanity of separating and tareing assunder my Negroes' several families." The "inconvenience" Laurens mentioned lay in lost labor owing to enslaved peoples' resistance to family separations: they varyingly pleaded for reunification, refused to work, grieved themselves sick, and fled. Laurens's sense of humanity was also self-interested. "I cannot be deaf to their cries least a time should come when I should cry & there shall be none to pity me," he decided. Other planters were more strategic; they knew disrupting families could be bad for business. Runaway advertisements in the *South Carolina Gazette* routinely explained that the fleeing person went in search of a relative. Preserving the family ties of enslaved people could pay a long-term dividend in the form of fewer flights, greater emotional leverage, and more children. That last matter led some planters to force pairings or offer incentives to women who bore children. How much the marriages recorded by planters reflected emotional commitments between enslaved women and men is therefore unknowable. Charles Pinckney seemed to fall into the strategic camp. He understood that the value of his plantations depended on forced labor, and the more stable he could make that labor the better off he would be. An advertisement for one of his plantations further suggested Charles's mindset: he detailed the merits of the land followed by the skills of the people who accompanied the land and then described several pieces of furniture and a 150-gallon copper boiler suitable for brewing beer or refining sugar.[27]

To oversee the Pinckneys' ongoing interests in South Carolina, Charles turned to his brother William and nephew Charles, who'd taken to sometimes calling himself Charles Pinckney Jr. While William supervised the country estates, Charles Jr. managed his uncle's city rentals. He ran weekly advertisements in the *South Carolina Gazette* for properties to rent and laborers for hire, including "a handy wench, who is a very good seamstress; also a negro fellow, an exceeding good bricklayer."[28]

As Charles had anticipated from all his carefully laid plans, his South Carolina estate turned steady profits; he and Eliza spent accordingly. Absentee planters, freed of the day-to-day oversight of their colonial plantations, they enjoyed an easy life. The three Pinckney siblings and the Drayton brothers all thrived in England. The perils of smallpox behind them, none of them contracted so much as a cold the first winter.[29]

There was only one problem: Charles did not share Eliza's zeal for their new life in the imperial center. Eliza confided to Anne Ashby Manigault in the spring of 1754 that she felt disappointed and bewildered because, despite all the happy adventures they had experienced in their first year in England, Charles still had "many [y]earnings after his native land." He wanted to go home. She thought they were already there.[30]

CHAPTER 9

"a home after her own heart"

Eliza and Charles Pinckney's friends admired their marriage; they seemed so close and loving, "this Happy Couple, enjoying all the Sweets of an agreeable Life." But even the best of marriages can sometimes be an ordeal. Eliza and Charles's travels to England in the mid-1750s proved they were no exception. Not only did they disagree about the charms of England. They also seemed at odds over exactly what kind of trip they'd made: was it a temporary visit, or a permanent move?[1]

A wayfarer her whole life, Eliza had gotten good at making a home wherever she lived. By nature, she was flexible and optimistic and quick to make friends. Besides, she loved being in England. If she had her way, she would not go back to South Carolina. Charles, slower to adapt, felt more apprehensive and unsettled. He missed South Carolina right away and soon began to talk about an early return. When he got sick in February 1754, his friends speculated that the illness gave him "a new Cause of Dislike to England."[2]

Eliza aired out her and Charles's disagreement with Anne Ashby Manigault. She confided to Anne in early 1754 that Charles remained "not quite satisfied" with England. Eliza hoped she could coax him into staying longer. No one could have been treated more warmly, she insisted: "Never strangers had more reason to like a place." Anne already knew about the couple's problem from her gossipy son, Peter. He predicted that Charles would prevail over

Eliza. "I believe," Peter told Anne, "all that his Lady will be able to say, will not put honest Carolina out of his head."[3]

Though she did not share Charles's discontent, Eliza understood it. He was frustrated by experiencing the imperial context of his colonial wealth and power. In Charles Town he was a gentleman of the first order; he lived in the most impressive house in the city and led a lifestyle unsurpassed in luxury. In London, he was a middling-rank outsider, reminded daily of how real English aristocrats lived. That new reality hit Charles harder than it did Eliza. His political position made things worse. In South Carolina, Charles had been at the center of power, holding high offices and commanding respect. His life there, Eliza recalled, "was a continual course of active virtue." Before they departed from the colony, Charles Town residents placed a notice in the *South Carolina Gazette* publicly offering Charles their "hearty Thanks" for his "excellent and learned" work as chief justice. A subsequent issue of the newspaper bade a fond farewell to "the Honorable CHARLES PINCKNEY, Esq." "We cannot omit," the editor added, "saying that he was a true Father of his Country that his Absence is a Loss to Carolina and that her Sons mourn that Loss."[4]

Charles's appointment in the imperial center was to be South Carolina's agent to the Board of Trade. In Charles Town that sounded very important. It was not.

The powerful men who managed Britain's global empire merely added Charles's name to a long list of colonial agents who occasionally offered brief reports. (North America was not a top priority.) Charles appeared before the Board of Trade when called but wielded no power. As Eliza gently put it, Charles's influence "was circumscribed within much narrower bounds." In fact, his appointment was shakier than most colonial agents'. Soon after he arrived in London, Charles learned that the South Carolina Assembly had refused to go along with the governor and Royal Council in certifying his appointment. He felt humiliated, and on two continents. He lashed out, blasting his opponents for trying to "pull down Pinckneys pride, and humble it in the dust!" "It is impossible," Charles insisted, "my pride, (you See I am not ashamed to own I have pride) is founded on too Solid a base to be so tumbled." Charles resolved to promote South Carolina's interests as best he could, despite the controversy. In the haphazard way common among colonial administrations, he operated, in his words, as "public Agent of the Province," with the support of the governor and Royal Council. He vowed to pursue "the good of our Country"—by which he meant South Carolina. But he was hurt, deeply.[5]

Charles tried to hide his embarrassment from Eliza but couldn't. She knew him by heart. She worried: he'd always been so sweet and cheerful. Now frustrations and fears crowded his mind. Unable to help, she bore witness to "his secrete grief."[6]

The prospect of settling in, of making the transition from visitors to residents, proved challenging for the couple, too. They moved to the metropole anticipating living as English gentry. In South Carolina that had essentially meant purchasing Englishness: clothes, housewares, food, books, and cultural activities. But Eliza and Charles soon discovered that the process of moving culturally from provincial to metropole was not quite so transactional. They could buy only so much of an English genteel identity. They would no longer live at the pinnacle of society, as they had done in Carolina. But they could live genteelly—and happily—nonetheless. It would just take time.[7]

They searched at length for a house that felt like a home. After a short stint in the house on Southampton Street in London, they briefly rented a place in Richmond. Eight miles southwest of London, Richmond was a lovely and fashionable village, near the royal gardens at Kew, and with a wide green on the town square. The Thames runs through Richmond, offering easy access to central London. But it didn't suit the couple: "We don't think of continuing at Richmond after our term in this house is up," Eliza said. By late 1753 the Pinckneys were looking in earnest for a house in London, but at a loss to find anything that fit their tastes at a price they were willing to pay. They searched every possibility between Temple Bar and Westminster to find an unfurnished house, which Eliza much preferred. They could secure only a furnished one. It was on Craven Street, which happened to be the most popular street for prominent North Americans living in London. Benjamin Franklin lived on Craven Street during his long residence in England. Eliza pronounced the house "a very good one in a very good street." Peter Manigault took notice that at £120 per year, the Pinckneys paid "Tip-Top rent."[8]

Craven Street put the couple back in the center of London. Charles could easily walk to Whitehall, if anyone bothered to call him. They were close again to people and places they knew. George Morley, Eliza's long-standing English agent, operated out of Somerset House, just east of their neighborhood. Ten minutes' walk along the Thames past Somerset was the Inns of Court, the center of legal training in England. South Carolinians favored Middle Temple. The Pinckneys' nephew Charles had studied there, and Peter

Manigault was a student. Later, both Charles Cotesworth and Thomas Pinckney pursed their educations at Middle Temple.

The Pinckneys didn't stay long on Craven Street, either. The next year they moved again, out of rental houses entirely. With an added infusion of capital from the settlement of Charles's late brother Thomas's estate, the Pinckneys bought a house—they called it a villa—in Ripley, a small village twenty-five miles southwest of London. They settled there in the summer of 1754.

Ripley was farther from London than Richmond and without river access. But the village lay on a well-maintained coach road that ran between London and the Royal Naval station at Portsmouth. Travel to London was reliable and safe, if slower than from Richmond. The Pinckneys' new house sat across from the village green, on the road toward London, just a quick walk north of the tavern and shops that formed the village center. To the rear of the white, two-story brick house was a large garden, perfect for Eliza's botanical interests. The Pinckneys remained in Ripley for nearly four years. It became to Eliza, her relatives said, "a home after her own heart."[9]

Eliza's favorite friend from her school days, Katherine Martin Carew, lived fifteen miles to the east. Again, Eliza's friendships afforded entry into English social networks. Katherine had married exceptionally well, to Lord Nicholas Carew, and resided at her husband's ancestral home, Beddington. For five hundred years the Carew family lived on the majestic estate. Also called Carew Manor, Beddington had one of the best-known private gardens in all of England. Dating back to the mid-sixteenth century, the gardens at Beddington included a lake, hunting grounds, even an orangery—the first in England. Katherine's father-in-law built an enormous dovecote, with 1,360 nesting boxes for pigeons, a fashionable food. The awe-inspiring centerpiece of the Carews' home was their grand hall and banqueting room, boasting a hammerbeam roof similar to the arched ceilings at Hampton Court and Middle Temple.[10]

After the Pinckneys moved to Ripley, Eliza and Katherine visited regularly—sometimes just for breakfast—and wrote openly affectionate letters when apart. Eliza delighted in the renewal of their friendship: "Begun at a very early time of life," their connection was marked by "great affection" and "great sincerity."[11]

The Pinckneys' Ripley villa was nothing on a par with the Carews' Beddington estate. But it was a thoroughly reputable home, in line with their neighbors in Ripley and appropriate to their station in life. In the first year of their residence, they added a separate laundry, granary, and dovecote as well as a new coach house for the his-and-her carriages they bought.

Eliza resumed her botanical interests at the Ripley villa, sparing no expense. The Ripley property was walled, and the house mostly surrounded by gardens. Charles bought expensive garden glasses—globes to place over individual plants. Serious and well-to-do English gardeners used glassware to protect nonindigenous plants from wind, rain, and cold while letting in sunlight. The Pinckneys also bought framed glass, to be propped up tent-style to protect larger beds. Peaches, apricots, and grapes grew in their gardens. At some point, Eliza planted a cedar tree in the backyard. She was putting down roots again, literally, for something solid, something to last.[12]

Eliza and Charles brought few household items with them from North America. The expense was too great. Instead, the couple sold a lot of personal items in the weeks before their departure, including books, china, and furniture. They replaced all those things in England, where they enjoyed easier access to a greater diversity of more up-to-date goods. Charles meticulously tallied his and Eliza's household expenses, down to the penny.[13]

The ledger shows how zealously the couple went about acquiring the trappings of a genteel lifestyle once they settled down in Ripley. Workmen trekked in and out of their home: blacksmiths, masons, metalworkers. Local craftsmen hung wallpaper, laid brick, grafted fruit trees, and cut glass. The Pinckneys updated the ceilings of the villa, repainted the walls, and laid new tile. They bought fancy saddles and bridles for their horses and even paved their coach house. Only the best would do. They hired prominent upholsterers to design curtains and chair coverings and skilled carpenters to build bedroom furniture. Among their purchases: a large mahogany table for their breakfast area, an imported Turkish carpet, half a dozen new mahogany chairs, and an eight-day clock—it needed winding only once a week. Such material goods signaled the Pinckneys' stylishness and refinement. Their new neighbors could read their worthiness in their housewares, put on display at dinner parties and social gatherings they hosted. They bought a monogrammed silver tea service, a red leather box to hold a special set of candlesticks, scores of silver place settings and cups and glasses, stacks of table linens, sets of china in purple, blue and white, yellow, and orange, hand-crafted pewter chafing dishes, and three punch bowls.[14]

Eliza and Charles settled into their English village, but they never strayed too far from their dependence on American slavery. Enslaved Carolinians lived with the family and labored for them in Ripley. Colonial elites routinely

Figure 7. Silver teapot, c. 1753, owned by Eliza Lucas Pinckney. Courtesy of The Charleston Museum, Charleston, South Carolina.

forced enslaved people to accompany them abroad. Eliza and Charles would not have gone to England without at least a personal maid for her and a "body servant" for him. Mary Ann remained in South Carolina with Prince and Beck, so another woman—or perhaps a young girl—accompanied Eliza across the Atlantic, attended to her clothes, set up her varied houses, and minded her children when they were not at school. Eliza's reliance of enslaved labor was so reflexive and her entitlement so deep that she never bothered to record the woman's name in her writings. To supplement forced black labor, and perhaps in a nod to English tradition, the couple also hired servants. Charles's copious records from Ripley list expenditures for the rooms occupied by their "maids" and "Men Servants." Who these people were remains a mystery, but their responsibilities in such a large house can easily be imagined.

At her new Ripley home, Eliza focused on her family and on friendships with her neighbors. As she had done upon moving to South Carolina in the late 1730s, she immersed herself in a neighborhood of established well-to-do women and befriended them. She entertained and took up cooking, with her characteristic zeal for improvement and productivity. Dick remained in South Carolina, so she could not rely on his culinary expertise. As was her wont,

Eliza created a record of what she learned from her friends, this time in a personal recipe book. The collection of recipes included both food and medicines. Sometimes the line between the two blurred: she recommended up to a quart a day of coffee brewed with milk instead of water to cure consumption.[15]

A well-connected woman with young children, Eliza collected medicinal recipes for childhood ailments—croup, whooping cough, and thrush—from leading doctors on both sides of the Atlantic. Her botanical pursuits and hands-on experience with sick enslaved people afforded Eliza further insights into medical treatments. She felt prepared to treat most everyday ailments, including fevers, toothaches, jaundice, and flux. The interventions were not always effective—a person with dysentery did not need a purgative—but Eliza's medical concoctions were up to date and in line with scientific knowledge at the time. When Thomas suffered from a swollen gland in his face, she learned how to make soothing poultices. The recipe book also showed Eliza's interest in her appearance: she made hand cream, shampoo to grow hair longer, and a recipe for lightening tanned skin (washing with lemon and salt before bedtime).[16]

But most of Eliza's recipes were for elaborate meals, learned from her English friends. They taught her how to make roasts with carrots, turnips, and mushrooms, topped with rich gravies, to pickle mackerel, bake mince pie and bread pudding, and preserve berries. She made almond milk and peach brandy. From her orangery, she produced orange marmalade. She learned, too, how to preserve imported lemons and cook with spices acquired from across the globe. While she experimented with gravies and gelatins, Eliza especially liked preparing desserts: cakes, puddings, and pies, as well as fruit jams. She kept a list of favorite easy desserts. Raspberry jam with fresh cream "makes a pretty dish," she noted, and apples roasted in liquor and topped with cream were a delicious treat for cold winter nights, of which she and Charles enjoyed many in the English countryside.[17]

Eliza was happy in Ripley, with her new friends and her new life. She also doted on her children, as she raised them to be genteel, educated, and pious. She felt lucky about the children; two years passed before any of them suffered a significant illness. She put all of them, including Thomas as soon as he could read, to daily Bible study. They had to memorize the daily collect from the Anglican Book of Common Prayer, too. And she set a strong example of personal piety.[18]

Charles took the lead in ensuring that all the boys got a proper education. His and Eliza's expectations were high, and they spared no cost. At first, Charles hired a private tutor to get Charles Cotesworth and the Drayton brothers up to speed on their studies. Then he sent the three of them to a prestigious academy in Camberwell, a village two miles south of the Thames. Charles Cotesworth was only seven when the family arrived in England in 1753, but Charles had already observed enough about the boy's temperament and intellect to imagine a career for him: the law. Charles Cotesworth "seemd to have capacity and inclination" for legal pursuits, his father bragged. As for little Thomas, his father concluded that he "was too young to determine any thing in relation to him." By the time Thomas was six or seven, Charles expected to be able to "consult his Genius." When Thomas got old enough to go to school, he joined the older boys at the Camberwell school. Later the Pinckney and Drayton boys attended Westminster School, one of the most prestigious boarding academies in London. In time, Charles Cotesworth and Thomas pursued advanced studies at Oxford and legal training at Middle Temple.[19]

None of those schools accepted girls. Eliza took responsibility for Harriott's education. From a young age, Harriott was, like her mother, "fond of learning." Following the example of her own father, Eliza took pride in her daughter's intellect and resolved to "indulge her in it." Harriott's later writings and conduct indicate that she was well educated. She penned elegant, eloquent letters as a young woman and understood botany and finance, just like her mother.[20]

Perhaps because she was so happy in Ripley and had so much to lose—or maybe it came with her stage of life—Eliza began to worry more. Now in her mid-thirties, she had lived long enough to see random events suddenly steal happiness. Past tragedies made her more fearful than she'd been before she and Charles had the children. When Thomas suffered from a swollen facial gland in the winter of 1755, Eliza consulted three doctors and insisted on going to London for treatment. When a fever followed, she dropped all socializing and even stopped corresponding with friends. Eliza said the illness reminded her of "the unstableness and uncertainty of all human happiness." She worried, too, about her friends. When Katherine Martin Carew left Ripley one blustery evening, Eliza watched the skies with dread as a storm built. Though she knew Katherine traveled over a well-known road in a sturdy coach with six horses, Eliza could not stop worrying. She paced and fretted until well past 1:00 A.M.[21]

Conversely, life in Ripley gradually lightened some of Charles's unease. The villa felt more permanent, and the neighborhood more like his country estate in South Carolina. He got used to life as an absentee planter. Away from London, he could escape the constant reminders of the grandeur of imperial society and his modest place in it. By 1755, Charles had put aside his plans to cut short the family's time in England and joined Eliza in considering making their move permanent. They would, they agreed, remain in their Ripley house at least until Charles Cotesworth and Thomas finished their educations. Perhaps they might stay for good.

The trip, the passing years, her growing responsibilities to her children—it all carried Eliza farther from her relatives in Antigua. She loved her mother and siblings no less, but the longing subsided. So much happened, and it was so difficult to keep Ann and Polly and Tommy and George up to date on her life. She tried mightily to maintain correspondences. Eliza thought of her letters as conversations and a space for discussing ideas, and it bothered her when her relatives' missives were too superficial, too brief, or too slow to arrive in London. Exasperated with Polly at one point, she said that a letter from her only sister was "almost as great a rarity as a cake of Ice" from Antigua. She wrote to her South Carolina friends, too, especially to Anne Ashby Manigault and Mary Wood Wragg. Still, her life was in England now, with Charles and the children, in her Ripley villa with her English lifestyle.[22]

The money, though, still flowed from South Carolina. Eliza and Charles neither cast aside their provincial roots nor lost sight of their colonial enterprises. Indeed, as they settled into Ripley for the long term, they continued to actively promote their South Carolina interests.

The Pinckneys met Princess Augusta again, in early 1755. This time, they visited her at Leicester House, in London. The couple brought another present, this one owing to Eliza's botanical experiments in South Carolina. The 1755 visit made the Charles Town newspaper. In April 1755, the *South Carolina Gazette* reported that Charles Pinckney had called on Princess Augusta. According to the newspaper, Charles presented her with "Silk Damask of the Growth and Product of his own Plantation in that Province, and dyed a fine blue with CAROLINA INDIGO." It was, of course, Eliza's experiments that made the gift possible, and she certainly would have accompanied Charles. "Her Royal Highness," the *South Carolina Gazette* proudly proclaimed, "declare[d] her Satisfaction in seeing such Improvements made in the Produce of our Colonies" and promised "that she will honour it with her own Wearing."[23]

Princess Augusta wearing South Carolina silk dyed with South Carolina indigo was no accident. Before Eliza left the province, in addition to selecting her birds, she carefully packed up the silk thread produced at Belmont. She carried it to London's silk weavers, designers, and tailors at Spitalfields. (In the eighteenth century, many London's neighborhoods, sometimes even individual streets, were segregated by trades.) French Huguenots had started the silk industry at Spitalfields, manufacturing cloth, creating designs, and ultimately producing housewares and attire from the luxurious fabric. By the time Eliza returned to England in 1753, Britons had taken over most of what the French began. Eliza was not unique in her fascination with silk. Throughout the Atlantic World, well-off women wore silk to signal their gentility and good taste. Women also managed silkworks throughout the empire. At Spitalfields, some women designed the patterns woven into silk fabrics.[24]

The enslaved people at Belmont had managed to cultivate enough silk to create fabric for three dresses. One was a beautiful, rich salmon adorned with cream-colored floral patterns. Another was bright yellow, with gold trimming. And the third was indigo blue.[25]

The dresses had great meaning to Eliza, far beyond their stylishness. They showcased the bounty of the North American colonies and the promise of Eliza's agricultural innovations. Once worn, they became a walking advertisement for her, for South Carolina, for the British Empire. Generations of Pinckney women passed down tales of those silk dresses and what they meant to their ancestor. The way they remembered the story, Eliza, not Charles, showed the silk dresses to the princess "in order that her highness might see what the province was capable of producing." Eliza kept one of the dresses for herself: the salmon floral. The other two she gave away, as a means of advertising her agricultural experiments. The recipients reflected the social world Eliza and Charles inhabited in England—and her savvy. Eliza gave one of the Belmont silk dresses to Lord Chesterfield, the famous English writer and bon vivant. The other went to the mother of the future king of England.[26]

As provincials living in the metropole, Eliza and Charles had to navigate between interconnected but different and sometimes competing worlds: English, colonial, American. Perhaps fittingly, or at least poetically, an imperial war sparked in the American provinces drew them out of the metropole and back to South Carolina.

In the summer of 1754, North Americans, in pursuit of western lands and without imperial approval, sparked a violent collision with French soldiers in the backcountry of Virginia and Pennsylvania. A little-known lieutenant in the Virginia militia named George Washington led a misguided effort to secure colonists' land claims. He was routed and surrendered on July 4. Notified

Figure 8. Eliza Lucas Pinckney's dress, made in London of South Carolina silk, was passed down and worn by later generations of Pinckney and Horry women. Courtesy of The Charleston Museum, Charleston, South Carolina.

of this ignominious defeat, King George II's leading minister, the Duke of Newcastle, reacted to the news with "an alarm that verged on panic." He sought funds to support the defense of Virginia as he opened diplomatic talks on the Continent. Resolved to defend its colonies' western borders and citizens, Britain sent General Edward Braddock to North America, to serve as commander of the armed forces of all the imperial holdings.[27]

The British Americans, it turned out, did not like being commanded. They were decidedly provincial, committed not to imperial or continental interests but to local concerns. Colonial assemblies as well as soldiers on the ground balked at Braddock's command. Imperial leaders were nonplussed. Braddock lost his life in July 1755, mortally wounded at the Battle of Monongahela while trying to capture Fort Duquesne, near present-day Pittsburgh. Sixty of Braddock's eighty-six officers were killed or wounded. The panicked remains of his army fled east, soon followed by droves of white settlers. Leaders in London were staggered at this shocking defeat.[28]

The Pinckneys were distressed, too. Although the fighting took place far from the South Carolina Lowcountry, trade disruptions and fear of the conflict spreading into the Southeast drew the rapt attention of Carolinians on both sides of the Atlantic. In late 1755, Charles became consumed with filing reports with the Board of Trade on behalf of fearful Carolinians. Eliza also closely followed the "late alarming accts of the strides the French are making." She, like Charles, feared the mounting conflict "may too soon very materially affect" their colonial interests. If the violence were to spread to South Carolina, it would further disrupt commodities markets. Worse still, combatants might overrun the Pinckneys' plantations and abet the flight of enslaved people. A war could destroy their livelihood.[29]

South Carolina was the least of Britain's concerns. In 1756, the North American conflict ricocheted into Europe. In January, Britain struck an alliance with Prussia; in May, France allied with Austria. With that, fifty-year-old alliances were inverted. France, hoping to curtail British colonial expansion, signaled that it might invade England. England moved to fortify its coasts. This left fewer resources for the overseas colonies on the mainland of North America and in the Caribbean, and at East India Company outposts in Calcutta and Madras. As these provinces became more vulnerable to attack, their profitability tumbled.[30]

Charles Pinckney looked out the window one morning and saw forty-four wagons loaded with munitions roll by. The supplies were bound for the coast, part of the massive mobilization for war with France. Eliza felt the flow of bad news turn her and Charles's happy life in Ripley into "gloomy anxiety."[31] They followed the news with growing alarm. By early 1757 minor battles in the interior of North America had ignited a global war—unprecedented in its scope. In March, Lord Loudon, the new commander in North America, intent on keeping his troop movements a secret from the French, embargoed all nonmilitary traffic from American ports. Trading activities in port cities, including Charles Town, ground to a halt. Economic chaos ensued. Though South Carolina remained far from the fighting, the colony, dependent on Atlantic trading, took a direct and crippling hit.

Events cascaded. Amid the escalating war, Charles Pinckney got word that his opponents in the South Carolina Assembly had finally succeeded in formally removing him from any power in England by appointing a new agent: James Wright. Around the same time that he learned of this ouster, Charles heard that his brother William had suffered a stroke. It was, Charles concluded, time to go back to South Carolina. The decision to depart was his alone. "Upon our continual alarms from abroad," Eliza explained, "Mr. Pinckney came to a resolution to return to Carolina."[32]

Eliza did not object. The stakes of staying were too high. It was one thing to wait out Charles's personal unhappiness, as she'd done in 1754. But now, remaining in England jeopardized the family's financial future. They could not take the risk of continuing as absentee planters. Together, Eliza and Charles decided they would return to South Carolina for two years only, and during that time "dispose of the greatest part of what he has there and fix it in a more secure . . . part of the world": England. Because their return to the province was only temporary, the couple decided not to sell their Ripley villa.[33]

Eliza told Katherine Martin Carew that the mere thought of recrossing the Atlantic filled her with "melancholy apprehensions." Once again, she would have to leave behind friends she had carefully cultivated. The sociable neighborhood of Ripley, the connections to all the interesting women she'd befriended, would be reduced to sporadic epistolary conversations. Most painful, she couldn't see Katherine. "Be assured," Eliza promised her, "what ever part of the world Providence alots me I shall ever retain the most affectionate regard for you." Eliza would always love Katherine, she vowed, "be the distance between us ever so great."[34]

Despite her reluctance to leave England and her fear of the Atlantic crossing, Eliza never considered staying behind. She was Charles's wife. She would go where he went.

What of the children? Their parents faced an anguishing choice. Charles Cotesworth was eleven, Harriott nine, and Thomas not quite seven when their parents decided to return to Carolina. Should they carry the children with them into a war zone? Or leave them behind? "You can judge," Eliza told Katherine, "what I have suffered" at the impossible choice. The boys, Eliza and Charles finally concluded, should stay at their studies. Thomas was a bit young to be left abroad, but only a bit. Eliza had been sent to England at age ten, as had her brother Tommy. The Drayton brothers were nine and ten when they left South Carolina. The Pinckneys had developed a strong support network that the boys could draw on and many friends to watch out for them. Charles Cotesworth was mature and responsible; he would take care of Thomas. But Eliza and Charles couldn't decide about Harriott. At first, Eliza wanted to carry her with them to South Carolina. Then, she thought better of it. She and Charles went round and round, weighing the choice.[35]

Eliza could hardly believe how fast her life was changing. In 1753, she and Charles "left a fine and flourishing Collony in profound peace, a Collony so valuable to this nation that it would have been lookd upon as absurd to have the least doubt of its being protected and taken care of in case of a war." Then, Eliza recalled, "I looked upon an Estate there as secure as in England." By 1757, everything had changed. If the Pinckneys remained in England, they might lose everything they had in South Carolina. Eliza concluded that the war made the necessity of a return "plain to every body ever so little acquainted with American affairs." There was that word again—American—Eliza's interests and her identity rooted in a place to which she had no wish to return.[36]

The war that sparked the Pinckneys' exodus from England then stalled their plans. It took nearly a year for them to leave. Thomas got a bit older, big enough to join Charles Cotesworth and Billy and Charles Drayton at school. The four boys were all admonished to make their parents proud and not to worsen the anguish of separation with foolish misbehavior.[37]

In the spring of 1758, Secretary of State William Pitt restructured Britain's military campaign in North America in an attempt to placate the still-obstreperous colonists whose parochialism had bogged down the war effort. It worked. By early 1758 Britain began to prevail on the high seas. More ships and a better-supplied navy gave them the edge against the French in the Atlantic. Trade—and the prospects of travelers—began to stabilize. In that window of opportunity for a safer crossing, Charles finalized their passage.[38]

Eliza carefully packed up her salmon and cream silk dress. Made in England from Carolina grown silk, it was going back across the Atlantic.[39] She also packed a new portrait of Charles, commissioned during their stay in Ripley. Eliza apparently chose not to sit for one. She never said why she decided to forgo a portrait commemorating her five-year residence in England. Portraits were popular at the time in elite circles, and London presented plenty of opportunities to hire a first-rate portraitist. North American couples liked to display their paintings side by side; they signaled wealth and power. Eliza seemingly demurred.[40]

In the end, Eliza and Charles decided to take Harriott with them. Separating was heartbreaking to the siblings. Harriott was rendered an only child, lonely without her brothers. Thomas and Charles Cotesworth lost their playmate, the middle child who connected them. Before they left and hoping to give the siblings some solace, Eliza and Charles hired an artist to create miniature silhouettes of all three children. Harriott took the silhouettes of Charles Cotesworth and Thomas to South Carolina. She wore the "shadows of my Brothers" on a pair of bracelets, which, Harriott said, could not "be bound nearer my arms" than her brothers were "to my heart."[41]

On March 12, 1758, Eliza Lucas Pinckney once again embarked on an ocean voyage she dreaded. She left behind another home she had made in another part of the British Empire. But this trip was worse than the ones before. The ship was sailing into the middle of a war. She, Charles, and Harriott might end up captives, or they might perish at sea. And if she survived? She would still be an ocean away from her sons, depending on chance to determine when—or whether—they might reunite.

As the ship headed out onto the Atlantic Ocean, Eliza knew how Charles Cotesworth and Thomas felt, for she, too, a lifetime before, had been left behind by a parent. Now, for the first time, she also understood how her father had felt. What could possibly be worse?

PART FIVE

A Widow Patriarch

CHAPTER 10

"oppressed with bitter Anguish"

Eliza, Charles, and Harriott Pinckney landed safely back in Charles Town on May 19, 1758, after a ten-week Atlantic crossing. They had been abroad for five years, and the city had changed in their absence. New, majestic brick houses dotted the expanded cityscape. St. Michael's church was going up on the southeast corner of Broad and Meeting. The grand Statehouse, opposite the church on the northwest corner, was midconstruction, too. Newcomers had entered the planter-merchant class and taken up positions of power in the colony. Other parts of the city felt comfortably familiar. It was still "an agreeable & polite place" where gentility reigned. The docks hummed with business as vessels entered every day, from Europe, Africa, and the Caribbean, and mainland ports including Boston, New York, Pensacola, and Mobile. Charles Town still bore "the appearance of a fair."[1]

The Pinckneys were greeted by beloved old friends. Eliza and Charles arrived in "great spirits," she proclaimed, and their friends received them "with great joy."[2]

Eliza's joy was short-lived. Charles's brother William couldn't come to town to welcome them. His stroke had been worse than Eliza and Charles knew. The couple set out to tour their properties and were shocked by the state of things. In William's debilitation, every plantation had fallen into disarray, badly mismanaged, Eliza quickly saw, by "ignorant or dishonest Over Seers."[3]

Charles Pinckney was fifty-eight when he made the crossing from England to South Carolina, fairly old for a man in that era, and doubtless weakened by the ordeal. Traveling around the swampy Lowcountry as summer hit its stride was not the wisest of decisions. In June, he got sick. Eliza and Charles probably thought their travels lay behind his first symptoms: the fever, headache, and chills might simply be part of reacclimating to South Carolina's weather and water. But he kept getting worse.

By late June, Eliza knew what Charles was up against: malaria. Colonial South Carolina's long summers and low-lying marshlands created an ideal breeding ground for mosquitoes and for malaria; the region routinely experienced outbreaks. The first signs of the disease are mild. As it deepens, however, sufferers become terribly fatigued, their fever spikes, and they have bouts of violent vomiting and diarrhea. The skin can become jaundiced and the body can convulse. Eliza had recipes for treating these symptoms: purgatives for the fever and jaundice, pennyroyal to ease stomach distress, and laudanum. But to her and other colonial Americans, the disease—and a cure—remained a mystery. Not until the late nineteenth century did physicians discover that parasites caused malaria and mosquitoes transmitted it. Hoping that a change of air might improve Charles's health, Eliza moved him around to various friends' houses. He only got sicker. As she cared for Charles, she tried to manage their businesses, too, and keep up their many obligations through correspondence. But his suffering sapped her resolve. "Sleepless nights and an aching heart," Eliza confided to a friend, "makes me very unfitt for this imployment." When she tried to write, she had "such a tremor upon my nerves I can but just hold my pen."[4]

With Eliza constantly at his bedside, Charles fought for his life for three weeks. He died at his friend Jacob Motte's Mount Pleasant estate, on July 12, 1758, a month shy of his fifty-ninth birthday. Eliza recorded the date in her catalogue of important days to commemorate. It was the last day she ever added to her list and, she said, "the most afflictive one I ever saw." It must have occurred to Eliza when she married a much older man that she was likely to outlive him. But knowing that intellectually and experiencing it were two entirely different matters. She held Charles's funeral at St. Philip's, where they had worshiped for many years and where she had always found comfort in her faith. Now, bitterness crowded out any solace. She was a thirty-five-year-old widow, with three little children to raise. She resented every part of widowhood, including burying Charles, as she put it, "in this unworthy land."[5]

Charles's death shattered Eliza. Ten months later she finally found the strength to write to Katherine Martin Carew. Katherine's letters from England had lain unanswered for months. "Could you not guess, my much loved friend, when I neglected you, that the greatest of human Evils had befallen me?" Eliza began. Then she unburdened herself: "I was deprived of what my soul held most dear upon Earth." Soon it would be a year since Charles died, and still, Eliza confided, "My Nights have passed in tears and my days in sighs without a single exception." "'Tis not in the power of words to paint my distress," Eliza told Katherine. Yet write she did, despite her still raw grief.[6]

The news had to be told, over and over again, to kin, friends, and business associates across the Atlantic. Sometimes when recounting Charles's last days, Eliza found herself paralyzed by sorrow. She broke down in the middle of some letters, confessing, "the violence of pain" was more than she could bear: "My Eyes fail and I can write no more." After a break, she took up her pen again. Eliza felt she had to personally write her far-flung friends about Charles's passing. Still committed to keeping her letterbook, she wrote each heartbreaking letter twice. "'Tis a painful task to have these dismal letters to coppy," she explained, "but it seems there is a necessity for it."[7]

In letter after letter, she narrated Charles's death, which, she insisted, he met with unflagging grace and Christian resignation. Woven into the story of his last days was his inherent goodness and her abiding love. Charles was, Eliza insisted, "the best of men of husbands and of Fathers." He had made her the happiest woman on earth, she insisted, and she had no desire beyond him. Charles's death was "the most distressful Event that ever did or could happen to me in this world." She said she would carry the memory of their love to her grave.[8]

How in the world could she tell her sons—twelve and eight years old, and an ocean away—that their father was dead? Charles had always doted on his children, more than most fathers in that era. They came late in his life, and he was grateful to God for blessing him and Eliza with Harriott and the boys. As he lay dying, the thought of leaving behind the children gave Charles his greatest anguish.[9]

As she pondered explaining Charles's death to the boys, Eliza recollected a conversation she'd had with Thomas at their home in Ripley. She and Charles had just begun to talk about leaving England. Thomas was only six at the time. He woke one morning and, alone with his mother, suddenly asked of her a favor. He wanted her to promise that if she and his father went to South Carolina and either of them died, the other would not tell him. As

Eliza remembered that poignant conversation with her youngest child, she felt utterly lost. Should she even tell the boys?[10]

She must have remembered her own pain upon accidentally learning of her father's death, when a sense of betrayal deepened her grief. Her mother and her husband had conspired to keep the news from her for honorable reasons, to be sure. Still, the deception hurt. Did she want to repeat that mistake with her sons? And could she really expect to keep Charles's death from them? With all the Carolinians in and out of London, surely someone would innocently offer condolences. How long could such a secret be kept?

Eliza wanted to hold and console her boys, but she couldn't. Instead, she began a terrible letter: "How shall I write to you! What shall I say to you! My dear, my ever dear Children!" Every word she penned brought anguish. "I have," she forced herself to continue, "a tale to tell you that will peirce your tender infant hearts."[11]

Written to inform the boys of their father's passing, the letter also marked the first of many advisory letters Eliza sent them as they pursued their studies in England. She began with heartfelt assurances that their father had loved them better than life itself. Then she introduced a decades-long refrain: Charles Cotesworth and Thomas's father had led an honorable, accomplished life, setting for his children "a great and good example." "Let it be a comfort to you," she urged, "as long as you live that you had such a father!" The boys should devote themselves to becoming worthy to be called Charles Pinckney's sons.[12]

Eliza presented Charles's life—and his death—as a lesson in Christian faith. Charles had served God his whole life. He met death without fear and "went like a Lamb into eternity." It fell to Eliza and her children to follow his example and to accept his death as God's will. The loss was severe and irremediable. But Charles Cotesworth and Thomas should, their mother told them, hold on to the biblical assurance that, in time, the family would be reunited in heaven.[13]

She apparently sensed the hollowness of the letter to comfort her sons. Doubting herself and thinking again about her early morning talk with Thomas, she sent her letter under cover to the boys' schoolmaster. She asked him and Rebecca Evance to decide together whether and when to share the letter with Charles Cotesworth and Thomas. Rebecca was a friend and longtime Belmont neighbor who had relocated to England. She acted as the boys' guardian and surrogate mother, and Eliza trusted her to know what to do. Overwhelmed and uncertain—rare for Eliza—she admitted, "I am not capable to think for my self." Hoping to send some small comfort to bridge the vast distance, she shipped with her letters a large barrel of South Carolina rice, which she knew her boys loved.[14]

In the depths of her despair, Eliza saw that she could not avoid certain family and business matters, starting with providing for Charles Cotesworth and Thomas. She sent one of her first letters after Charles's passing to George Morley, her and Charles's business manager in London—now hers alone. She directed him to provide Rebecca Evance with however much money she needed for the boys. With no more explanation of her authority than the quick assertion of it, Eliza assured George that she would gratefully repay him. She also urged friends in England and Carolinians traveling to the metropole to look in on her sons and try to cheer them up.[15]

The other Charles Pinckney, Eliza's nephew, was, besides little Harriott and her incapacitated brother-in-law William, her sole remaining relative in South Carolina. He rushed to help Eliza with administrative matters as she reeled from grief. They kept in steady contact in the months after Charles's death. The younger Charles never forgot his uncle's love and support. He was a faithful friend to Eliza, in the fullest, eighteenth-century sense of that word: watching out for her, smoothing the rough spots when he could, and advocating for her interests.[16]

Excepting unavoidable responsibilities, Eliza retreated into a shell of her former self, consumed by resentment and heartbreak. "Earth," she told her mother, "has no more charms for me." Ann, fifteen hundred miles away in Antigua, doubtless wanted to hold and console her child, too, but couldn't. When grief over Charles's death and pity for her fatherless children overwhelmed Eliza, she confided in her friends about her hopelessness and anger: "My soul is oppressed with bitter Anguish beyond the power of words to utter."[17]

Eliza lost all interest in the clash of imperial powers that had so captivated her when she lived in England. She also ignored tensions roiling the South Carolina interior, as Cherokee leaders resisted settler encroachments. Ordinarily, Eliza kept close watch on political disruptions that threatened her family's interests. But these were no ordinary times. She withdrew from society and chose not to reside at any of her and Charles's properties. Being surrounded by memories of Charles was more than she could bear. Instead, she took Harriott and retreated to the home of her friend Mary Golightly, where they lived for several months.[18]

When the longing for Charles became unbearable, Eliza turned to her religious faith for perspective. God, she reasoned, had given her Charles's love and blessed them with three wonderful children and fourteen years of happiness together. God would watch over Charles Cotesworth, Harriott, and Thomas. She needed to submit to God's design: it was, Eliza believed, a necessary, if also nearly impossible, act of faith. She prayed for the strength to carry on, if only for her children's sake. Sometimes she fell short. "My sorrow," she confided to a friend, revealed "how little truely Christian fortitude I have possessed." Faith did not end Eliza's unhappiness. But, in time, it helped her recover the will to persevere.[19]

By the spring of 1759, Eliza started to crawl out of her grief. She finally took notice of the war with the Cherokee on South Carolina's frontier and the one spiraling across Europe, especially the financial implications. She decamped from Mary Golightly's house to begin what she called "my own solitary habitation in Charles Town." The move to the city was essential, she said, "on account of business."[20]

As Eliza came to terms with being left alone without "the best of men and of husbands," she focused on the fact that she had three children to raise and a vast estate to run. She realized that she could no longer afford to have "my thoughts intirely taken up with my own melancholy concerns."[21] Eliza made a vow to herself, her God, and her children: she would devote the rest of her life to pursuing the children's best interests. By marshaling all her talents to benefit Charles Cotesworth, Harriott, and Thomas, she could prove "how much, how truely, I loved and honoured" Charles.[22]

Devotion to her children and their long-term financial security led Eliza to make one of the most surprising decisions of her life: to stay in South Carolina. So much argued for a return to England in 1759. She had wanted to remain in the metropole in the first place. Her boys and her closest friends were there, and Charles left her the Ripley estate in his will. Meanwhile, everywhere she turned in the Lowcountry, she ran into painful reminders of her loss. Eliza's English friends, upon hearing of Charles's death, expected her imminent return. When, they wanted to know, should they look for her arrival? Eliza's first impulse was to flee the heartrending memories now stamped on South Carolina and to reunite with her sons. "My heart is with them," she told her English friends. But she didn't go.[23]

As she studied her family's financial situation, Eliza saw that a quick departure would be irresponsible. "The Case then stands thus," she reasoned: either the children "must suffer in their interests, or I in my mind." "Cruel alternative!" she concluded, "But I do not hesitate."[24] Besides, she couldn't go back to her former life in England. What would be the point? Charles was gone, and there could be no more carefree days exploring medieval castles, no romantic evenings at the theater in London, no vacations in Bath, no adventures and no joy without him. The fear of another dangerous ocean crossing paralyzed her. What if she died on the voyage? What would happen to her and Charles's children?

Instead, Eliza decided to follow through on the plan she and Charles had devised before they left England. She would leave the colony only once the family's future rested on a rock-solid foundation. She wanted to acquire enough money for her and the children to live the rest of their lives in England "in a retired, comfortable, and decent way." Closing out her holdings in South Carolina might take several years, she speculated. By the mid-1760s, she anticipated, she could think about returning to the metropole, this time for good.[25]

Eliza could not shrewdly divest herself of her Carolina interests any sooner because of the staggering scope of Charles's estate. Besides the East Bay mansion, he owned three other residences in Charles Town: two on the bay and another on Colleton Square. Those were the larger houses with city lots. He also referred in his will to "the rest of my houses, Lands, and Tenements" in the city—rental and investment properties. And those were just the parts of his estate located in the city. He also listed nine plantations, thousands upon thousands of acres, stretching across the Lowcountry into the interior of the colony and south toward Georgia. The plantations included fifteen hundred acres at Port Royal, five hundred acres along the Savannah River, the eleven-hundred-acre estate Ashepoo (Auckland), the nearly one-thousand-acre Pinckney Island, and Belmont.[26]

Eliza took charge of it all.

To fulfill her responsibilities as a loving mother and devoted widow, Eliza Lucas Pinckney returned to the work she had undertaken half a lifetime ago. Once again, she became the independent steward of her family's fortune and future.

Though the magnitude of her properties was exceptional, Eliza did not otherwise stand out in South Carolina as a young widow independently managing a family business. Men married later than women, and the unhealthful environment drove down life-expectancy rates. The Lowcountry was home to many white women widowed in their thirties and forties. And fewer than half those widows ever remarried. Some young widows turned their properties and businesses over to brothers or brothers-in-law and waited for sons to come of age and take charge. But others, like Eliza, stepped into the role of business owner, planter, and head of household, to become, in effect, the family patriarch. Some working widows, like Eliza, ran large rice and indigo plantations. They bought and sold land, shipped commodities, and advertised for runaway slaves. Middling-rank widows took charge of print and millinery shops, taverns, and ferries. Free black women also ran their own businesses in Charles Town, usually working as laundresses and seamstresses and boardinghouse keepers.[27]

White widows of Eliza's class needed to take up typically male roles while continuing to fulfill traditionally female roles—caring for children, households, and family reputations—and without directly challenging the hierarchical structure of colonial society. For some women, this was a taxing, scary change. But Eliza knew how to supervise plantations, trade commodities, and command enslaved people. As important, she understood how to carry her authority in ways advantageous to her interests and acceptable to elite society. She had learned how to balance being a respectable lady and a savvy planter as a young woman. She didn't want to return to that kind of life without Charles, but she was certainly able.[28]

Charles clearly wanted Eliza to remain an independent woman. In his will he gave her Belmont, a house in Charles Town on Colleton Square, and the estate in Ripley. (He bequeathed the East Bay residence to Charles Cotesworth.) She also collected, for the rest of her life, one-third of all the rental profits from Charles's other Charles Town properties. The other two-thirds, alongside the remaining real estate, she held in trust for her children. In his will, Charles empowered Eliza to spend money however she saw fit to educate and maintain the three children. Anything above that he requested she invest in land and slaves "as she shall think proper." His trust in Eliza to ensure the future of the Pinckneys was commonplace among rich Carolinians. In their wills, most men of property left their wives outright ownership of some part of their estate—not simply a life interest—and responsibility for overseeing their minor children's inheritances. This gave widows a greater share of autonomy to adjust to financial fluctuations and pursue new opportunities. The implicit focus of both the testator and the trusted beneficiary was on family and securing a legacy of wealth and prominence. Other planters even used similar language as Charles Pinckney. Mary Hyrne Smith's husband, for example, authorized her to manage a similarly vast estate as "she thinks fit."[29]

Charles's will granted Eliza such far-reaching authority that she didn't bother formally proving it, which would have required a time-consuming inventory. She was luckier than most widows in that Charles owed only a few debts, and those were easily settled by Eliza outside of court. Except for bequeathing a handful of personal items and small amounts of money to kin and friends, Charles left everything—and everyone—he owned to Eliza and his three underage children. Charles also named Eliza his executrix. She controlled everything: the estate, her properties, and the children's inheritances.

There was, she saw, "no body to call me to account."[30] She intended to keep it that way. Several factors influenced Eliza's decision never to remarry. There was, to start, her deep love for Charles; he was irreplaceable. And, thanks to her exclusive command over so large an estate, she had the financial wherewithal to remain single if she wished. The children mattered, too. An unwise remarriage could jeopardize their future. The fear of creating rival heirs, of squandering estates, and of causing tensions kept some elite Carolinians from remarrying. The prominent merchant Henry Laurens was widowed in his forties and decided to remain permanently single because, he said, "[I] had no desire to hazard an alienation of my affections from our Children by a Second Marriage." In her choice to remain single, then, Eliza took the path followed by the majority of elite Carolinians. Still, she was relatively young, only thirty-five when widowed, and in her fourteen-year marriage she'd lost none of the refined qualities and capacious interests that made her so attractive in South Carolina gentry circles. Had she felt the slightest inclination, Eliza could have remarried in short order. But, she insisted, "a second marriage never once enter'd into my head."[31]

There were certainly suitors. Ambitious men in South Carolina surely dreamed of winning Eliza's hand (and estate). At least one man made an offer. The gossip reached as far as Ripley, where Eliza's curious friends quickly wrote for confirmation: Had she remarried? Absolutely not, she replied. The man was quite well-off, so the match, as Eliza put it, "must have been to my advantage." But the courtship ended before it started. "Indeed," she told her Ripley friends, "I did not think it could have got air enough to have wafted it to England."[32]

She never named this mystery suitor, probably to protect her privacy and the rejected man's reputation. It may have been the most powerful man in the colony, Governor William Henry Lyttelton. He was two years younger than Eliza, single, and a highly educated English gentleman. Charles had known him and thought well of him. Before William left England, Charles recommended him to his South Carolina friends, praising his character and expressing confidence that he would make a fine governor. While sailing to his post, William was captured by French privateers and briefly held captive at Brest—the same location Eliza's father had been imprisoned in the 1740s. Perhaps Eliza learned from William's experiences what her father's last days may have entailed. In any event, William and Eliza corresponded and visited throughout 1759–1760. William matched her vague description of the man she rejected. He certainly would have advanced her rank and wealth—and few men in South Carolina fit that bill. Whether or not Governor Lyttelton developed (unreciprocated) romantic feelings for Eliza, the two of them became good friends. He updated her on imperial politics. She kept a close watch over his actions in the Cherokee War. He directed his London agent to cover some of Eliza's sons' school expenses. She forwarded letters from him to her contacts in England. Their friendship affirmed Eliza's prominence in Lowcountry society and her ability to cross traditional gender boundaries. A friend to the governor, a go-between for diplomatic matters, an independent manager of a family empire, Eliza saw no reason to become again a wife.[33]

Eliza had her work cut out for her in late 1759 as she reentered the world of commercial planting. Her nephew Charles had ably handled her and Charles's city properties during their years in England. The plantations were another matter entirely. Eliza was disinclined to criticize her incapacitated brother-in-law, but she insisted on "things being deferently conducted" after she took charge. She hired a manager to direct each overseer, and she supervised him. "It requires great care, attention and activity to attend properly to a Carolina Estate," Eliza quickly rediscovered. She relied on drivers and overseers, supervised by her new manager, to run things on her far-flung properties. She visited and coordinated but did not involve herself in on-the-ground operations outside of Belmont. Her work was heavily administrative: coordinating transatlantic shipments, fronting bills of exchange, corresponding with factors, ship captains, and overseers.[34]

Planters across the English Atlantic who operated on the scale Eliza did often required weekly statistics from their overseers, which they studied to track enslaved individuals' output and sick days. Some planters adopted double-entry bookkeeping to manage work logs. Productivity was at the forefront of enslavers' minds, and they went to great lengths to push workloads and increase profits. George Washington, for example, used a pocket watch to time the people he enslaved at Mount Vernon. An Antiguan planter captured the mindset: "A plantation ought to be considered as a well-constructed machine, compounded of various wheels, turning different ways, and yet all contributing to the great end proposed." It is easy to imagine Eliza, characteristically meticulous and now set on restoring her plantations and family fortune, embracing this attitude and these practices.[35]

She also thought of her work as a helpful distraction from her heartbreak. Visiting the various plantations got her outdoors, gave her exercise, and put her among people. By the spring of 1760, some of Eliza's optimism began to return. She decided that staying busy was good for her. Without her planting interests, she speculated, "I might have sunk to the grave by this time."[36]

As she had done at every other major transition in her life, Eliza found solace in a network of female friends. Mary Golightly, Mary Mackenzie Drayton, Margaret Glen Drayton, Mary Wood Wragg—they all comforted and sustained her in the early years after Charles's death. Her nephew Charles Pinckney continued to offer support and advice, too. New friends, starting with the royal governor, advanced her interests while brightening her days.

Even though she kept busy with work and friends, grief shadowed her. In fact, Eliza never fully recovered the easy aplomb that marked her youthful plantation management. "My mind," she confessed in February 1760, "has been in such a strange situation." Sometimes sadness over the loss of Charles engulfed her. Other times, she worked to the point of distraction. She often felt whipsawed between being a conscientious business manager and grief-stricken widow. She endured agonizing setbacks. When Harriott got sick in the summer of 1760, Eliza fell back into despondency. The weight of her grief again became nearly unbearable and took a toll on her health. "I look more like a walking Ghost than any thing else," she realized. She got sick herself in 1760, from what she never disclosed. But she took four months to recover. Fear of dying and leaving her children orphans surely worsened her physical pain.[37]

She pushed on: through recurring bouts of despair; through self-recriminations for failing to surmount her grief; through Harriott's and her illnesses; through the painful separation from her sons. At times, Eliza found comfort in her faith that God would protect Charles Cotesworth, Harriott, and Thomas. She tried to live out her pledge to submit to God's will. Other times, she faltered and blamed it on personal, spiritual weakness. When her steady prayers failed to end her anguish, she saw that as another failing. She blamed herself when her emotions clouded her reason.[38]

Working through her grief, Eliza ensured that the family enterprise thrived. She took pride in her success. Her management of the Pinckney interests showed, she decided, "how capable women are both of friendship and business." She was gratified to think that her work might "raise the reputation of . . . my sex in general."[39]

Raising the reputation of her "sex in general" depended on the systematic brutalization of African American women and their families. Eliza felt no identification or solidarity with them. The Pinckneys' return to South Carolina and Charles's sudden death brought major changes to the communities of enslaved people at their varied properties, in the form of Eliza's determination to have planting operations "deferently conducted." Charles's death also sparked anxieties about being separated from loved ones. With no knowledge of the Pinckneys' finances, enslaved people must have feared that they would be sold to satisfy Charles's creditors: that happened regularly in South Carolina. Instead, they were divided according to his perception of their families. Charles named in his will at least eighty-five enslaved women, men, and children, parceled out to Eliza and the children. The first individuals named all went to Eliza: Mary Ann and her children, Prince and Beck, and Dick the cook. Still, the white people kept quiet about their importance. No surnames were given as Charles distributed families to his heirs: adults and children lawfully granted to children, in perpetuity. Harriott inherited Sego and Kate and their five children. Charles Cotesworth received three generations of one family: Helena, her three children, and two grandchildren, along with any other future descendants. Eliza kept Quorqe and his wife, Daphne, their daughter Onia, and Onia's three children, including her son, named after his grandfather and called Little Quorqe. Eliza voiced no misgivings about owning these families. It was pervasive in South Carolina. As one visitor summed it up, "The laborious business is here chiefly done by black slaves of which there are great multitudes."[40]

Until Charles Cotesworth, Harriott, and Thomas turned twenty-one (or married), Eliza retained complete authority over the enslaved people at all the Pinckney family plantations. Charles expressly empowered Eliza "to work and labour her own or any of her Children's Slaves" in any place or way "as she shall think fit." She did just that: putting everyone to work in her various homes and rice and indigo fields, making sure that she and her children grew wealthier and lived in the style their late father intended for them.[41]

Recommitted to her leadership of the family, Eliza divided her time between Belmont and her house in Charles Town. At Belmont, she dove back into her botanical pursuits. "I am my self head gardener," she told one English friend. "I have room enough to exercise my Genius." This necessarily entailed exercising her mastery, too. The gardens and fields at Belmont reflected Eliza's design, but the plans materialized only through the work of enslaved women and men. If they failed to fulfill her vision, she said she "could not help being very angry."[42] Mary Ann and Dick and the other enslaved people who worked in the house at Belmont learned to read predictors of her moods. They came to understand, for example, that a letter arriving from George Morley, her English agent, could, Eliza told George, "put their Mistress in great good humour." Most enslaved people experienced Eliza's authority from a distance, on plantations miles from her and under the physical command of her overseers and drivers. But the people assigned to housework at Belmont and in Charles Town saw her daily, and they directly endured her whims and, no doubt, her wrath.[43]

When Eliza was in Charles Town, she required the labor of a half-dozen women just to prepare her meals. Mary Ann apparently traveled with Eliza between the country and city houses, and she led the efforts. Daphne and Onia baked bread. "Young Ebba" worked with her mother or grandmother, "old Ebba," who tended the poultry, fetched wood, and scrubbed pots, alongside Pegg, who also milked the cows. Without a note of irony Eliza proclaimed, "Nobody eats the bread of idleness when I am here." Eliding the brutality required to compel enslaved people to work for her, day and night, she also declared, "Nor are any overworked."[44]

She took care of enslaved people's health to protect her children's financial futures. When smallpox raged through Charles Town in 1760, Eliza retreated to Belmont, determined to keep "my people" out of the city and away from the epidemic. She began inoculating the enslaved people at Belmont, using procedures she found superior to efforts in Charles Town. Though Carolinians had mostly overcome their inoculation fears by 1760, they were ill-prepared for the outbreak. Doctors were overworked and underskilled, and by the time the outbreak ran its course, 10–12 percent of Charles Town's population died. At Belmont, after inoculating dozens of enslaved people, Eliza supervised an impromptu smallpox hospital for workers who contracted mild cases of the disease from inoculation. (She and Harriott retained lifelong immunity.) Fifteen people contracted smallpox at Belmont, and only one man, who caught it naturally rather than through Eliza's inoculation, died. Eliza identified him only as "a valuable Carpenter."[45]

It took her more than two years, but Eliza gradually learned to manage her mourning. By 1760, she was back to administering her family business, to trafficking people and commodities across the Atlantic, to experimenting with crops and socializing with friends and caring about politics. Eager for financial stability, she gladdened at the British conquest of New France in September 1760. More relief came as South Carolina and British forces prevailed over the Cherokee, ending several years of sporadic violence and asserting colonial power in Cherokee country. She worried about escalating taxes under new imperial policies driven by those expensive wars. "We are a young colony," she reminded her English friends, and the Atlantic Ocean did not "throw up sands of gold" on South Carolina's shoreline. These were concerns common to every Lowcountry planter-patriarch: wealth, security, respect in the larger empire. After two years of overwhelming grief, Eliza accepted her new reality and met the new decade with newfound resolve.[46]

CHAPTER 11

Cultivating a Legacy

Everything Eliza Lucas Pinckney did in the 1760s centered on her children. The first time she had been an independent planter-patriarch, in the 1730s and 1740s, Eliza worked hard to fulfill a family duty, too. Then it had been to her father. Now it was for her children. Eliza declared that on the three of them rested "all the happiness I have or desire upon Earth."[1]

She had to look forward, for there was no looking back. By the 1760s, the family Eliza had been born into didn't exist anymore. She lost both of her brothers and her mother within a few years of Charles's death. Her brother Tommy died in Antigua in 1756. Eliza probably learned of his death only after she had resettled in South Carolina. Eliza's mother, Ann, passed away in the fall of 1759, and her brother George Jr. died just a few months later. Polly, alone in Antigua, married a man named John Atkinson in March 1762 and thereafter disappeared from Antiguan records. Most likely, Polly Lucas Atkinson died in the early 1760s. If she had lived, Eliza would have written her and preserved copies of those letters. Eliza, the first born of the Lucas siblings, became the sole survivor. The story of the Lucas family, prominent in Antiguan politics and society for four generations—across nearly the colony's whole history—ended with her.[2]

The last of one prominent family, Eliza determined to ensure the long-term renown of another. She resolved that the Pinckney name—the reputation, the wealth, and the power—would not be diminished on her watch.

When she set her cap for something Eliza was seldom deterred. For this mission, however, she needed the commitment of her children. Charles Cotesworth, Harriott, and Thomas had to prove themselves good stewards of their family name. That started with becoming accomplished students, faithful Christians, and honorable and refined young people. Eliza, a single parent acting as both mother and father, did everything in her power to foster their success.[3]

Eliza never moved back to England. In the early 1760s, the lingering French and Indian War militated against her return. "When," she pressed her friend Wilhelmina-Catharine King in February 1762, "shall we have peace?" Eliza knew she could not risk the ocean crossing so long as the war continued. It kept her, she complained, "immovably fixt" in South Carolina. But there were other factors, too. The family interests in South Carolina required her sustained attention. And she liked her work. She took comfort in hearing positive reports about Charles Cotesworth and Thomas. When their schoolmasters wrote to compliment the boys' character and study habits, Eliza felt elated. Seeing them would be better, of course, but that was a happiness, she decided, "which for their sakes I must not yet injoy."[4]

By the time the European powers finalized the peace treaty ending the global conflict in February 1763, Eliza had stopped talking about returning to the metropole. Charles Cotesworth turned seventeen and Thomas thirteen that year. They were safe, healthy, and thriving. Her good friend and former neighbor Rebecca Evance faithfully treated them like her own children. The brothers had managed five years in England, and all their instructors praised their intellectual talent and drive to succeed. Eliza learned to live with the distance.[5]

Though Harriott and the boys grew up separated by the Atlantic, all three bore the mark of their formidable mother and her high expectations. Eliza spared no expense in raising them in what she deemed the proper style. Wilhelmina-Catharine King shipped Harriott the latest fashions from London. Before she turned twelve, Harriott showed off her specially made, imported clothes in Charles Town. Harriott, Eliza happily reported, "has an opportunity of seting the fashion."[6] Money was no object when it came to Charles Cotesworth and Thomas, either. Eliza's English contacts knew to provide whatever the boys needed, and she gladly paid. Eliza routinely sent special treats to them, including at one point a box of pomegranates, which she knew they liked. The shipment signaled Eliza's immersion in a transatlantic net-

Figure 9. Eliza Lucas Pinckney's brooch, including diamonds, emeralds, and rubies. Courtesy of The Charleston Museum, Charleston, South Carolina.

work of trade and friendship: at her direction, the ship captain who transported the box to England carried it to Eliza's business agent, who passed it to Rebecca Evance, who gave it to Charles Cotesworth and Thomas. Eliza also made sure her sons had plenty of pocket money. She steadily increased the amounts as they grew older, with more expensive tastes and, no doubt, friends to impress. Whatever the children needed, she said, "I shall always chearfully acquiesce."[7]

Eliza indulged her own tastes, too. She hired a Charles Town jeweler to design a pin adorned with diamonds, rubies, and emeralds. She acquired specially crafted fabric to decorate her bedroom; she slept under a patterned canopy featuring indigo plants. She wore an exquisite pair of satin shoes, trimmed in silver braid and dyed—what else—blue. She and Harriott imported Persian fabric, French shoes, Chinese dinnerware, English silver services. Meanwhile, Charles Cotesworth and Thomas hired tailors and socialized in high style.[8]

If she perhaps spoiled the children materially, Eliza never stopped reminding them of the weighty responsibilities they owed to their late father and to her. Over and over again, Eliza taught the three siblings about duty, achievement, and loyalty. As she put it: "Be good children, mind your learning, and love one another." Eliza calculated each child's success exactly as she did her own: by their growing in "Virtue, Religion, and learning." She expected them all to become devout Christians, of the Anglican persuasion. Christian duty called on them to be patient, kind, honest, and hopeful. While Charles Cotesworth and Thomas received a more extensive formal education than Harriott—suitable for future careers in law and government service—the foundational values Eliza instilled in her children did not vary.[9]

No matter how consistently parented, siblings inevitably have their own unique experiences within their families. In the Pinckney family, Harriott was the only girl and the only sibling to live in the household after Eliza became a single mother. Charles Cotesworth, the eldest, bore the first and greatest responsibility. Thomas, the youngest, lived the longest in England, including for several years apart from everyone else in the family. These experiences shaped the three siblings' character and their relationships with their supremely devoted mother.

Harriott Pinckney was not quite ten when she left her brothers and moved to what felt to her like a strange land. She'd been born in South Carolina, but she was so young when the family left for England that she had few, if any, memories of the place. Having spent her whole childhood—or at least the part she could remember—in the imperial center, Harriott shared her mother's letdown upon returning to South Carolina. Echoing Eliza's language, Harriott complained to an English friend about the "want of entertaining subjects in this remote corner of the world."[10]

Mother and daughter grew extraordinarily close after Charles died. Though friends offered comfort during that terrible ordeal, the two of them endured together the anguish of his passing and turned toward each other as they mourned. They continued to live alone together for more than a decade. When Eliza fell so ill in 1760 that she stayed in her bedroom for four months, Harriott was just twelve, without her brothers and watching her only parent suffer. She later confessed that witnessing Eliza's long illness "damped in me every cheerful thought & prevented every agreeable imployment."[11]

Harriott seemed determined to avoid adding to her mother's troubles. Perhaps she inherited Eliza's character, or maybe it was just her resolve. Either innate or practiced, Harriott became the child her mother wanted. She was sensible, curious, lively, intelligent, and loving.

That Harriott sparked to her studies pleased Eliza to no end. "She is fond of learning," Eliza bragged, "and I indulge her in it." Educating Harriott gave Eliza tremendous pleasure. It was, she told her friends, "one of the greatest Businesses of my life." Eliza chose an agricultural metaphor to describe supervising Harriott's education. "I have an excellent soil to work upon," she said, and confidence that "the fruit will be answerable to my indeavours in the cultivation."[12]

Eliza handled some of Harriott's education herself. She taught her, for example, how to write to their English friends, cultivating proper letter-writing practices as well as important social connections. She inspired in Harriott curiosity about the larger world, including the political scene. At age twelve, Harriott wrote to her mother's friend Wilhelmina-Catharine King to describe the Cherokee leaders who came to Charles Town on a diplomatic mission and thanked King for updating her about political news in England. Eliza hired private tutors to teach Harriott mathematics, French, and Latin. "My chief employments," Harriott explained in 1763, centered on reading, writing, math, French, geography, and music. With no suitable drawing master available for hire in Charles Town, Harriott was forced to temporarily give up "hope of arriving at any great perfection of it." She focused instead on music, which she loved.[13]

Eliza raised Harriott to be both a genteel woman and a skillful planter. She did not appear to want Harriott to lead a life like hers, as an independent planter, but she prepared her for it, just in case. Parts of Harriott's training matched that of a typical wealthy Carolina daughter, to ready her to be a refined, sophisticated wife; other preparations were less conventional. Eliza did not leave her at boarding school in London, even though Harriott was the same age Eliza had been when she began her English studies. Instead, she kept Harriott close. That is not to say that Harriott's youth was rigidly circumscribed. She traveled about the Lowcountry with friends and pursued her special interests in geography and music. At age sixteen, Harriott had access to her own money, apparently a good deal of it. She still wore the bracelets with the silhouettes of her brothers. Now, however, she wanted miniature portraits, set in gold, for new bracelets. She directed Charles Cotesworth to find a skilled painter and jeweler in London. She would send the money; he just needed to tell her the price.[14]

Besides a sense of autonomy and self-determination, Eliza encouraged Harriott's interest in botany and in agricultural experiments, appropriate in case she ever needed to run the family business. Mother and daughter restarted the silkworks at Belmont. Their finished fabric, Harriott remembered late in her life, was considered by English consumers the equal of any available on the international market. Harriott also liked managing the family dairy—which, like the silkworks, involved direct oversight of enslaved women and men. Her mother gladly supported Harriott's interest.[15]

From her mother, Harriott learned how to command enslaved people. Eliza bragged about Harriott's ability to ensure that workers heeded her directions. She seemed quite pleased that her daughter showed no hesitation when extracting labor from enslaved men, women, and children.[16]

In so many ways, Harriott became her mother's daughter. She even started her own letterbook in 1759, when she was just eleven years old, copying and preserving letters she sent to her brothers and friends. She sometimes served as her mother's secretary, copying Eliza's letters. In the 1760s, Harriott began her own recipe book, borrowing twenty-six recipes from Eliza to start. She tried to replicate her mother's determined optimism, too. Like Eliza, Harriott needed to practice that trait. She often cut herself off from writing about sad events to pivot to sunnier topics.[17]

As she matured from a girl to a young woman, Harriott Pinckney was not only intelligent and vivacious but physically attractive, too: tall, pretty, and slender, with blue eyes and curly light brown hair. Those superficial qualities added to her education and sophistication and her family wealth to make Harriott very desirable in the South Carolina marriage market.[18]

Eliza gave Harriott the romantic advice she had followed as a young woman. Harriott parroted to a friend her mother's maxim: "Guard *well* your Heart." A smart woman avoided superficial seductions and entertained only suitors of piety, intellect, and decency, from good families and with bright futures. Many of Harriott's friends couldn't wait to get married, but, like her mother before her, Harriott saw no need to hurry. Charles Cotesworth quizzed Harriott in 1766, as she neared her eighteenth birthday: Did she have any serious suitors? Didn't she want to marry soon? Her answer revealed a young woman every bit as self-confident and forceful as her mother had been. "I find myself so happy as I am," she informed her brother, "that I shall not be in a hurry to sign myself by any name other than . . . Harriott Pinckney."[19]

That changed when Harriott met Daniel Huger Horry Jr. An only child and descended from a prominent Huguenot family, Daniel had been formally educated in England. He was well connected, handsome, and wealthy. Ten years older than Harriott, he'd long since inherited a family fortune made from growing rice along the South Santee. Though he owned several plantations and a house in Charles Town, he made his principal home at Hampton

Plantation, around thirty-five miles northeast of Charles Town. When he began to court Harriott in 1767, Daniel Horry was a recent widower and childless. His first wife, Judith Serré, had died in 1765, not quite six years into their marriage. Daniel acquired a good deal of property, including Hampton, from Judith.[20]

Harriott Pinckney married Daniel Huger Horry Jr. on February 15, 1768, a few months shy of her twentieth birthday. Harriott insisted that she preferred marrying an older man. She found the local men her age flighty. Daniel's feelings, she pronounced, were "guided by more judgment and seek a more solid Basis." She seemed to be channeling her mother's views of her father, from twenty-five years before.[21]

To seal their union, Daniel and Harriott sought the approval of the head of the family and administrator of Harriott's inheritance. Eliza gladly gave it. She liked Daniel and thought him a worthy husband for Harriott. Though Eliza controlled the family finances, colonial society was so patriarchal that when the marriage announcement appeared in the February 19, 1768, edition of the *South Carolina Gazette*, Harriott was listed as the daughter of Charles Pinckney, deceased. The account made no mention of Eliza, for the past decade Harriott's only parent and nearly daily companion.[22]

Unlike their sister, Charles Cotesworth and Thomas spent the 1760s some four thousand miles away from their mother. To guide them toward proper manhood, Eliza had to overcome the distance of an ocean. She also needed to cross traditional boundaries dividing maternal and paternal responsibilities.

The years-long separation of a mother from her young sons, bridged only by spotty letters, was neither unusual nor controversial in the eighteenth century. Children routinely spent large parts of their formative years separated from their family of origin. Enslaved children or their parents could be sold on a whim or simply moved about to serve the financial interests of owners. Poor and working-class white children labored from a young age, too, sometimes in long-term apprenticeships. Rich parents like Eliza bought European educations for their children, leaving sons to grow to adulthood in the care of surrogate parents and schoolmasters. The very nature of the British Empire depended on separating children from parents, through the exploitation of enslaved families as well as the training of colonial aristocrats. Eliza spent five years of her girlhood in England. So Charles Cotesworth and Thomas didn't have particularly unusual coming-of-age experiences. The channel linking

Eliza and the boys was typical, too: carefully crafted letters. Writing was so important in that era that a cottage industry emerged around penmanship exercises and epistolary guidebooks. Letter writers not only minded their prose style but also selected the right kind of stationery and filled the pages to the margins. All three of the Pinckney siblings mastered that craft, following the example set by their exceptionally prolific mother.[23]

What was unusual about the arrangement was that the Pinckney boys' mother took charge of their formal education. Typically, fathers—or male surrogates when fathers died—supervised boys' education. Mothers wrote to sons at school, but they generally left decisions and oversight to men. Charles Cotesworth and Thomas Pinckney became the sons their father had imagined because of their mother's vigilance. Assuming the responsibility of a father, Eliza corresponded with Charles Cotesworth and Thomas's teachers, as the boys made their way from school to school, up through the ranks of England's finest centers of learning. Their future happiness, Eliza believed, depended in large measure on the right kind of education. So she urged schoolmasters and tutors and surrogate parents to give them "the utmost attention," reminding them that the boys had lost "their best friend and example."[24]

Eliza did everything in her power to fill that gap, replacing her late husband as their benefactor, counselor, and role model. Responsible fathers (and father figures) created a protective and advantageous network for young men under their charge. Eliza slid into that role, too. She kept up strong connections with her English friends, not only for her own emotional and financial well-being but also to protect Charles Cotesworth and Thomas. Her Ripley and London contacts kept her updated on her boys—nearly always sending good news. Whenever leading Carolinians Eliza knew traveled to London, she asked them to check on her sons.

Though she drew on this network, Eliza remained the ultimate judge of her sons' progress. She studied their letters to glean how much they learned and how closely they hewed to her vision of dutifulness, piety, and accomplishment. Her advisory letters left an indelible mark on her boys. When friends abroad reported that Charles Cotesworth and Thomas were thriving, Eliza felt relieved and proud. But, as mourning has a way of doing, sadness about losing her husband accompanied the joy. Charles missed out on opening precious envelopes sealed by beloved sons. And so, even as Eliza treasured the boys' letters, she thought with longing about Charles. How happy they would have been reading together about their sons' English adventures.[25]

Charles Cotesworth understood even as a young boy that as the firstborn child he bore the first responsibility for his siblings and for the Pinckney family's future. He didn't know how fast he would need to grow up and assume part of those duties until 1758, when he learned the crushing news of his father's passing. Barely thirteen years old, he showed remarkable maturity. Right away he wrote to ten-year-old Harriott, urging her to do everything she could to comfort Eliza. He promised Harriott that he and Thomas would do the same. "Let us vye with one another," Charles Cotesworth urged his siblings, "in shewing our reverence for the memory of the best of Fathers, by loving, honouring, and chearfully obeying, the best of Mothers."[26]

Eliza never wanted her sons to forget their "best of Fathers." They didn't. Far from forgotten, Charles cast a long shadow over their lives, Charles Cotesworth's in particular. Charles Cotesworth scoured Charles's books for marginal comments, searching for some insight into his father's mind. All his life Charles Cotesworth retold stories from his boyhood, cherishing the few memories he retained of being with his father.[27]

Eliza used Charles's vision for his firstborn son to lay out a specific set of expectations for Charles Cotesworth. Charles had made patently clear in his will the character he expected Charles Cotesworth to adopt and the education he wanted the boy to attain. Charles expressly wanted him "to become the head of his family" once he reached the age of majority. This meant providing "service and advantage to his country" as well as honoring "his Stock and Kindred." Hoping to instill his own devout Christian faith in his namesake, Charles wrote in his will that he expected Charles Cotesworth to "employ all his future abilities in the service of God, and his Country; in the Cause of virtuous liberty as well religious as Civil." He spoke directly from the grave: "Let not my Son slight or disregard these solemn Admonitions of his Father." Throughout the 1760s, as Charles Cotesworth grew from a boy to a man, Eliza repeatedly reminded him of the weight of her and Charles's expectations. He needed to ready himself to fulfill his duty. Shortly after Charles Cotesworth turned fifteen, Eliza told him again: "Though you are very young, you must know the welfair of a whole family depends in a great measure on the progress you make."[28]

He quailed at the thought of disappointing her. Far from lackadaisical, Charles Cotesworth pursued his education so doggedly that Eliza started to worry about his health. He worked on, to honor his father's legacy and acquire the best education his mother's money could buy: Westminster, Christ Church College at Oxford, Middle Temple. Eleven years he studied, his mother advising, hoping, and sometimes fretting across the ocean.[29]

Eliza worried more about Charles Cotesworth than she did about Harriott. Or perhaps she simply wrote more about her concerns. No other correcting communication was possible: no disapproving looks, no whispered counsel, no firm reprimands, no punishments. When Charles Cotesworth reached his teenage years, Eliza repeatedly warned him that he had arrived at a dangerous time in life. He might make irreversibly bad choices about money or love or pick up a drinking or gambling habit that would ruin his reputation. She worried, too, about his quick temper and directed him to get it under control.[30]

All her apprehensions came to naught. Charles Cotesworth, no less than Harriott, was a dutiful, obliging child who worked hard to make his mother proud. Not all Lowcountry parents were so fortunate with their sons. Charles Drayton, the younger of the two brothers Eliza and Charles took to England in 1753, frustrated and grieved his father. The young man rarely wrote home. "I hardly know I have such a Son," John Drayton complained. When John did hear from Charles, it was nearly always bad news. Instead of focusing on his studies, Charles spent recklessly and socialized constantly. "No man on earth has been so long for Education as he & benefited so poorly," John Drayton concluded after years of trying to cajole Charles into behaving. When John finally threatened to cut off Charles's funding if he failed to straighten up, Charles became belligerent and, his hurt father said, "behaved Extremely Ill to me." In sharp contrast, when Charles Cotesworth completed his studies and prepared to return to South Carolina, Eliza could honestly say that he had never once troubled her. He was just the man she had hoped he would become: worthy of being called Charles Pinckney's son.[31]

Thomas, the youngest of the three siblings, was not quite eight when his parents left him in England. He lived the longest apart from his mother—fourteen-plus years in total. In some ways Charles Cotesworth raised him as much as Eliza, who expected Thomas to follow his older brother's lead. In his will, Charles Pinckney repeated for Thomas the plans and admonitions he laid out for Charles Cotesworth. Eliza often wrote to the brothers together, anticipating that Charles Cotesworth, four and a half years older, would set the example for his little brother. Thomas perhaps felt like an afterthought sometimes, always in Charles Cotesworth's wake. But he didn't rebel. Instead, Thomas dutifully followed Charles Cotesworth into the finest schools in England. He became a standout Hellenist, consistently ranking first among his classes. He read Greek his entire life, for pleasure, and impressed even his best-educated peers with his outstanding mastery. He developed a wry sense of humor, too. Perhaps Thomas saw these as ways of escaping the shadow of his brother, of standing out in his mother's mind.[32]

In the mid-1760s, Thomas and Charles Cotesworth sent home new portraits. Eliza showed them off to all her friends. People who had not seen Charles Cotesworth since he left South Carolina in 1752 could easily recognize him. But Thomas had changed so much that even Harriott and Eliza were hard-pressed to identify him. Distance did not sap Thomas's determination to be every bit as responsive to his mother's expectations as his older siblings. Like Charles Cotesworth and Harriott, he did everything in his power to honor his father and please his mother.[33]

As the 1760s passed by, single mother and planter-patriarch Eliza Lucas Pinckney watched with pride as her children grew into responsible, accomplished adults. Following her expectations and example, they also remained devoted to one another. Perhaps the sibling connections ran all the deeper for the family's geography: Charles Cotesworth and Thomas alone together, Harriott always isolated from them.

With an eye toward the long-term success of her family, Eliza impressed upon her three children the imperative to love and take care of one another. The lesson stuck. Six years into the separation from her brothers, Harriott's longing was palpable. "'Tis no small Mortification to me," she said, "to be at this painfull distance from my dear Brothers who I long much to see." Charles Cotesworth did all he could to watch over Thomas. For the rest of his life, Thomas recalled their boyhood bond with love and gratitude. "I never felt myself as fatherless as I should have done," Thomas reflected, because Charles Cotesworth "always felt a paternal responsibility towards me, when we were alone at school."[34]

Charles Cotesworth, Harriott, and Thomas remained close partners and confidants their whole lives. As Harriott reached her teenage years, she took on the responsibility of kin guardian for the sibling set. She was the one in charge of ensuring the three of them remained close and responsive to one another's interests. Kin guardian was a role usually filled by women in the eighteenth century. It carried authority. Harriott didn't hesitate to upbraid her brothers when they failed to write home as often as she expected. When her friend Rebecca Izard visited England in 1766, Harriott sent along a scolding: "If you should see a youth call'd Chars. Pinckney, let him know that he has a mother and Sister in this part of the World to whome he is very dear, that would be glad to hear from him often." When she fell behind in her letters, her brothers did some scolding of their own. This was all gentle joking, but aimed at ensuring that the three of them stayed close emotionally, despite the miles and years apart.[35]

Harriott played matchmaker for her brothers, too. "Lock up your heart . . . till you come here," she told Charles Cotesworth in 1766. There were many "fine Girls," in Charles Town, she promised, immediately adding, "and fine fortunes too." Marrying locally was the strong preference of South Carolina elites, all the better to cement business ties and family finances. Harriott already had two or three women in mind for each of her brothers. Whomever Charles Cotesworth and Thomas married, Harriott made clear they needed to live in South Carolina. That way, the siblings, separated in their youth, could grow old together.[36]

As she worked in the 1760s to set her family's future on a sure foundation, Eliza Lucas Pinckney gradually accepted that South Carolina would be her permanent home. Sometimes she still envied her English friends. In her romantic memories of the metropole, they lived at the center of the world, "in the midst of Scenes of entertainment and pleasure," while she occupied a "remote Corner of the Globe." Despite her wealth and renown in South Carolina, her many beloved friends, and all the imported fineries, to the self-consciously cosmopolitan Eliza, the colony still felt "distant from every thing that is new and entertaining." South Carolina was her home, but was Carolinian her identity? Eliza equivocated. "All Countrys are now to me alike," she announced in the wake of Charles's death. "Nor do I prefer any one to another."[37] Certainly, Eliza counted herself "a very Loyal Subject" of the British crown and continued to idealize the metropole and all things royal. She was elated when Wilhelmina-Catharine King sent her lengthy descriptions of the coronation of the new king, twenty-two-year-old George III, in the fall of 1760, and of the royal wedding, just ten months later. Eliza was the first Carolinian to acquire such details about the young Queen Charlotte. Her friends and neighbors felt a bit jealous, which Eliza relished. Within a half-hour of Eliza's opening Wilhelmina-Catharine's letter, the governor arrived at her home to find out about Queen Charlotte. Eliza proudly read the description to him, and she read it again and again over the following days as other curious Carolinians called on her.[38]

After she gave up the idea of moving permanently to England, Eliza continued to nurse hopes of visiting her sons. Perhaps they might all travel to

Geneva, a splendid place for the brothers to finish their educations. But that trip seemed more improbable with each passing year. Eliza's children were growing up, and she was becoming, in her words, "an old woman in the Wilds of America."[39]

Still, much of Eliza's life in the 1760s was as she desired and designed it, and, aside from the continued separation from her sons, mostly fulfilling. The estate thrived under her able financial management and systematic exploitation of enslaved laborers. The children were all she had hoped for. It was not the life she had dreamed of, for Charles was missing from it. And it was sometimes volatile. South Carolina was roiled, multiple times in the 1760s, by tensions with the imperial center over tax policies, starting with the Stamp Act of 1765. Leaders in Parliament saw the innovations as essential to pay debts accrued during the French and Indian War, but assemblymen in South Carolina—and political leaders along the Atlantic seaboard—denounced the new taxes. Opposition on the streets of Charles Town to the Stamp Act took a direful turn: when the first ship carrying the stamped paper arrived in the harbor, upset locals erected a gallows on the corner of Broad and Church Streets, and a crowd hanged and burned in effigy the Stamp Tax collector and physically threatened several local officials. The street violence—some real, much theatrical—didn't sit well with many elites, nor did the stalled trade that followed the political turmoil. The Stamp Act Crisis also revealed class divisions between white Carolinians, with middling-rank residents and artisans adopting a more aggressive defense of their rights than the wealthiest planters and merchants. With opposition engulfing North America, Parliament repealed the hated tax in 1766. That year, Eliza's friend Peter Manigault was elected speaker of the South Carolina Assembly. He led assemblymen in formally thanking George III for his "great goodness" and proclaiming South Carolinians "a loyal and a grateful people." But another crisis unfolded in 1767–1768, over the Townshend Acts. Those taxes sparked boycotts across North America, including in South Carolina, and more financial setbacks for commercial planters such as Eliza Lucas Pinckney.[40] There was further tumult emanating from the backcountry. White farmers, called "Regulators," organized against Lowcountry elites dominating the colonial government and failing to support—or even acknowledge—the needs of backcountry residents. The Regulators pushed for local courts and sheriffs and for fair representation in the assembly. In addition to these widespread disruptions, Eliza also suffered through personal losses. In the winter of 1767–1768, two of her closest friends, Mary Wood Wragg and Ann Murray, died within three weeks of each other.

Their deaths, Harriott said, sat "very heavy" on her mother. But as Eliza reflected on all she had, she felt sanguine. She could say something rare in colonial South Carolina, and rarer still for any eighteenth-century woman: "I live agreeable enough to my own taste."[41]

The year 1769 brought big changes to Eliza's life and to her family. Her eldest child was called to the bar in England in January. Charles Cotesworth was just shy of his twenty-third birthday and as distinguished as any rich colonial could be in London. Still, he was a colonial there. In South Carolina, he could be at the pinnacle of society. His education complete, Charles Cotesworth knew it was time to rejoin his mother and sister.[42]

Harriott Pinckney Horry cheered her brother's plans to move back, as she put it, to "your own Country." She longed for him and eagerly awaited his return. Eliza was happy, too, but apprehensive about Charles Cotesworth's voyage home. She told him to pick a good ship for his passage but not tell her the name—the anxiety of knowing was too great to bear. Shortly before he departed England, the family finally submitted Charles's will to a court. Charles Cotesworth could then lawfully claim his inheritance once he reached South Carolina.[43]

Fifteen-plus years of living in England had turned Charles Cotesworth Pinckney into a firm American. While his mother remained cosmopolitan, fluid, even ambivalent about the national and political part of her identity, Charles Cotesworth was clear about his. Daily living his provincial status likely lay behind his self-identity and drove his fierce advocacy of colonial rights.[44]

Charles Cotesworth arrived back in Charles Town in the spring of 1769 and moved into the East Bay mansion—no longer the finest residence in the city but quite an impressive home for a twenty-three-year-old single man. His family name assured him quick entry into the inner circles of power. In November, barely six months after his arrival in the colony, he was elected to the South Carolina Assembly. Charles Cotesworth also took charge of his inheritance, freeing Eliza from some of her responsibilities. Harriott and Daniel Horry already managed Harriott's inheritance, and Harriott aided Eliza with Thomas's share of the estate.[45]

Eliza must have been so proud of her firstborn son. He had become the man she and Charles had imagined when he was just a little boy, with the character and abilities she'd carefully groomed. Surely she felt relief, too. Charles Cotesworth had dodged all the pitfalls of an entitled youth spent abroad. Eliza could trust him, as she did Harriott, to be a faithful partner in protecting the Pinckney name and fortune.

She became a grandmother in 1769. Harriott delivered a baby boy, Daniel Horry, at Eliza's house in Charles Town in August. He was hailed by everyone—parents, grandmother, and uncles—as "a little Cherubim sent from Above to fill our hearts with Joy and Gratitude." Harriott and the baby stayed with Eliza for several weeks after the delivery. Charles Cotesworth visited often, and he, like Eliza, was instantly captivated with the baby, the first member of a new generation of their family. The next came in short order: a girl, Harriott Pinckney Horry, born in October 1770.[46]

An adoring and hands-on grandmother, Eliza delighted in her new role. Still, missing Charles tempered her joy. Death had cheated him out of another family milestone and cheated Eliza out of sharing it with him.[47]

Not long after Harriott Jr.'s birth, Thomas made the Atlantic crossing to visit South Carolina. He turned twenty-one in October 1771, and Harriott told him that he needed to join her and Charles Cotesworth in assuming responsibility for his "own private affairs." The family wanted to divide up their varied lucrative properties, so Thomas took a break from his studies. He stayed around eighteen months, from the fall of 1771 until the spring of 1773, before returning to England to complete his education.[48]

For the first time in thirteen years, Eliza got to see, to hold, to hear the voice of her youngest child. Since leaving him in England in 1758, she had read and heard plenty of reports, but she had seen only the one unrecognizable portrait, painted when Thomas was around fifteen. Now she met a man, tall and lean, quiet but charmingly witty, self-controlled and thoroughly sophisticated. Harriott could not find the words to express her happiness at seeing her "much loved & long absent Brother." Thomas didn't really know his mother or his sister; he had been so little when they parted. His relationship with his mother had been mediated through advisory letters and stories passed across the ocean. Now they met face to face. As Eliza and Thomas got reacquainted, Charles Cotesworth could bridge any emotional clumsiness. The four of them—Eliza, Charles Cotesworth, Harriott, and Thomas—quickly formed a tight bond that remained unbroken as long as they lived.[49]

Eliza's family now ran three generations. They were happy, healthy, and reunited, with more wealth than any of them needed. They migrated between lavish households: Hampton, Belmont, and the Charles Town houses, their every need attended wherever they went by scores of enslaved people.

The Pinckneys, and South Carolina elites generally, felt justifiably confident in their power and prosperity in the early 1770s. France had been removed from the interior, Spain pushed south, and the Cherokees defeated. Trade thrived. As a symbol of the centrality of import-export businesses to the colony's success, leaders constructed a majestic new customs house, called the Exchange. Dominating the waterfront while signaling the colony's English bona fides, the grand Palladian design intentionally resembled exchanges in Bristol and London. Lowcountry residents bragged about their economy's unrivaled, seemingly unstoppable growth. They lived, some boasted, in "the most thriving Country perhaps on this Globe." At minimum South Carolinians felt that theirs was the finest colony in North America.[50]

Some lingering resentments festered over imperial tax policies. But the crises of the 1760s—over the Stamp Tax and the Townshend Acts—calmed. Even anger over the disturbing violence on Boston Common, the so-called "massacre," which seemed to portend a violent collision between the North American provinces and the metropole, faded after a Massachusetts jury acquitted the British soldiers involved in the fracas in the early winter of 1770. Great Britain made important concessions to the colonies, and harmony returned. Around that same time, Lowcountry politicians acceded to some of the backcountry farmers' demands for new courts, judges, and sheriffs and more equitable representation in the assembly. Lowcountry elites maintained firm control over the colonial government, but the agreement sufficed to stabilize regional rivalries.[51]

Eliza Lucas Pinckney turned fifty in late December 1772. Surrounded by her successful, loving, dutiful adult children, she could breathe a sigh of relief. She had achieved all that she'd set her mind to, yet again. She had protected her family's business and reputation and built a strong legacy for her heirs. She'd taught her children to be faithful Christians and ensured that they acquired every skill necessary to thrive in colonial society. Now Charles Cotesworth, Harriott, and Thomas would take care of their own inheritances. Eliza didn't need to fill multiple roles any longer or be the family patriarch.

Her early fifties were filled with happy milestones. Eliza and Harriott cried when Thomas sailed back to England to complete his education, but they believed this last, brief separation necessary for Thomas to reach his full potential. He sent updates confirming their high hopes. "I am," Thomas assured his family in April 1774, "blending the Gentleman with the Scholar."[52]

Charles Cotesworth got married in September 1773 to Sarah Middleton. Eliza approved of the loving and lucrative match. Sarah, whom everyone called Sally, was the daughter of Henry Middleton, as rich and powerful as any man in South Carolina. She grew up at Middleton Place, one of the most palatial estates in British America. Charles Cotesworth ably assumed the roles his parents had long ago planned for him: holding public office, pursuing a career in the law, and heading a family. He was elected to serve in the South Carolina Assembly, which had eclipsed the Royal Council and assumed the lion's share of authority over colonial politics. Interrelated elite assemblymen focused on their shared values: controlling the enslaved majority of South Carolinians and advancing their financial interests. A surprised visitor from New England watched as the members "conversed, lolled, and chatted much like a friendly jovial society." Charles Cotesworth fit right in. He had acquired during his years in England exactly the sophistication Carolinians admired. His English credentials helped launch a law practice, too. He and Sally spent most of their time at the East Bay mansion—the first Pinckneys to occupy the stately home since the 1750s, when Eliza and Charles had left for England.[53]

Eliza, so long the center of her family, wasn't any longer. Charles Cotesworth's expanding familial role in the early 1770s included relieving his mother of some of her business obligations. He, not Eliza, represented the Pinckney family with London creditors. Harriott, raising two toddlers, took on more emotional responsibilities within the family. In a pattern common when adult children have their own children, Harriott's son and daughter shifted the focus of the Pinckney family.

If Eliza pined for the past, she didn't show it. Instead, she felt proud of her children and grandchildren and happy to enter a new phase of her life. Supremely secure in her wealth and status, she entertained her grandchildren, socialized with friends, and pursued her botanical experiments, including her silkworks. When Thomas dreamed of home, he saw his mother "very busy planting at Belmont."[54]

The early 1770s were a good time to be rich and leisured—independent—in South Carolina. The colony's economy hummed. In a single year, Lowcountry planters exported 130,784 barrels of rice and 1,000,000 pounds of indigo. Residents of Charles Town continued to number among the wealthiest people in North America, and their economy was the fastest-growing in the English Atlantic World. The Pinckneys and other elites used the profits from their slave-produced commodities to keep buying their English identity: importing

English housewares, food, and clothing, patronizing English plays and concerts, constructing English-styled residences and public spaces. The St. Cecilia Society hosted spectacular concerts for its rich and cosmopolitan subscribing members. A grand new theater on Church Street mounted scores of plays: seventy-seven in the 1773–1774 season alone. Every part of well-off Carolinians' lifestyle reflected their intentional consumption to effect English identity.[55]

Eliza remained the head of her own households, in Charles Town and at Belmont, while also frequently visiting Harriott at Hampton. A package Eliza sent Harriott reveals her lifestyle: pastries for her grandson; a shaving case for her son-in-law and a suitcase for Harriott; imported cloth, cutlery, and food, including one hundred limes. She also sent a copy of *The Inflexible Captive,* a play written by someone with whom the independent-minded mother and daughter probably identified: the English playwright Hannah More.[56]

Though she held fewer familial responsibilities after her children came of age, family remained Eliza's top priority—and her greatest joy. "I love my Children above all sublunary beings," she insisted. Having lost a child early in life and known many mothers forced to bury children, Eliza remained vigilant about Harriott, Thomas, and Charles Cotesworth's health, even after they were all grown up. "My fears," she told them, "are always awake about you."[57]

She showered her grandchildren with love and attention. Daniel often stayed with his grandmother in the early 1770s, and the two grew close. Eliza taught him to be devoted to his relatives, just as she'd taught her own children. Under her watchful eye, the little boy wrote letters to his Uncle Thomas in England. Eliza also scrutinized Harriott's mothering, including cautioning her, in the timeless way of grandmothers, to make sure little Daniel wore a hat on cool days.[58]

Harriott and Charles Cotesworth doted on their mother and even competed a bit to see who could be most attentive. When Harriott and Daniel sent Eliza "plenty of eatables," Charles Cotesworth and Sally brought "more wine . . . than I have room for." Thomas couldn't match his siblings' daily attentions, but he made certain that his conduct in England pleased his mother. "My Children," Eliza bragged in the summer of 1774, "are determined I shall live well." And live well she did. Having achieved all her goals and retired from the full-time demands of being a planter-patriarch, Eliza relished the comfortable life she had carefully made for herself and her posterity. The future seemed so secure.[59]

PART SIX

Revolution and War

CHAPTER 12

A Gathering Storm

As Eliza Lucas Pinckney welcomed home her youngest child—for good, at long last—in late 1774, dread clouded their reunion. South Carolina, alongside the other mainland colonies, was engulfed in a political firestorm. Fifteen months before, British officials had passed the Tea Act. Designed to protect the East India Company while appeasing the volatile North Americans who kept resisting parliamentary tax measures, the law actually lowered the cost of tea in the American colonies. In London, the act seemed a reasoned measure. Radicals in Boston and other North American seaports didn't see it that way. They feared the implications of the law for local merchants and for future colonial autonomy. Vigilantes fought the Tea Act with a ferocity and lawlessness that stunned the metropole. The most shocking spectacle took place in Boston, where a brazen mob destroyed £10,000 worth of tea. Resolved to at last bring their American provinces into order, Parliament passed the Coercive Acts. Until Massachusetts paid for the property destroyed on December 16, 1773, in the Boston "Tea Party," the colony would endure military occupation and strict trade prohibitions. The courts and assembly were closed, too. In response, representatives from most mainland colonies gathered in Philadelphia, in September and October 1774, in what they termed a Continental Congress. Created to coordinate resistance to the Coercive Acts, the Congress humbly petitioned King George III for redress. But if he failed to act, Congress called for a boycott of all trade with England, to commence in December

1774. George III and leaders in Parliament could hardly believe the bizarre claim out of an extralegal gathering in Pennsylvania that the American colonies—designed expressly to advantage the empire—were not subject to English law. Of course the Americans fell under parliamentary authority, and of course they had no right to boycott trade with the metropole.

Meanwhile, in South Carolina and other seaboard colonies, officially sanctioned government began to collapse. Royal Governor Charles Montagu twice dissolved the South Carolina Assembly before leaving the colony in disgrace. Montagu's successor, William Campbell, proved no more effective. By late 1774, extralegal committees, consisting of the same men who had served in the now-disbanded assembly, were, for all practical purposes, running South Carolina. The pattern, of extralegal institutions operating in the vacuum left by the collapse of royal governments, ran across North America throughout 1774. In January 1775, the extralegal group controlling South Carolina politics called for colony-wide elections to create a Provincial Congress. Elected members of the new congress—including Charles Cotesworth Pinckney—granted themselves authority to enforce the Continental Congress's call for nonimportation and nonexportation.[1]

Eliza watched these unprecedented events but failed to anticipate their full implications. Few Americans did, even among those at the forefront of the opposition movement. Despite the political tumult, Eliza, like most North Americans, went about her normal routine. The concerning events seemed to shift and evolve with disorienting speed. But surely these crises, like the ones before, would pass and peace return to the American colonies. Anything else was unthinkable. So, though she kept an eye on politics, Eliza remained focused primarily on family matters throughout 1774 and into early 1775. She had a new grandchild to fuss over: Sally and Charles Cotesworth's daughter, Maria Henrietta. Thomas's entry into Charles Town's social scene offered another distraction. Socializing continued apace despite the political uproar, and Thomas felt nervous but excited to attend a winter ball. "I am to make my first appearance as Beau in all my Glory (that is to say my best suit of Cloaths)," he told Harriott. It was a smashing entrance. He danced until 3:00 A.M. Just a few days later, he enjoyed a "Family Hop" at the Rutledges and attended a tea party at the Middletons that, "a Fidler being at hand . . . soon converted into a Cotillon."[2]

Eliza's family, like families across the eastern seaboard, did not see—could not imagine—what spring would bring. The Pinckneys' biggest worry in February 1775, despite all that had unfolded over the previous six months, was

Thomas's debut in court. Charles Cotesworth attended the session and immediately went to Eliza's house to give a full report. He entered while she was writing to Harriott. She stopped midsentence to hear the news. "Your brother has just been here," Eliza explained as she resumed writing. "He stept in from Court to let me know Tomm has spoke for the first time." Thomas won the case, Charles Cotesworth said, and conducted himself ably. Eliza was skeptical. "I have seen nobody yet to know how he spoke but his brother," she told Harriott, "and he, you know is very partial to him."[3]

Thomas shortly arrived at his mother's house with a less sanguine report. He'd felt awkward and confused and embarrassed. Other men in the community came to reassure Eliza. Charles Cotesworth's brother-in-law Edward Rutledge (they married sisters) visited that evening and insisted that the power of Thomas's ideas outweighed his nervousness. Edward promised Eliza that Thomas's clumsiness "would wear off in one Circuit." Obsessed with Thomas's reputation, Eliza sought other opinions. She told her nephew Charles Pinckney to ask his friends about Thomas's performance. He assured her that city powerbrokers thought Thomas had "acquitted himself extraordinary well, with great calmness and good sence," and acted "not at all confused, or flusterd." The family drama dissipated by the end of February. Eliza concluded that if Thomas made a less than shining start into his legal career, he would get better with practice. There was plenty of time, she imagined, for him to hone his skills.[4]

The commotion about Thomas passed and things returned to normal for the Pinckneys. In March 1775, Eliza was in Charles Town studying the market value of enslaved people. When one of her former Wappoo neighbors, Sarah Harvey Elliott, died and executors auctioned off the people she enslaved, Eliza was glad to see the price averaged £507 per person—an excellent sign for her own extensive investment in human trafficking. Thomas and Charles Cotesworth traveled together to check on their far-flung plantations, including Ashepoo (Auckland) and Pinckney Island. Harriott stayed at Hampton, tending to a sick child while hosting visitors.[5]

Suddenly, everything changed. In late April 1775, from the Massachusetts farming towns of Lexington and Concord came shocking news: colonial complaints against Britain had spiraled into armed combat. That fast, the unimaginable began to unfold.

War had been a near-constant presence throughout Eliza Lucas Pinckney's adulthood: imperial conflicts in the Caribbean, the French and Indian War, the Cherokee War, clashes between backcountry "Regulators" and tidewater governments. But no previous conflict had brought as much danger and devastation as she and her family endured in the American Revolutionary War. It completely upended Eliza's carefully planned, comfortable life.

The South Carolina Provincial Congress reconvened on June 1, 1775, incensed by the hostilities outside Boston, which they blamed wholly on the British government. Radicals controlling the extralegal legislatures along the seaboard, including in South Carolina, saw the cause of Massachusetts as their own. The Coercive Acts and the battles at Lexington and Concord had, Carolinians concluded, driven "an oppressed people to the use of arms!" They would stand together. Avowing their allegiance to the Second Continental Congress, members of the Provincial Congress mutually pledged their "lives and fortunes" to "resisting force by force." They would secure their rights, no matter the cost. Escalating the tensions were rumors that Britain planned to ally with Indian nations to suppress the colonies. In direct violation of imperial law, the South Carolina Provincial Congress ordered the raising of three regiments, totaling fifteen hundred soldiers.[6]

Charles Cotesworth and Thomas immediately joined the military, followed by their brother-in-law, Daniel Horry. Their wealth and long-standing immersion in English markets did not curb their zeal for the American cause. The Pinckney brothers were commissioned as captains and headed out to recruit soldiers. They were back in Charles Town as the summer heat broke. Alongside Francis Marion, Charles Cotesworth led forces to claim James Island, which the British abandoned on September 14, 1775. The next day, Royal Governor William Campbell fled his home on Meeting Street and took refuge on a British ship, the *Tamar*. With that, a hundred years of English authority over South Carolina came to an end.[7]

How far they had come, and so quickly. Not so long ago, Eliza was gushing at meeting Princess Augusta and the young crown prince, George. To Eliza's delight, Charles Cotesworth attended King George III's coronation while studying in London. Now, the men in the Pinckney family were organizing militias to fight British forces.[8]

It was a pattern replicated throughout North America in the summer of 1775: fiercely proud English subjects, asserting defense of their English rights, took up arms against the English government. Allegations that the British military was plotting with Indians and instigating slave uprisings helped to persuade some colonists to embrace the radical patriot movement. Reflecting widespread fears, South Carolina's self-appointed Council of Safety tried several enslaved people for planning rebellions in the summer of 1775. Events out of Virginia in the fall sealed the matter for others. In November 1775, the royal governor, Lord Dunmore, made a bold proclamation: enslaved Virginians who fought with the British would secure their freedom. Still, only fitfully—and fifteen months into the widening war—did the defiant colonists decide they should be independent Americans.[9]

Eliza Lucas Pinckney loathed war. She had lost her father to a military campaign; now she contemplated the horror of losing her sons. Even if everyone stayed safe, a war with Great Britain would, she understood, trigger catastrophic financial losses. What of the rice and indigo growing in their fields, the thousands of acres of land she and her children owned? Harriott Pinckney Horry saw it, too, and dreaded the "Evils of Indigence that stare us in the face."[10]

Clear-eyed about the costs of the war, the Pinckney women joined the men in supporting the patriot movement. Perhaps as she weighed her loyalties, Eliza thought of her father and grandfather and their bold stands against high-handed royal officials. More immediately, there was the threat to her sons and to her family. That carried the day. Eliza's priorities as the crises mounted did not waver: she stayed fixed on her family's well-being, wealth, and prominence. With that in mind, she and Harriott took over the family responsibilities and took up the patriot cause. In August 1775, while her brothers marshaled forces, Harriott corresponded with a relative about Americans' commitment. "Britain surely will be shortly taught," Elizabeth Trapier concluded, "in spite of all their base arts to disunite us that America determines to be free." She added, "it is beyond their force of arms to enslave so vast a Continent." Eliza, harboring fewer romantic notions about war, still urged young men, including her sons, to stand firm for the American cause. These were, she knew, extraordinarily trying times, and men needed to rise to the challenge. If worthy men declined serving when called, she asked, what would possibly become of America?[11]

Eliza captured the general reaction of Lowcountry elites. Most entered the contest with a mix of purposefulness and trepidation. At a service at St. Philip's as the Provincial Congress took charge of South Carolina, people wept in their pews at the thought of their loved ones entering a dangerous war. But, they concluded, armed conflict could not be avoided. They would proceed, despite sadness, with resolution.[12]

Charles Cotesworth numbered among the most fiercely committed, but he felt far from sanguine about Americans' prospects. In the fall of 1775 and into early 1776, he struggled to train a band of frustratingly unruly soldiers. Many drank and caroused, and a few, to his mortification, stole from civilians.

Despite his best efforts, his soldiers kept "lurking in the Dram shops" in Charles Town as he tried to run drills. Separation from his wife and child weighed on him, too. He worried about their safety and financial security as he waited for British forces to bring the war south. He feared for his own life, enough to make out his will.[13]

Thomas was single, twenty-five years old, and, thanks to Harriott, more carefree during the first year of the Revolutionary War than his older brother. Harriott and Thomas grew extraordinarily close during the war years. She took care of his properties and finances and held full discretionary power to pay bills, borrow money, and extend credit in his name. Thomas's greatest inconveniences were staying awake for occasional night patrol and "being separated from the Dear Charmers." Sometimes he was in camp with Charles Cotesworth, sometimes on recruiting trips, and sometimes socializing in Charles Town. Harriott became the constant in his life: his closest confidante and greatest comfort. Thomas adored Harriott, looked for any opportunity to see her, and missed her terribly when the war kept them apart. To stay connected, they wrote letters, the contents ranging easily, he bragged, "from Ethics and Metaphysics down to Scandal and Fiddle Faddle."[14]

Gender didn't matter much in Harriott and Thomas's relationship—nor did it generally among brothers and sisters in their social circle. The Pinckney family and the gentry class in general had long relied on capable women to run businesses and estates when men were absent. Female planter-patriarchs faced strict limits to their authority when it came to politics: they could not vote or hold political office. But in colonial South Carolina they enjoyed the confidence of their male kin and crossed nearly every other stereotypical boundary dividing male from female responsibilities.[15]

Thomas made fun of the idea that his sister should spend her time "reeling Cotton or knitting Stockings." Harriott was, he knew, capable of far more important things than "trotting from the Parlour to the Kitchen" and back again. He recommended that she spend less time on housework and more on quadratic equations. Their many letters to each other reflect the siblings' mutual trust and affection and Thomas's deep reliance on Harriott. The scope of that reliance during the war was sweeping, as reflected in a typical letter: "I shall esteem it a Favor if you will write a Letter to me informing the News both Public & Private, such as the Price of Goods . . . What Beauties are in Town, & how Rice sells . . . News from General Washington & how much I must give for a Genteel pair of Epaulets . . . any News of a French War, & . . . about my new Coat."[16]

As soldiers mustered, civilian authorities in South Carolina enforced radical political changes that ignited violence. In June 1775, the Provincial Congress, in addition to asserting their right to take up arms against Great Britain, declared those opposing their actions "persons inimical to the Liberty of the Colonies." South Carolina joined other mainland colonies in making loyalty to the British crown a crime. Anyone refusing to take an oath of allegiance could be lawfully banished. Overt resistance sparked swift and cruel retribution. While declaiming their devotion to liberty, patriot leaders not only brutalized enslaved people they suspected of seeking freedom, they also systematically threatened white neighbors who disagreed with them, seized their estates, and made them refugees. Loyalists faced only bad choices: submission, silence, violence, or exile.[17]

The loyalists' prospects got worse in early 1776. On January 6, after more than four months stuck on a ship in the harbor waiting to reclaim his authority, Governor Campbell gave up and sailed away. Then in late March, the Second Provincial Congress of South Carolina ratified a new constitution. John Rutledge was elected president of the independent state of South Carolina. Power rested securely in the hands of the patriots, who doubled down on forcing a loyalist exodus.[18]

The Pinckneys stood together as strong patriot supporters. But with loyalism criminalized, many other prominent Lowcountry families fractured along political lines. The Bulls, Draytons, Moultries, Heywards, Manigaults, Hugers, Wraggs, and even the Horrys divided, with some members embracing the American cause and others fleeing in fear for their fortunes and lives. More than two hundred Lowcountry families relocated to England by 1778.[19]

Loyalists weren't the only ones on the move. Terrified patriot women gathered up their children and evacuated Charles Town to escape the inevitable British attack. As the central port in the southern colonies, the city was an irresistible target.

In late 1775 Eliza and Harriott set out for Thomas's Ashepoo Plantation, about fifty miles southwest of Charles Town. For safekeeping, they packed up their family business papers and letters, including those written by Eliza's late husband. They left with heavy hearts: "Think with what reluctance I must leave the place," Harriott lamented, "when I leave in it my Husband, Brothers, and every male relation . . . exposed to every danger." She and her mother resolved to exercise "all our Fortitude to meet the Awfull Event with that decency and resignation becoming Xtians." Fear was palpable and pervasive.

Rumors ran like wildfire: about the size of the British force, the timing of an invasion, alliances with Indian nations, the fomenting of slave rebellions, and the viciousness of British and Hessian soldiers. Some of it was true, some false. But the dread of a devastating assault on their hometown was real, and fear traumatized people long before the war reached them.[20]

As white women moved out of Charles Town, fortifications went up, constructed mostly by enslaved men forced to labor for the patriot cause. Trenches and earthworks crisscrossed streets. Every house on the waterfront was demolished to aid the sentries. The city, in short order, became unrecognizable.[21]

By June 1776, Eliza moved again, with Harriott and Harriott's children, to a plantation in Colleton County owned by family friends Charles and Ann Elliott. Sally Middleton Pinckney took flight, too, with her toddler Maria Henrietta, to a Middleton family plantation along Goose Creek. Sally was pregnant again; she delivered a daughter named Harriott in December 1776. Charles Cotesworth, Thomas, and Daniel remained at their posts: the Pinckney brothers on James Island and their brother-in-law at Haddrell's Point.[22]

Expecting the British assault to commence at any hour, Thomas worried about Eliza: "I hope my Mother does not suffer herself to be low Spirited on this Occasion." Charles Cotesworth feared that Eliza might "be alarmed by hearing exaggerated reports" of the British fleet. He promised Eliza that he and Thomas faced no grave danger and that the men under his command would, if called into action, fight courageously and prevail. The brothers knew their mother was a worrier when it came to her children's well-being. But they also recognized her strength. They didn't need to protect her from the truth. Both Charles Cotesworth and Thomas wrote Eliza unvarnished accounts of their experiences throughout the long and violent Revolutionary War.[23]

Instead of launching a direct assault on Charles Town, the British set their sights on Sullivan's Island, at the entrance to the city's harbor and the site of a partially constructed fort. British ships commenced firing on the makeshift garrison at around 11:30 in the morning on June 28, 1776. The attack dismissed Carolinians' lingering hopes for a resolution with Great Britain. Outgunned and outmanned, the Carolinians held one key advantage: they had built their bastions out of palmetto trees. The soft, rather spongy wood kept Britain's cannonballs from causing much damage. The invaders kept firing all day, until after sunset. British commanders, stunned at their failure to break through the Carolinians' fortifications, gave the cease-fire order just after 9:00 P.M. The Carolinians—stunned themselves—had prevailed. So weighty was the triumph owing to the palmetto fortifications that Carolinians later put the tree in the center of their state flag.[24]

The Pinckney brothers watched from afar. Stationed at Fort Johnson, on James Island, Charles Cotesworth regretted he "was only a Spectator," distant from the "honor & danger" at Sullivan's Island. He and Thomas commiserated about the lost chance at glory. Thomas repeated Charles Cotesworth when he reported to Harriott that he had been among the "idle Spectators" to the "noble Action."[25]

Less than a week after the battle, members of the Second Continental Congress unanimously endorsed a radical proposition: the North America colonies were "Free and Independent States . . . Absolved from all Allegiance to the British Crown." Emboldened by the successful defense of Sullivan's Island (now called Fort Moultrie), South Carolina's patriot majority celebrated the Declaration of Independence on August 5, 1776. Before a large crowd at 1:00 in the afternoon, leaders read the text aloud and proceeded to the Exchange for celebrations.[26]

Slavery shaped every part of white South Carolinians' path from resistance to revolution in 1775–1776. At the end of 1775, more than 100,000 enslaved people lived in South Carolina, constituting a majority in the Lowcountry. Before the Revolutionary War, traffickers used Sullivan's Island as a "pest house" for newly arriving Africans. People were quarantined there at the end of the Middle Passage and before auctions to ensure that they did not carry infectious diseases into South Carolina. Charles Town's population, around 12,000, was half free and half enslaved. Whites' fears about enslaved Carolinians allying with Britain to orchestrate a widespread uprising encouraged radical opposition to the metropole. Among the complaints the Provincial Congress leveled that drove "an oppressed people"—how the white Carolinians saw themselves—to overthrow imperial authority was "the dread of instigated insurrections in the colonies."[27] The Exchange, where extralegal committees convened and revelers celebrated the Declaration of Independence, had been built by enslaved laborers to market slave-produced commodities. Patriot leaders forced enslaved men to erect the city's fortifications in 1776. Enslaved women cooked and cleaned for the soldiers and packed up for the white families fleeing town. South Carolina was not alone. The foundation of American freedom was American slavery. White men could be free and equal because they would never be black and enslaved, never part of the permanent, racially defined underclass in the American Republic.[28]

For Eliza and her family, dependence on slavery was ubiquitous and personal, too. Eliza felt vexed when any of the people she enslaved enjoyed free time, and she moved men and women and children between her varied properties to ensure greater productivity. She congratulated herself on wisely picking a very promising little girl to train as a future personal maid: "She is the most attentive little Negroe I ever knew." The Pinckneys stayed connected to one another in the early years of the Revolutionary War through the people they enslaved. Their sometimes-daily letters and the many supplies Eliza and Harriott sent to Thomas, Charles Cotesworth, and Daniel came via enslaved couriers, who ran the family's errands across the dangerous countryside. Even in flight, Eliza commanded a host of enslaved men and women: cooks, drivers, laundresses, and couriers. Harriott's management of Thomas's properties included his human property. As they joined the military to fight for liberty and freedom, Charles Cotesworth and Thomas relied on their "body servants" to shave and dress them.[29]

Zealous patriots, the Pinckneys had no intention of letting their new political allegiances compromise their old tradition of human bondage. In that regard, they were becoming an all-American family.

CHAPTER 13

The Hastening War

After the fiasco at Sullivan's Island, Britain refrained from undertaking another major incursion into South Carolina until late 1779. But the three-year absence of pitched battles did not mean that Eliza and her family enjoyed peace. No one knew when the British might strike again. Just days after the Second Continental Congress declared America's independence, Eliza asked Charles Cotesworth where she should move to keep safe. He couldn't say: "It is so uncertain when the Enemy will renew their attack." Rumors flew, mostly unfounded but deeply distressing. Worse still was the staggering financial costs of waging a war against the British Empire.[1]

In addition to wrecking the Pinckneys' finances, those ostensibly peaceful years scattered family members. In late 1776, Thomas headed out to recruit volunteers in North Carolina, Virginia, and Maryland. The "very Tedious, unsuccessful Journey" left him frustrated, homesick, disillusioned, and bored. As his duties carried him to the South Carolina backcountry, East Florida, and Georgia, his thoughts turned to Charles Town's social scene, to women in particular. Harriott, raising children and managing plantations, added another responsibility: courting for her absent younger brother. "If chance should throw my Charmer in your way," Thomas told her, "make strong love for me."[2]

Charles Cotesworth left South Carolina, too. Through family connections, he secured a position in George Washington's inner circle. But he found no more glory in the Continental Army than he had at Sullivan's Island.

When he returned to South Carolina, he kept his military rank but turned to politics. Because of his family name, he won whatever position he sought in the new state government. The Revolution made that work more time-consuming and more dangerous; he couldn't visit his mother or sister or wife and child when he wanted. And he couldn't always be sure where they had taken refuge. He continued to worry about South Carolinians' lack of preparations for an attack everyone knew was coming. Thomas Pinckney and Daniel Horry balanced dangerous military duties with high-stakes elected office, too. Daniel commanded a South Carolina regiment of light dragoons under Francis Marion and served in the South Carolina government. Thomas held a seat in the General Assembly, alongside his brother and brother-in-law, while continuing his military excursions.[3]

Eliza and Harriott ran the day-to-day family finances which, for South Carolinians, constituted the most chaotic and painful part of the Revolutionary War between 1776 and 1779. British blockades crippled the Lowcountry economy. Charles Town, "once the seat of pleasure and amusement" for the Pinckneys, endured "almost total stagnation of every kind of business."[4] What few items residents could import cost a fortune. Inflation was outrageous. Thomas decided to take some time off from his military service to practice law in late 1778, hoping that the fees might help him pay back debts that Harriott had covered for him. He earned next to nothing. Charles Cotesworth dreaded the consequences for the abysmally supplied soldiers under his command. On the eve of another ill-funded excursion he complained: "What can be more cruel than crowding eight, ten, and twelve men into one tent, or oblige those who cannot get in, to sleep in the heavy dews? What is more inconvenient than to have only one camp-kettle to ten, twelve or fifteen men? And in this hot climate to have one small canteen to six or eight men?"[5]

Everyone in the family grew weary of these wartime disruptions. Eliza tried to take comfort in her religious faith. She kept repeating to herself and her children aphorisms about providential design and God's omnipotence. "I exert my utmost resolution," she said. Still, she found it "impossible not to be anxious." And the worst was yet to come.[6]

In February 1778, Eliza learned, American diplomats coaxed France into recognizing their fledging country's independence. That alliance led France to declare war on England in March. France's entry into the war, in turn, forced Britain to recalibrate its strategy. What had started off as a worrisome local revolt was escalating into a global conflict; Britain sent troops into Central

America, the Caribbean, West Africa, and India while fearing an invasion of the metropole. North America was no longer their most pressing concern. To stave off threats to Britain's lucrative Caribbean colonies, commanders evacuated Philadelphia in the summer and sent troops to shore up the mainland southern provinces in the fall. South Carolina moved into Britain's crosshairs. Georgia was first, though, and Savannah fell in the last days of December 1778. "Can any be so weak-sighted as not to see that the war is hastening to us?" Charles Pinckney commiserated with his Aunt Eliza. Neither he nor his cousins felt hopeful about Carolinians' prospects. "If our Militia continue as supine as they have been," Thomas predicted, British forces would overrun South Carolina in a matter of weeks.[7]

With the long-dreaded invasion imminent, Eliza retreated to Hampton in the spring of 1779, where Harriott gathered her sister-in-law, Sally Middleton Pinckney, and a half-dozen other prominent women and their children. Across the state, white women holed up together, clinging to the illusion of security in numbers. Three generations of Manigault women fled together, and the Motte and Brewton women gathered, too. From reports out of New England and the mid-Atlantic, they had heard about the sadistic British and Hessian soldiers who waged war on civilians and communities, who violated women's homes and their bodies.[8]

The Pinckney brothers along with Daniel Horry joined an expedition heading south to try to wrest Savannah from the British. The British stayed one step ahead: a general led forces north in a bid to seize Charles Town. They didn't prevail, but they inflicted a tremendous amount of damage as they made their way through the countryside.

In early May 1779, a detachment of those British soldiers rode up to Thomas's Ashepoo Plantation (Auckland). Seeing the writing on the wall, Thomas's overseer fled into the swamp. The soldiers slaughtered the livestock, smashed furniture, destroyed Thomas's books and personal possessions, drank all his liquor, burned down the house, and rode off with his horses. Among the most treasured possessions lost: the papers of Thomas's late father. The records of a lifetime went up in smoke. Nineteen enslaved people left Ashepoo with the British soldiers. The rest of the African Americans, Thomas complained to his mother, "are now perfectly free & live upon the best produce of the plantation." The same thing happened across North America whenever British soldiers appeared.[9]

In June 1779, British General Henry Clinton offered an even better incentive than Lord Dunmore's transformational 1775 proclamation. Clinton announced that any enslaved person fleeing to British lines would be protected and could not be reclaimed by the rebels. Unlike Dunmore, Clinton added no requirement of taking up arms. Reports quickly spread far and wide. Some enslaved Carolinians read the exciting news in the *South Carolina Gazette,* while others learned about it from loyalists and traveling sailors. But most probably overheard about this new path to freedom in whispered conversations among their appalled enslavers, who perceived the Clinton proclamation as the fulfillment of their worst fears. Historians estimate that perhaps as many as 100,000 of the 500,000 people enslaved in North America escaped bondage, at least temporarily, during the war. A few people discussed plans to overthrow the institution of slavery, but far more, including the people at Ashepoo, fled their captors. Those who remained saw British soldiers humiliate and overawe enslavers, like the panicked overseer at Ashepoo. It was a window into the fragility of white power. Sometimes the way the British treated African Americans disappointed their hopes, but not their resolve to get free.[10]

Dinah numbered among the people enslaved at Ashepoo who seized the opportunity opened by the British incursions. She was thirty-six years old in 1779, and, according to the runaway advertisement Thomas bought trying to recapture her, "big with Child when she went away." Dinah also carried a child in her arms and took with her a thirteen-year-old daughter, Phillis.[11]

The year Dinah and her children escaped Ashepoo, British forces invaded Belmont, too. Soldiers ransacked Eliza's country mansion but left her buildings intact. Eliza calculated that Thomas, suffering greater losses than she, faced near total ruin. She tried to console him while also clearly explaining that her setbacks at Belmont left her unable to help him. Charles Cotesworth rose to the occasion. He immediately volunteered to divide his estate with Eliza and Thomas—an offer that Eliza fawned over but quickly rejected. "Independence is all I wish," Eliza told Thomas, with a reminder: "A little will make us that." Eliza allowed that her stage of life let her weather the tumult better than her son: "I can't want but little, nor that little long." And besides, she still had what mattered most. "While I have such children as I have," she proclaimed, "dare I think my lot hard."[12]

The safety of her family did not keep Eliza from complaining about being on the receiving end of British policy regarding enslaved Carolinians. Some had run away or followed the British army. Others ignored her directions. She found it exasperating: "They all do now what they please every where." It was, to say the least, not Eliza's finest hour. Then, in October, just four months later, she lent the state of South Carolina £4,000. It proved a savvy investment:

she collected 10 percent annual interest payments on the loan for the next ten years. But it came on the heels of poor-mouthing Thomas and rebuking people like Dinah, who wanted safety and freedom for their children, too.[13]

In the middle of their frustrations over Ashepoo and Belmont, the Pinckneys marked a happy milestone. Through letters and occasional visits and with the aid of Harriott, Thomas successfully courted Elizabeth Motte. Elizabeth, whom everyone called Betsey, was the daughter of Rebecca Brewton Motte, and Harriott's neighbor and friend. One of the Motte estates, Fairfield, was near Hampton. Betsey and Thomas wed in late July 1779, in a joyful if hasty break from the war. He was twenty-eight, she just seventeen. Betsey captivated Thomas; he praised "the Accomplishments of her Mind and the Graces of her Person." The money was good, too, and the ties between the two families ran deep. Betsey's aunt, Frances Brewton Pinckney, was married to Thomas's cousin, Charles Pinckney, Eliza and Charles's favorite nephew. Thomas's father had died at Betsey's grandfather's house in Mount Pleasant in 1758.[14]

Betsey's mother, Rebecca Brewton Motte, was every bit as savvy and formidable as Eliza Lucas Pinckney, and even richer. Rebecca's brother, Miles Brewton, died at sea with his family in 1775. Miles left Rebecca his city home, the finest in all of Charles Town, as well as several other properties, including Mount Joseph, a thirteen-hundred-acre plantation on the Congaree River with more than 240 enslaved laborers. Rebecca's husband, Jacob Motte Jr., died in January 1780, leaving her his land, too. On the eve of the British invasion of South Carolina, Rebecca Brewton Motte numbered among the richest people—some say she was the richest—in the state of South Carolina. Like Eliza, Rebecca was an independent planter-patriarch and head of a prominent family. After Betsey and Thomas's wedding, Betsey stayed with her mother at her Charles Town home as Thomas returned to his military post, to await the inevitable.[15]

As he set out for South Carolina just after Christmas 1779, British General Henry Clinton, commander of the southern campaign, understood, "This is the most important hour Britain ever knew." By winning back the southern provinces he could save his country's claim over North America and, at last, break the Continental Army. The strategy was precise, the force designed to overwhelm. By March 1780, as far as Charles Town residents could see, British warships filled the sea. At least one hundred vessels under the command of Admiral Mariot Arbuthnot trained their weapons on the city. The mistakes of 1776 would not be repeated. General Clinton, leading an army of ten thousand men, moved relentlessly up the Sea Islands along the southern coastline. The circle tightened, and American General Benjamin Lincoln, trying to defend Charles Town with no more than five thousand troops, found himself cut off by land and sea.[16]

Before he ordered the first weapons fired, Clinton, now commanding a force of fourteen thousand, gave Lincoln the chance to surrender. Lincoln refused. After a brief shelling on April 13, Lincoln reconsidered. He recommended that civilian leaders accept whatever the British offered to save their city and preserve his army to fight another day. Charles Cotesworth Pinckney led a small, adamant minority who disagreed. South Carolina must never surrender, he insisted. His exceedingly bad judgment prevailed.[17]

On May 9, 1780, Clinton and Arbuthnot unleased the full force of their military might on Charles Town. Two hundred cannon fired at once. As William Moultrie watched the bombardment, he found it spectacularly horrifying. It looked to him "as if the stars were tumbling down." There was no relief that night from the endless whizzing cannon balls, concussing of mortar, exploding magazines, raging fires, and, under it all, cries of the dying. Patriot forces fought all night long, but to no avail. Britain held all the advantages. Dawn revealed the carnage, grim even to seasoned Hessian soldiers. Mutilated bodies riddled the streets, with random limbs scattered about and "people burnt beyond recognition, half-dead and writhing like worms." Charles Town fell in less than forty-eight hours. The surrender, on May 11, 1780, marked Britain's greatest triumph of the entire war and the patriots' most devastating loss. Along with the most important port and largest city south of Philadelphia, Lincoln surrendered his entire army: seven generals, scores of officers, and more than five thousand soldiers with all their weapons and supplies.[18]

Commanders of the occupying forces set up their offices in the most majestic house in town, owned by Rebecca Brewton Motte. Thomas Pinckney's young bride Betsey was there with her mother and two sisters when British soldiers unceremoniously moved in. Refusing to abandon her property, Rebecca kept her daughters in the attic to protect them from the soldiers. From Rebecca Brewton Motte's parlor, General Clinton assumed he had conquered South Carolina. He offered full pardons to residents who reaffirmed their allegiance to George III and soon departed, leaving Lord Cornwallis in command and charged with the minor matter of subduing the countryside.[19]

George Washington knew what he had lost when Charles Town fell. But he also understood two fundamental truths about the war that Clinton and

Cornwallis missed: first, occupation of cities did not equal victory; second, a protracted contest worked in the patriots' favor. The money and manpower required to hold South Carolina would tax British resources and, in the long term, advantage the Americans. This became the wager: Carolinians would provoke and endure unspeakable carnage to bleed the British Empire into surrender.[20]

The story of the American Revolution, in popular imagination and a good deal of scholarship, unfolds as a noble (if incomplete or flawed) transformation in politics and ideology. The founders' bold vision of American representative democracy triumphed over the inheritable hierarchy of the monarchical world of Europe. Accepting John Adams's assessment, the war becomes a consequence, almost an afterthought to the Revolution: "Radical Change in the Principles, Opinions Sentiments and Affection of the People, was the real American Revolution." Patriotic statues and romantic paintings of the "Founding Fathers"—all velvet knee-britches and powdered wigs, gathered in legislative halls writing the creeds of a nation—reinforce the widespread perception that the Revolution was reasoned, peaceful, admirable. Perhaps the ideas were, but the war required to affirm them was assuredly not. The military contest to secure American independence was far from an orderly, all-male affair.[21]

In the summer of 1780, Eliza Lucas Pinckney met the Revolutionary War—bloody, chaotic, and cruel—face to face. What she endured and witnessed shifts our focus from men to women, from seats of political power to the countryside, and from high-minded political theories to the hard realities of war.

CHAPTER 14

"shatter'd and ruin'd"

The Revolutionary War that raged across North America between 1775 and 1783 was, like all wars, a living hell. The most sustained and vicious fighting took place in the last years and in the southern states, where British forces assailed the environment and economy, not just the rival army. Patriots matched them step for step.

In 1780–1782, Eliza Lucas Pinckney lived through a civil war more vicious, sweeping, and catastrophic than anyone imagined possible. British forces expelled her from her city house and seized Belmont. Her rental houses were confiscated, too, "fill'd with Hessians, and refugees" and horribly damaged, while she was taxed at exorbitant rates. To her mortification, Eliza found herself without "a place to lay my head." Soldiers carried off her cattle and cut down her timber. Her children all suffered, each in a uniquely horrible way, and Eliza felt powerless to help them. A lifelong slaveholder, she professed, without irony, never to have seen before such "insolence of power, and wanton cruelty!" The people she enslaved—who constituted her most valuable property—fled, refused to work, joined the British, and were impressed into public works. By the end of the war Eliza's estate lay "shatter'd and ruin'd." "I experienced a large share of the bitter potion dealt out," she reflected. Still, Eliza knew she was far from alone and luckier than many of her friends and neighbors, who paid for the patriot cause with their or their relatives' lives.[1]

In the aftermath of the May 1780 bombardment, death washed over Charles Town. "Wherever you turn," one occupying British soldier reported, "the weeping widow and fatherless child pour out their melancholy tales." And the city was just the start. Resentments over the occupation of Charles Town fueled vengeance, which begat cruelty. In the backcountry, guerrilla fighters on both sides ignored command structures and defied established rules of war. British commanders also openly advocated a war of attrition and wholesale destruction. In 1780–1781, South Carolina was the site of almost one-fifth of all battlefield deaths in the entire Revolutionary War. Meanwhile, anarchy disrupted households, communities, and institutions. Lawlessness became the new normal. Seasoned General Nathanael Greene was shocked by the "savage fury" of both sides: "Which of the two was most barbarous it is impossible to say." Vigilante mobs bent on revenge lowered the threshold for acceptable violence. Trying to break the will of their opponents, they raided private homes, wantonly slaughtered livestock, burned farmland. Commanders like Greene likened the insurgents to "beasts of prey." Nothing was sacred: combatants raped women, rummaged through sepulchers, slaughtered surrendering opponents, and left their corpses to rot. Packs of wolves scavenged for the dead, adding yet another danger for the living. People stopped eating their hogs because they also roamed the countryside feeding on abandoned cadavers. In September 1781, William Moultrie secured parole to visit his plantations. The trip was, he said, "the most dull, melancholy, dreary ride that any one could possibly take." He rode across a ravaged landscape, riddled with animal carcasses, burned-out houses, and, to his anguish, the bones of unburied soldiers.[2]

Most people in the war zone were civilians. Coordinated battles between uniformed soldiers inflicted high casualties but were the outlier in the southern campaigns. The plantations and farms where men waged South Carolina's civil, guerrilla war were mostly populated by women and children. Deployments and wartime deaths made South Carolina's white households decidedly female-centered even before the fall of Charles Town, before thousands more men became prisoners of war. Then, the war moved out of the occupied city and spiraled into the homes of women and past all control.[3]

The (few) surviving accounts from South Carolina women are harrowing. Eliza Wilkinson, for example, kept a record of her "day of terror"—the first of many—in June 1780. She heard horses thundering toward her home and then the shouts of riders. Within minutes, British troops burst into her house.

Terrified and helpless before the armed soldiers, she watched them ransack her house, taking even the women's jewelry, and destroying everything else. One woman refused to part with her wedding ring; she relented only when a soldier pointed his pistol at her. Soldiers came and went when they pleased, returning to prey on women again and again. During another raid on her home, Eliza Wilkinson heard a commotion and looked out the window to see a three-legged bloody pig racing by, soldiers in hot pursuit. They'd hacked off the poor animal's leg while it was still alive.[4]

This women's war, even for elites like Eliza Lucas Pinckney and Eliza Wilkinson, was defined by scarcity and deprivation, disease and violence, occupation and exile. Soldiers took over women's homes, forcing them to wash and cook for them. They took everything they could carry when they moved on to the next house. Raids to destroy crops and livestock and shortages of food were not simply a consequence of the war but an intentional policy. British troops tried to break the will of patriot women and, by extension, men. They threatened and terrorized women who stood fast in their convictions. In one macabre spectacle, when a woman refused to cooperate with the British, soldiers forced her and her children to watch as they exhumed her husband's body.[5]

It went on and on and on. "Our nights," one woman explained, "were wearisome and painful; our days spent in anxiety and melancholy." Often women could not tell friend from foe; they felt both confused and terrified whenever they saw riders in the distance. Among their fears: being raped. When women were sexually assaulted, they usually couldn't bear to admit it. In 1777, the Continental Congress called for a report of rapes occurring in the war, but few women would come forward. Rumors abounded, however, about rapes perpetrated on both sides, against women and girls of all ages, and as a tactic of war.[6]

On top of enduring the ravages of war, with many men dead and many more away from home, white women also needed to learn to operate outside their normal roles. And they had to do so without the security of domestic spaces and family ties they usually relied upon. Many women far less experienced with running plantations and farms than Eliza and Harriott learned to make do in a world that felt at once absent of and overrun by men: too few protectors and too many predators. They turned to female kinship and friendship networks to protect themselves and their family assets. The Pinckney women, for example, secreted away everything from horses to gold. But the chaos of war disrupted those support systems, too, deepening women's frustra-

Figure 10. John Trumbull, Charles Cotesworth Pinckney (1746–1825), 1791. Oil on wood panel. National Portrait Gallery, Smithsonian Institution; gift of Elise Pinckney.

tion and anxiety. This wartime entry into new roles with new responsibilities was not about the occasional outlier, either. Changes in women's roles went far beyond the temporary oversight of deputy husbands and widows to build a society-wide, years-long pattern: independent women operated as farmers, business managers, planters, and heads of households. Some women, of course, had been doing that long before the war. The number of powerful property-owning women such as Eliza Lucas Pinckney and Rebecca Brewton Motte stunned the British and deepened their difficulties. By holding on to farms, businesses, and plantations and keeping them even sporadically functioning, these independent women—old hands and newcomers alike—undercut Britain's campaign to control the countryside, which extended the war's cruelties and suffering.[7]

Besides her personal losses, Eliza grieved for her children, each of whom faced his or her own tribulations during the war. As Charles Cotesworth, Harriott, and Thomas suffered, Eliza lived out the adage that a parent is only as happy as her least happy child. Her inability to end their misery weighed heavily on Eliza and felt like a failing. But she did succeed in keeping the four of them a tight-knit group, determined to weather the war together and rebuild their family wealth on the other side.[8]

As Charles Town fell, Charles Cotesworth Pinckney, the commander of Fort Moultrie, bore the humiliation of surrendering the fort and became a prisoner of war. Confined at Haddrell's Point, he fell ill. British officials granted him a temporary parole to move to his cousin Charles Pinckney's estate, Snee Farm. Charles kept Snee Farm from being confiscated by agreeing to renounce his patriot allegiance. Cousin Charles's twenty-two-year-old son and namesake, a zealous soldier for the patriot cause, broke with his father and was imprisoned by the occupying military.[9]

Approached by royal officials to follow Charles's path and reassert his loyalty to the British crown, Charles Cotesworth flatly refused. In retaliation, his wife and children—ages six, four, and one—were forced to vacate the East Bay mansion. Eliza was ousted from her city house, too; soldiers confiscated it along with everything else the family owned in Charles Town. The Pinckneys numbered among scores of Carolinians whose holdings were seized: the British confiscated more than one hundred estates and five thousand enslaved people.[10] Then, in October 1780 Charles Cotesworth's infant son and namesake got sick. Still under British custody, with his letters screened and his visits restricted, Charles Cotesworth relied on his mother, seasoned in lay medicine, for news about the boy's worsening health and advice about treatments. "I am anxious, exceedingly anxious about the fate of my poor Child," he wrote her. Until the baby recovered, Charles Cotesworth wanted candid updates from Eliza at least once a day. He knew his mother: "You who are the most affectionate of Parents, will easily account for my anxiety." Eliza understood exactly how it felt to watch, helplessly, as a precious baby suffered. She could not spare him the grief she knew too well: Charles Cotesworth Jr. died in early 1781.[11]

Through these ordeals, Charles Cotesworth followed the example of resolution his mother had set for him her whole life: "I entered into this Cause

Figure 11. Walter Robertson, Harriott Pinckney Horry (1748–1830). Graphic reproduction of a miniature. Courtesy of the Frick Art Reference Library.

after much reflection, & through principle," he said. Nothing he endured in the occupation changed his mind about the righteousness and the necessity of the patriot cause: "My heart is altogether American."[12]

Harriott Pinckney Horry's troubles during the 1780–1782 occupation were of a different sort entirely. After Charles Town fell, her husband was able to come home to Hampton Plantation because he, like Eliza's nephew Charles Pinckney, renounced his allegiance to the American cause. Daniel Horry was hardly alone. Nearly two thousand Charles Town residents signed oaths of allegiance that summer. Still, he put Harriott in a tight position: one brother imprisoned and the other still fighting while he took the easy way out. The contrast was stark. Charles Cotesworth vowed to Edward Rutledge, "If I had a vein that did not beat with love for my country, I myself would open it."

Reluctant to exacerbate tensions between the sister he adored and her husband, Thomas told Eliza that he felt sorry to hear about Daniel's capitulation, but saw a silver lining: Daniel might help protect the women in the family.[13]

Eliza seemed less forgiving of her son-in-law's vanishing patriotism. After 1780, she rarely mentioned Daniel in any of her letters, even though she lived with him and Harriott at Hampton for several months during the occupation. When she wrote her sons, she sent along her and Harriott's love, often adding greetings from the children, but not Daniel. In fact, he dropped out of nearly all the family correspondence. If Daniel had ever managed to make his way into the tight circle of Eliza, Harriott, Thomas, and Charles Cotesworth, he became an outsider after 1780. There were other, earlier hints at trouble in their marriage. Harriott quit having children in 1770, at age twenty-two.

Unlike with Charles Cotesworth's heartbreak over losing his son, Eliza had no experience to draw on for counseling Harriott. She and Charles never faced a serious disagreement, and he certainly never did anything to embarrass her or alienate her from her family and friends. In a convenient departure from an increasingly tense scene, Daniel left South Carolina in 1781, to take his and Harriott's son to England for his formal education. As more and more Carolinians either suffered in British prison camps or lived in exile, relatives left behind looked askance at those who cast off their allegiances in exchange for an easier life. Men who, as one refugee put it, "thro' fear, or Self Interest, have meanly submitted" deserved the disdain of their neighbors.[14]

Harriott's troubles deepened after the war, when Daniel paid the price, literally, for his waffling allegiances. As the British evacuated, state leaders confiscated the property of some loyalists and imposed steep fines on many others. With her husband standing to lose everything, Harriott wrote directly to state officials. "If Mr. Horry is so guilty as to deserve this forfeiture," she reasoned, "I hope it will be remember'd that it is impossible to separate him from the many innocent ones connected with and who must suffer with him." Seizing Daniel's assets would, she explained, only add to "the many Injuries and mortifications which myself, my Mother and brothers with their Families have suffer'd . . . from our attachment to our Country." Thanks to her appeal and family name, Daniel forfeited only 12 percent of his and Harriott's estate. Prominent men in Charles Town gossiped about Daniel's embarrassment and noted that "had it not been for the many Virtues of the Pinckneys, his Estate would have unquestionably been confiscated."[15]

Figure 12. John Trumbull, Thomas Pinckney (1750–1828), 1791. Oil on wood panel. National Portrait Gallery, Smithsonian Institution; gift of Elise Pinckney.

Thomas Pinckney, who fought during the 1780 siege of Charles Town, managed to get around British lines before the city fell. He could not risk a stop at Hampton to see Eliza and Harriott as he raced into the backcountry, British soldiers in pursuit. "The trial is at present rather severe," he confessed to Harriott. But he remained resolute. Like Charles Cotesworth, Thomas vowed to stand firm in his principles, "let my fate be what it may." Thomas planned to head north and join the Continental Army, but he never made it out of South Carolina.[16]

Whatever respect Eliza had for her wobbly son-in-law must have evaporated in August 1780 when she heard from Thomas that while fighting in the Battle of Camden he had been shot in the leg. British forces routed the Americans in the backcountry town, and Thomas, the bones in his leg shattered, nearly bled to death. By incredible coincidence, one of Thomas's English schoolmates, Charles McKenzie, saw Thomas lying among the wounded and abandoned rebels. Charles persuaded British surgeons to treat Thomas, saving him from near-certain death. With massive casualties among their own ranks, the British generally had neither the resources nor the will to care for their opponents. As for dead soldiers, they were routinely piled onto wagons and carted off to be pitched into trenches. Once rescued by his former classmate, Thomas received care commensurate with his social and military rank. "My Treatment," he concluded, "has been humane, Politic, and attentive from the British officers into whose Hands I have fallen."[17]

Technically a prisoner of war and still clinging to life, Thomas was taken to the house of Ann Legardere Clay, where she had gathered a group of her female kin. After some debate, the British surgeons decided not to amputate Thomas's leg. He remained bedfast at Clay's house for three weeks, then endured a slow and painful recovery. In late September 1780 the wound remained a purulent mess. Thomas confided to Harriott that he looked like a skeleton: "My Legs are literally no thicker than a Stout Man's Wrist." Thomas had inherited his mother's optimism. Despite the painful injury he reported some good news: "I have hopes of retaining my Leg."[18]

Betsey Motte Pinckney was nine months pregnant with her first child when Thomas was shot. After the triage in Camden, she became Thomas's nurse while caring for their infant son, Thomas Jr. It must have been a rude awakening to the hard realities of war for the newlyweds. For months Betsey pulled out splinters of bone as they worked their way through Thomas's leg. She could barely stand it; at one point she fainted while trying to extract shards.[19]

When he got strong enough to travel, Betsey moved Thomas to one of her mother's plantations, Mount Joseph. The trip was excruciating, and he arrived too weak to sit upright. Rebecca Brewton Motte had moved the women in her family to Mount Joseph after decamping from the house in Charles Town. As with Ann Legardere Clay's home in Camden and Harriott's Hampton, Mount Joseph was home to a group of female kin and friends. Gathered for protection from the raging war, women across South Carolina took care of patriot soldiers too sick to make it to military prisons in British-occupied Charles Town. The Motte home had been a makeshift hospital for some time when Thomas arrived, and the women provided skillful care. Still, for Thomas to escape deadly infections was a minor miracle. A year later, Thomas's leg remained too weak for him to mount his horse. He took it all in stride. After he relocated to his mother-in-law's house, Thomas started corresponding with his ten-year-old nephew, Daniel Horry. "I suppose you are curious to know the Situation of my Leg," Thomas wrote the boy. So he mailed him one of the bone fragments that Betsey removed.[20]

Eliza, staying mostly at Hampton, did all she could for Thomas from afar. He refused her overtures to come to Camden, insisting that it was too dangerous for her to travel to "such a place of sickness, filth and wretchedness." If Eliza chafed at being excluded from her son's day-to-day care, she didn't show it. She sent medical advice and loving letters to Thomas and Betsey, and when she learned that he lacked his "body servant," she sent two enslaved men, John and Moses, to attend to him. Eliza also coached Betsey about dealing with the overwhelming situation. She offered her daughter-in-law timeless wisdom: "The greatest favor you can do him, will be to take care of your self, and bear with an equal mind your present trials."[21]

Then, just as Thomas began to recover some strength, Betsey got so sick that the Pinckneys and Mottes feared she might die. Besides worrying about Betsey, Eliza agonized over what losing her might do to Thomas. She knew the devastation of burying a beloved mate, and she, Charles Cotesworth, and Harriott prayed that Thomas might be spared that heartbreak. Thankfully, Betsey recovered, and within a few months she got pregnant again. She delivered her daughter, named Elizabeth Brewton Pinckney, in 1781, the fourth member of the next generation of Pinckneys born in war.[22]

In the summer of 1781, Eliza and Harriott found themselves, again, living alone together and separated by hundreds of miles from Charles Cotesworth and Thomas. In July, the Pinckney brothers evacuated South Carolina as part of a prisoner exchange. Exiles and refugees spilled across North America and the Atlantic World during the war years: loyalists and patriots, civilians and prisoners of war, black, white, and Indian. Charles Cotesworth and Thomas joined a large contingent of Carolinians exiled to Philadelphia. Five hundred seventy Carolinians—two-thirds of them women and children—moved there by the end of 1781. In the eyes of patriots, those families had refused to "Sully their honour & Conscience by taking protection."[23]

Of course, the Pinckneys were hardly refugees in the twenty-first-century sense of the word. In the eighteenth century, rank-and-file prisoners of war were often treated little better than animals, with moldy, maggot-filled food thrown at them as if they were hogs. Lice covered prisoners, head to toe. Untreated wounds festered with gangrene, water turned putrid, and the disregard for corpses was profane. The stench of camps was nauseating. The Pinckney brothers' military and social rank enabled them to escape the brutality meted out to average soldiers and sailors. As he waited to move north, for example, Charles Cotesworth regularly received letters and supplies from Eliza, Harriott, and Sally, including rum and home-cooked food. He had the wherewithal to strike up a correspondence with his nephew, Daniel Horry, and coach him on penmanship. He even retained his enslaved "body servant." The man named Fortune, he explained, "has waited upon me ever since the commencement of the present War."[24]

Charles Cotesworth and Thomas were forced to leave South Carolina, but they did so in the style befitting gentlemen. The two brothers sailed with their wives and children to Philadelphia, joined by Charles Cotesworth's brother-in-law, Edward Rutledge, and his family. (Sally Middleton Pinckney's sister Henrietta was married to Edward.) The easy passage took only eight days. A rich friend lent the Carolinians a house, where they all lived together. They socialized with local elites and members of the Confederation Congress. Thomas kept making progress. That summer he could walk a mile without giving out, though he still required a cane. They all remained in Philadelphia for most of the rest of the war, shielded by their wealth and rank from the worst of the conflict.[25]

Wealth did not buy women on the home front as much ease. Sometimes it put them in greater jeopardy. Because women provided medical treatment and supplies and even spied for the rebels, they became legitimate targets in Britain's campaign to subdue South Carolina. British forces also knew that otherwise resolute patriot commanders might be cowed—or at least humiliated—to learn how much their kinswomen suffered. The tactic should have felt familiar to slaveholders: they routinely brutalized the wives, daughters, and mothers of defiant black men.

Eliza could have evacuated with her sons, but she stayed behind with Harriott in 1781–1782 to weather wave after wave of danger, depredation, and indignity. She could not do justice in her letters to "the deplorable state of our Country." Soldiers on both sides continued to take whatever they wanted whenever they wanted. At one point in 1782, a band of British soldiers demanded Harriott's jewelry, among the last possessions she had been able to keep hidden. There seemed no bottom to the financial collapse. When Thomas and Charles Cotesworth left, the Continental dollar had already fallen in value to the British pound from 125:1 to 700:1.[26]

In time, the terror of war gave way to heroic family tales, passed across the generations by Pinckney women, about Pinckney women. For the rest of her life, Harriott Jr. remembered being fast asleep at the foot of her Grandmother Eliza's bed, at the height of the war, when Mary Motte, Betsey Motte Pinckney's sister, ran screaming into the room, chased by soldiers. Eliza jumped from the bed and hid Mary under her covers. As Harriott Jr. remembered the story in the nineteenth century, Eliza stood up to the soldiers, who "shrank abashed" before her. Perhaps. Or that might be a sanitized version of events to both honor and obscure what happened to women in the war.[27]

In another often-retold family memory, late one night, Harriott, heading a household of women at Hampton, heard the dreaded horse hooves in the distance. To her great relief, it was American General Francis Marion. The thankful women fed him dinner. Afterward, gratified to find a safe respite, General Marion fell asleep. Then Harriott heard more horses. As Banastre Tarleton pounded on her door, Harriott shook Marion awake, then rushed him out the back and stalled Tarleton. Tarleton searched Horry's home and discovered the ruse, but too late to catch Marion. The family story ends there, without ever saying what punishment Harriott received.[28]

Betsey Motte Pinckney's family told heroic stories of women in the war, too. In the spring of 1781, British soldiers confiscated Rebecca Brewton Motte's estate, Mount Joseph. The main house became a British command center. For the second time, Rebecca was compelled to vacate her home and provide for the British officers who moved in. In May 1781, patriot commanders Francis Marion and Henry "Light-Horse Harry" Lee decided that their best chance of countering the British lay in setting fire to Motte's house. They could then kill or capture the fleeing forces. Rebecca not only agreed to the scheme but, the family legend went, helped set the fire, becoming a folk hero in South Carolina.[29]

How many other South Carolina women suffered and sacrificed during the ordeal of 1780–1782? We will never know, because the historical record of their lives (if any ever existed) is lost. But the women who wrote their way into history—Eliza Wilkinson, Rebecca Brewton Motte, Harriott Pinckney Horry, and Eliza Lucas Pinckney—give a revealing glimpse.

"Fortitude," Eliza proclaimed in the midst of the occupation of South Carolina, "is as much a female as a masculine virtue." She was often afraid and sometimes miserable and generally furious at having to sacrifice so much of what she had devoted her life to creating. She had taken great pains to diversify her holdings in the 1760s and early 1770s, intentionally purchasing, she explained, "different kinds of property, and in four or five different parts of the Country." She'd been a supremely conscientious businesswoman. The war took it all. The lifestyle Eliza so meticulously created—the careful investments, the lavish homes, the seemingly rock-solid wealth—lay in shambles. She felt humiliated—and angry—to admit in the spring of 1782 that she lacked the money to pay a modest £60 bill. "A strange concurrance of circumstances must happen," she marveled, "before a person so situated, as I was, should become thus destitute of the means of paying a small debt." Her migraines returned, and she knew why: "My poor head always suffers for the feelings of my heart." But Eliza did not lose her confidence in the American cause or her resolve to rebuild her family legacy.[30]

Amid the tribulation, Eliza could see the war turning in America's favor. Although Cornwallis's surrender at Yorktown did not stop the fighting in South Carolina, the British controlled less and less of the state. By early 1782, they barely held Charles Town and that, as George Washington had predicted, required massive, unsustainable expenditures. Instead of subduing the rebels, Britain's total war campaign had enflamed them and hardened their resolve to exact revenge and win independence at any cost.

Eliza fully expected that when the British evacuated South Carolina she would reclaim her assets. That included the scores of people she enslaved. When Eliza calculated a way out of her family's financial free fall, she knew the answer: slavery. She thought it foolish, if not impossible, to try to sell enslaved laborers in the middle of the British occupation. Not only had they "behaved so infamously and even those that remaind at home so Insolent and quite their own masters," but the war so destabilized the slavery market that "it must be absolute ruin to sell at this time." Eliza was a patient woman. She would wait out the turmoil. The Americans would prevail, she believed, and when that happened, Eliza expected the value of her chattel to stabilize and her racial power to be reasserted.[31]

In August 1782, the commander of British forces in Charles Town received the order that everyone anticipated: vacate South Carolina. Nobodies from the edge of nowhere had defeated the world's greatest military. "I wish to the Lord they were gone to the Devil," said Edward Rutledge. But the unprecedented exodus took more time than anyone wanted. The relocation of massive numbers of people, black and white, civilians and soldiers, commenced in early October. In two months, more than nine thousand loyalists left South Carolina. Including soldiers and sailors and the smaller-scale evacuation from Savannah, Britain evacuated more than twenty thousand people in two months. "It is impossible to describe what Confusion people of all denominations seem to be in," marveled one loyalist soldier.[32]

Charles Cotesworth and Thomas got home shortly before the evacuations began. Eliza had not seen them or any of her grandchildren, except for Harriott Jr., in more than a year. There was yet another member of the next generation of Pinckneys. Sally Middleton Pinckney became pregnant in Philadelphia and delivered her third daughter in 1782. Eliza was thrilled to meet another Eliza Lucas Pinckney: "my little namesake," the baby's doting grandmother cooed.[33]

Within days of the first departures, the Pinckneys began planning a celebration. Eliza felt chastened by the prospect before her. Independence came at a punishing price. But she was proud of the American triumph and ready to look toward the future. Charles Cotesworth asked Harriott to buy "a pipe of good Madeira Wine, the older the better, Some Port wine, a Hogshead of Rum, a Hogshead of Porter, a double Gloucester Cheese." Like his mother, he anticipated that slavery would endure. In addition to all the alcohol, he needed Harriott to buy blankets and cloth for the people he enslaved.[34]

African Americans in the city were making their own plans, which did not include serving wine and cheese to their enslavers. The most startling scene in the devastated city beset with demoralized soldiers and traumatized civilians unfolded outside the Statehouse. General Alexander Leslie, responsible for the evacuation, agreed to return to white Carolinians the enslaved people under British protection—except for those individuals who had been promised freedom or feared retribution if left behind. Since personal testimony offered the only basis for determining promises and fears, Leslie appointed a board to interview claimants. Hundreds of black people lined up to testify to their right to freedom and get out of South Carolina. Some wore the English finery they had taken as they fled the homes of their former captors. They were joined in line by some white enslavers who had secured passes to enter the still-occupied city, in a futile effort to persuade the black people they had held in bondage to remain. Slave owners' complicity in inverting the social order grew out of desperation. By the war's end some twenty-five thousand enslaved people were "missing" from South Carolina—nearly one-quarter of the total black population. Some died from disease and deprivation, but most left to seek freedom.[35]

On December 14, 1782, the final British fleet weighed anchor and headed out to sea, charting courses for the Caribbean, England, Florida, and Canada. The elected governor of the state of South Carolina rode into Charles Town around 3:00 that afternoon. After two and a half years of military rule, civilian government was restored. Elites who returned to their perch cheered the departure. "I am in perfect rhapsody," proclaimed Eliza Wilkinson. "Really all nature smiles; these sons of plunder being driven away, has given life to every thing." Eliza Lucas Pinckney and her children felt just the same—save for Daniel Horry. His troubles were just starting. Edward Rutledge thought him "truly to be pitied . . . and ten Thousand Times more wretched" than anyone he knew. Having gambled on the British and lost, Daniel surrendered 12 percent of his wealth as a punishment for his disloyalty to the American cause. His in-laws kept him from losing much more.[36]

It turned out that Eliza's troubles weren't over, either. Two months after the British evacuated, her house at Belmont burned down. The fire, the Pinckneys concluded, started because of "the Carelessness of the Negroes who were cutting wood there." Perhaps. That same month the lead carpenter at Belmont, a man named Quaco, left on a fishing boat never to return. More likely than an accident, Quaco or someone he fled with had set the fire, as a step toward justice, or at least retribution. How much authority Eliza and other Lowcountry slave owners would be able to reassert in the new American Republic remained unclear.[37]

In the summer of 1783, Eliza, now a grandmother seven times over, penned the most cheerful letter she had written in years. She wrote it for her grandson, Daniel Horry, at his studies in England. "We have just heard of the Arrival of the Definitive Treaty of Peace in America!" she announced. "With the utmost gratitude to Heaven I received the glad Tidings."[38] Although her family had endured staggering losses during the war, Eliza felt only relief "when I see my dear children after being exposed to variety of suffering, danger, and Death, alive and well around me!" As she reflected on the fortitude Charles Cotesworth, Harriott, and Thomas showed during the war, Eliza told her grandson, "my heart overflows with gratitude to their great preserver, for continuing to me such children!" Fortunes could be rebuilt; family mattered most.

She was thinking a lot about the future of her family that summer. She told her grandson about the harrowing ordeal she and her children lived through. But Eliza still chose looking forward rather than back. "The change is so great and sudden!" Eliza explained, "it appears like a dream . . . that peace with all its train of blessings are return'd." Now she and her descendants could be happy. Ignoring any mention of Daniel's father except for one throwaway line at the end of the letter, Eliza offered up Charles Cotesworth and Thomas as models for the boy's future. History might not present Daniel with an opportunity such as his uncles had met, but, Eliza counseled, "you may be guided by the same principles of true honour and real virtue that have always actuated them." Following the high standards embodied by his uncles would, Eliza promised Daniel, honor his mother. "No pleasure," she explained, "can equal that which a mother feels when she knows her children have acted their part well through life."

Eliza believed the duty young Daniel owed was to his mother and the example he should follow came from his uncles—not his father. Daniel was a Pinckney after all, by blood if not surname. His grandmother let him know that she was counting on him, as the oldest of the next generation, to carry a proud legacy forward into a new age, in a new country.

PART SEVEN

Peace at Last

CHAPTER 15

Happy under Her Own Vine and Fig Tree

Even as she and her relatives toasted the British evacuation of Charles Town shortly before Christmas 1782, Eliza Lucas Pinckney could not ignore the turmoil afflicting the newly independent country: farms and fields devastated, relatives scattered, lifelong friends estranged, businesses collapsed. Like their neighbors and countrymen, the Pinckneys struggled to rebuild their fortunes in the mid-1780s.

The first years after the Revolutionary War were stamped by grievous personal losses, too. Eliza's favorite nephew, Charles Pinckney, died in 1782, shortly before the British evacuation. Sally Middleton Pinckney, Charles Cotesworth's wife, died less than two years later, in May 1784. Sally was so young, two months shy of her twenty-eighth birthday. She had been pregnant five times in her eleven-year marriage, burying two sons and delivering three healthy daughters. Her death was probably related to her final pregnancy—Eliza's namesake granddaughter. Charles Cotesworth was left at age thirty-eight with their girls: ten-year-old Maria Henrietta, Harriott, age seven, and the toddler Eliza Lucas. Grief-stricken and unsure what to do with these daughters, he followed the common course of young widowers: he sent them to live with his mother and sister. When Alice DeLancey Izard saw Harriott Pinckney Horry that winter, she thought her friend's daughter looked "melancholy, & no wonder. I dare say, she will spend the remainder of her life with him, in taking care of his Children." In fact, Harriott welcomed helping her brother and the motherless nieces she loved.[1]

Harriott's husband, Daniel, died in the fall of 1785, probably of acute liver failure. He bore all the symptoms: abdominal pain, disorientation, vomiting, and most telling, jaundice. Harriott nursed Daniel as his skin turned "as yellow as the darkest orange." Eliza, sensing the gravity of the situation, carried Harriott Jr. to Charleston—the city got its new name in 1783, to symbolize Carolinians' rejection of the British monarchy. Harriott Jr. was fifteen, nearly grown, but still, no one wanted her to watch her father die. Charles Cotesworth, still raw from the grief of losing his wife, stayed with Harriott but saw that nothing could be done for his brother-in-law.[2]

Harriott, like her mother before her, needed to write her son in England to tell him the horrible news. She couldn't bear to do it. Eliza, who had finished a far harder letter to her sons thirty years before, carried the burden. After several weeks, Harriott followed up. "I know," she wrote Daniel, "the pain you must have felt on the loss of a Parent who had always shewn you so much fondness." And, of course, she did. Daniel was just a little older than Harriott had been when her father died.[3]

Eliza's family was broken, again: two of her three children widowed, five of her grandchildren mourning a dead parent. That she had lived it all before probably brought her little comfort. No perspective can blunt the heartbreak of inconsolable children.

None of this robbed Eliza of her fundamental optimism. She continued in the 1780s and early 1790s to follow the advice she gave others: be "happy in your situation" and meet life's obstacles with "chearfulness and ease of mind." Eliza kept her boundless curiosity about the natural world, too. When enslaved fishermen at one of Thomas's plantations netted a large catfish just as it spawned, Betsey knew the specimens would intrigue her mother-in-law. She rushed to gather up the eggs and send them, preserved in rum, to Eliza.[4]

But by the time the Revolutionary War ended, Eliza was in her sixties—an old woman in South Carolina—and slowing down. She didn't want to live alone anymore out in the countryside at Belmont. Her house there burned at the end of the war, and she never rebuilt. In early 1786, Thomas and Charles Cotesworth, acting on her behalf, took out an advertisement in the Charleston newspaper offering to lease the Belmont property. It was "in planting order, with every necessary building in good repair." It lacked only a willing planter, which Eliza no longer was. That part of her life was over. She stayed at her city home and with Harriott, at Hampton.[5]

Even as her world narrowed, Eliza chose to live the last stage of life with sunniness and confidence. In the spring of 1786 she wrote an old friend a reflective letter about her long life. When she was young, Eliza observed, her friends had mostly been older than she. The prospect of aging, she said, never bothered her, except for one thing: the loss of friends. "Out living those we loved is what gives the principal gloom to long protracted life," Eliza concluded. So as she aged, she made younger friends, whom she now treasured. She doted on her grandchildren, growing up so fast. She thought about their future more than her own.[6]

Having arrived at what she cleverly called "this formidable period," Eliza neither pined for the past nor feared what lay ahead. Instead, she felt grateful for the life she'd made: satisfied. "I regret no pleasures that I can't enjoy," she proclaimed, "and I enjoy some that I could not have had at an early season." She worried a great deal about her erratic grandson Daniel Horry. He seemed determined to waste his life and dash her hopes. But her own children had become exactly the kind of people she had hoped for, and her other grandchildren seemed promising. "And what," she reflected, "is there in youthful enjoyments preferable to this."[7]

Eliza's only longing was for Charles. Thirty years after his death, she still missed her "ever dear Mr. Pinckney whose virtues I still revere whose memory I tenderly love." Time could never take that from her.[8]

Eliza did not take the lead in rebuilding the Pinckney family's fortune after the Revolutionary War. Her accomplished, independent children loved her and respected her, but they no longer needed her, at least not in the same way. She, in turn, trusted them and so gradually moved to the periphery. She admired how her children met postwar challenges and saw that they set a strong course for the family's long-term success. They were, in her eyes, "every thing the fondest parent could hope or desire." She was glad to be mostly retired, and, using the common biblical parlance of aging eighteenth-century patriarchs, said she was happy to be living under her own vine and fig tree.[9]

Charles Cotesworth, Harriott, and Thomas went forward to new adventures, in a new nation, but following family values instilled by their mother. All three were bookish and curious about the world. Charles Cotesworth's daughter said he read nearly constantly, from the moment he rose in the morning, whenever he had a spare moment, even "while he walked about and made his toilet." Thomas, too, made books "the companions of his life." The three siblings all regularly attended St. Philip's and St. Michael's and raised their children in the church. Charles Cotesworth often served on the St. Philip's vestry, and he was president of the Charleston Bible Society. All three liked botany and dabbled in medicine. They experimented with new crops and new technologies. They regimented their lives, paraded their power and wealth, and recorded their thoughts for posterity.[10]

After the war ended, Charles Cotesworth Pinckney began speculating in land with his brother-in-law, Edward Rutledge, and rededicated himself to his law career. The decade after the Revolution proved a lucrative time to be an attorney. Everyone was suing: to reclaim confiscated estates, recover prewar debts, and secure soldiers' pensions. Land disputes and bankruptcies multiplied, and families divided over wartime losses and the estates of fallen soldiers. Charles Pinckney had been right when he judged his first son ideally suited for a legal career. Charles Cotesworth was a meticulous thinker with an unsurpassed mastery of the law. He made an intimidating opponent, and his practice thrived.

Unlike Eliza and Harriott, Charles Cotesworth didn't choose to remain single after his mate died. It was harder for men to contemplate crossing into women's realm than vice versa. Whereas the women in the family decided they could manage just fine on their own after being widowed, Charles Cotesworth wanted and needed a second wife. In July 1786 he married Mary Stead. Thirty-four years old and descended from two prominent Lowcountry families, Mary was well educated and cosmopolitan from a youth spent in Europe. She fit right in with the Pinckneys. Mary and Charles Cotesworth never had any children together; she helped Harriott raise his daughters and traveled with him on his political assignments. A skillful leader, Charles Cotesworth eventually rose to the highest echelons of power in the new nation. He attended the Philadelphia Convention that drafted the U.S. Constitution. He was at the center of creating the South Carolina state constitution, too, as was Thomas Pinckney. In the late 1790s, Charles Cotesworth served as U.S. minister to France. He ran, unsuccessfully, for president of the United States in 1804 and 1808.[11]

Thomas Pinckney rode the circuit with Charles Cotesworth in the mid-1780s. His and Betsey's children visited Hampton regularly and for long stretches, growing up with their cousins and under the watchful eye of Grandmother Eliza. Reflecting the family's close connections—and adding to genealogical confusion—Betsey and Thomas named three of their children Thomas, Harriott, and Charles Cotesworth. As his plantation enterprise stabilized, Thomas immersed himself in state and national politics. He was brilliant and witty as well as supremely refined and always of "unruffled temper and perfect self-control": an ideal politician. He was elected governor of

South Carolina in February 1787. Charles Cotesworth, bursting with pride for his brother, bragged about the news to Eliza. Thomas also served in the late 1780s and early 1790s, at various times, in the South Carolina legislature, in the U.S. House of Representatives, and as the U.S. ambassador to Great Britain. Like his father before him, Thomas endured occasional setbacks and embarrassments. But his admirable service to his country greatly enhanced the Pinckney name.[12]

Eliza had worried so much about Thomas and Charles Cotesworth as they grew up abroad, with only her advisory letters to connect them to her. Now she felt pride and relief. They had turned out to be model men with sterling reputations who earned the trust of their countrymen. Their political appointments carried them to New York and Philadelphia and then across Europe. President George Washington offered both brothers federal judicial appointments and key diplomatic assignments. The Pinckney brothers' father and Grandfather Lucas had been important men, but only in their small corner of the English Atlantic. Thomas and Charles Cotesworth were statesmen who represented their country on the world stage.

Eliza was just as proud of her daughter: an independent woman and her mother's child in so many ways. Supremely responsible and capable, Harriott Pinckney Horry ran the vast Horry estate with skills unsurpassed by any planter-patriarch in South Carolina. "A Corrispondance between the factor and me seems to be just the thing that suits my Genius," Harriott recognized. Only thirty-seven when Daniel died and highly desirable as a wife, she rejected any thought of remarriage. Like her mother, Harriott remained an independent planter-patriarch for the rest of her life, until old age required her to rely on Harriott Jr. to run the family estate.[13]

In 1790, Harriott was probably the richest woman in South Carolina and one of the richest people in the state. In the economy of the eighteenth century, enslaved persons were the surest, most lucrative "property." When her husband Daniel died in 1785, assessors valued his estate at Hampton at £17,692. More than £15,000 of that derived from slavery. According to the first U.S. census in 1790, Harriott held 340 enslaved people at Hampton. They made Hampton one of the largest commercial agricultural enterprises in the entire South and Harriott the fourth-largest slaveholder in South Carolina. She enslaved more people than nearly all the powerful men in Charleston, including Henry Laurens, Gabriel Manigault, Senators Pierce Butler and Ralph Izard, and her two brothers.[14]

As their mother had taught them, the siblings acted as a fiercely unified team. Harriott occupied the center of the family businesses and caregiving, and her brothers respected her as an equal. They especially relied on her when politics consumed too much of their time or required them to leave South Carolina. In 1785, for example, Thomas got distracted with state politics—sucked into the "Vortex of the State House," he complained. Betsey was busy with their little children, and Harriott rose to their aid, advising Thomas about the best way to manage their estate. Thomas deferred to Harriott when it came to dealing with overseers, renters, and hired workers, and he avoided signing agreements until she weighed in. Thomas's overseers, including William Frazer, who managed Fairfield, reported to Harriott. William wrote to Harriott no differently than he would an experienced male planter: "You will be pleased to judge in this Case & write me what you think most proper to be done in this Situation of the Matter." Harriott also held final authority on matters related to controlling enslaved people at her brother's plantations. In October 1792, William updated Harriott about an ongoing conflict between two enslaved men who worked as drivers, Philander and Moses. William wanted to strip Moses of his responsibilities and mete out a violent "punishment as an example to others." But he knew he should not act without Harriott's permission.[15]

Trust among the three siblings was rock solid. They relied on in-laws, too, including Edward Rutledge. He and Charles Cotesworth remained friends and business partners long after Sally died. Equally trusted was Betsey Motte Pinckney's sister, Frances "Fanny" Motte Middleton. Harriott, Thomas, and Betsey partnered with Fanny on several ventures. Fanny was another young widow who led an independent life. When her husband died the year after their 1783 wedding, he left her with an infant son and a lot of complicated business interests. Fanny dove into the responsibilities, managing several plantations along the South Santee. In 1797, after her sister Betsey died, Fanny became Thomas Pinckney's second wife. But for fifteen years, she ran her own large estate. Like Eliza Lucas Pinckney and Harriott Pinckney Horry, Fanny Motte Middleton was supremely competent and very ambitious. At one of her plantations, enslaved men ran a rice mill, and she contracted with her neighbors and relatives to use it. In a typical transaction in 1790, Thomas revealed the group's dynamics: "Mrs. Middleton is beating with her Mill & will load your Schooner next Trip if," he told Harriott, "you chuse it." For expediency and for economy, Harriott owned her own vessels to move her crops and the people she enslaved around Lowcountry waterways. Ownership in this proposed transaction is key: women owned both the mill and the boat, and they made the decisions about how to use their property. Thomas, the only man in this network of women, acted as the go-between, conveying information for two rice planters who happened to be women. This was not unusual. Men routinely relied on their sisters and sisters-in-law and treated them as equal partners.[16]

The power and wealth held by such female planter-patriarchs as Harriott Pinckney Horry and Fanny Motte Middleton often required nonelite white men to defer to their authority. In the 1790s, white Americans increasingly moved toward stricter gender roles, idealizing white women as "republican mothers." "Proper" women managed the moral and educational preparation of their children and operated solely in the domestic domain, spurning politics and other participation in the "public"—increasingly, that is, the man's—world. Southern female planter-patriarchs stood apart, however. Though women like Harriott and Fanny did not attempt to vote or hold office, they confidently entered into business dealings and plantation management, just as their mothers had done.[17]

Soon enough, then, Eliza's children rebuilt their fortunes and climbed back to their perch of privilege. In the last years of her life, Eliza was again, her descendants bragged, "respected, admired, at the head of society in Carolina."[18]

The whole state, in fact, rebounded from the catastrophic Revolutionary War with remarkable speed. Visitors marveled at the turnaround. Johann David Schoepf, a German naturalist and physician, traveled across the United States in 1784. "Recovery is more rapid here," Johann saw when visiting South Carolina, "than in any of the other states; commerce is almost as flourishing and as extended as before the disquiets, and there is every reason to expect further." Charleston's private clubs, theaters, and other civic centers had reopened. Elites were again parading in the latest European fashions. "The ladies bestow much attention upon their dress," Johann noticed, "and spare no cost to obtain the newest modes from Europe. Milliners and hair-dressers do well here and grow rich." The rice and indigo fields again provided "abundant sources of wealth for many considerable families who therefore live their lives to the enjoyment of every pleasure and convenience." Timothy Ford, a New Jersey native who moved to South Carolina in 1785 to read law with his rich Lowcountry brother-in-law, likewise marveled at Charleston's fast recovery. Timothy was contemptuous of Carolinians' unabashed flaunting of slavery: "Accustomed to have every thing done for them they cannot or will not do anything for themselves." But he admired the stately town houses of Charleston and the enchanting estates that dotted the countryside. Ford was soon seduced by what he had initially maligned as the "luxury and dissipation" of slaveholders. He hunted in the mornings and danced and dined in the evenings, welcomed into the homes of leading Charlestonians, including the Pinckneys. Many days were whiled away in leisure. "Thursday we spend in romping about the plantation," Timothy recorded in his diary, "& in viewing the negroes at work at the rice."[19]

By 1790, the Pinckneys were as rich and powerful as ever, living in the sumptuous residences that visitors extolled. Charles Cotesworth and Mary Stead Pinckney owned various plantations across the Lowcountry, including Pinckney Island, and their Charleston home, tended by twenty enslaved workers. Harriott Pinckney Horry added a grand portico on the western entrance to her house at Hampton and improved the grounds. She owned a second home in Charleston, where thirty-four enslaved people lived and worked. Thomas Pinckney owned several homes, too. His Fairfield estate looked down on the South Santee River from the highest bluff in the area. The great house at Eldorado was designed to evoke a French chateau and was surrounded by English gardens. In the early 1800s, after he had lost his first wife and married his sister-in-law Fanny Motte Middleton, he lived part of the time at Fanny's stunning neoclassical Charleston mansion on George Street. It had a four-story self-supporting staircase that alone cost $14,000 when it was built in the late 1790s.[20]

Slavery underlay it all. After the Revolution, the Pinckney family, like Lowcountry elites generally, retained an unshakable commitment to slavery. Nothing in the Revolutionary era rhetoric about equality changed the racial attitudes of most white Carolinians. On that front, it seemed as if the Revolution had never happened. In the 1780s and 1790s, many states tried to reconcile the principles of the Revolution with their laws, gradually abolishing slavery. Outside of South Carolina and Georgia, there was widening recognition that continuing to hold people in bondage in an ostensibly free republic was hypocritical. But in the deep South, elites rebuilt their stately houses and sprawling plantations on slave labor—in fact and metaphorically.[21]

In 1785, Charles Cotesworth Pinckney published an essay in a local newspaper arguing that enslaved people were "the strength of this country" and "constituted its riches." No threat to the future of slavery, he concluded, could be tolerated. In May 1787, he carried that conviction to Philadelphia, where he served as a delegate to the convention that created the U.S. Constitution. Charles Cotesworth and Mary used the trip as a delayed honeymoon and left his three daughters with Harriott and Eliza. They took three enslaved people with them: Jenny, George, and Fortune, who had been Charles Cotesworth's "body servant" for years. The trip north turned into a terrible ordeal. Both Charles Cotesworth and Mary got horribly seasick and Mary developed a crippling fear of water. Before they even landed in Philadelphia, the couple made up their mind: "We shall return to Carolina by Land."[22]

At the Philadelphia Convention, Charles Cotesworth's signal contribution centered on protecting the future of slavery. He served with his second cousin Charles Pinckney (the namesake son of his cousin Charles) and kinsmen John Rutledge and Pierce Butler. Once there, the South Carolinians affirmed that their state would not cast off its long history of gentry power and racial hierarchy just because Americans had won their independence from Great Britain. Charles Cotesworth, the second-highest-ranking military officer at the convention, after George Washington, threatened to upend the meeting unless the Constitution protected slavery. "Property in slaves," he announced, "should not be exposed to danger, under a government instituted for the protection of property."[23]

For Charles Cotesworth and other deep South delegates, there would be none of the handwringing of the Virginians. Though never acting on their convictions, powerful slaveholders from Virginia routinely lamented the immorality of bondage, the betrayal of their newly treasured ideals, and the corruption of white children. Thomas Jefferson bemoaned the "unhappy influence on the manners of our people," especially the white children of enslavers like himself: "The parent storms, the child looks on, catches the lineaments of wrath . . . and thus nursed, educated, and daily exercised in tyranny, cannot but be stamped by it." He never wrote about what enslavement did to his children by Sally Hemings. Patrick Henry, another lifelong slaveholder, condemned slavery as an "abominable practice" that Christians should feel ashamed to tolerate. He judged the "violence and tyranny" antithetical to the teachings of the Bible, to just political principles, and to basic humanity. He conceded that he could manufacture no valid excuse for the fact that he enslaved people: "I will not, I cannot justify it." The Carolinians did. They invented pro-slavery politics in the crucible of the Revolutionary era. Eventually, it metastasized across the South.[24]

The Pinckneys and other Lowcountry elites wanted to resume as many of their traditions as soon as possible. Governor Thomas Pinckney presided at the

South Carolina Ratification Convention, affirming his brother's work at the Philadelphia meeting. He also led the state to reopen trade with English merchants and to adopt a lenient approach to reintegrating loyalists. His leadership, his relatives concluded, "had a happy effect in healing the breaches" among prominent South Carolinians who had divided over the Revolution. As the population of South Carolina shifted west, the Lowcountry continued to dominate the legislature, holding far more seats than was proportionally fair and setting state policies accordingly. In 1790, Charles Cotesworth played a key role in redesigning the state constitution, and he championed traditional moneyed interests. He and other Charleston elites had to compromise with their Upcountry counterparts on representation in the legislature and on moving the state capital from Charleston to Columbia. But there were no debates about slavery. Upcountry politicians fully embraced the racial values of Lowcountry elites.[25]

By 1790, Eliza Lucas Pinckney had become more a spectator in the life of the family than a leader. She admired the Constitution her sons championed and thought it in the best interest of her country—and her slaveholding family. But politics no longer interested her much. Eliza's last years were the most peaceful she ever had, the only ones unmarred by war. Though some things had changed radically—a new government, the end of imperial rule—South Carolina in the early 1790s remained fundamentally the same in most regards, especially the hierarchy that placed families like the Pinckneys at the top of society. The new state and new American Republic felt familiar and comfortable to the now retired planter-patriarch.

The Pinckneys faced setbacks, of course, and Eliza reasserted her authority when she thought it necessary. She was no doubt furious when Charles Cotesworth got into a scrape with a local hothead named Daniel Huger in 1785, just a year after Sally died. The two men decided to fight a duel, and Huger shot Pinckney in the thigh, though the wound was not serious. As doctors patched him up, Eliza monitored his treatment. The family kept the matter as quiet as they could. But it is easy to imagine the blistering rebuke Eliza dished out to her usually levelheaded and now middle-aged son. A widowed father of three little girls, engaging in a blood feud. How foolish and out of character! What would his daughters do without him? Charles Cotesworth learned his lesson. Later in life he called on the Society of the Cincinnati to work to end "this odious custom."[26]

Far more troubling was Eliza's only misbehaving grandchild, Daniel Horry. Like his grandmother and his uncles before him, Daniel grew up in

England, at a pricey boarding school far from his relatives. He was unlike them in every other regard. He complained constantly about being sent to England for his education, rebelled against his teachers, and mailed home slapdash, unintelligible letters. He fairly hemorrhaged money, hiring carriages to transport him to London plays and tailors to dress him in the latest style. He refused to shake what his frustrated mother called his "Fopperies."[27]

While Eliza left most matters to her grown children, she dove into the family effort to coach Daniel toward leading a respectable life. It was, she believed, important to the family's future that he try to become, in the language of the age, an "ornament to your family and Country." She held up Thomas and Charles Cotesworth as examples of responsible manhood, and cajoled, admonished, complained, and begged Daniel to follow their virtuous example. "You are," she reminded him, "in the way of one of the greatest advantages in life a liberal Education." His indifference to that education grieved her.[28]

When Daniel turned eighteen in the summer of 1787, he decided to indulge in a grand tour of Europe, not so much finishing his studies as abandoning them. Charles Cotesworth and Thomas, still hoping for a reversal in Daniel's character, asked their powerful friends for letters of introduction. In 1790, George Washington wrote the Marquis de Lafayette that it would be "a particular favor" to him to if Lafayette would meet the young man. Daniel used the entrée to court and marry Lafayette's grandniece, Eleanore Marie Florimonde de Fay la Tour de Maubourg. Around that time, Daniel made a highly unusual decision. Dropping his father's given name in favor of one that linked him to his maternal relatives, he proclaimed himself Charles Lucas Pinckney Horry—Pinckney Horry, for short. The name change did nothing to erase the character flaws.[29]

An outlier in a family of dutiful, accomplished men and women, Daniel remained the one great disappointment of his grandmother's old age. By 1790, Eliza had ten grandchildren, and she adored them. She was keen for them to share her religious faith, too. She quizzed them about the Bible passages employed in each Sunday sermon and carefully explained the parts she thought they misunderstood. She helped Harriott take care of what Harriott called "all our Children"—her daughter, Charles Cotesworth's three girls, and sometimes Thomas's children, too. Charles Cotesworth, Harriott, and Thomas trained their children to love and honor their Grandmother Eliza. As soon as they could write, they learned to carefully pen letters to their "dear Grandmama." Her granddaughter Maria Henrietta said, "All that she thought, and said, and did, was right."[30]

But there was no mistaking that Harriott, not Eliza, now headed the female-centered family. Wherever their political offices carried them, Thomas and Charles Cotesworth made sure to write to their mother, describing their adventures. But it was Harriott's advice and aid they solicited. They sent their aging mother jars of jelly and jugs of wine—treats to show their love. The brothers doted on their mother, but they didn't depend on her any longer. Even on gardening matters—long Eliza's purview—they relied on Harriott. Eliza developed a new curiosity about snails, and her children and grandchildren collected and shipped them to her. But this was a casual pastime of an old woman, not an entrepreneurial "scheme."[31]

Eliza had grown up with a sickly mother, a responsibility rather than a resource for her daughter, unable to lead the Lucas family in her husband's absence. Eliza was lucky to remain healthy nearly her whole life, aside from occasional migraines, but she also seemed resolved to be a positive and active presence in her children's and her grandchildren's lives even as they grew past needing her. She didn't allow the violence of the Revolutionary War to remake her into a fearful person. Even as time narrowed her world, she tried to remain curious and optimistic and engaged.

Old age sometimes tested that resolve. It was Christmas 1790, and Eliza was very excited. Thomas and Charles Cotesworth were back home with their wives and as free of political entanglements as they had been in more years than she could count. Everyone was healthy. And her treasured friend Mary Mackenzie Middleton was coming from England for the holidays. The Pinckney and Mackenzie women had become friends in the 1750s. Thirty-plus years had passed, including the Revolution, "without the least abatement of esteem or affection." Eliza loved Mary and happily awaited her return to South Carolina. Harriott was hosting a Christmas dinner at Hampton, with Mary as the guest of honor. Eliza had a thousand questions for Mary. She knew that she was traveling on the *Britannia*, but arrivals were never precisely timed. So Eliza sent an enslaved messenger into town to wait at the harbor and each day report back to Hampton. At last, just a few days before Christmas, the *Britannia* arrived. The unnamed man raced back to Hampton. But the news he brought devastated Eliza. Mary was dead, three weeks past. Every day Eliza waited, her friend lay in a watery grave. (With no safe way to transport the dead, ship captains dumped bodies at sea.) Instead of a Christmas celebration, Hampton's residents fell into mourning. Eliza couldn't bear to write to Mary's relatives, so Harriett did, explaining how much Eliza grieved for poor Mary. It never got easier for Eliza to lose a beloved friend.[32]

The hardest tradeoff of aging, though, turned out to be that long life claimed Eliza's independence. In the last five years of her life, she either quit writing or quit preserving her letters. Did her hands shake too much, or did her eyes fail her? Did later generations of Pinckney women toss aside the scribblings of an old woman collecting snails? Or did Eliza quietly turn over the duties of correspondence to Harriott? Harriott kept all her letters now; she was responsible for important business matters and the well-being of a large extended family.

Gradually, the story of Eliza's life moved out of her hands, beyond her control. Her children became her guardians, watching her health, managing her days, making more of her decisions. When Eliza got sick in the spring of 1790, for example, her doctor talked not to her but to Charles Cotesworth. Harriott—not Eliza—received the doctor's treatment plan. Eliza appeared to resist her children handling her and was a less than compliant patient. "Do prevail on [her]," Charles Cotesworth urged Harriott, "to attend to his advice."[33]

The closest relationship in the last decade of Eliza's life was with Harriott. They became friends as much as mother and daughter. They shared the same interests, a love of nature, of discovery, and of family. Harriott called Eliza "my much loved parental friend." Time tilted the dynamic of their relationship: Harriott grew up in Eliza's household, and Eliza grew old in Harriott's. If Harriott asserting her independence as a young woman and Eliza losing hers to age caused strains, that was not the story of their life together. Their bond was marked by mutual admiration and love. Mother and daughter stood side by side for the last great adventure of Eliza Lucas Pinckney's life.[34]

They waited on the sprawling front porch between the imposing white columns, in outfits fashioned just for the occasion. It was early May 1791, and the women at Hampton dressed that morning in bright summer colors. Harriott wore Eliza's prized salmon dress, made in England in the 1750s of silk grown at Belmont and transported back across the ocean to be worn on special occasions just like this. On top of their flowing dresses, they added identical sashes, decorated with the coat of arms of the United States, an eagle bearing a shield and gripping thirteen arrows in one talon and an olive branch in the other, and the motto "e pluribus unum." They wore matching headbands, too. They had attended to every detail of their appearance and the house, for nothing so grand had ever happened at Hampton. The most important man in America was coming for breakfast.[35]

Figure 13. Eliza Lucas Pinckney lived much of the last decade of her life at Hampton Plantation, her daughter Harriott Pinckney Horry's estate. Photo by author.

The president's visit was Harriott's doing; Eliza was a helper and a bystander by then. On April 14, 1791, Harriott Pinckney Horry wrote to George Washington, claiming by her actions a place at the forefront of American gentry culture and reflecting her identity as an independent planter-patriarch. "I heard with great pleasure that your Excellency proposed favoring this part of the Continent with a visit, and as my house on the Santee is in your route to Charleston," she hoped he would "do me the honor of making it a stage" during the journey. The letter was short, as there was no need for special appeals or introductions. President Washington knew Harriott's brothers well. But Harriott did not trade on her brothers' renown. She left no doubt: Hampton was *her* house, and it made a fitting "stage" for President Washington. She was right.[36]

Hampton was a large and elegant estate, similar to George Washington's Mount Vernon, which was also designed to impress guests. Harriott preferred mahogany furniture. She owned mahogany bookshelves, chairs, and dining tables and half a dozen mahogany beds and dressers. Gold-leaf mirrors hung from her walls, brass fixtures adorned the fireplaces. She walked on carpets woven in Turkey, decorated her windows with curtains made of cloth from China, rested on French sofas. She entertained guests in the east wing grand hall, which ran the width of the house. Light streamed in from windows running along three sides of the room, which was bordered with an elaborately carved cornice and topped with a turquoise ceiling. Harpsichord music filled the hallways, card tables could be brought out for lazy afternoon games. The rear entrance of the Georgian mansion opened onto gardens and then sloped down toward Wambaw Creek. More than thirty horses grazed in the fields, a carryover from Harriott's late husband's racing days. Magnolias and live oaks, draped in Spanish moss, flanked the road entry. A particularly large oak tree hid the view of her newly completed sweeping portico until visitors were nearly upon the house. It bothered Harriott that the tree diminished the awe for first-time guests. Perhaps, she thought, she would order it removed in the fall.[37]

George Washington accepted Harriott Pinckney Horry's offer: Hampton would be the first place he stopped as he made his way toward Charleston in May 1791. The trip was part of a series of journeys the president took to visit every state in the union. He hoped to bind the country together and to determine, he said, "how well the Inhabitants are disposed to support the General Government." Charleston, where he stayed a full week, was the longest stop on his two-month-plus trek.[38]

While Eliza and Harriott put the finishing touches on Hampton, Thomas Pinckney rode out to Georgetown to meet the president. George Washington spent Friday, April 29, at William and Mary Motte Alston's plantation. Mary was Thomas's sister-in-law, the sister of his wife Betsey. Thomas, George, and a handful of dignitaries left the Alston estate early Saturday morning, around 6:00, bound for Hampton. George rode in his carriage, Thomas on horseback. President Washington was consumed with appearances, and on his southern tour he adopted a specific routine as he entered each new locale. At a discreet spot near his destination, he halted the caravan, left his carriage, changed into his full military uniform, and mounted a white horse for the last, short leg of the day's journey.[39]

Not long before, the sound of approaching horses had spread fear through the women of Hampton. Now, they felt elation. As the party appeared in the distance, Eliza stood on one side of Harriott, Harriott Jr. on the other, with Charles Cotesworth's three daughters around them. George Washington walked up the steps to greet them around 11:00 A.M. Breakfast was waiting. The enslaved cooks at Hampton had been up for hours, preparing a feast they could not eat.[40]

Harriott was the host. Eliza "assisted her in entertaining the President."[41] The conversation came easy, for the three had much in common. They were planters and entrepreneurs, fascinated by the natural world and agricultural innovations. George, like Eliza, had shrewdly diversified his business interests in the 1750s. They were both aging patriots, too, he ten years younger than she. He must have talked commerce with Harriott. She commanded slightly more enslaved workers at Hampton than he did at Mount Vernon. Charles Cotesworth's two youngest daughters were around the same age as Washington's twelve-year-old step-granddaughter, Nelly, whom he and Martha were raising. The Pinckney girls probably played the harpsichord for him, reminding him of Nelly. He stayed most of the day.

As George and Harriott strolled across Hampton, she pointed out the vexing oak tree and described her plans to remove it. He had reoriented the front of Mount Vernon to impress visitors, so he understood her thinking. But he liked the beautiful tree. He told her he wouldn't think of cutting it down, and so she didn't. The tree, now called the Washington Oak, still stands at Hampton, more than two hundred years after the president's visit.[42]

The next morning's newspaper in Charleston announced the imminent arrival of President Washington. He had dined the day before "at Mrs. Horry's"—everyone knew who she was. In Lowcountry circles, Harriott was as well regarded as her brothers.[43]

The Pinckneys remained at the center of the action when President Washington visited Charleston. Eliza's grandnephew, Charles Pinckney, was governor of South Carolina. Given to vanity, Charles relished the glory of serving as the president's primary host. George declined Charles's repeated pleas to stay at his home—as he did every such offer. Disappointed, Charles resolved to miss no chance to squire George about town and stay in the spotlight. In advance of his arrival, Governor Pinckney assured President Washington that "the people of this country feel themselves on this occasion so strongly bound by every principle of Gratitude and affection that no exertion will be wanting on their part to render your stay among us as agreeable as possible." And none was.[44]

Charlestonians knew how to celebrate. In anticipation of Washington's visit the legislature repaired roads and bridges. City leaders hired the prominent painter John Trumbull to commemorate the visit. Residents washed the city sidewalks. Poets and writers penned orations. Business owners blanketed the city with banners welcoming the president. A special platform was erected at the Exchange, just for Washington to speak. The president's entry by sea was stunning. Men wearing matching light blue silk jackets—dyed with indigo—rowed Washington into the harbor. Musicians sailed alongside in two boats, serenading him. More than forty other vessels were filled with spectators jostling to see the president. Music wafted out of St. Philip's Church, competing with a marching band.[45]

Every day brought new displays of Charlestonians' patriotism, wealth, and refinement. George Washington could not help being impressed. He proclaimed the people he met "wealthy—Gay—& hospitable." As he was accustomed to doing at Mount Vernon, he elided the enslaved people in Charleston and all their labor that lay behind his enjoyments.[46]

Often joined by Charles Cotesworth and Thomas, George toured battlefields and fortifications and explored the city's architecture and commerce. Each night special lanterns hung on ships in the harbor, to light up the sea. Other illuminations sparkled across the city. Residents crowded into the streets to attend balls, banquets, concerts, and parties. Five hundred people sat down to a 10:30 P.M. supper after an evening of dancing at the Exchange. Nearly a thousand attended a concert at the St. Cecilia Society.[47] Charles Cotesworth and Thomas attended private events with the president, too, including a gathering for the Society of the Cincinnati. (Washington, Alexander Hamilton, and the Pinckney brothers were the organization's first four national presidents.) George was clearly more impressed by Eliza's sons than her grandnephew, the grasping governor. While making his way back to Mount Vernon, he wrote Charles Cotesworth and asked him to join the United States Supreme Court. He graciously declined, but eventually agreed to serve as minister to France. In the fall of 1791, the president persuaded Thomas to become minister to Great Britain, a position Charles Pinckney, Eliza's grandnephew, had unsuccessfully lobbied to get.[48]

Eliza would have been unable to contain the pride she felt in all three of her children that summer. She was doubtless gratified to meet George Washington, too. She always loved socializing with interesting and important people. But her mind was on the future of her family. And that future was, she saw, rock solid. That Harriott, Charles Cotesworth, and Thomas had earned the respect of the president of the United States fulfilled her highest hopes. In 1791, Eliza Lucas Pinckney was a mother serene in the knowledge that her children "acted their part well through life."[49]

CHAPTER 16

One Last Journey

Eliza Lucas Pinckney was nearing seventy years old when her youngest son—in his forties and not so young any longer—accepted appointment as United States minister plenipotentiary to Great Britain. Thomas sailed to England in 1792 as his country's highest-ranking diplomat. Unlike his father forty years before, Thomas was not going to London to appeal to powerful men. Instead, he would number among them. The prestigious appointment brought some unwelcome repercussions. Betsey did not want to go; she wept when Thomas told her the news, and she was crying when they left Charleston. And the move, Thomas complained, "deranges every domestic plan I had formed." Still, he knew he could depend on Harriott to manage his affairs in his long absence. In the course of his diplomatic duties, Thomas met regularly with King George III. Decades before, Eliza had visited the young heir to the throne as a deferential subject; Thomas now attended royal levees as the ambassador of his country. Ever witty, Thomas quipped about occasional frustrations of his duties, including George III's efforts to steer their conversations toward "the weather or other topic equally important."[1]

Eliza had been healthy her whole life, aside from her recurring headaches, but shortly before Thomas sailed to England, she developed a rash and a fever that wouldn't go away. Charles Cotesworth eventually diagnosed it as erysipelas, sometimes called St. Anthony's fire. Though a hopeful lot, Eliza's children understandably worried. Erysipelas can spread to the bloodstream and prove fatal. All three siblings corresponded about Eliza's health that spring, with Charles Cotesworth and Harriott trying to keep Thomas up to date. In late May, a much-relieved Charles Cotesworth assured Thomas that Eliza was on the mend. The health reprieve proved short-lived.[2]

Sometime in the summer of 1792, Eliza discovered a tumor in her breast. "We sent to the Northward for Leeches to apply to my Mothers Cancer," Charles Cotesworth wrote Thomas in London. Charles Cotesworth and Harriott had sought out one of the top physicians in the most medically advanced city in America, Philadelphian Dr. William Shippen Jr., to find the best kind of leeches. "But," Charles Cotesworth continued, "Dr. Shippen says there are none of the right sort there they having the same defect that ours have, not sticking to the flesh."[3]

Thomas would have felt the dread filling the Pinckney household as soon as he read the letter. As Harriott and Charles Cotesworth scrambled for a solution, they spared no expense or trouble. The search for proper leeches in Philadelphia having failed, Charles Cotesworth asked Thomas to scour London. Having consulted with experts, he offered specific advice to his younger brother about shipping the leeches across the Atlantic: "To preserve their lives, the water must be changed once a day at least," while adding that "we have had them live a week here in the same water without dying." He urged Thomas to "enquire on this subject of some experienced Apothecary." Upset over his mother's diagnosis, America's most important diplomat went running around London looking for leeches.[4]

The Pinckney siblings grew increasingly desperate in 1792–1793. Charles Cotesworth queried all his connections and found out that the most innovative cancer treatments in America were being undertaken by Dr. James Tate in Philadelphia. Tate, Charles Cotesworth learned, was "famous for the great Cures he has made in eradicating Cancers without either the Knife or Caustic." Even George Washington lauded his skills. Dr. Tate, the president said, "is possessed of the valuable secret of curing Cancerous complaints."[5]

Cutting off or burning away her tumors was not an option for Eliza. At age seventy, she was not strong enough to endure the agony of breast surgery. The English writer Fanny Burney underwent an operation for breast cancer when she was in her fifties, and she graphically described it to her sister. Wine was the only painkiller she received. "When the dreadful steel was plunged into the breast, cutting through veins, arteries, flesh, nerves," Burney recounted, "I began a scream that lasted unintermittingly during the whole time of the incision, and I almost marvel that it rings in my ears still! So excruciating was the agony. . . . I then felt the knife rankling against the breastbone, scraping it! This performed, while I remained in utterly speechless torment." The doctor, Fanny remembered, was "pale nearly as myself, his face streaked with blood and its expression depicting grief, apprehension, and almost horror."[6] Abigail Adams Smith, the daughter of Abigail and John Adams, also underwent breast cancer surgery. She was in her forties when the famous physician Benjamin Rush told her and her stricken parents that "there was no chance for her Life, but by an immediate operation." The surgery took four doctors and an agonizing twenty-five minutes—without anesthesia—followed by nearly an hour dressing the wound. The doctors removed Abigail's entire breast, and though the wound started to heal in four or five weeks, she was so weakened by the procedure that she remained at her parents' home for months.[7]

Harriott and Charles Cotesworth seized on Dr. Tate's noninvasive approach. He was part of a cohort of Philadelphia physicians seeking cures for cancer. Tate sometimes performed cancer surgeries, but he also used arsenic and a combination of pills—of unknown makeup—and tincture applications. Harriott and Charles Cotesworth didn't probe the details. Tate seemed to them the best of their dwindling options.

Then they faced a bigger obstacle: Eliza refused to go to Philadelphia. Charles Cotesworth tried mightily to pay Dr. Tate to come to South Carolina, but he could not be bought. It was, the doctor repeatedly explained, "impossible for him to leave Pennsylvania where he had many Patients without drawing upon himself very heavy censure."[8]

Dr. Tate would gladly treat Eliza, he said, but she had to come to Philadelphia, and the sooner the better. Whatever eighteenth-century doctors misunderstood about cancer, they knew it metastasized. Trying to counter Eliza's reluctance, Dr. Tate reported that "he had very lately cured a Lady of Seventy Years of age who had been in a most deplorable State." Eliza's local doctor, Matthew Irvine, agreed that Eliza's best chance lay in Philadelphia, and he "pressed this matter with great earnestness." Harriott and Charles Cotesworth "joined warmly in the requisition, & entreated her to consent to a voyage to Philadelphia in order to try the Efficacy of Tate's Remedies, of which we had heard such high accounts." Eliza held fast.[9]

By mid-April 1793, the cancer had progressed so far that Charles Cotesworth and Harriott could see several tumors. Hoping to coax his mother, Charles Cotesworth proposed that the entire family relocate to Philadelphia.

Money being no object, they could take care of Eliza together. Eliza did not want to leave South Carolina, certainly not via an ocean voyage. Any trip involved danger, many were violent, and some were deadly. Josiah Quincy traveled from New England to South Carolina and offered a harrowing if not unusual account of what sailing along the eastern seaboard entailed. On the best days, his seasickness was unbearable: "I was too weak to rise and in too exquisite pain to lie in bed." Two people carried him to the deck, where he vomited until he fainted. Then the ship sailed into a storm. "The scene," he recalled, "beggars all description." "The sea rose in mountains on each side," as the ship was tossed in the air and then deluged beneath waves. Josiah tied himself into his bed to avoid being hurled across his cabin. "In short," he concluded, "horror was all round us."[10]

Eliza knew the perils of the trip, from her own terrible voyage in the 1750s, from stories like Josiah Quincy's, and from the catastrophes that beset her friends and family over the years. Miles Brewton and his whole family drowned at sea on the way to Philadelphia in the 1770s. Charles Cotesworth and Mary had gotten violently ill on their ship to Philadelphia just a few years before. Mary Mackenzie Middleton's death on her Atlantic crossing remained a fresh wound.

Also, Eliza probably understood the futility of it all. She'd sat vigil with the terminally ill: her friend Elizabeth Lamb Pinckney, her son George and grandson Charles Cotesworth, her husband Charles. And she knew herself. A woman as self-aware and experienced with death as Eliza surely understood that the end of her life was near. But her children kept pleading.

So, against her better judgment, Eliza reluctantly consented to a dangerous voyage seeking a fanciful cure to placate her frightened children. She insisted that the family's future be protected at all costs. She already had one beloved child, Thomas, an ocean away from his siblings. She would not abide all three of them being gone from South Carolina at the same time, leaving no one to protect what she had spent a lifetime building and rebuilding. More to the point, she refused to wager all their lives on a fool's errand to Philadelphia. As Charles Cotesworth reported to Thomas, Eliza "said she would not by any means consent to risque us all at once." She needed Harriott. But under no circumstance could Charles Cotesworth make the trip. "She seemed positive on this point," Charles Cotesworth told Thomas: "only my Sister & Maria & the two Harriotts"—Harriott's daughter and his own—could go. Given no other choice, he said, "I acquiesced."[11]

Harriott Pinckney Horry immediately set to making plans. Since she was responsible for Thomas's business and planting interests during his diplomatic assignment, she needed to attend to those matters in addition to packing for the trip. She settled some accounts in town and made sure Thomas received a bill of exchange as well as precise information on the price she got for his rice.[12]

Harriott was terrifically organized. In advance of their travels, she catalogued everything they would need to take with them. During the trip she also carefully recorded all her expenditures. She made sure to carry plenty of supplies, starting with medicine for onboard the ship and once they reached Philadelphia. She packed boxes of clothes, including "sea clothes" for her and Eliza; music and books; towels, tablecloths, eighteen pillows, even mattresses. She shipped livestock, rum and brandy, and lots of food, including raspberry vinegar, capers, limes, and mangoes—all they might want during their journey.[13]

Harriott also chose the enslaved women and men she forced to go with her. She picked three women: Sibby, Hannah, and Dye, probably for the nursing care they could provide Eliza in between cleaning and cooking for everyone. She took Ned and Isaac, too, to run errands and gather firewood and do other physical labor. Sibby was perhaps the oldest person on the trip except for Eliza. After the Philadelphia trip, Hannah, Ned, and Isaac disappeared from the historical record. They probably all died as they'd lived: enslaved by some of the Pinckneys. Sibby died at Hampton in 1796. Dye was young and probably Harriott's personal maid. When she drew up her will in 1828, Harriott left Dye a £10 life annuity in her will "in consideration of her past services." But she did not emancipate Dye.[14]

The Pinckney women showed no reluctance about transporting enslaved people to Philadelphia, the seat of the still-new federal government, although they knew about the growing antislavery convictions there. Pennsylvania legislators had recently passed a law freeing enslaved people who resided in the state more than six months. This posed a risk for slaveholders moving to the country's capital and presented an opportunity to the people they enslaved. On the other hand, even the president of the United States held people in bondage in Philadelphia. George and Martha Washington were attended in their residence and at official events by enslaved workers—"servants" became the preferred euphemism. The Washingtons devised a way of skirting the Pennsylvania law: they cycled men and women back to Mount Vernon, restarting again and again the clock on their eligibility for emancipation.[15]

Perhaps Harriott thought that she would not remain in Philadelphia long enough for the law to take effect. In any event, she had never gone anywhere or done much of anything without slave labor. She wasn't going to start while trying to save her mother's life.[16]

Harriott had never visited Philadelphia, but she could draw on her brothers' experience. Charles Cotesworth and Thomas knew the city. They had lived there together in the last stages of the Revolutionary War, Charles Cotesworth had been there all summer in 1787, and Thomas visited in 1792 on his way to London. Harriott also turned to South Carolina friends to make her plans. Charlestonians temporarily residing in Philadelphia for political office or business congregated together. Some wealthy Lowcountry families even bought stately brick town houses in a fashionable downtown neighborhood on Spruce Street, around Ninth and Tenth Streets. They called it Carolina Row.[17]

Harriott contracted with Mary Williams, who ran a boardinghouse at Spruce and Third Streets, to rent four rooms: two bedchambers, a parlor for greeting guests, and a drawing room. For $45 per week, Williams provided everything except liquor, candles, firewood, linens, and "provisions for my Negroes." The Pinckney women would be near Carolina Row but not at the center of it, close enough to get any help they needed but in a quieter location for Eliza's much-hoped-for recovery.[18]

News of Eliza Lucas Pinckney's imminent departure for Philadelphia quickly spread. Friends in Charleston and Philadelphia and even London shared with the Pinckney siblings their hope, as one friend put it, that "Mrs. Pinckney may reap the advantages expected from the assistance of an emanant Phisician at that Place."[19]

They all rose early, before the dawn, on Wednesday, April 10, 1793. They boarded the *Delaware* in the first morning light. The captain, James Art, was trustworthy. He regularly made the trip between the two port cities. Traveling with Eliza and Harriott were Harriott's daughter Harriott Jr., who was twenty-two, and Charles Cotesworth's two oldest daughters, Maria Henrietta, who was around nineteen, and sixteen-year-old Harriott. It was fitting that Eliza made this trip in the company of kinswomen, as so much of her life had been so female-centered.

The granddaughters who escorted Eliza ranged, coincidentally, from age sixteen to twenty-two—the very years that Eliza had been left to manage her family holdings in her own youth. On this trip, as with every other in her seventy years, she was attended every step by people she and her family enslaved. They headed north on the Atlantic, just as she'd done when she left Antigua.

Eliza first entered the South Carolina colony on the eve of the 1739 Stono Revolt—the largest uprising ever on the mainland of North America. She and her family moved from Antigua, in part, because of an aborted slave rebellion on that Caribbean island. More than fifty years later, she left South Carolina just as the greatest slave uprising in modern history reached Charleston's shores. It started in late April 1791, on Saint-Domingue, a French colony in the Caribbean. Within weeks, 100,000 people were involved in an islandwide fight for freedom, and the movement kept growing. The revolutionaries eventually overthrew white domination and created Haiti, the first republic in world history led by formerly enslaved black people. It was the last and most transformative of the eighteenth-century Atlantic Revolutions, and it terrified enslavers. "The scourge which is now laying waste [to] the most valuable French possessions in America," one dispatch warned, "threatens all the neighbouring Colonies." White refugees from Haiti fled to South Carolina from late 1791 through 1793. Perhaps Eliza saw some of the ships from the deck of the *Delaware*.[20]

Captain Art set sail at 8:00 A.M., but a headwind forced him to turn back. They weighed anchor at Sullivan's Island until the evening. Both Harriott and Eliza got terribly sick. The next morning, the ship managed to make it out onto the high seas, but even Captain Art found the waters "very rough, disagreeable," and everyone was seasick. Harriott ruefully recorded that when the *Delaware* entered the gulf stream on Friday "we tumbld dreadfully all night with a head wind." Saturday and Sunday brought no relief. As they skirted Cape Hatteras, North Carolina, the seas remained "very boistrous." On Sunday, Harriott saw a waterspout rising in the distance. Captain Art said it was the largest he'd ever seen, and it was headed straight for the *Delaware*. The ship, Harriott explained in her understated way, "was put about." Then the waterspout suddenly dissipated, and the voyagers carried on.[21]

A week into her journey, Harriott found no relief from her ordeal. Since leaving Charleston, she groused, "we have had the most dismal passage." Captain Art ruefully concurred. He told Harriott he "never had yet so violent a passage." During these dangerous, trying days, Harriott found little time to elaborate on their ordeal in her travel journal—of course, she kept a written record of this important trip. The entries were quick and practical and mostly bleak. While she made no mention of her mother's health, it is not difficult to imagine how challenging it would have been. Eliza was already weakened by the cancer when they left Charleston, and a week on a storm-tossed sea would make even the healthiest traveler sick. Two days of relative calm, on April 17 and 18, probably gave Harriott a chance to stabilize her mother, to tend to her daughter and nieces, and to recover herself.[22]

On Friday, April 19, Captain Art sailed onto the Delaware River. The Pinckney women passed through New Castle and Wilmington, Delaware, and then Chester, Pennsylvania. Harriott breathed a huge sigh of relief: "We went up gent[ly] with the tide and without wind." The calm allowed her time to reflect on her surroundings. It's easy to picture Harriott pointing out to her mother the beauty of the countryside and agricultural improvements made by mid-Atlantic farmers. As they glided up the Delaware River, Harriott marveled at the "fine fields of Wheat and the fruit trees in bloom," the verdant rolling hills, and the cherry blossoms near Wilmington. On the New Jersey side of the river, however, "there is the greatest difference in the world in the appearance of the Country." That landscape left Harriott decidedly unimpressed. "On the Jersey side," she recorded, "appears poor sandy land very little cultivated and poorly settled." At long last they arrived in Philadelphia. It was 8:00 on Saturday morning, April 20, and, to Harriott's great frustration, "the weather miserably bad."[23]

During the voyage, Eliza's health deteriorated to the point that she was too weak to walk. Harriott noted in her journal that her mother was "very sick and obliged to be lifted in a chair into the boat"—no doubt by Ned and Isaac. The water churning in the harbor rocked the smaller boat as they made their way toward the dock. South Carolina friends waited for Eliza's arrival. Alice DeLancey Izard, wife of U.S. Senator Ralph Izard, had sent her coach to meet the Pinckneys. It stood at the ready and immediately carried the women to their boardinghouse. Alice came straightaway to visit Eliza. No one could have imagined, sitting together that dreary April day, what the future would hold for these two families. In time, Alice's son Ralph married the youngest of Charles Cotesworth's daughters, the one named Eliza after her grandmother.[24]

Though doubtless heartened by at last being off that dreadful ship, Eliza remained grievously ill. "My mother," Harriott closed the day's entry, "continued sick all day." Dr. William Shippen Jr. visited on Eliza's first day in the city. Eliza "had a bad night" and he came back again on the twenty-first and examined her breast. Two days later, Dr. James Tate arrived.[25]

Women representing the leading families of Philadelphia also came calling. They offered whatever help they could to Eliza and her main caregiver,

Harriott. Eliza's visitors read like a who's who of Philadelphia society: wives of congressmen and senators; women from the prominent Shippen, Willing, and Powel families; female representatives from the family of Chief Justice Benjamin Chew, who lived within a block of the Pinckneys' boardinghouse; Elizabeth Schuyler Hamilton, whose husband was secretary of the Treasury. Abigail Adams would surely have visited, but she was not in Philadelphia that spring. The most important men in the city came, too, including Supreme Court Justice James Iredell, Alexander Hamilton, Congressman Lambert Cadwalader, General Benjamin Lincoln, the wealthy businessman William Bingham, and President George Washington. Because Martha Washington was sick, she did not visit in the first days after Eliza's arrival in Philadelphia. When a week passed and she had still not recovered, George came himself. It was only a few weeks past his second inaugural, a modest event that had taken place in the Senate chambers on March 4, 1793. Busy with varied political and diplomatic matters, he made time to show his respects to Harriott and Eliza. The president, Harriott wrote in her journal, was "extremely kind & said as Mrs. Washington was sick he offered in her name as well as his own every thing in their power to serve us." He urged Harriott to be candid and see "no ceremony" in seeking what she and her mother needed.[26]

As soon as they settled in, Harriott wrote to Charles Cotesworth. In her absence, he'd taken charge of the family interests in South Carolina while maintaining his legal practice. He was also responsible for passing all news on to Thomas in London. In the meantime, he waited.[27]

Thomas waited, too, but the waiting was harder for being longer. In his worry, Thomas misplaced the cypher he and other diplomats used for discussing confidential matters in code. Thomas was mortified. Perhaps, he sheepishly confessed to Secretary of State Thomas Jefferson, he had mailed it to someone by accident. Jefferson revised the code and sent Thomas a replacement.[28] And Thomas had another problem. He wanted to tell Daniel/Pinckney Horry face-to-face the concerning news about his grandmother's health, but his nephew kept stalling on a visit. Thomas told Harriott that he had avoided mentioning the situation in letters, "as I have been so long in expectation of telling him in person of all our domestic concerns." Thomas was worried about Eliza's feelings more than anything else. He hoped that Eliza understood that her grandson's silence was owing to ignorance of her health rather than indifference.[29]

As promised, as soon as Charles Cotesworth got Harriott's letter, he wrote to Thomas. Their mother's passage, he reported, "was very boisterous, & has much weakened her." After making land, she was "tormented" for several days with relentless vomiting. Dr. Tate judged Eliza so weak that he "was unwilling to undertake the cure."[30]

Even in her frail state, Eliza Lucas Pinckney remained a woman to be reckoned with. Perhaps she had come too far and endured too much to give up. Or maybe she just wanted to fight to live, to get back home to South Carolina. Either way, Dr. Tate proved no match: "Mother expressed so much anxiety that he should attempt it that he has consented." Still, Charles readied his younger brother for what might come next. Because of their mother's terrible weakness, "we have to apprehend the greatest misfortune that can befall us."[31]

Thomas was once again far away, just as he'd been as a boy. But now he was a man, with many wealthy and powerful friends in Philadelphia. He told them to stand ready to help his mother and sister. The week of their arrival in town William Ward Burrows, a South Carolina native living in the city, assured Thomas that he had received Thomas's letter and that he and his wife had already visited Eliza and Harriott and "shall be happy if we can in any Measure be instrumental to their Comfort or Pleasure." William had also spoken with Drs. Shippen and Tate, and he promised Thomas that Eliza was getting the best care possible. But, William added, Eliza's age and the advanced state of her cancer worried the physicians: "They think had it been known to them any time sooner from its earliest Appearance, they would soon have eradicated it."[32]

Outside Mary Williams's boardinghouse, Philadelphia buzzed with activity. Exploring it would have delighted Eliza, if only she had been healthy and strong. The largest city in the United States, with more than 42,500 residents, it was a model of innovation and public amenities. Streetlamps lit paved roads, and residents enjoyed public water pumps and verdant parks. Charles Willson Peale ran the country's first museum in Philadelphia. The cultural center of the country, Philadelphia was home to the Philosophical Society and the Library Company. Philadelphia was richly diverse. The booming economy and Atlantic Revolutions drew immigrants from Scotland, Germany, Ireland, France, and Haiti. Philadelphia's streets crowded with famous former revolutionaries and luminaries from all the states. John Bill Ricketts had recently opened his circus—the first ever in America—to the enchantment of Philadelphians. Among other breathtaking feats, Ricketts could juggle oranges while standing astride two horses as they galloped around in a circle. Performers also included a tightrope walker, acrobats, singers, and a circus clown. President Washington, a masterful horseman, bought tickets for his whole family. Philadelphians were also intrigued that summer by the planned construction of the permanent federal city. The week the Pinckney women arrived, commissioners considered an architect for the main hotel of Washington, DC. Ten designs were presented, "so varied in their beauties, as to astonish the collection of gentlemen who were present at the pleasing exhibition." The commissioners ultimately chose a drawing by Charlestonian James Hoban. There was a foreign policy crisis brewing, too, around the arrival in Philadelphia of "Citizen Genêt" on May 17, 1793. Edmond Charles Genêt first entered the United States in Charleston, coincidentally, two days before Harriott and Eliza left.[33]

Inside the boardinghouse on Spruce Street, the world fell away. Harriott took no notice of Philadelphia. She mentioned in her journal none of the sights and sounds of the city and, uncharacteristically, offered no comparison to her hometown. Caring for her mother consumed her. On May 7: "My mother very ill a continual sick Stomach and reching." Eliza couldn't keep down the medicine Dr. Tate prescribed. Dr. Shippen took another tack, which seemed to alleviate her vomiting, but she remained, Harriott recorded, "extremely weak." The next day Eliza quit vomiting enough to take Dr. Tate's medicine, and "tho' her stomach appears considerably stronger she does not in general increase in strength." Alas, Harriott admitted, the treatment "hitherto produced no effect."[34]

Eliza woke up feeling stronger on May 9. Harriott used the reprieve to take one short break from her caregiving. Alice DeLancey Izard picked up her and the three young women for a carriage ride about town. Dye, Sibby, and Hannah, who had been working the whole time, took charge of Eliza. Harriott "saw several good houses," including where the Washington family lived. But her heart wasn't in sightseeing. So Alice took her to the city hospital, known then as the "bettering house." It was located on Spruce, between 10th and 11th Streets, and was America's first government-sponsored hospital, dating back to the 1730s. Ostensibly, Izard carried the Pinckney women to the hospital "to walk in the gardens." Harriott, for a moment returning to her old self, marveled at "the greatest number of Tulips I ever saw." But the trip was more strategic than relaxing. Dr. Tate had long urged Harriott to visit patients there, "to see some of his cancerous patients who were cured, and some who were then under care." Tate thought she might benefit from directly asking his patients about their treatments.[35]

As Harriott considered her mother's dire straits, she wondered whether she had made the wrong decision in bringing her to Philadelphia. Was Eliza facing a cure worse than the disease? Carrying her so far for medical care was unusual. Most sick people were treated at home, by female kin and, occasionally, local doctors they knew and who visited their homes. Harriott worried about the newness of what she was doing for her mother—or was it to her? But the afternoon she visited Dr. Tate's patients, she met two women who eased her mind. One woman had "scars and seams on her breast," which Harriott took as a physical sign that her cancer "must have been bad indeed." The other, who'd had "a large Tumor in her breast" now seemed "half cured and in a fair way of doing well." Harriott said she "rec'd much satisfaction from seeing them." Perhaps she was doing the best by her mother after all.[36]

The next day, Harriott returned to the quiet world inside the boardinghouse, to caring for her mother, who remained "very sick indeed and extremely weak." There was hope, though. Dr. Tate "perceived that his Medicine began to operate upon the Cancer."[37]

And then Harriott went silent. The last two weeks of Eliza's life were unspeakably awful. Harriott stopped making even cursory notes in her journal. Too busy or too devastated to commit her experiences to paper—a reversal of a generations-long family tradition—Harriott did not return to writing until June 10. She penned only this: "From the above mentioned time [May 10] till the 26th May my dear Mother continued to suffer extremely with the sick Stomach and vomiting, and for several hours was in great agony when it pleased Almighty God to take her to him self."[38]

Another week passed before Harriott wrote anything more in the journal. How she got word to Charles Cotesworth in Charleston is unclear. Perhaps she had someone deliver the sad news in person. That was, of course, not possible with Thomas. Harriott asked their friend William Ward Burrows to write to Thomas on her behalf. Burrows, unsure what letters and information might have reached Thomas in London, began at the beginning. Eliza had come to Philadelphia with her daughter and three granddaughters for cancer treatment. But "her Age & other Infirmities" complicated her medical care. During the Pinckneys' stay in Philadelphia, William assured Thomas, "The Family received every Attention from the most respectable Part of the City, and no Attention was wanting." "Yet nothing," he continued, "could avert the Stroke of Death." William wanted to make sure Thomas understood that he was not writing on his own accord, but at Harriott's direction. Charles Cotesworth wrote Thomas, too, as soon as he got the news. It was, he said, an "irreparable loss." But, Charles Cotesworth recommended, the three siblings should resolve to bear their loss with fortitude—to act the way their mother raised them.[39]

When he read the letters from America, Thomas immediately wrote to Harriott. He longed for his sister and begged her to come to England. The trip from Philadelphia would not be too bad, he promised. But Harriott was already gone. Sharing Charles Cotesworth's impulse, she left Philadelphia determined to escape the sad reminders of her mother's painful death, to take her daughter and nieces to see another part of the country.[40]

It was lucky timing. Within weeks of their departure, yellow fever struck Philadelphia. It raged across the city, with upward of fifty people a day dying. Ricketts's circus became a charnel house; city leaders quarantined some patients in his building but provided no care. By the end of the summer, five thousand people—nearly 12 percent of the city's population—had succumbed to the epidemic. As cadavers piled up in the streets, almost 40 percent of residents fled in fear. The city government collapsed, and most state and federal officials evacuated. Even the Washington family left in early September. The outbreak didn't end until the cold weather came. By then, the most elegant city in North America was pockmarked with vacant houses, failed businesses, and overcrowded graveyards. Cemeteries, one observer said, looked "like ploughed fields," as grave diggers buried corpses on top of one another and in mass graves.[41]

The Pinckney women escaped the fever, but not their heartache. The trip, Harriott told Alice DeLancey Izard, was "a very pleasant ride through a delightful country." But it did nothing to erase the loss of her mother and, in fact, made Harriott miss Eliza more: "Accustomed as I had been for so many years to receive particular satisfaction from . . . amusing my dear Mother with an Acct. of every thing I saw or heard abroad," the trip only brought "a renewal of my grief."[42]

Eliza, who had stopped writing years earlier, didn't get to tell her own story about the trip that carried her out of South Carolina and, eventually, took her life. She disappeared from her own narrative. Harriott was too grief-stricken to write about her passing. There is no account of her funeral, either, though family legend held that President Washington served as a pall bearer at his own request. There is no record of where Eliza is buried. She was somewhere, for some time, in St. Peter's Churchyard in Philadelphia. Exactly where and for how long remains a mystery.

The date Eliza was buried is clear: May 27, 1793. May 27 had been a very special day to Eliza since 1744. It was her wedding anniversary, the day "The Almighty bless'd me with the best of husbands and the most amiable of men."[43]

In her youth, Eliza had often thought about her death. "How I shall conclude this last action of human life God only knows," she told her brother Tommy. "But," she added, " 'tis a scene that has been often acted over in my imagination." When she was young, Eliza claimed that she didn't dread death. She imagined she would pass peacefully: "resign this breath with ease and Comfort," like drifting off to sleep. Death, she decided with all the wisdom of her twenty years, was merely "changing a mortal for an immortal habitation."[44]

Fifty years passed. Now death was upon her, and so far from the Lowcountry home she had made and loved. Eliza found neither ease nor comfort as the tumors ravaged her body. There would be no drifting off to sleep.

Bedfast in the grip of cancer, there was only suffering and time. As she slipped in and out of consciousness, she must have dreamed about the long adventure that had been her life: of warm breezes that swept across the central plain of Antigua and sticky summer nights in Charleston and the stench of indigo vats; of the many "schemes" of her youth that had made her rich and renowned; of the years in London with Charles and their happy little children; of the father she had adored and lost too soon and the dead baby who had been given his name; of her sister and her brothers, long passed, and the long train of friends she had made and treasured and then left behind or buried; of the ordeal of the Revolution, which looked as if it would break her family but didn't; of nearly losing Thomas in the war; of the pride of watching President Washington ride up for breakfast at Harriott's home; of the white family she had led and the black families—too many to count—she had used for her own gain. Did the flood of soothing memories carry with them regrets? Did she think about Dick or Mary Ann? Was there any hint of a moral awakening? Did it occur to her, in the last hours of her life, that Dye and Sibby and Hannah, enslaved women she'd looked down on her whole life, were now looking down on her?

When the love of her life died in 1758, Eliza had felt certain that memories of his "affection and tenderness" would "remain to my latest moment." She accepted a lifetime of longing as the cost of their love. She called it "the Luxury of grief." She was equally sure that there would be, after this world, "a Union of Virtuous souls where there is no more death, no more separation, but virtuous love and friendship to endure to Eternity!"[45]

Sometime on May 26, 1793, the "great agony" she had endured for weeks at last gave way. If her faith was well-founded, Eliza walked again through the forests of Wappoo, breathing in "the scent of the young mirtle and Yellow Jesamin." And across thirty-five years was Charles, once again, just a heart-beat away.[46]

Epilogue

Like many people of many faiths, Eliza Lucas Pinckney believed in an afterlife. Her religion promised that her God waited in heaven to welcome true Christians. Eliza's friends said that her "whole life was like the Milky way with stars, thick-set with the genuine fruits of sincere piety and active benevolence." In Eliza's perception of how salvation worked, faithful Christians such as she could "have a well grounded hope of a blessed immortality." She never calculated the moral costs of over a half-century of human bondage but felt confident that she would number among the redeemed. Still, she conceded, only God knew for certain.[1]

What Eliza could control, she did, and with the help of her descendants, she secured a different kind of afterlife. The earliest letters she sent from South Carolina to her father in Antigua still survive, fragile sheets of paper housed at the South Carolina Historical Society Archives at the College of Charleston and the David M. Rubenstein Rare Book and Manuscript Library at Duke University. They open a treasure trove of writings that illuminate the life and mind of a colonial planter-patriarch turned American patriot who also happened to be a woman. The Charleston Museum, which Eliza's eldest son Charles Cotesworth helped found, owns several of her personal belongings, including her bed canopy adorned with images of the indigo plants she so zealously cultivated. Her canary yellow dress, elegantly crafted in London from silk raised at Belmont, is in the permanent collection of the Smithsonian Institution's National Museum of American History.

Eliza's salmon and cream silk dress survives, too. Generations of Pinckney women passed it down and laced it up to parade in civic celebrations in Charleston. As they sweated under the blistering Carolina sun, the fabric started to discolor and break down. Time did its work, too. The sun's rays and the weight of the dress left it faded and frayed at the seams. In 2017, the Eliza Lucas Pinckney chapter of the National Society of the Daughters of the American Revolution raised $23,000 to conserve the damaged dress, housed at the Charleston Museum. The project was important enough to the organization that it hired the renowned textiles expert who helped restore George Washington's military tent—the centerpiece of Philadelphia's Museum of the American Revolution.[2]

In the still small village of Ripley, England, the house the Pinckneys owned during their sojourn to the imperial center survives. It has been expanded over time, divided into residences, and is now home to several owners. They call it Ripley House. In the northwest corner of the property stands a stunning nearly three-hundred-year-old tree, planted by an Atlantic wayfarer who loved gardening and things made to last.[3]

So much of Eliza Lucas Pinckney's literary, material, and botanical legacy remains. Where is Eliza? Harriott intended her mother's burial spot in St. Peter's Churchyard to be temporary. Once she completed her northeastern travels and the summer heat passed, she would return to Philadelphia to supervise the exhumation of her mother's remains and transport her back to South Carolina, to be reinterred at St. Michael's. But then yellow fever struck, making it impossible for Harriott to pursue her plans. On top of the mortal danger posed by returning to Philadelphia, towns and cities, even some states, passed laws forbidding the entry of coaches, travelers, and vessels coming from the city. Harriott had to return to South Carolina without her mother's remains.[4]

Two years later, Harriott wrote to her Philadelphia friend William Ward Burrows for help with what she called "a melancholy piece of business." "The removal of the remains of my dear Mother," Harriott explained to William, "has ever been on my mind." Now she and her brothers needed to "trespass on your goodness" to supervise the exhumation. Harriott left William no room to decline. "We shall," she wrote, "be much obliged to you to have it done as soon as possible." The next mention of Eliza's remains appears in Harriott's will, from March 29, 1828. "It is my desire," she wrote, "that I may be buried in St. Michaels Church yard at the feet of my honored mother."

Lined up against an exterior wall of St. Michael's, beneath an arched window, stand matching grave markers for Harriott Pinckney Horry, her daughter and son-in-law, Charles Cotesworth Pinckney, and his three daughters. There is no marker—and no space—for Eliza. Nor is there any visible gravestone for her at St. Philip's, where Thomas and Fanny are buried.[5] It seems unlikely that a woman of Harriott Pinckney Horry's resolve and resources, with her deep devotion to her mother, would simply drop the matter. Perhaps Harriott succeeded in reburying Eliza's remains in South Carolina and Eliza's gravestone is no longer legible. Such edifices pockmark the graveyards at St. Michael's and St. Philip's. Or could the three siblings have simply lost sight of their mother? In looking forward to the family's future did they fail to look after their mother's final resting place?

It probably would not distress Eliza that her tomb vanished. She was not a sentimental woman. Except for longing for Charles, she didn't look back in life. She never returned to Antigua, never visited her father's or her siblings' graves, and for all her love of Charles, the location of his grave is a mystery, too. That she is lost in death connects Eliza to the great majority of eighteenth-century women. We glimpse their names but cannot recover much of their lives. Eliza made sure that didn't happen to her. She wrote herself into history. What really mattered to her—her family, her reputation, her wealth, and her writing—transcended time.[6]

Eliza would have felt supremely satisfied with the obituary that appeared in her hometown newspaper. It so precisely captured the life she cultivated that she could have written it herself. Usually the *South Carolina Gazette* mentioned only the basic facts of a person's death—typically one or two lines. Eliza's was ten times longer than any other death notice, for woman or man, in that issue of the weekly newspaper. The author even took Eliza's side on the matter of chasing a cure for cancer all the way to Philadelphia. She had been coaxed into the trip, the writer explained, by "the importunate solicitations of her friends." They pressed her into the trip because they felt "anxious for the preservation of so valuable a life." The writer didn't sentimentalize Eliza's last days: "She met death in the midst of the most excruciating pain." But having led a life of "rational, liberal, and pure" religious faith, she passed, readers were assured, "with a truly Christian fortitude." Borrowing from the English poet Thomas Tickell's elegy to a friend—a man—the obituary proclaimed: "She taught us how to live, and, oh too high a price for knowledge! taught us how to die."[7]

The eulogist called her Mrs. Elizabeth Pinckney. She was neither familiarly Eliza nor derivatively Mrs. Charles Pinckney, though the obituary opened by mentioning her late husband. While also nodding to her famous sons, the bulk of the piece centered squarely on her:

> This all accomplished lady, possessed, in a most eminent degree, all the amiable and engaging qualities, united to all the virtues and graces, which embellish and exalt the female character.—Her manners had been so refined, by a long and intimate acquaintance with the polite world, her countenance was so dignified by serious contemplation and devout reflection . . . that it was scarcely to behold her without emotions of the highest veneration and respect. Her understanding, aided by an uncommon strength of memory, had been so highly cultivated and improved by travel and extensive reading, and was so richly furnished, as well with scientific, as practical knowledge, that her talent for conversation was unrivalled, and her company was sedulously sought after by all, without distinction of age or sex.[8]

"Mrs. Elizabeth Pinckney" would have been pleased, too, by the way her three children conducted themselves after she died. Her grasping grandnephew, Charles Pinckney, leapt out the window of an abandoned building in Washington, DC, in 1820 after he was caught having sex with a local woman who was not his wife. The disgraced congressman decided not to seek reelection. There were no such scandals among Eliza's upstanding children. Nor were there embarrassments from any of the grandchildren, save for Daniel/Pinckney Horry, and he lived in Europe and in relative obscurity. Charles Cotesworth, Harriott, and Thomas got to grow old together. All three retired in their seventies, on grand estates spread across Lowcountry South Carolina. At the twilight of their lives they gathered with their children and grandchildren for Sunday dinners, often telling stories about the most famous member of their illustrious family.[9]

Eliza's descendants learned from her children to look up to her as the founder of the family. "Never," they said, "was there a daughter that more fully repaid the thousand cares bestowed on her" than Harriott Pinckney Horry. Charles Cotesworth's daughter always remembered that it was Eliza who "planted the seeds of religion and virtue" in her father's heart. Thomas's love of botany and agricultural experiments were, his grandson concluded, "natural in a son of Eliza Lucas." That narrative traversed the generations. Eliza's great-great-granddaughter, Harriott Horry Ravenel, remembered that she and her siblings and cousins grew up hearing stories from Eliza's grandchildren, "the old people to whose conversation I listened in childhood and youth, drinking in their endless tales of the old times." Looking back across four generations, Ravenel saw Charles Cotesworth and Thomas's service to their country as "the result of her [Eliza's] life-work." Ravenel interpreted Harriott's accomplishments, too, as a reflection of Eliza: Harriott "inherited her mother's business talent."[10]

The stories Eliza's descendants passed down about her life read as if she left them a script. And in a way, she did. Charles Cotesworth began the effort of curating a legacy for Eliza to transcend time while she was alive. In 1785, he asked his mother to record her memories of working on indigo cultivation. He wanted to make sure she got her due credit. Eliza complied, and Charles Cotesworth passed her letter to David Ramsay, the first historian of the American Revolution. In *The History of South Carolina* (1809), he put Eliza at the center of the story about indigo and the colonial economy. Over time, her partnership in producing indigo with several Lowcountry men (including her future husband) was condensed in favor of a great-woman narrative: Eliza Lucas invented indigo! In 1989, Eliza's agricultural innovations—starting with indigo—earned her induction into the South Carolina Business Hall of Fame. She was the first woman ever honored at the annual black-tie affair.[11]

Harriott, meanwhile, preserved Eliza's dresses and the story of her silkworks at Belmont. She passed on the dresses and the memories to Harriott Jr., who passed them to her daughters, and so on. Descendants handed down books, furniture, jewelry, and housewares, too. When Eliza's grandchildren retold family stories about the Revolutionary War, they could point to the chair Francis Marion sat in before Harriott and Eliza secreted him away from Banastre Tarleton. "Kept," later generations knew, "as relics of the story."[12]

Generations of Pinckney women safeguarded Eliza's writings, too. Through hurricanes, wars, fires, relocations, sudden deaths, and family disagreements, Eliza's descendants protected the record she created of her life and, with it, her story of the eighteenth-century Atlantic World. In 1850, Harriott Pinckney Holbrook—Harriott Pinckney Horry's granddaughter—privately published part of Eliza's writings. Ten years later, a Charleston printer published a family history written some decades earlier by Charles Cotesworth's daughter, Maria Henrietta Pinckney. In 1896, Harriott Horry Ravenel turned her family's oral histories and carefully preserved letters into a full-length biography of Eliza. In venerating and commemorating Eliza's life, the nineteenth-century Pinckneys followed a pattern common among members of well-to-do southern families, who crafted celebratory books about idealized eighteenth-century patriarchs—usually men—that wove together historical narratives with letters, oral traditions, and memories.[13]

Meanwhile, descendants began to deposit Pinckney family papers at professionally maintained archives, to ensure preservation for posterity and academic historians. Apparently because the letters had been divided among various heirs, the eighteenth-century family correspondence and parts of Eliza's writings are scattered across the East Coast, including at Duke University, the Library of Congress, and the South Carolina Historical Society. In 1972, descendant Elise Pinckney made Eliza's earliest letters widely available for the first time, in a professionally edited volume. In 2008, Constance B. Schulz led a team of scholars working at the University of South Carolina to create comprehensive digital editions of the Pinckney papers. In a move at once surprising and inevitable, they started with the women. The writings of men in the family came second.[14]

From these carefully crafted and carefully curated records it is possible to rediscover the remarkable life of Eliza Lucas Pinckney and in so doing reimagine the Age of Revolution. Men in powdered wigs deliberating in legislative halls or dashing across battlefields dominate our impressions of the eighteenth century. It must have been a man's world, right? Wives might help out from time to time—there is even a term for it, "deputy husbands." But mostly they hid behind their bonnets and minded children while towering men transformed the Atlantic World. The invention of a female political identity in the wake of American independence—"republican motherhood"—didn't fundamentally change women's status.

Eliza's life subverts this story. And she was not alone. Just in her extended family, there were Harriott Pinckney Horry, Rebecca Brewton Motte, Fanny Motte Middleton Pinckney, and others. Were they the exceptions? Or the rule? The more we look, the more we see families and communities across the Atlantic World run by ruthless planter-patriarchs, savvy entrepreneurs, sophisticated gatekeepers to rank and refinement, and revered heads of households, "sought after by all, without distinction of age or sex." These powerbrokers were white and rich and mostly men. But not always.[15]

Eliza asked the question when she was only nineteen. From her first Lowcountry plantation, she watched a comet blaze across the night sky and wondered, "Why not a woman?"

Notes

INTRODUCTION

1. W. T. Lynn, "The First Comet of 1742," *Observatory* 30 (1907): 284–285; *Pennsylvania Gazette*, 3 March 1742; Eliza Lucas to Mary Bartlett, c. March/April 1742, *The Papers of Eliza Lucas Pinckney and Harriott Pinckney Horry: Digital Edition*, ed. Constance B. Schulz, http://rotunda.upress.virginia.edu/PinckneyHorry (hereinafter DE). Because her name changed over the course of her life and to avoid confusion with her relatives, I have adopted the use of "Eliza." I follow a similar practice for men and women throughout the book. I have occasionally silently corrected misspellings or expanded common abbreviations (such as "which" to replace "wch") if those changes in no way alter Eliza's voice or meaning. For Eliza's life in South Carolina, see also Sam S. Baskett, "Eliza Lucas Pinckney: Portrait of an Eighteenth-Century American," *South Carolina Historical Magazine* 72 (October 1971): 207–219; Barbara L. Bellows, "Eliza Lucas Pinckney: The Evolution of an Icon," *South Carolina Historical Magazine* 106 (April–July 2005): 147–165; David L. Coon, "Eliza Lucas Pinckney and the Reintroduction of Indigo Culture in South Carolina," *Journal of Southern History* 42 (February 1976): 61–76; Eliza L. Martin, "Eliza Lucas Pinckney: Production and Consumption in the Atlantic World," *World History Connected* 7 (February 2010), https://worldhistoryconnected.press.uillinois.edu/7.1/martin.html; Constance B. Schulz, "Eliza Lucas Pinckney and Harriott Pinckney Horry: A South Carolina Revolutionary-Era Mother and Daughter," in *South Carolina Women: Their Lives and Times,* vol. 1, ed. Marjorie Julian Spruill, Valinda W. Littlefield, and Joan Marie Johnson (Athens: University of Georgia Press, 2009), 79–108; Kacy Dowd Tillman, "Eliza Lucas Pinckney as Cultural Broker: Reconsidering a South Carolina Legacy," *Southern Studies* 18 (Fall–Winter 2011): 49–66; Paula A. Treckel, "Eliza Lucas

Pinckney: 'Dutiful, Affectionate, and Obedient Daughter,' " in *Developing Dixie: Modernization in a Traditional Society,* ed. Winfred B. Moore, Jr., Joseph F. Tripp, and Lyon G. Tyler, Jr. (Westport, CT: Greenwood, 1988), 219–234; and the July 1998 special edition of the *South Carolina Historical Magazine*. Margaret F. Pickett, a living history interpreter with the National Park Service, also published *Eliza Lucas Pinckney: Colonial Plantation Manager and Mother of American Patriots, 1722–1793* (Jefferson, NC: McFarland, 2016). Eliza has been the subject of at least one dissertation: Megan Hatfield's excellent "A Family upon the Deep Blue Sea: The Atlantic Life of Eliza Lucas Pinckney," Ph.D. diss., University of Miami, 2015.

2. Eliza Lucas to Mary Bartlett, c. 1742, DE.
3. Eliza Lucas to Mary Bartlett, c. June 1742, *The Letterbook of Eliza Lucas Pinckney, 1739–1762,* ed. Elise Pinckney (Columbia: University of South Carolina Press, 1997), 41 (hereinafter *Letterbook*).
4. Special thanks to Anne Boylan for sharing her research into twentieth-century radio programs. Eliza Lucas was the subject of two programs: *Self-Reliance,* 9 April 1936, and *The Indigo Girl,* 27 December 1948, accessible at http://archive.org/details/OTRR_Cavalcade_of_America_Singles. Anne Boylan, "Usable Pasts: Representing Women's History to Popular Audiences in the 1930s United States," unpublished essay in author's possession.
5. Eliza Lucas to Elizabeth Lamb Pinckney, undated, *Letterbook,* 66.
6. Eliza Lucas Pinckney, "Days sett apart to be rememberd," DE. For an eighteenth-century New England woman's written life, see Catherine A. Brekus, *Sarah Osborn's World: The Rise of Evangelical Christianity in Early America* (New Haven: Yale University Press, 2013). The centerpiece of Eliza's writings was her letterbook, the copied compilation of letters she sent across the Atlantic World. It is housed at the South Carolina Historical Society Archives, College of Charleston. Leather-bound and 8 by 12½ inches, it runs to more than 250 pages. At some point someone removed some pages, now housed at the David M. Rubenstein Rare Book and Manuscript Library, Duke University. "The Letterbooks of Eliza Lucas Pinckney and Harriott Pinckney Horry," DE.
7. Eliza Lucas Pinckney to James Kirkpatrick, February 1760, *Letterbook,* 131; "Marriages and Death Notices from the City Gazette," *South Carolina Historical and Genealogical Magazine* 21 (October 1920), 159. For a similar case in Virginia, see Ami Pflugrad-Jackisch, " 'What Am I but an American?': Mary Willing Byrd and Westover Plantation during the American Revolution," in *Women in the American Revolution: Gender, Politics, and the Domestic World,* ed. Barbara B. Oberg (Charlottesville: University of Virginia Press, 2019), 171–191.
8. For the history of biography, see Scott E. Casper, *Constructing American Lives: Biography and Culture in Nineteenth-Century America* (Chapel Hill: University of North Carolina Press, 1999); Hermione Lee, *Biography: A Very Short Introduction* (New York: Oxford University Press, 2009); Nigel Hamilton, *How to Do Biography: A Primer* (Cambridge: Harvard University Press, 2008).
9. Eliza Lucas Pinckney to Daniel (Charles Lucas Pinckney) Horry, 7 August 1783, DE.

10. Eliza Lucas Pinckney to George Keate, February 1762, *Letterbook*, 181. For women's/dual biographies, see Patricia Brady, *Martha Washington: An American Life* (New York: Viking, 2005); Woody Holton, *Abigail Adams, A Life* (New York: Free Press, 2009); Cynthia A. Kierner, *Martha Jefferson Randolph, Daughter of Monticello: Her Life and Times* (Chapel Hill: University of North Carolina Press, 2012); Jill Lepore, *Book of Ages: The Life and Opinions of Jane Franklin* (New York: Knopf, 2013); Rosemarie Zagarri, *A Woman's Dilemma: Mercy Otis Warren and the American Revolution*, 2nd ed. (Malden, MA: Wiley Blackwell, 2015). This pattern held in Linda Colley, *The Ordeal of Elizabeth Marsh: A Woman in World History* (New York: Random House, 2007); Erica Armstrong Dunbar, *Never Caught: The Washingtons' Relentless Pursuit of Their Runaway Slave, Ona Judge* (New York: Atria, 2017); Louisa Thomas, *Louisa: The Extraordinary Life of Mrs. Adams* (New York: Penguin, 2016). Patricia Cleary, *Elizabeth Murray: A Woman's Pursuit of Independence in Eighteenth-Century America* (Amherst: University of Massachusetts Press, 2000); Charlene M. Boyer Lewis, *Elizabeth Patterson Bonaparte: An American Aristocrat in the Early Republic* (Philadelphia: University of Pennsylvania Press, 2012); and Ann M. Little, *The Many Captivities of Esther Wheelwright* (New Haven: Yale University Press, 2016), provide powerful exceptions.

1. *BORN TO PRIVILEGE*

1. Carol Walter Ramagosa, "Eliza Lucas Pinckney's Family in Antigua, 1668–1747," *South Carolina Historical Magazine* 99 (July 1998), 243; Herman Moll, "The Island of Antego" (London: Thomas Bowles and John Bowles, c. 1732), Harvard Map Collection, Harvard University; R. B. Sheridan, "The Rise of a Colonial Gentry: A Case Study of Antigua, 1730–1775," *Economic History Review* 13, no. 3 (1961), 355, appendix 1; Harriet Simons Williams, "Eliza Lucas and Her Family: Before the Letterbook," *South Carolina Historical Magazine* 99 (July 1998), 263.
2. *The Laws of the Island of Antigua: Consisting of the Acts of the Leeward Islands, Commencing 8th November 1690, ending 21st April 1798; and the Acts of Antigua, Commencing 10th April 1668, ending 7th May 1804*, 2 vols. (London: Samuel Bagster, 1805), 1: 178; Vere Langford Oliver, *The History of the Island of Antigua*, 3 vols. (London: Mitchell and Hughes, 1894–1899), 1: xcvi, lxxxviii; *Journal of the Commissioners for Trade and Plantations, from January 1722–3 to December 1728* (London: His Majesty's Stationery Office, 1928), 271; 10 April 1724, *Calendar of State Papers, Colonial, America and West Indies*, vol. 34 (quotation). Calendar of State Papers accessed through British History Online, www.british-history.ac.uk.
3. Williams, "Eliza Lucas and Her Family," 260–261.
4. Stephanie E. Jones-Rogers demonstrated the compatibility of femininity and violence in *They Were Her Property: White Women as Slave Owners in the American South* (New Haven: Yale University Press, 2019). See also Edward B. Rugemer, *Slave Law and the Politics of Resistance in the Early Atlantic World* (Cambridge: Harvard University Press, 2018); Caitlin Rosenthal, *Accounting for Slavery: Masters and Management* (Cambridge: Harvard University Press, 2018); Randy M. Browne,

Surviving Slavery in the British Caribbean (Philadelphia: University of Pennsylvania Press, 2017).

5. Williams, "Eliza Lucas and Her Family," 262; Ramagosa, "Eliza Lucas Pinckney's Family," 249. Ramagosa found only 5 percent of children listed as born to a courtesan.
6. Eliza Lucas to George Lucas, c. 1740, DE.
7. For early Antiguan history, see David Barry Gaspar, *Bondmen and Rebels: A Study of Master-Slave Relations in Antigua with Implications for Colonial British America* (Baltimore: Johns Hopkins University Press, 1985); Natasha Lightfoot, *Troubling Freedom: Antigua and the Aftermath of British Emancipation* (Durham, NC: Duke University Press, 2015). For Eliza's family in Antigua, see Williams, "Eliza Lucas and Her Family"; Ramagosa, "Eliza Lucas Pinckney's Family."
8. For the tumult that defined the early Caribbean, see Richard Dunn, *Sugar and Slaves: The Rise of the Planter Class in the English West Indies, 1624–1713* (New York: Norton, 1971), 118; Jan Rogozinski, *A Brief History of the Caribbean: From the Arawak and Carib to the Present* (New York: Facts on File, 1992).
9. William Byam, 1668, quoted in Sheridan, "The Rise of a Colonial Gentry," 347. For John Lucas's acquisition of land, see Ramagosa, "Eliza Lucas Pinckney's Family," 239.
10. For context, see Natalie Zacek, "Rituals of Rulership: The Material Culture of West Indian Politics," in *Material Culture in Anglo-America: Regional Identity and Urbanity in the Tidewater, Lowcountry, and Caribbean,* ed. David S. Shields (Columbia: University of South Carolina Press, 2009), 115–126.
11. Petition of John Lucas, 27 January 1699, *Calendar of State Papers, Colonial, America and West Indies,* vol. 17 (first and second quotations); John Lucas to Robert Lucas, 28 April 1698, *Calendar of State Papers, Colonial, America and West Indies,* vol. 16 (third and fourth quotations); John Lucas to Robert Lucas, 28 April 1698, *Calendar of State Papers, Colonial, America and West Indies,* vol. 16 (last quotation). For the Codrington controversy, see also John Lucas to Robert Lucas, 25 April 1698, *Calendar of State Papers, Colonial, America and West Indies,* vol. 16; John Lucas to Edward Walrond, 23 June 1698, *Calendar of State Papers, Colonial, America and West Indies,* vol. 16; Petition of John Lucas to Council of Trade, 9 January 1699, *Calendar of State Papers, Colonial, America and West Indies,* vol. 17; John Lucas, 16 March 1699 and 17 March 1699, *Calendar of State Papers, Colonial, America and West Indies,* vol. 17. For John Lucas's work in the legislature, see John Lucas, Speaker, and Christopher Codrington, Governor, 1 July 1692, *The Laws of the Island of Antigua,* 1: 89; *The Laws of the Island of Antigua,* 1: 6, 75, 165.
12. Dunn, *Sugar and Slaves,* 144 (first quotation); *Some Instances of the Oppressions and Male Administration of Col. Parke, late Governor of the Leeward Islands, with an Account of the Rise and Progress of the Insurrection at Antegoa, and Remarks on a Paper intituled, Truth brought to light, or Murder will out* (London, n.d.) (second and third quotations); Oliver, *The History of the Island of Antigua,* 1: lxxxi–lxxxii; *Antigua and the Antiguans: A Full Account of the Colony and its Inhabitants from the Time of the Caribs to the Present Day, Interspersed with Anecdotes and Legends. Also, an Impartial View of Slavery and the Free Labour Systems; the Statistics of the Island, and Biographical Notices of the Principal Families,* 2 vols. (London: Saunders and Otley, 1844), 1: 39, 43,

68–79; Matthew Mulcahy, *Hubs of Empire: The Southeastern Lowcountry and British Caribbean* (Baltimore: Johns Hopkins University Press, 2014), 191. See also *The history of Col. Parke's administration whilst he was Captain-General and Chief Governor of the Leeward Islands; with an account of the rebellion in Antego: Wherein he, with several others, were Murther'd on the 7th of December, 1710. By Mr. George French* (London, 1717). Parke had some defenders; see *Truth brought to Light; or, Murther will out; Being a Short, but True, Account of the most horrid, barbarous, and bloody MURTHER and REBELLION committed at Antego in the West-Indies, against Her Majesty and Her Government* (London: John Morphew, 1713). For context, see Natalie Zacek, "Sex, Sexuality, and Social Control in the Eighteenth-Century Leeward Islands," in *Sex and Sexuality in Early America,* ed. Merril D. Smith (New York: New York University Press, 1998), 190–214; Helen Hill Miller, *Colonel Parke of Virginia: "The Greatest Hector in the Town"* (Chapel Hill: Algonquin, 1989).

13. Eliza Lucas to Mary Bartlett, c. 1742, DE; Eliza Lucas Pinckney to George Keate, February 1762, DE.

14. The following description draws from Rogozinski, *A Brief History of the Caribbean,* 131–136; Dunn, *Sugar and Slaves,* 191–198; Mulcahy, *Hubs of Empire,* 46–48. See also Jennifer L. Morgan, *Laboring Women: Reproduction and Gender in New World Slavery* (Philadelphia: University of Pennsylvania Press, 2004), 146–151; Rugemer, *Slave Law and the Politics of Resistance,* 19–22; Susan Dwyer Amussen, *Caribbean Exchanges: Slavery and the Transformation of English Society, 1640–1700* (Chapel Hill: University of North Carolina Press, 2007), chapter 3. For the history of sugar, see also Sidney W. Mintz, *Sweetness and Power: The Place of Sugar in Modern History* (New York: Penguin, 1985); James Walvin, *Sugar: The World Corrupted, From Slavery to Obesity* (New York: Pegasus, 2018).

15. Williams, "Eliza Lucas and Her Family," 260–261.

16. Mulcahy, *Hubs of Empire,* 46.

17. For punishments, see Browne, *Surviving Slavery in the British Caribbean*; Edward B. Rugemer, "The Development of Mastery and Race in the Comprehensive Slave Codes of the Greater Caribbean during the Seventeenth Century," *William and Mary Quarterly* 70 (July 2013): 429–458. For a 1692 alleged slave conspiracy with wider implications, see Jason T. Sharples, "Discovering Slave Conspiracies: New Fears of Rebellion and Old Paradigms of Plotting in Seventeenth-Century Barbados," *American Historical Review* 120 (June 2015): 811–843. The 2010s brought an outpouring of scholarship on slavery in the Caribbean and English Atlantic. Exemplary works include Amussen, *Caribbean Exchanges*; Browne, *Surviving Slavery in the British Caribbean*; Michael Guasco, *Slaves and Englishmen: Human Bondage in the Early Modern Atlantic World* (Philadelphia: University of Pennsylvania Press, 2014); Brooke N. Newman, *A Dark Inheritance: Blood, Race, and Sex in Colonial Jamaica* (New Haven: Yale University Press, 2018); Simon P. Newman, *A New World of Labor: The Development of Plantation Slavery in the British Atlantic* (Philadelphia: University of Pennsylvania Press, 2013); Daniel B. Rood, *The Reinvention of Atlantic Slavery: Technology, Labor, Race, and Capitalism in the Greater Caribbean* (New York: Oxford University Press, 2017); Rugemer, *Slave Law and the Politics of Resistance.*

18. Robert Robertson, *A short account of the hurricane, that pass'd thro' the English Leeward Caribbee Islands, on Saturday the 30th of June 1733. With remarks. In a letter from an inhabitant of His Majesty's Island of Nevis, to a gentleman in London* (London, 1733), 15.
19. For family ties and gentry culture, see Sheridan, "The Rise of a Colonial Gentry."
20. For another well-educated woman, see Rosemarie Zagarri, *A Woman's Dilemma: Mercy Otis Warren and the American Revolution*, 2nd ed. (Malden, MA: Wiley Blackwell, 2015), 3–4, 12–13. See also Ann M. Little, *The Many Captivities of Esther Wheelwright* (New Haven: Yale University Press, 2016), 101.
21. Megan Hatfield emphasized the importance of moving in "A Family upon the Deep Blue Sea: The Atlantic Life of Eliza Lucas Pinckney," Ph.D. diss., University of Miami, 2015. For Antigua's population, see Gaspar, *Bondmen and Rebels*, 218.
22. Eliza Lucas to Mary Boddicott, 2 May 1741, DE.
23. Eliza Lucas to George Lucas, 2 May 1744, DE. No physical remains of the school survive. Williams, "Eliza Lucas and Her Family," 266. For women studying botany, see Susan Scott Parrish, *American Curiosity: Cultures of Natural History in the Colonial British Atlantic World* (Chapel Hill: University of North Carolina Press, 2006), chapter 5; Ann B. Shteir, *Cultivating Women, Cultivating Science: Flora's Daughters and Botany in England, 1760–1860* (Baltimore: Johns Hopkins University Press, 1996).
24. Eliza Lucas to Mary Boddicott, 14 December 1743, DE.

2. *TROUBLE BACK HOME*

1. *Antigua and the Antiguans: A Full Account of the Colony and its Inhabitants from the Time of the Caribs to the Present Day, Interspersed with Anecdotes and Legends. Also, an Impartial View of Slavery and the Free Labour Systems; the Statistics of the Island, and Biographical Notices of the Principal Families,* 2 vols. (London: Saunders and Otley, 1844), 1: 68, 66.
2. Robert Robertson, *A detection of the state and situation of the present sugar planters, of Barbadoes and the Leward Islands; With an Answer to this Query, Why does not England, or her Sugar Islands, or both, make and settle more Sugar Colonies in the West-Indies? Written in the month of December 1731, by an inhabitant of one of his Majesty's Leward Caribee Islands; and humbly Dedicated to the Right Honourable Sir Robert Walpole* (London: J. Wilford, 1732), 48–49. See also Vere Langford Oliver, *The History of the Island of Antigua,* 3 vols. (London: Mitchell and Hughes, 1894–1899), 1: xcvi; *Antigua and the Antiguans,* 1: 68; Richard Dunn, *Sugar and Slaves: The Rise of the Planter Class in the English West Indies, 1624–1713* (New York: Norton, 1971), 34.
3. Robert Robertson, *A short account of the hurricane, that pass'd thro' the English Leeward Caribbee Islands, on Saturday the 30th of June 1733. With remarks. In a letter from an inhabitant of His Majesty's Island of Nevis, to a gentleman in London* (London, 1733), 4–6 (quotations), 19.
4. Quoted in David Barry Gaspar, *Bondmen and Rebels: A Study of Master-Slave Relations in Antigua with Implications for Colonial British America* (Baltimore: Johns Hopkins University Press, 1985), 224.
5. Natasha Lightfoot, *Troubling Freedom: Antigua and the Aftermath of British Emancipation* (Durham, NC: Duke University Press, 2015), 25; Carol Walter Ramagosa,

"Eliza Lucas Pinckney's Family in Antigua, 1668–1747," *South Carolina Historical Magazine* 99 (July 1998), 246; Gaspar, *Bondmen and Rebels*, 223 (quotation).

6. For planter culture, see Dunn, *Sugar and Slaves*. For Nevis, see Keith Mason, "The Absentee Planter and the Key Slave: Privilege, Patriarchalism, and Exploitation in the Early Eighteenth-Century Caribbean," *William and Mary Quarterly* 70 (January 2013): 79–102. For material consumption, see David S. Shields, ed., *Material Culture in Anglo-America: Regional Identity and Urbanity in the Tidewater, Lowcountry, and Caribbean* (Columbia: University of South Carolina Press, 2009).
7. James Gamble, 24 March 1735, in Oliver, *The History of the Island of Antigua*, 3: 156; Harriet Simons Williams, "Eliza Lucas and Her Family: Before the Letterbook," *South Carolina Historical Magazine* 99 (July 1998), 271–272, 261, fn. 4.
8. For Antiguan laws, see *The Laws of the Island of Antigua: Consisting of the Acts of the Leeward Islands, Commencing 8th November 1690, ending 21st April 1798; and the Acts of Antigua, Commencing 10th April 1668, ending 7th May 1804*, 2 vols. (London: Samuel Bagster, 1805), 1: 158–164, 214–231. For the Caribbean, see Edward B. Rugemer, "The Development of Mastery and Race in the Comprehensive Slave Codes of the Greater Caribbean during the Seventeenth Century," *William and Mary Quarterly* 70 (July 2013): 429–458; Edward B. Rugemer, *Slave Law and the Politics of Resistance in the Early Atlantic World* (Cambridge: Harvard University Press, 2018). For Virginia, see Edmund S. Morgan, *American Slavery, American Freedom: The Ordeal of Colonial Virginia* (New York: Norton, 1975); Ira Berlin, *Many Thousands Gone: The First Two Centuries of Slavery in North America* (Cambridge: Harvard University Press, 1998), chapters 1 and 5; Anthony S. Parent, Jr., *Foul Means: The Formation of a Slave Society in Virginia, 1660–1740* (Chapel Hill: University of North Carolina Press, 2003); Allan Kulikoff, *Tobacco and Slaves: The Development of Southern Cultures in the Chesapeake, 1680–1800* (Chapel Hill: University of North Carolina Press, 1986).
9. For fears of plots, see Jason T. Sharples, "Discovering Slave Conspiracies: New Fears of Rebellion and Old Paradigms of Plotting in Seventeenth-Century Barbados," *American Historical Review* 120 (June 2015), 816–817. For recent interpretations that deemphasize resistance, see Randy M. Browne, *Surviving Slavery in the British Caribbean* (Philadelphia: University of Pennsylvania Press, 2017); Justin Roberts, *Slavery and the Enlightenment in the British Atlantic, 1750–1807* (New York: Cambridge University Press, 2013).
10. Between 1730 and 1735, seventy-five enslaved Antiguans were executed for crimes, including thirty-nine for flight. David Barry Gaspar, " 'To Bring Their Offending Slaves to Justice': Compensation and Slave Resistance in Antigua, 1669–1763," *Caribbean Quarterly* 30 (September–December 1984): 45–59. For deprivations, see Letter from Antigua, 4 August 1736, *South Carolina Gazette*, 6 November 1736.
11. *A Genuine Narrative of the Intended Conspiracy of the Negroes at Antigua. Extracted from an Authentic Copy of a Report, made to the Chief Governor of the Carabee Islands, by the Commissioners, or Judges appointed to try the Conspirators* (Dublin: R. Reilly, 1737), 4; *Antigua and the Antiguans*, 1: 91. For analysis, see Gaspar, *Bondmen and Rebels*, 222–226. Court is known today in Antigua as Prince Klaas and is a national

hero. See also Mike Dash, "Antigua's Disputed Slave Conspiracy of 1736," www.Smithsonian.com.

12. For a chart of slave conspiracies and uprisings, see Jan Rogozinski, *A Brief History of the Caribbean: From the Arawak and Carib to the Present* (New York: Facts on File, 1992), 158–160.
13. Excerpt from report by John Vernon, Ashton Warrer, and Nathanial Gilbert, 30 December 1736, *South Carolina Gazette*, 12 February 1737 (first quotation); Robert Arbuthnot quoted in Gaspar, *Bondmen and Rebels*, 19 (second quotation). There are conflicting reports of the date of the dance. I adopt the date given in the judges' official report. For a description of the dance, see *A Genuine Narrative of the Intended Conspiracy of the Negroes at Antigua*, 6–9. For the significance of dance, see Katrina Dyonne Thompson, *Ring Shout, Wheel About: The Racial Politics of Music and Dance in North American Slavery* (Urbana: University of Illinois Press, 2014).
14. *A Genuine Narrative of the Intended Conspiracy of the Negroes at Antigua,* 9 (quotations); Gaspar, *Bondmen and Rebels,* 4.
15. *A Genuine Narrative of the Intended Conspiracy of the Negroes at Antigua,* 10, 3, 6.
16. Letter from Antigua, 24 October 1736, *South Carolina Gazette*, 11 December 1736.
17. *Antigua and the Antiguans,* 1: 107 (first and second quotations); "Extract of a Letter from Antigua," *Virginia Gazette*, 27 May 1737 (third quotation).
18. Letter from Antigua, 13 December 1736, *South Carolina Gazette*, 30 April 1737; "Extract of a Letter from Antigua," *Virginia Gazette*, 27 May 1737 (quotation); David Barry Gaspar, "The Antigua Slave Conspiracy of 1736: A Case Study of the Origins of Collective Resistance," *William and Mary Quarterly* 35 (April 1978), 309, 311, fn. 14.
19. "Extract of a Letter from Antigua," 24 October 1736, *Virginia Gazette*, 8 April 1737. See also *South Carolina Gazette*, 24 September 1737. For context of the punishment of alleged conspirators and rebels, see Rugemer, *Slave Law and the Politics of Resistance*, 67–102; Sharples, "Discovering Slave Conspiracies." For gendered dimensions of resistance and revolt, see Jennifer L. Morgan, *Laboring Women: Reproduction and Gender in New World Slavery* (Philadelphia: University of Pennsylvania Press, 2004), chapter 6.
20. Ramagosa, "Eliza Lucas Pinckney's Family," 247. Gaspar, *Bondmen and Rebels*, 32–33, lists all convicted people and their enslavers.
21. Excerpt from report by John Vernon, Ashton Warrer, and Nathanial Gilbert, 30 December 1736, *South Carolina Gazette*, 12 February 1737. See also *Boston Weekly News-Letter*, 24 March–1 April 1737.
22. Eliza described their friendship when they reconnected through letters. Eliza Lucas to Katherine Martin Carew, 2 September 1743, DE. See also Eliza Lucas to Mary Boddicott, 2 May 1741, DE.
23. *New-England Weekly Journal*, 9 April 1737. See also "Extract of a Letter from Antigua," *Virginia Gazette*, 27 May 1737; *New York Weekly Journal*, 6 December 1736; *New York Gazette*, 29 November 1736. For out-migration, see Robertson, *A detection of the state and situation of the present sugar planters*, 91.
24. Eliza Lucas to Mary Boddicott, 2 May 1741, DE; Eliza Lucas to Mrs. Pearson, 30 June 1742, DE; Eliza Lucas to George Lucas, 2 May 1744, DE. For refinement and material

expressions of gentility, see Steven C. Bullock, *Tea Sets and Tyranny: The Politics of Politeness in Early America* (Philadelphia: University of Pennsylvania Press, 2017); Richard L. Bushman, *The Refinement of America: Persons, Houses, Cities* (New York: Knopf, 1992), 3–203; Cary Carson, *Face Value: The Consumer Revolution and the Colonizing of America* (Charlottesville: University of Virginia Press, 2017); Cynthia A. Kierner, *Beyond the Household: Women's Place in the Early South, 1700–1835* (Ithaca, NY: Cornell University Press, 1998), especially 40–55; Shields, *Material Culture in Anglo-America*; Jennifer Van Horn, *The Power of Objects in Eighteenth-Century British America* (Chapel Hill: University of North Carolina Press, 2017). Most girls' educations were circumscribed for gendered roles they filled as adults. See Catherine Kerrison, *Claiming the Pen: Women and Intellectual Life in the Early American South* (Ithaca, NY: Cornell University Press, 2006), 11–19, 84–86; Kierner, *Beyond the Household*, 59–65; Cara Anzilotti, *In the Affairs of the World: Women, Patriarchy, and Power in Colonial South Carolina* (Westport, CT: Greenwood, 2002), 85–87.

3. *"IN A STRANGE COUNTRY"*

1. 5 February 1737, *Calendar of State Papers, Colonial, America and West Indies*, vol. 43 (accessed through British History Online, www.british-history.ac.uk); Harriet Simons Williams, "Eliza Lucas and Her Family: Before the Letterbook," *South Carolina Historical Magazine* 99 (July 1998), 272.
2. See also Williams, "Eliza Lucas and Her Family," 278.
3. Williams, "Eliza Lucas and Her Family," 274 (first quotation); Eliza Lucas to Katherine Martin Carew, 2 September 1743, DE (second quotation). George Lucas, living at Wappoo, advertised for a lost horse in the *South Carolina Gazette*, 25 August 1739.
4. Quotation in "Neu-gefundenes Eden. Oder Aussfürlicher Bericht von Sud und Nord Carolina, Pensilphania, Maryland, und Virginia" (published for the Helvetische Societdt, 1737), 111. See also H. Roy Merrens and George D. Terry, "Dying in Paradise: Malaria, Mortality, and the Perceptual Environment in Colonial South Carolina," *Journal of Southern History* 50 (November 1984): 533–550. For the 1730s beginning a golden age for South Carolina commerce, see George C. Rogers, Jr., *Charleston in the Age of the Pinckneys* (1969; Columbia: University of South Carolina Press, 1980). For colonial South Carolina, see S. Max Edelson, *Plantation Enterprise in Colonial South Carolina* (Cambridge: Harvard University Press, 2006); Lorri Glover, *All Our Relations: Blood Ties and Emotional Bonds among the Early South Carolina Gentry* (Baltimore: Johns Hopkins University Press, 2000); Jack P. Greene, Rosemary Brana-Shute, and Randy J. Sparks, eds., *Money, Trade, and Power: The Evolution of Colonial South Carolina's Plantation Society* (Columbia: University of South Carolina Press, 2001); Emma Hart, *Building Charleston: Town and Society in the Eighteenth-Century British Atlantic World* (Charlottesville: University of Virginia Press, 2010); Tom Hatley, *The Dividing Paths: Cherokees and South Carolinians through the Revolutionary Era* (New York: Oxford University Press, 1995); Daniel C. Littlefield, *Rice and Slaves: Ethnicity and the Slave Trade in Colonial South Carolina* (Urbana: University of Illinois Press, 1981); Robert Olwell, *Masters, Slaves, and Subjects: The Culture of Power in the*

South Carolina Low Country, 1740–1790 (Ithaca, NY: Cornell University Press, 1998); Ryan A. Quintana, *Making a Slave State: Political Development in Early South Carolina* (Chapel Hill: University of North Carolina Press, 2018).

5. Eliza Lucas to Mary Boddicott, 2 May 1740, DE; Eliza Lucas to Thomas Lucas, 22 May 1742, *The Letterbook of Eliza Lucas Pinckney, 1739–1762,* ed. Elise Pinckney (Columbia: University of South Carolina Press, 1997), 39 (hereinafter *Letterbook*). For other wayfaring families, see Patricia Cleary, *Elizabeth Murray: A Woman's Pursuit of Independence in Eighteenth-Century America* (Amherst: University of Massachusetts Press, 2000); Linda Colley, *The Ordeal of Elizabeth Marsh: A Woman in World History* (New York: Random House, 2007); Susan Clair Imbarrato, *Sarah Gray Cary, from Boston to Grenada: Shifting Fortunes of an American Family, 1764–1826* (Baltimore: Johns Hopkins University Press, 2018).
6. *South Carolina Gazette*, 11 June 1744.
7. Eliza Lucas to Thomas Lucas, 22 May 1742, *Letterbook*, 39–40.
8. For South Carolina slave codes, see Edward B. Rugemer, *Slave Law and the Politics of Resistance in the Early Atlantic World* (Cambridge: Harvard University Press, 2018), 35–36, 51–74, 102; Edward B. Rugemer, "The Development of Mastery and Race in the Comprehensive Slave Codes of the Greater Caribbean during the Seventeenth Century," *William and Mary Quarterly* 70 (July 2013), 430, 454–457.
9. *South Carolina Gazette*, 4 December 1736; Official Report on Antigua Slave Conspiracy, 30 December 1736, *South Carolina Gazette*, 12 February 1737. See also Letter from Antigua, 24 October 1736, *South Carolina Gazette*, 11 December 1736.
10. *South Carolina Gazette,* 25 January 1739.
11. Peter H. Wood, *Black Majority: Negroes in Colonial South Carolina from 1670 through the Stono Rebellion* (New York: Norton, 1974), 314–315.
12. "An Account of the Negroe Insurrection in South Carolina," in *The Colonial Records of the State of Georgia*, ed. Allen D. Candler, William L. Northern, and Lucian L. Knight (Atlanta: Byrd, 1913), 22: 232–236. Reprinted in *Stono: Documenting and Interpreting a Southern Slave Revolt,* ed. Mark M. Smith (Columbia: University of South Carolina Press, 2005), 13–15.
13. "Report of the Committee Appointed to Enquire into the Causes of the Disappointment of Success in the Late Expedition against St. Augustine," 1 July 1741, in *Journal of the Commons House of Assembly*, ed. J. H. Easterby et al., 10 vols. (Columbia: Historical Commission of South Carolina, 1953–1989), 3: 83–84. Reprinted in Smith, *Stono*, 28–29.
14. Wood, *Black Majority*, 319 (first quotation); *Journal of the Commons House of Assembly*, 2: 98 (second quotation); *Journal of the Commons House of Assembly*, 3: 83–84 (third quotation). For details of the rebellion, see Smith, *Stono*; Wood, *Black Majority*, 314–317; Rugemer, *Slave Law and the Politics of Resistance*, 111–113.
15. "An act for the better ordering and governing Negroes and other slaves in this Province," 10 May 1740, in *The Statutes at Large of South Carolina,* vol. 7, ed. Thomas Cooper and David J McCord (Columbia: A. S. Johnston, 1840), 397–417. For excerpts, see also Smith, *Stono*, 20–27. For analysis see Wood, *Black Majority*, 324–325; Rugemer, *Slave Law and the Politics of Resistance*, 113–116. Important overviews of

enslavement in South Carolina include Ira Berlin, *Many Thousands Gone: The First Two Centuries of Slavery in North America* (Cambridge: Harvard University Press, 1998), chapters 3, 6, 11; Philip D. Morgan, *Slave Counterpoint: Black Culture in the Eighteenth-Century Chesapeake and Low Country* (Chapel Hill: University of North Carolina Press, 1998); Littlefield, *Rice and Slaves*; Olwell, *Masters, Slaves, and Subjects*; Quintana, *Making a Slave State*.

16. Rugemer, *Slave Law and the Politics of Resistance*, 114 (including quotation).
17. Journal of Colonel William Stephens, 13 September 1739, in Smith, *Stono*, 4; Eliza Lucas to Katherine Martin Carew, 2 September 1743, DE.
18. Eliza Lucas to Mary Boddicott, 2 May 1740, DE.
19. Eliza Lucas to Mary Boddicott, 2 May 1740, DE. For Fanny Fayerweather, see Williams, "Eliza Lucas and Her Family," 268; "Fanny Fayerweather," DE; John Carney, "In Search of Fayerweather: The Fayerweather Family of Boston," *New England Historical and Genealogical Register* 144 (April 1990): 157–159. Elizabeth Murray also moved to North America in 1739; she managed her brother's North Carolina household at age fourteen while he served in the War of Jenkins' Ear. Cleary, *Elizabeth Murray*, 33–34.
20. Matthew Mulcahy, *Hubs of Empire: The Southeastern Lowcountry and British Caribbean* (Baltimore: Johns Hopkins University Press, 2014), 162; Cara Anzilotti, *In the Affairs of the World: Women, Patriarchy, and Power in Colonial South Carolina* (Westport, CT: Greenwood, 2002), 96–98.
21. Eliza Lucas to Mary Bartlett, c. 1745, DE. For kinship in South Carolina, see Glover, *All Our Relations*. For Georgia, see Ben Marsh, *Georgia's Frontier Women: Female Fortunes in a Southern Colony* (Athens: University of Georgia Press, 2007), especially 36–42.
22. Eliza Lucas to Mary Boddicott, 2 May 1740, DE. For women's roles, see Cynthia A. Kierner, *Beyond the Household: Women's Place in the Early South, 1700–1835* (Ithaca, NY: Cornell University Press, 1998).
23. Eliza Lucas to George Lucas, 2 May 1744, DE.
24. Eliza Lucas to George Lucas, c. 1740, DE.
25. *A Detection of the State and Situation of the Present Sugar Planters, of Barbadoes and the Leeward Islands* (London: J. Wilford, 1732), 53; Eliza Lucas to George Lucas, 2 May 1744, DE.

4. *PUTTING DOWN ROOTS*

1. Eliza Lucas to Miss Livingston, c. 1743, *The Letterbook of Eliza Lucas Pinckney, 1739–1762*, ed. Elise Pinckney (Columbia: University of South Carolina Press, 1997), 62 (first quotation; hereinafter *Letterbook*); Eliza Lucas to Elizabeth Lamb Pinckney, c. 1741, DE.
2. Eliza Lucas to Mary Boddicott, 2 May 1740, DE.
3. Eliza Lucas to George Lucas, c. 1740, *Letterbook*, 10–11. See also Eliza Lucas to Mary Bartlett, c. January 1742, *Letterbook*, 27.
4. Eliza Lucas to Mary Boddicott, 2 May 1741, *Letterbook*, 14.

5. For reliability mattering more than gender, see also Ellen Hartigan-O'Connor, *The Ties That Buy: Women and Commerce in Revolutionary America* (Philadelphia: University of Pennsylvania Press, 2009), 70, 194.
6. Matthew Mulcahy, *Hubs of Empire: The Southeastern Lowcountry and British Caribbean* (Baltimore: Johns Hopkins University Press, 2014), 102, 126; Jennifer L. Morgan, *Laboring Women: Reproduction and Gender in New World Slavery* (Philadelphia: University of Pennsylvania Press, 2004), 105, 111.
7. See Eliza Lucas to George Lucas, 4 June 1741, *Letterbook*, 16; Eliza Lucas to George Lucas, 23 April 1741, *Letterbook*, 13; Eliza Lucas to Starrat, 16 October 1741, *Letterbook*, 23; Eliza Lucas to William Murray, 11 November 1741, *Letterbook*, 24.
8. For plantations as business enterprises, see Justin Roberts, *Slavery and the Enlightenment in the British Atlantic, 1750–1807* (New York: Cambridge University Press, 2013); Caitlin Rosenthal, *Accounting for Slavery: Masters and Management* (Cambridge: Harvard University Press, 2018).
9. For debates about rice knowledge, see Daniel C. Littlefield, *Rice and Slaves: Ethnicity and the Slave Trade in Colonial South Carolina* (Urbana: University of Illinois Press, 1981), 98–106; S. Max Edelson, *Plantation Enterprise in Colonial South Carolina* (Cambridge: Harvard University Press, 2006), 53–62; Morgan, *Laboring Women*, 161–165. For producing rice, see also Mulcahy, *Hubs of Empire*, 97–99. For task vs. gang systems, see Philip D. Morgan, *Slave Counterpoint: Black Culture in the Eighteenth-Century Chesapeake and Low Country* (Chapel Hill: University of North Carolina Press, 1998), 179–194.
10. Planters had few qualms about putting enslaved women to fieldwork. Morgan, *Laboring Women*, especially 150.
11. Eliza Lucas to William Murray, c. July 1742, *Letterbook*, 54. For white women and slaveholding, see Thavolia Glymph, *Out of the House of Bondage: The Transformation of the Plantation Household* (New York: Cambridge University Press, 2008), chapter 1; Stephanie E. Jones-Rogers, *They Were Her Property: White Women as Slave Owners in the American South* (New Haven: Yale University Press, 2019). For the Caribbean, see Hilary McD. Beckles, "White Women and Slavery in the Caribbean," *History Workshop* 36 (Autumn 1993): 66–82; Marisa J. Fuentes, *Dispossessed Lives: Enslaved Women, Violence, and the Archive* (Philadelphia: University of Pennsylvania Press, 2016), especially 74–77, 86.
12. Eliza Lucas to George Lucas, 1 June 1742, *Letterbook*, 50.
13. *The Laws of the Island of Antigua: Consisting of the Acts of the Leeward Islands, Commencing 8th November 1690, ending 21st April 1798; and the Acts of Antigua, Commencing 10th April 1668, ending 7th May 1804*, 2 vols. (London: Samuel Bagster, 1805), 1: 91, 101.
14. Eliza Lucas to Richard Boddicott, undated, *Letterbook*, 65.
15. Her situation was unusual but not unique. For other examples, see Susan Hanket Brandt, "Marketing Medicine: Apothecary Elizabeth Weed's Economic Independence during the American Revolution," in *Women in the American Revolution: Gender, Politics, and the Domestic World*, ed. Barbara B. Oberg (Charlottesville: University of Virginia Press, 2019), 60–79; Kit Candlin and Cassandra Pybus, *Enterprising Women:*

Gender, Race, and Power in the Revolutionary Atlantic (Athens: University of Georgia Press, 2015); Patricia Cleary, *Elizabeth Murray: A Woman's Pursuit of Independence in Eighteenth-Century America* (Amherst: University of Massachusetts Press, 2000); Linda Colley, *The Ordeal of Elizabeth Marsh: A Woman in World History* (New York: Random House, 2007); Ami Pflugrad-Jackisch, " 'What Am I but an American?': Mary Willing Byrd and Westover Plantation during the American Revolution," in Oberg, *Women in the American Revolution*, 171–191.

16. For the importance of family letters, see William Merrell Decker, *Epistolary Practices: Letter Writing in America before Telecommunications* (Chapel Hill: University of North Carolina Press, 1998); Konstantin Dierks, *In My Power: Letter Writing and Communications in Early America* (Philadelphia: University of Pennsylvania Press, 2009); Sarah M. S. Pearsall, *Atlantic Families: Lives and Letters in the Later Eighteenth Century* (New York: Oxford University Press, 2008); Steven M. Stowe, "The Rhetoric of Authority: The Making of Social Values in Planter Family Correspondence," *Journal of American History* 73 (March 1987): 919–933; Tamara Plakins Thornton, *Handwriting in America: A Cultural History* (New Haven: Yale University Press, 1996); Michael Zuckerman, "Penmanship Exercises for Saucy Sons: Some Thoughts on the Colonial Southern Family," *South Carolina Historical Magazine* 84 (July 1983): 152–166.
17. David Ramsay, *The History of South Carolina, from Its First Settlement in 1670 to the Year 1808,* 2 vols. (Charleston: 1809), 2: 411. For analysis, see Cynthia A. Kierner, *Beyond the Household: Women's Place in the Early South, 1700–1835* (Ithaca, NY: Cornell University Press, 1998), especially 44, 56; Lorri Glover, *All Our Relations: Blood Ties and Emotional Bonds among the Early South Carolina Gentry* (Baltimore: Johns Hopkins University Press, 2000), especially 108; Elizabeth M. Purden, "Investing Widows: Autonomy in a Nascent Capitalist Society," in *Money, Trade, and Power: The Evolution of Colonial South Carolina's Plantation Society,* ed. Jack P. Greene, Rosemary Brana-Shute, and Randy J. Sparks (Columbia: University of South Carolina Press, 2001), 344–362. For women planters, see also Pflugrad-Jackisch, " 'What Am I but an American?' "; Mary Beth Norton, *Liberty's Daughters: The Revolutionary Experience of American Women, 1750–1800* (New York: Little, Brown, 1980), 26–33.
18. For South Carolinians' affinity for Englishness, see Emma Hart, *Building Charleston: Town and Society in the Eighteenth-Century British Atlantic World* (Charlottesville: University of Virginia Press, 2010), especially 130–141; Jennifer Van Horn, *The Power of Objects in Eighteenth-Century British America* (Chapel Hill: University of North Carolina Press, 2017), especially 216. For gentry culture and gender values, see Cara Anzilotti, *In the Affairs of the World: Women, Patriarchy, and Power in Colonial South Carolina* (Westport, CT: Greenwood, 2002); Glover, *All Our Relations*, chapters 3–4; Catherine Kerrison, *Claiming the Pen: Women and Intellectual Life in the Early American South* (Ithaca, NY: Cornell University Press, 2006); Kierner, *Beyond the Household*, chapters 1–2; Cary Carson, *Face Value: The Consumer Revolution and the Colonizing of America* (Charlottesville: University of Virginia Press, 2017).
19. Eliza Lucas to Mary Boddicott, 2 May 1740, DE.
20. Anne King Gregorie, "Cemetery Inscriptions from Christ Church Parish," *South Carolina Historical and Genealogical Magazine* 21 (April 1920), 73; Randy J. Sparks,

Africans in the Old South: Mapping Exceptional Lives across the Atlantic World (Cambridge: Harvard University Press, 2016), 24.

21. Eliza Lucas to Mary Boddicott, 2 May 1740, DE.
22. Eliza Lucas to Mary Bartlett, c. 1742, *Letterbook*, 34–35.
23. Eliza Lucas to Mary Bartlett, c. June 1742, *Letterbook*, 46.
24. Eliza Lucas to Mary Bartlett, c. May 1742, *Letterbook*, 38. See also Eliza Lucas to Mary Bartlett, c. 1741, Harriott Horry Ravenel, *Eliza Pinckney* (New York: Charles Scribner's Sons, 1896), 28.
25. Ravenel, *Eliza Pinckney*, 43–44. See also Lynn B. Harris, *Patroons and Periaguas: Enslaved Watermen and Watercraft of the Lowcountry* (Columbia: University of South Carolina Press, 2014). Drayton Hall and Middleton Place survive today. The Ashley River Road is a National Scenic Byway.
26. Eliza Lucas to George Lucas, Jr., July 1741, DE; Eliza Lucas to George Lucas, Jr., c. 1742, *Letterbook*, 52; Eliza Lucas to Thomas Lucas, c. 1743, DE.
27. Eliza Lucas to George Lucas, Jr., July 1741, *Letterbook*, 17 (first quotation); Eliza Lucas to George Lucas, Jr., c. 1742, *Letterbook*, 45 (second quotation). See also Eliza Lucas, c. September 1742, *Letterbook*, 56.
28. Eliza Lucas to Mary Bartlett, c. 1742, DE. For George Lucas's library, see Eliza Lucas to Mary Boddicott, 2 May 1740, DE. Family libraries were a common source of young women's self-education. Kerrison, *Claiming the Pen*, chapter 4; Kierner, *Beyond the Household*, 65.
29. Eliza Lucas to Mary Bartlett, c. 1742, *Letterbook*, 34. For Garden's school, see Shawn Comminey, "The Society for the Propagation of the Gospel in Foreign Parts and Black Education in South Carolina, 1702–1764," *Journal of Negro History* 84 (Autumn 1999): 360–369; Robert Olwell, *Masters, Slaves, and Subjects: The Culture of Power in the South Carolina Low Country, 1740–1790* (Ithaca, NY: Cornell University Press, 1998), 119–121; Fred E. Witzig, *Sanctifying Slavery and Politics in South Carolina: The Life of Reverend Alexander Garden, 1685–1756* (Columbia: University of South Carolina Press, 2018), chapter 6. For the 1740 law, see Kerrison, *Claiming the Pen*, 12; Edward B. Rugemer, *Slave Law and the Politics of Resistance in the Early Atlantic World* (Cambridge: Harvard University Press, 2018), 116. For reading and writing, see Anzilotti, *In the Affairs of the World*, 87; Gloria L. Main, "An Inquiry into When and Why Women Learned to Write in Colonial New England," *Journal of Social History* 24 (Spring 1991): 579–589.
30. Eliza Lucas to Mrs. H., c. 1742, *Letterbook*, 49; Eliza Lucas to George Lucas, January 1742, *Letterbook*, 25.
31. Eliza Lucas to Mary Bartlett, c. 1742, *Letterbook*, 34–35.
32. Eliza Lucas to Mary Boddicott, 2 May 1740, DE. See also Eliza Lucas to Mary Boddicott, 14 December 1743, DE.
33. Eliza Lucas to Mary Bartlett, c. 1742, DE.
34. Mary Boddicott knew about the headaches from Eliza's days in boarding school. Eliza Lucas to Mary Boddicott, 2 May 1741, *Letterbook*, 14; *Letterbook*, 12, fn. 16. For migraines later in her life, see Charles Cotesworth Pinckney to Harriott Pinckney Horry, 8 October 1782, DE.

35. Eliza Lucas to George Lucas, 4 June 1741, *Letterbook*, 15.
36. Eliza Lucas to Mary Boddicott, 29 June 1742, *Letterbook*, 42.
37. Eliza Lucas to Mary Bartlett, c. June 1742, *Letterbook*, 41. No will written by Eliza Lucas survives.
38. Eliza Lucas to Mary Bartlett, c. June 1742, *Letterbook*, 41.
39. Eliza Lucas to Mary Bartlett, c. April 1742, *Letterbook*, 36 (first and second quotations); Eliza Lucas to Mary Bartlett, c. May 1742, *Letterbook*, 39; Eliza Lucas Pinckney to [Charles Cotesworth Pinckney], 10 September 1785, DE (last quotation). Eliza described her memory of his encouragement in this letter. See also Eliza L. Martin, "Eliza Lucas Pinckney: Production and Consumption in the Atlantic World," *World History Connected* 7 (February 2010), http://worldhistoryconnected.press.uillinois.edu/7.1/martin.html; Emily Bowles, " 'You Would Think Me Far Gone in Romance': Eliza Lucas Pinckney and Fictions of Female Identity in the Colonial South," *Southern Quarterly* 42 (Summer 2004): 35–51. Jane Colden (1724–1776), often celebrated as America's first female botanist, was likewise encouraged by her father. Susan Scott Parrish, *American Curiosity: Cultures of Natural History in the Colonial British Atlantic World* (Chapel Hill: University of North Carolina Press, 2006), 196–200.

5. *A BRILLIANT SCHEME*

1. Eliza Lucas to George Lucas, 3 February 1744, *The Letterbook of Eliza Lucas Pinckney, 1739–1762*, ed. Elise Pinckney (Columbia: University of South Carolina Press, 1997), 58 (first quotation; hereinafter *Letterbook*); Eliza Lucas to Mary Bartlett, c. 1742, DE (second quotation).
2. For an excellent exploration of indigo, see Andrea Feeser, *Red, White, and Black Make Blue: Indigo in the Fabric of Colonial South Carolina Life* (Athens: University of Georgia Press, 2013).
3. Joyce E. Chaplin, *An Anxious Pursuit: Agricultural Innovation and Modernity in the Lower South, 1730–1815* (Chapel Hill: University of North Carolina Press, 1993), 193–196; David L. Coon, "Eliza Lucas Pinckney and the Reintroduction of Indigo Culture in South Carolina," *Journal of Southern History* 42 (February 1976), 62–63; Eliza L. Martin, "Eliza Lucas Pinckney: Production and Consumption in the Atlantic World," *World History Connected* 7 (February 2010), https://worldhistoryconnected.press.uillinois.edu/7.1/martin.html; Feeser, *Red, White, and Black Make Blue*, chapter 5. For a contemporary description, see Charles Woodmason, "Art of Manufacturing Indigo, and of Distinguishing the Best," *Gentleman's Magazine* (June 1755): 256–259.
4. Coon, "Eliza Lucas Pinckney," 63. For rice production, see S. Max Edelson, *Plantation Enterprise in Colonial South Carolina* (Cambridge: Harvard University Press, 2006), chapter 2; Daniel C. Littlefield, *Rice and Slaves: Ethnicity and the Slave Trade in Colonial South Carolina* (Urbana: University of Illinois Press, 1981).
5. Eliza Lucas to George Lucas, July 1740, DE; Eliza Lucas to George Lucas, 4 June 1741, DE.
6. Marriage Settlement, May 1744, DE. For Quash's life, see also Feeser, *Red, White, and Black Make Blue*, chapter 7.

7. Eliza Lucas to Mary Bartlett, c. 1742, DE (quotation); Eliza Lucas Pinckney to [Charles Cotesworth Pinckney], 10 September 1785, DE. See also George Lucas to Charles Pinckney, 12 July 1745, DE; George Lucas, Article of Agreement, 12 July 1745, DE.
8. Eliza Lucas Pinckney to [Charles Cotesworth Pinckney], 10 September 1785, DE; Eliza Lucas to George Lucas, 14 October 1741, *Letterbook*, 22; Feeser, *Red, White, and Black Make Blue*, 100–105. For enslaved skilled artisans, see S. Max Edelson, "Affiliation without Affinity: Skilled Slaves in Eighteenth-Century South Carolina," in *Money, Trade, and Power: The Evolution of Colonial South Carolina's Plantation Society*, ed. Jack P. Greene, Rosemary Brana-Shute, and Randy J. Sparks (Columbia: University of South Carolina Press, 2001), 217–255.
9. Eliza Lucas to George Lucas, 25 July 1740, *Letterbook*, 10; Coon, "Eliza Lucas Pinckney," 68–73; "Agricola," *South Carolina Gazette*, 23 December 1745. For context regarding colonial women and botany, see Susan Scott Parrish, *American Curiosity: Cultures of Natural History in the Colonial British Atlantic World* (Chapel Hill: University of North Carolina Press, 2006), chapter 5, especially 201–208.
10. J. Harold Easterby and Ruth S. Green, eds., *The Journal of the Commons House of Assembly*, vol. 9, *28 March 1749–19 March 1750* (Columbia: Historical Commission of South Carolina, 1962), 99 (quotation). See also Chaplin, *An Anxious Pursuit*, 187–208; Justin Roberts, *Slavery and the Enlightenment in the British Atlantic, 1750–1807* (New York: Cambridge University Press, 2013), especially 90.
11. Eliza Lucas Pinckney to George Lucas, c. 1744, DE; Feeser, *Red, White, and Black Make Blue*, 6, 49–51.
12. Coon, "Eliza Lucas Pinckney," 71; Matthew Mulcahy, *Hubs of Empire: The Southeastern Lowcountry and British Caribbean* (Baltimore: Johns Hopkins University Press, 2014), 103; Henry Laurens to Sarah Nickelson, 1 August 1755, *The Papers of Henry Laurens,* 16 vols., ed. David R. Chesnutt et al. (Columbia: University of South Carolina Press, 1968–2003), 1: 309 (quotation); Edward McCrady, *The History of South Carolina under the Royal Government, 1719–1776* (New York: Macmillan, 1899), 267–268. For context see S. Max Edelson, "The Characters of Commodities: The Reputation of South Carolina Rice and Indigo in the Atlantic World," in *The Atlantic Economy during the Seventeenth and Eighteenth Centuries: Organization, Operation, Practice, and Personnel,* ed. Peter A. Coclanis (Columbia: University of South Carolina Press, 2005), 349–355.
13. Letter from Antigua, 24 October 1736, *South Carolina Gazette*, 11 December 1736; "An act for the better ordering and governing Negroes and other slaves in this Province," 10 May 1740, in *The Statutes at Large of South Carolina,* vol. 7, ed. Thomas Cooper and David J. McCord (Columbia: A. S. Johnston, 1840), 397–417.
14. Eliza Lucas to George Lucas, 7 January 1743, *Letterbook*, 57. For owners' court appearances, see also Robert Olwell, *Masters, Slaves, and Subjects: The Culture of Power in the South Carolina Low Country, 1740–1790* (Ithaca, NY: Cornell University Press, 1998), chapter 2, especially 95–96. For examples of other women running estates and businesses, see Susan Hanket Brandt, "Marketing Medicine: Apothecary Elizabeth Weed's Economic Independence during the American Revolution," Ami Pflugrad-Jackisch, " 'What Am I but an American?': Mary Willing Byrd and Westover Plantation

during the American Revolution," Kaylan M. Stevenson, " 'Until Liberty of Importation Is Allowed': Milliners and Mantuamakers in the Chesapeake on the Eve of the Revolution," all in *Women in the American Revolution: Gender, Politics, and the Domestic World,* ed. Barbara B. Oberg (Charlottesville: University of Virginia Press, 2019).

15. Thomas Dale to Thomas Birch, 25 November 1734, Thomas Dale Papers, South Caroliniana Library (hereinafter SCL); Eliza Wilkinson to Mary P., 20 September 1782, Eliza Wilkinson Papers, SCL.
16. Eliza Lucas to George Lucas, c. April 1740, *Letterbook,* 6. For marriage patterns among elite Carolinians, see Cara Anzilotti, *In the Affairs of the World: Women, Patriarchy, and Power in Colonial South Carolina* (Westport, CT: Greenwood, 2002), chapter 3; Lorri Glover, *All Our Relations: Blood Ties and Emotional Bonds among the Early South Carolina Gentry* (Baltimore: Johns Hopkins University Press, 2000), 9–10, 47–49, 60–70; Jennifer Van Horn, *The Power of Objects in Eighteenth-Century British America* (Chapel Hill: University of North Carolina Press, 2017), chapter 4.
17. John Lloyd to Richard Campion, 9 May 1794, John Lloyd Letterbook, SCL; Mabel L. Webber, ed., "Extracts from the Journal of Ann Manigault, 1754–1781," *South Carolina Historical and Genealogical Magazine* 20 (April 1919), 139–140.
18. Descendants said Eliza never sat for a portrait. Harriott H. Ravenel to Mrs. Rose, 10 March n.y., David O. Percy Transcription, Harriott Ravenel Smythe Family Papers (hereinafter Smythe Family Papers), South Carolina Historical Society (hereinafter SCHS). For analysis of portraits, see Maurizio Valsania, *Jefferson's Body: A Corporeal Biography* (Charlottesville: University of Virginia Press, 2017), 45–48; Van Horn, *The Power of Objects,* 16–18, chapter 4; Cary Carson, *Face Value: The Consumer Revolution and the Colonizing of America* (Charlottesville: University of Virginia Press, 2017), 88–90, 156–157.
19. Eliza Lucas to George Lucas, c. April 1740, *Letterbook,* 6.
20. Eliza Lucas to George Lucas, c. April 1740, *Letterbook,* 6; Eliza Lucas to Mary Bartlett, c. January 1742, *Letterbook,* 27.
21. Eliza Lucas to Mrs. H., c. June 1742, *Letterbook,* 48.
22. Eliza Lucas to George Lucas, 11 November 1742, *Letterbook,* 57.
23. Eliza Lucas to George Lucas, 8 September 1742, *Letterbook,* 55.
24. Eliza Lucas to George Lucas, January 1742, *Letterbook,* 25; Eliza Lucas to Mary Boddicott, 29 June 1742, *Letterbook,* 42; Eliza Lucas to George Lucas, 24 September 1742, *Letterbook,* 56; Eliza Lucas to George Lucas, 7 January 1743, *Letterbook,* 58; Eliza Lucas to George Lucas, Jr., c. 1742, *Letterbook,* 45 (first quotation); Eliza Lucas to George Lucas, 10 February 1743, DE (second quotation).
25. Eliza Lucas to Mary Boddicott, 29 June 1742, *Letterbook,* 42; Eliza Lucas to Thomas Lucas, 30 June 1742, *Letterbook,* 43.
26. Eliza Lucas to Mary Woodward Chardon, c. 1743, *Letterbook,* 68; Eliza Lucas to Thomas Lucas, c. 1743, *Letterbook,* 70–71.
27. Eliza Lucas to Mary Boddicott, 14 December 1743, *Letterbook,* 69.
28. Eliza Lucas to Mary Bartlett, c. 1742, DE (quotations); Eliza Lucas to Mary Bartlett, c. April 1742, *Letterbook,* 36.

29. Eliza Lucas to Miss Dunbar, 11 April 1743, DE (quotation); Eliza Lucas to Mary Boddicott, 14 December 1743, *Letterbook*, 69.
30. Eliza Lucas to Mary Boddicott, 14 December 1743, *Letterbook*, 70.
31. For concerns about Elizabeth's health, see Eliza Lucas to Elizabeth Lamb Pinckney, c. 1741, *Letterbook*, 19; Eliza Lucas to Mary Bartlett, c. 1742, *Letterbook*, 34.

6. *"I HAVE CHANGED MY CONDITION IN LIFE"*

1. Eliza Lucas Pinckney to Katherine Martin Carew, 11 January 1745, DE.
2. Eliza Lucas Pinckney to Fanny Fayerweather, c. 1744, DE. See also Harriott Horry Ravenel, *Eliza Pinckney* (New York: Charles Scribner's Sons, 1896), 93–94. For their marriage, see also Barbara L. Bellows, "Eliza Lucas Pinckney: The Evolution of an Icon," *South Carolina Historical Magazine* 106 (April–July 2005), 154–156; Constance B. Schulz, "Eliza Lucas Pinckney and Harriott Pinckney Horry: A South Carolina Revolutionary-Era Mother and Daughter," in *South Carolina Women: Their Lives and Times,* vol. 1, ed. Marjorie Julian Spruill, Valinda W. Littlefield, and Joan Marie Johnson (Athens: University of Georgia Press, 2009), 87–88; Anne Firor Scott, "Self-Portraits: Three Women," in *Uprooted Americans: Essays to Honor Oscar Handlin,* ed. Richard L. Bushman et al. (Boston: Little, Brown, 1979), 64–66.
3. Frances Leigh Williams, *A Founding Family: The Pinckneys of South Carolina* (New York: Harcourt Brace Jovanovich, 1978), 5–6.
4. George C. Rogers, Jr., *Charleston in the Age of the Pinckneys* (1969; Columbia: University of South Carolina Press, 1980), 120; "Biographical Sketches of Principal Correspondents," DE; Marvin R. Zahniser, *Charles Cotesworth Pinckney, Founding Father* (Chapel Hill: University of North Carolina Press, 1967), 4–5; Charles Cotesworth Pinckney, *Life of General Thomas Pinckney* (1895; Memphis: General Books, 2012), 2; Mabel L. Webber, "The Thomas Pinckney Family of South Carolina," *South Carolina Historical and Genealogical Magazine* 39 (January 1938), 15–18; Ravenel, *Eliza Pinckney*, 73–74, 86–87; Williams, *A Founding Family*, 7.
5. Webber, "The Thomas Pinckney Family," 21; A. S. Salley, Jr., "Col. Miles Brewton and Some of His Descendants," *South Carolina Historical and Genealogical Magazine* 2 (April 1901), 133–138; Pinckney, *Life of General Thomas Pinckney*, 2; Ravenel, *Eliza Pinckney*, 87.
6. Eliza Lucas to Miss Thomas, c. 1740, DE.
7. Eliza Lucas to George Lucas, 1 June 1742, *The Letterbook of Eliza Lucas Pinckney, 1739–1762,* ed. Elise Pinckney (Columbia: University of South Carolina Press, 1997), 51 (hereinafter *Letterbook*); Eliza Lucas to Elizabeth Lamb Pinckney, c. 1741, *Letterbook*, 19; Eliza Lucas to Mary Bartlett, c. 1742, *Letterbook*, 35 (last quotation). See also Eliza Lucas to Charles Pinckney, 6 February 1741, *Letterbook*, 12. For shared books, see Eliza Lucas to Mary Bartlett, c. March/April 1742, DE; Eliza Lucas to Charles Pinckney, c. 1741, *Letterbook*, 21. For southern women and literary culture, see Catherine Kerrison, *Claiming the Pen: Women and Intellectual Life in the Early American South* (Ithaca, NY: Cornell University Press, 2006).
8. Eliza Lucas to Mary Bartlett, c. June 1742, *Letterbook*, 41; Eliza Lucas to Charles Pinckney, c. 1741, *Letterbook*, 21; Eliza Lucas to Mary Bartlett, c. 1742, *Letterbook*, 38.

See also Eliza Lucas to Charles Pinckney, 6 February 1741, *Letterbook*, 12; Eliza Lucas to George Lucas, 1 June 1742, *Letterbook*, 51.

9. Eliza Lucas to Charles Pinckney, c. 1743, DE; Eliza Lucas to Charles Pinckney, c. 1742, DE; Eliza Lucas to Thomas Lucas, c. 1743, *Letterbook*, 70.
10. Eliza Lucas to Elizabeth Lamb Pinckney, c. 1743, DE; Eliza Lucas to Mary Bartlett, c. May 1743, *Letterbook*, 61–62. For the Middletons, see "Middleton of South Carolina," *South Carolina Historical and Genealogical Magazine* 1 (July 1900): 228–262. For Crowfield, see Michael Trinkley et al., "Archaeology at an Eighteenth-Century Slave Settlement in Goose Creek, South Carolina," Chicora Foundation Research Series 57 (Columbia, SC: Chicora Research Foundation, 2003), 9–14, https://www.chicora.org/pdfs/rs57-Crowfield%20Slave%20Settlement.pdf.
11. Eliza Lucas Pinckney to Mary Bartlett, c. 1745, DE.
12. Eliza Lucas Pinckney to Katherine Martin Carew, 11 January 1745, DE; Eliza Lucas Pinckney to Mary Bartlett, c. 1745, DE; Eliza Lucas to George Lucas, 2 May 1744, DE.
13. Eliza Lucas Pinckney to George Lucas, 2 June 1744, DE.
14. Smith quoted in Cara Anzilotti, *In the Affairs of the World: Women, Patriarchy, and Power in Colonial South Carolina* (Westport, CT: Greenwood, 2002), 71; Henry Laurens to Mathias Holmes, 20 May 1763, *The Papers of Henry Laurens,* 16 vols., ed. David R. Chesnutt et al.(Columbia: University of South Carolina Press, 1968–2003), 3: 461 (regarding Eleanor Austin; hereinafter *Papers of Henry Laurens*); Joseph W. Barnwell, ed., "Diary of Timothy Ford, 1785–1786," *South Carolina Historical and Genealogical Magazine* 13 (October 1912), 192. See also Lorri Glover, *All Our Relations: Blood Ties and Emotional Bonds among the Early South Carolina Gentry* (Baltimore: Johns Hopkins University Press, 2000), 68–69, 95–102; Anzilotti, *In the Affairs of the World*, 67–74.
15. Eliza Lucas Pinckney to George Lucas, 2 June 1744, DE.
16. Marriage Settlement, May 1744, DE. For women's legal status, see Marylynn Salmon, *Women and the Law of Property in Early America* (Chapel Hill: University of North Carolina Press, 1986). For coverture, see Tim Stretton and Krista J. Kesselring, eds., *Married Women and the Law: Coverture in English and the Common Law World* (Montreal: McGill-Queen's University Press, 2013). For marriage settlements, see Anzilotti, *In the Affairs of the World*, 145–148.
17. Eliza Lucas to George Lucas, 2 May 1744, DE.
18. Eliza Lucas, Private Prayers, 25 May 1744, DE.
19. Changing names was common in early America and often deeply meaningful. See Camilla Townsend, *Pocahontas and the Powhatan Dilemma* (New York: Hill and Wang, 2004); Edward E. Andrews, "In Occramar Marycoo's Hand: Naming and the Journey of an African Moses," unpublished essay in author's possession.
20. Mabel L. Webber, ed., "Abstracts of Marriage Bonds of South Carolina, December 1743–November 1744," *South Carolina Historical and Genealogical Magazine* 19 (July 1918), 134; Eliza Lucas Pinckney to Charles Pinckney, c. 1744, DE; Eliza Lucas Pinckney to Fanny Fayerweather, c. 1744, DE; Charles Pinckney to Peter Manigault, 8 April 1756, DE; Charles Pinckney to Ann Mildrum Lucas, c. 1744, DE. In the 1730s

the average marriage age for white women in South Carolina was seventeen. In the 1740s it rose to nineteen. Anzilotti, *In the Affairs of the World*, 73. For courtship, see Kerrison, *Claiming the Pen*, 144–150; Jennifer Van Horn, *The Power of Objects in Eighteenth-Century British America* (Chapel Hill: University of North Carolina Press, 2017), chapter 4. For weddings, see Julia Cherry Spruill, *Women's Life and Work in the Southern Colonies* (1938; New York: Norton, 1972), 86–87, 94–95, 110–112; Cynthia A. Kierner, *Beyond the Household: Women's Place in the Early South, 1700–1835* (Ithaca, NY: Cornell University Press, 1998), 52. Little of Eliza and Charles's courtship and marital correspondence survives.

21. Margaret Manigault to Gabriel Manigault, 20 November 1792, Manigault Family Papers, SCL; Gabriel Manigault to Margaret Manigault, 6 December 1791, Manigault Family Papers, SCL; Oliver Hart to Ann Hart, 12 June 1781, Oliver Hart Papers, SCL; Thomas Dale to Thomas Birch, 17 November 1732, Thomas Dale Papers, SCL. For marital relationships, see Kathleen M. Brown, *Good Wives, Nasty Wenches, and Anxious Patriarchs: Gender, Race, and Power in Colonial Virginia* (Chapel Hill: University of North Carolina Press, 1996), especially 334–342; Glover, *All Our Relations*, especially 67–70; Kerrison, *Claiming the Pen*, 150–153; Kierner, *Beyond the Household*, 164–168; Mary Beth Norton, *Liberty's Daughters: The Revolutionary Experience of American Women, 1750–1800* (New York: Little, Brown, 1980), chapter 2; Daniel Blake Smith, *Inside the Great House: Planter Family Life in Eighteenth-Century Chesapeake Society* (Ithaca, NY: Cornell University Press, 1980), chapter 4; Van Horn, *The Power of Objects*, chapter 4.
22. Eliza's descendants insisted that "no one seems to have been at all scandalized," but that appears more aspirational than accurate. Ravenel, *Eliza Pinckney*, 68.
23. Eliza Lucas Pinckney to Mary Bartlett, c. 1745, DE. For Charles's absence from his law practice, see also *South Carolina Gazette*, 26 December 1743.
24. Eliza Lucas Pinckney to Sarah Lamb Bartlett, 7 March 1745, DE. Charles Pinckney left money to Sarah Lamb Bartlett and Mary Bartlett in his will.
25. Eliza Lucas to George Lucas, Jr., c. 1742, *Letterbook*, 52.
26. Eliza Lucas Pinckney, Resolutions, DE.
27. Eliza Lucas Pinckney to Charles Pinckney, c. 1744, DE.
28. Williams, *A Founding Family*, 11; Eliza Lucas Pinckney to George Lucas, c. July 1744, DE.
29. Eliza Lucas Pinckney to George Lucas, 2 June 1744, DE.
30. Eliza Lucas Pinckney to Ann Mildrum Lucas, c. October 1744, DE; Ravenel, *Eliza Pinckney*, 101–102.
31. For sericulture, see Zara Anishanslin, *Portrait of a Woman in Silk: Hidden Histories of the British Atlantic World* (New Haven: Yale University Press, 2016), 28, 38, chapter 7; Joyce E. Chaplin, *An Anxious Pursuit: Agricultural Innovation and Modernity in the Lower South, 1730–1815* (Chapel Hill: University of North Carolina Press, 1993), 158–165.
32. Eliza Lucas Pinckney to George Lucas, c. 1744, DE; Ravenel, *Eliza Pinckney*, 100.
33. Eliza Lucas Pinckney to George Lucas, c. 1744, DE.
34. See Ravenel, *Eliza Pinckney*, 100, 102; Eliza Lucas Pinckney to George Lucas, c. 1744, DE. The Digital Edition editors speculate that Charles took over managing the Lucas

properties after he and Eliza married, but note that some business papers in the 1740s–1750s were in Eliza's hand. They conclude: "To what degree she remained involved may never be fully determined." "Lucas Family Plantation Management," DE.

35. Jill Lepore observes, "Marriage determined the whole course of every woman's life." Jill Lepore, *Book of Ages: The Life and Opinions of Jane Franklin* (New York: Knopf, 2013), 52. Martha Custis to John Hanbury and Company, 20 August 1757, in Joseph E. Fields, ed., *"Worthy Partner": The Papers of Martha Washington* (Westport, CT: Greenwood, 1994), 6. See also Patricia Brady, *Martha Washington: An American Life* (New York: Viking, 2005), chapter 4. For the Izards, see Ralph Izard to Alice DeLancey Izard, 28 December 1782, Ralph Izard Papers, SCL. For Mercy Otis Warren, see Rosemarie Zagarri, *A Woman's Dilemma: Mercy Otis Warren and the American Revolution,* 2nd ed. (Malden, MA: Wiley Blackwell, 2015), especially 4, 79.
36. Eliza Lucas Pinckney to George Lucas, c. 1744, DE. For examples of continued engagement, see Eliza Lucas Pinckney to George Lucas, miscellaneous letters 1744, DE; George Lucas, Article of Agreement, 6 July 1744, DE.
37. Richard Boddicott to Charles Pinckney, 22 April 1745, DE; Eliza Lucas Pinckney to George Lucas, 2 June 1744, DE. William Murray to Eliza Lucas Pinckney, January 1745, DE, is his last letter to Eliza.
38. Williams, *A Founding Family*, 12; Eliza Lucas Pinckney to Mary Bartlett, June 1745, DE.
39. George Lucas to Charles Pinckney, 22 May 1745, DE; George Lucas, Jr., to Charles Pinckney, 21 October 1745, DE.
40. Webber, "The Thomas Pinckney Family," 16.
41. George Lucas to Charles Pinckney, 23 December 1745, DE; Charles Pinckney to George Lucas, 28 August 1745, DE; Ann Mildrum Lucas to Charles Pinckney, 30 January 1746, DE.
42. Ann Mildrum Lucas to Charles Pinckney, 30 January 1746, DE (quotations); George Lucas to Charles Pinckney, 30 January 1746, DE. For pregnancies, see Anzilotti, *In the Affairs of the World*, 82–83, 93; Glover, *All Our Relations*, 26–27. For analysis, see Norton, *Liberty's Daughters*, chapter 3; V. Lynn Kennedy, *Born Southern: Childbirth, Motherhood, and Social Networks in the Old South* (Baltimore: Johns Hopkins University Press, 2009), chapters 2–3; Nora Doyle, *Maternal Bodies: Redefining Motherhood in Early America* (Chapel Hill: University of North Carolina Press, 2018), chapters 1–2, especially 83–84; Kathleen M. Brown, *Foul Bodies: Cleanliness of Early America* (New Haven: Yale University Press, 2009), 191–194; Katy Simpson Smith, *We Have Raised All of You: Motherhood in the South, 1750–1835* (Baton Rouge: Louisiana State University Press, 2013), 95–99; Cynthia M. Kennedy, *Braided Relations, Entwined Lives: The Women of Charleston's Urban Slave Society* (Bloomington: Indiana University Press, 2005), chapter 10; Jennifer L. Morgan, *Laboring Women: Reproduction and Gender in New World Slavery* (Philadelphia: University of Pennsylvania Press, 2004), chapter 4; Sara Collini, "The Labors of Enslaved Midwives in Revolutionary Virginia," in *Women in the American Revolution: Gender, Politics, and the Domestic World,* ed. Barbara B. Oberg (Charlottesville: University of Virginia Press, 2019), 19–38.

43. George Lucas to Charles Pinckney, 30 January 1746, DE.
44. Eliza Lucas Pinckney to Mary Boddicott, 20 May 1746, DE.
45. Eliza Lucas Pinckney to Mary Bartlett, 20 May 1746, DE; Journal of Anne Ashby Manigault, March–April 1758, Manigault Family Papers, SCL.
46. Eliza Lucas Pinckney to Mary Bartlett, 2 December 1747, DE.
47. Eliza Lucas Pinckney to Mary Bartlett, 20 May 1746, DE. For the couple's childrearing, see also Steven C. Bullock, *Tea Sets and Tyranny: The Politics of Politeness in Early America* (Philadelphia: University of Pennsylvania Press, 2017), 203–208. For elite childrearing, see Anzilotti, *In the Affairs of the World*, 79–83; Smith, *Inside the Great House*, chapters 2–3.
48. Eliza Lucas Pinckney to Polly Lucas, c. December 1747, DE; William Read to Jacob Read, 18 December 1795, Jacob Read Papers, SCL; Henry Laurens to Lachlan McIntosh, 7 March 1763, *Papers of Henry Laurens,* 3: 362.
49. Eliza Lucas Pinckney to Polly Lucas, c. December 1747, DE.
50. *Antigua and the Antiguans: A Full Account of the Colony and its Inhabitants from the Time of the Caribs to the Present Day, Interspersed with Anecdotes and Legends. Also, an Impartial View of Slavery and the Free Labour Systems; the Statistics of the Island, and Biographical Notices of the Principal Families,* 2 vols. (London: Saunders and Otley, 1844), 1: 109; Vere Langford Oliver, *The History of the Island of Antigua,* 3 vols. (London: Mitchell and Hughes, 1894–1899), 3: 320; Eliza Lucas to George Lucas, c. 1740, *Letterbook,* 11.
51. Eliza Lucas Pinckney to Mary Bartlett, 2 December 1747, DE; Carol Walter Ramagosa, "Eliza Lucas Pinckney's Family in Antigua, 1668–1747," *South Carolina Historical Magazine* 99 (July 1998), 256, fn. 59; Williams, *A Founding Family*, 12–13. For grief over infant death, see also Smith, *We Have Raised All of You*, 163–164.

7. *FAITH AND SELF-GOVERNMENT*

1. Eliza Lucas to Mary Bartlett, c. March 1742, DE; Eliza Lucas to Thomas Lucas, c. 1743, *The Letterbook of Eliza Lucas Pinckney, 1739–1762,* ed. Elise Pinckney (Columbia: University of South Carolina Press, 1997), 63 (first quotation; hereinafter *Letterbook*); Eliza Lucas to Thomas Lucas, c. 1743, *Letterbook*, 71 (second quotation).
2. Charles Woodmason, "An Account of the Churches in South Carolina, Georgia, North Carolina, and the Floridas, 1765," in *The Carolina Backcountry on the Eve of the Revolution: The Journal and Other Writings of Charles Woodmason, Anglican Itinerant,* ed. Richard J. Hooker (Chapel Hill: University of North Carolina Press, 1953), 70 (first quotation); "Journal of Josiah Quincy, Jr.," *Proceedings of the Massachusetts Historical Society* 49 (October 1915–June 1916), 444 (second quotation). Originally built on the corner of Meeting and Broad, the first St. Philip's, a wooden structure, was nearly destroyed by a hurricane in 1710. A new brick building, called the Second Church, was built in a nearby location, on Church Street. That church burned in 1835. It was rebuilt and still stands today. Anna Wells Rutledge, "The Second St. Philip's, Charleston, 1710–1835," *Journal of the Society of Architectural Historians* 18 (October 1959): 112–114. For context, see Louis P. Nelson, "The Diversity of Countries: Anglican Churches in Virginia, South Carolina, and Jamaica," in *Material Culture in*

Anglo-America: Regional Identity and Urbanity in the Tidewater, Lowcountry, and Caribbean, ed. David S. Shields (Columbia: University of South Carolina Press, 2009), 74–101.

3. Robert Olwell, *Masters, Slaves, and Subjects: The Culture of Power in the South Carolina Low Country, 1740–1790* (Ithaca, NY: Cornell University Press, 1998), chapter 3, especially 104.
4. For the Enlightenment in America, see Henry F. May, *The Enlightenment in America* (New York: Oxford University Press, 1976), parts 1–2; Susan Scott Parrish, *American Curiosity: Cultures of Natural History in the Colonial British Atlantic World* (Chapel Hill: University of North Carolina Press, 2006). For Anglicanism in South Carolina, see S. Charles Bolton, *Southern Anglicanism: The Church of England in Colonial South Carolina* (Westport, CT: Greenwood, 1982); Louis P. Nelson, *The Beauty of Holiness: Anglicanism and Architecture in Colonial South Carolina* (Chapel Hill: University of North Carolina Press, 2008), especially chapter 6; Olwell, *Masters, Slaves, and Subjects,* chapter 3. Bolton reached a similar conclusion about Eliza's religious values. Bolton, *Southern Anglicanism,* 156. For Anglicanism in Virginia, see Lauren F. Winner, *A Cheerful and Comfortable Faith: Anglican Religious Practice in the Elite Households of Eighteenth-Century Virginia* (New Haven: Yale University Press, 2010). For comparison to a New England woman, see Catherine A. Brekus, *Sarah Osborn's World: The Rise of Evangelical Christianity in Early America* (New Haven: Yale University Press, 2013). For early American women and religion generally, see Marilyn J. Westerkamp, *Women and Religion in Early America, 1600–1850: The Puritan and Evangelical Traditions* (New York: Routledge, 1999). For individualism in religious traditions, see also Ruth H. Bloch, "Religion, Literary Sentimentalism, and Popular Revolutionary Ideology," in *Religion in a Revolutionary Age,* ed. Ronald Hoffman and Peter J. Albert (Charlottesville: University Press of Virginia, 1994), 323–329.
5. Eliza Lucas Pinckney, Private Prayers, DE (first and third quotations); Eliza Lucas to George Lucas, Jr., c. 1742, *Letterbook,* 51. For eighteenth-century ideals of womanhood, see Cynthia A. Kierner, *Beyond the Household: Women's Place in the Early South, 1700–1835* (Ithaca, NY: Cornell University Press, 1998), 25–34. Megan Hatfield defines Eliza as a "rational Christian" shaped by "Enlightenment optimism." Hatfield, "A Family upon the Deep Blue Sea: The Atlantic Life of Eliza Lucas Pinckney," Ph.D. diss., University of Miami, 2015, 136.
6. *Letterbook,* 9–10, fn. 11 (quotations); *South Carolina Gazette,* 8–15 January 1741; Fred E. Witzig, *Sanctifying Slavery and Politics in South Carolina: The Life of Reverend Alexander Garden, 1685–1756* (Columbia: University of South Carolina Press, 2018), 18–19, 70, 84–87, 95–96, 116–117, 133–138; Randall Balmer and Lauren F. Winner, *Protestantism in America* (New York: Columbia University Press, 2002), 14; Bolton, *Southern Anglicanism,* 4, 50–55, 138–139; Nelson, *The Beauty of Holiness,* 302–303. See also Nelson, *The Beauty of Holiness,* chapter 6; Witzig, *Sanctifying Slavery and Politics,* 33–34; Rhys Isaac, *The Transformation of Virginia, 1740–1790* (Chapel Hill: University of North Carolina Press, 1982), especially 58–65; Winner, *A Cheerful and Comfortable Faith.*
7. Hugh Bryan, quoted in Harvey H. Jackson, "Hugh Bryan and the Evangelical Movement in Colonial South Carolina," *William and Mary Quarterly* 43 (October

1986), 602. For the Great Awakening in South Carolina, see also Peter N. Moore, *Archibald Simpson's Unpeaceable Kingdom: The Ordeal of Evangelicalism in the Colonial South* (Lanham, MD: Lexington, 2018); Witzig, *Sanctifying Slavery and Politics*, chapters 4–6. For evangelicals and elites after the Revolution, see Christine Leigh Heyrman, *Southern Cross: The Beginnings of the Bible Belt* (New York: Knopf, 1997).

8. Eliza Lucas Memorandum, 11 March 1742, *Letterbook*, 30 (first quotation); Eliza Lucas to Mary Bartlett, c. March 1742, DE (second quotation). For evangelical challenges to gentry worldviews in Virginia, see Isaac, *The Transformation of Virginia*, 161–177.
9. Eliza Lucas to George Lucas, Jr., c. 1742, *Letterbook*, 52 (quotation). Louis P. Nelson points to Eliza as illustrative of South Carolina Anglicans; see *The Beauty of Holiness*, 222–223, 248. For teaching enslaved girls to read, see Eliza Lucas to Mary Bartlett, c. 1742, DE. For the religious lives of enslaved South Carolinians, see Olwell, *Masters, Slaves, and Subjects*, chapter 3; Philip D. Morgan, *Slave Counterpoint: Black Culture in the Eighteenth-Century Chesapeake and Low Country* (Chapel Hill: University of North Carolina Press, 1998), 420–437, 610–648. Catherine A. Brekus finds a similar attitude in her biography *Sarah Osborn's World: The Rise of Evangelical Christianity in Early America* (New Haven: Yale University Press, 2013), 237.
10. Eliza Lucas to Mary Bartlett, March 1742, DE (first quotation); Eliza Lucas to George Lucas, Jr., c. 1742, *Letterbook*, 53 (second quotation). For analysis, see Nelson, *The Beauty of Holiness*, 219–221. Mercy Otis Warren likewise saw no contradiction between religion and reason. Rosemarie Zagarri, *A Woman's Dilemma: Mercy Otis Warren and the American Revolution*, 2nd ed. (Malden, MA: Wiley Blackwell, 2015), 18.
11. Eliza Lucas to George Lucas, Jr., c. 1742, *Letterbook*, 52–53 (quotation); Eliza Lucas to Thomas Lucas, c. 1743, *Letterbook*, 70; Eliza Lucas Pinckney, Private Prayers, 28 December 1746, DE.
12. Eliza Lucas Pinckney to Mary Bartlett, 2 December 1747, DE.
13. Frances Leigh Williams, *A Founding Family: The Pinckneys of South Carolina* (New York: Harcourt Brace Jovanovich, 1978), 13.
14. "The Ichnography of Charles-Town, at High Water," 1739 map by George Hunter, digital access at https://collections.leventhalmap.org/search/commonwealth:hx11z600p. For an excellent introduction to eighteenth-century Charleston, see Emma Hart, *Building Charleston: Town and Society in the Eighteenth-Century British Atlantic World* (Charlottesville: University of Virginia Press, 2010).
15. Robert Pringle, c. 1769, quoted in Olwell, *Masters, Slaves, and Subjects*, 35; George C. Rogers, Jr., *Charleston in the Age of the Pinckneys* (1969; Columbia: University of South Carolina Press, 1980), 99. For context, see Emma Hart, "Building Charleston: The Expansion of an Eighteenth-Century British Atlantic Town"; and Martha A. Zierden, "The Archaeological Signature of Eighteenth-Century Charleston," both in Shields, *Material Culture in Anglo-America*.
16. For middling-rank influences in Charles Town, see Hart, *Building Charleston*, especially chapter 6; Ellen Hartigan-O'Connor, *The Ties That Buy: Women and Commerce in Revolutionary America* (Philadelphia: University of Pennsylvania Press, 2009).

17. For Charles Town as an urban center, see Hart, *Building Charleston*, chapter 1; Rogers, *Charleston in the Age of the Pinckneys*; S. Max Edelson, *Plantation Enterprise in Colonial South Carolina* (Cambridge: Harvard University Press, 2006), chapter 4; Olwell, *Masters, Slaves, and Subjects*; Nicholas Michael Butler, *Votaries of Apollo: The St. Cecilia Society and the Patronage of Concert Music in Charleston, South Carolina, 1766–1820* (Columbia: University of South Carolina Press, 2007); Cynthia M. Kennedy, *Braided Relations, Entwined Lives: The Women of Charleston's Urban Slave Society* (Bloomington: Indiana University Press, 2005), especially chapter 8. For port cities, see Jennifer Van Horn, *The Power of Objects in Eighteenth-Century British America* (Chapel Hill: University of North Carolina Press, 2017); Hartigan-O'Connor, *The Ties That Buy*; Shields, *Material Culture in Anglo-America.*
18. Olwell, *Masters, Slaves, and Subjects*, 222.
19. For the town's architecture, see Olwell, *Masters, Slaves, and Subjects*, chapter 1. For St. Philip's and St. Michael's, see also Bolton, *Southern Anglicanism*, 74–76.
20. Eliza Lucas to Mary Boddicott, 2 May 1740, DE (first quotation); Eliza Lucas to Thomas Lucas, 22 May 1742, *Letterbook*, 39 (second quotation).
21. Hart, *Building Charleston*, 138–139. See also Cary Carson, *Face Value: The Consumer Revolution and the Colonizing of America* (Charlottesville: University of Virginia Press, 2017), 146–147; R. C. Nash, "Domestic Material Culture and Consumer Demand in the British Atlantic World: Colonial South Carolina, 1670–1770," in Shields, *Material Culture in Anglo-America*, 221–266.
22. Edward McCrady, *The History of South Carolina under the Royal Government, 1719–1776* (New York: Macmillan, 1899), 239–240; Hart, *Building Charleston*, 68–71.
23. George Fenwick Jones, ed., "John Martin Boltzius' Trip to Charleston, October 1742," *South Carolina Historical Magazine* 82 (April 1981), 98–102. For other visitors' impressions, see Jennie Holton Fant, ed., *The Travelers' Charleston: Accounts of Charleston and Lowcountry, South Carolina, 1666–1861* (Columbia: University of South Carolina Press, 2016); T. P. Harrison, ed., "Journal of a Voyage to Charlestown in So. Carolina by Pelatiah Webster in 1765," *Publications of the South Carolina Historical Society* (Charleston, 1898): 1–18; "Journal of Josiah Quincy, Jr."; Joseph W. Barnwell, ed., "Diary of Timothy Ford, 1785–1786," *South Carolina Historical and Genealogical Magazine* 13 (July 1912), 132–147.
24. A thorough description, including Charles's specifications, is in Alice R. Huger Smith and D. E. Huger Smith, *The Dwelling Houses of Charleston, South Carolina* (Philadelphia: Lippincott, 1917), 361–374.
25. George Lucas, Jr. to Charles Pinckney, 21 October 1745, DE.
26. Harriott Horry Ravenel, *Eliza Pinckney* (New York: Charles Scribner's Sons, 1896), 111–112 (including quotations); Rogers, *Charleston in the Age of the Pinckneys*, 68; Smith and Smith, *Dwelling Houses*, 361–363, 367–371.
27. Ravenel, *Eliza Pinckney*, 111 (quotations); Smith and Smith, *Dwelling Houses*, 362, 367, 369.
28. Ravenel, *Eliza Pinckney*, 112. Most of the household goods were seized during the Revolutionary War, and the house burned during the Civil War. In 2018 controversial plans to build a hotel on the site threatened the archaeological evidence still buried

on East Bay Street. Robert Behre, "One of Charleston's Most Intriguing Archaeological Sites Could Be Lost Forever," *Post and Courier*, 16 July 2018.

29. For women and gentility, see Kierner, *Beyond the Household*, 37–48; Cara Anzilotti, *In the Affairs of the World: Women, Patriarchy, and Power in Colonial South Carolina* (Westport, CT: Greenwood, 2002), chapter 2; Van Horn, *The Power of Objects*.
30. Eliza Lucas Pinckney to Mary Bartlett, c. June 1745, DE.
31. Ravenel, *Eliza Pinckney*, 112.
32. Marriage Settlement, May 1744, DE; George Lucas to Charles Pinckney, 22 May 1745, DE; Eliza Lucas Pinckney to George Lucas, c. 1745, DE. For Quash's life, see also Andrea Feeser, *Red, White, and Black Make Blue: Indigo in the Fabric of Colonial South Carolina Life* (Athens: University of Georgia Press, 2013), chapter 7. For enslaved skilled artisans, see also S. Max Edelson, "Affiliation without Affinity: Skilled Slaves in Eighteenth-Century South Carolina," in *Money, Trade, and Power: The Evolution of Colonial South Carolina's Plantation Society*, ed. Jack P. Greene, Rosemary Brana-Shute, and Randy J. Sparks (Columbia: University of South Carolina Press, 2001), 217–255.
33. George Lucas to Charles Pinckney, 17 September 1745, DE; Eliza Lucas Pinckney to George Lucas, miscellaneous letters 1745, DE; George Lucas to Charles Pinckney, 12 April 1746, DE.
34. Bill of Sale, Charles Pinckney, 5 January 1750, DE; Marriage Settlement, May 1744, DE; Daniel Huger Horry, Jr. Estate Inventory, 16 January 1786, DE. For challenges to families under slavery, see Jennifer L. Morgan, *Laboring Women: Reproduction and Gender in New World Slavery* (Philadelphia: University of Pennsylvania Press, 2004), 104–105, 123–128, 133–139; Matthew Mulcahy, *Hubs of Empire: The Southeastern Lowcountry and British Caribbean* (Baltimore: Johns Hopkins University Press, 2014), 129; Gregory E. O'Malley, *Final Passages: The Intercolonial Slave Trade of British America, 1619–1807* (Chapel Hill: University of North Carolina Press, 2014), 45; Justin Roberts, *Slavery and the Enlightenment in the British Atlantic, 1750–1807* (New York: Cambridge University Press, 2013), chapter 6.
35. Bill of Sale, Charles Pinckney, 5 January 1750, DE. For enslaved Anglican converts, see Olwell, *Masters, Slaves, and Subjects*, 122–126, 130–131.
36. Manumission of John Williams, 12 May 1750, DE. For free blacks, see Peter H. Wood, *Black Majority: Negroes in Colonial South Carolina from 1670 through the Stono Rebellion* (New York: Norton, 1974), 100–103; Olwell, *Masters, Slaves, and Subjects*, 45; Robert Olwell, "Becoming Free: Manumission and the Genesis of a Free Black Community in South Carolina, 1740–1790," *Slavery and Abolition* 17 (April 1996): 1–19.
37. *South Carolina Gazette*, 4 June 1750; *South Carolina Gazette*, 20 August 1763; Wood, *Black Majority*, 102–103; Feeser, *Red, White, and Black Make Blue*, 106–107.
38. Eliza Lucas Pinckney, Resolutions, DE. The exact date she composed her resolutions is unknown.
39. Eliza Lucas Pinckney, Resolutions, DE.
40. Ravenel, *Eliza Pinckney*, 138; Glen quoted in Jonathan Mercantini, "The Great Carolina Hurricane of 1752," *South Carolina Historical Magazine* 103 (October 2002), 354.

41. Ravenel, *Eliza Pinckney*, 139; *South Carolina Gazette*, 19 September 1752 (quotations).
42. Matthew Mulcahy, " 'Melancholy and Fatal Calamities': Disaster and Society in Eighteenth-Century South Carolina," in *Money, Trade, and Power: The Evolution of Colonial South Carolina's Plantation Society*, ed. Jack P. Greene, Rosemary Brana-Shute, and Randy J. Sparks (Columbia: University of South Carolina Press, 2001), 287; Mercantini, "The Great Carolina Hurricane of 1752," 355–356.
43. Ravenel, *Eliza Pinckney*, 139–140.
44. Eliza Lucas Pinckney, "Days sett apart to be rememberd," DE.
45. Williams, *A Founding Family*, 15.
46. Eliza Lucas Pinckney, "Days sett apart to be rememberd," DE.
47. McCrady, *History of South Carolina*, 279; *South Carolina Gazette*, 27 September 1752.
48. McCrady, *History of South Carolina*, 281. See also Peter Manigault to Gabriel Manigault, 25 August 1753, Manigault Family Papers, SCL.
49. Ravenel, *Eliza Pinckney*, 135.
50. Ravenel, *Eliza Pinckney*, 135–136; Charles Cotesworth Pinckney, *Life of General Thomas Pinckney* (1895; Memphis: General Books, 2012), 5.
51. Eliza Lucas Pinckney, Resolutions, DE.

8. *BECOMING AN AMERICAN IN LONDON*

1. Eliza Lucas Pinckney, Resolutions, DE; *South Carolina Gazette*, 12 April 1753.
2. *South Carolina Gazette*, 17 July 1793. For contemporaries of Eliza who temporarily moved abroad, see Woody Holton, *Abigail Adams, A Life* (New York: Free Press, 2009); Susan Clair Imbarrato, *Sarah Gray Cary, from Boston to Grenada: Shifting Fortunes of an American Family, 1764–1826* (Baltimore: Johns Hopkins University Press, 2018); Charlene M. Boyer Lewis, *Elizabeth Patterson Bonaparte: An American Aristocrat in the Early Republic* (Philadelphia: University of Pennsylvania Press, 2012); Louisa Thomas, *Louisa: The Extraordinary Life of Mrs. Adams* (New York: Penguin, 2016); Patricia Cleary, *Elizabeth Murray: A Woman's Pursuit of Independence in Eighteenth-Century America* (Amherst: University of Massachusetts Press, 2000).
3. *South Carolina Gazette*, 12 April 1753.
4. Eliza Lucas Pinckney to Mary Wood Wragg, c. 1753, DE. For the Wraggs, see Wragg Family Papers, SCHS; Alexia Jones Helsley, "William Wragg," *South Carolina Encyclopedia*, www.scencyclopedia.org.
5. William Henry (Billy) Drayton was born in September 1742 and Charles in December 1743. Charlotta Bull Drayton died two weeks after delivering Charles. John Drayton thereafter married Margaret Glen, sister of James Glen, who succeeded William Bull as governor of South Carolina. Henry A. M. Smith, "The Ashley River: Its Seats and Settlement," *South Carolina Historical and Genealogical Magazine* 20 (April 1919), 96; Keith Krawczynski, *William Henry Drayton: South Carolina Revolutionary Patriot* (Baton Rouge: Louisiana State University Press, 2001), 6–12; Edward McCrady, *The History of South Carolina under the Royal Government, 1719–1776* (New York: Macmillan, 1899), 474, 495; Kinloch Bull, Jr., *The Oligarchs in Colonial and Revolutionary Charleston: Lieutenant Governor William Bull II and His Family*

(Columbia: University of South Carolina Press, 1991), 51. For context, see Sarah M. S. Pearsall, *Atlantic Families: Lives and Letters in the Later Eighteenth Century* (New York: Oxford University Press, 2008), chapter 2.

6. Eliza Lucas Pinckney to Mary Wood Wragg, c. 1753, DE; Eliza Lucas Pinckney, "Days sett apart to be rememberd," DE.
7. Eliza Lucas Pinckney to Mary Wood Wragg, c. 1753, DE.
8. For a vivid description, see Elizabeth Fenn, *Pox Americana: The Great Smallpox Epidemic of 1775–82* (New York: Hill and Wang, 2001), 15–20. See also Kathleen M. Brown, *Foul Bodies: Cleanliness in Early America* (New Haven: Yale University Press, 2009), 126–131; Suzanne Krebsbach, "The Great Charlestown Smallpox Epidemic of 1760," *South Carolina Historical Magazine* 97 (January 1996): 30–37. Mortality rates in the colonial era are difficult to chart but perhaps one in three Euro-Americans who contracted smallpox died. The figures were far higher in Indian Country. For analyses and debates, see Alfred W. Crosby, "Virgin Soil Epidemics as a Factor in the Aboriginal Depopulation in America," *William and Mary Quarterly* 33 (April 1976): 289–299; David S. Jones, "Virgin Soils Revisited," *William and Mary Quarterly* 60 (October 2003): 703–742; Paul Kelton, *Cherokee Medicine, Colonial Germs: An Indigenous Nation's Fight against Smallpox, 1518–1824* (Norman: University of Oklahoma Press, 2015).
9. Genevieve Miller, "Smallpox Inoculation in England and America: A Reappraisal," *William and Mary Quarterly* 13 (October 1956), 491.
10. For overviews of London, see Julie Flavell, *When London Was Capital of America* (New Haven: Yale University Press, 2010); Elizabeth McKellar, *Landscapes of London: The City, the Country, and the Suburbs, 1660–1840* (New Haven: Yale University Press, 2014).
11. Peter Manigault to Anne Ashby Manigault, 8 December 1753, *South Carolina Historical and Genealogical Magazine* 32 (October 1931), 270 (quotation). The number of Carolinians traveling to the imperial center spiked after 1760. Flavell, *When London Was Capital of America*, 11. For information about the Pinckneys' travels, see also Peter Manigault to Anne Ashby Manigault, 9 May 1753, *South Carolina Historical and Genealogical Magazine* 32 (April 1931), 130; Peter Manigault to Anne Ashby Manigault, 16 May 1753, *South Carolina Historical and Genealogical Magazine* 32 (July 1931), 176. For ties and tensions between colonial and metropole cultures, see T. H. Breen, "An Empire of Goods: The Anglicization of Colonial America, 1690–1776," *Journal of British Studies* 25 (October 1986): 467–499; Steven C. Bullock, *Tea Sets and Tyranny: The Politics of Politeness in Early America* (Philadelphia: University of Pennsylvania Press, 2017); Cary Carson, *Face Value: The Consumer Revolution and the Colonizing of America* (Charlottesville: University of Virginia Press, 2017); George Goodwin, *Benjamin Franklin in London: The British Life of America's Founding Father* (New Haven: Yale University Press, 2016); Brendan McConville, *The King's Three Faces: The Rise and Fall of Royal America, 1688–1776* (Chapel Hill: University of North Carolina Press, 2006); Louis P. Nelson, *The Beauty of Holiness: Anglicanism and Architecture in Colonial South Carolina* (Chapel Hill: University of North Carolina Press, 2008); David S. Shields, ed., *Material Culture in Anglo-America: Regional Identity and Urbanity in the Tidewater, Lowcountry, and Caribbean* (Columbia:

University of South Carolina Press, 2009); Jennifer Van Horn, *The Power of Objects in Eighteenth-Century British America* (Chapel Hill: University of North Carolina Press, 2017).

12. Eliza Lucas Pinckney to Anne Ashby Manigault, c. February/March 1754, DE (first quotation); Peter Manigault to Anne Ashby Manigault, 24 June 1753, *South Carolina Historical and Genealogical Magazine* 32 (July 1931), 179 (second quotation); Eliza Lucas Pinckney to Mrs. Figg, c. December 1753/January 1754, DE (third quotation); Peter Manigault to Anne Ashby Manigault, 29 March 1754, *South Carolina Historical and Genealogical Magazine* 33 (January 1932), 57 (last quotation). See also Peter Manigault to Anne Ashby Manigault, 16 May 1753, *South Carolina Historical and Genealogical Magazine* 32 (July 1931), 176. Anne kept a diary detailing Lowcountry social events. See Mabel L. Webber, ed., "Extracts from the Journal of Ann Manigault, 1754–1781," *South Carolina Historical and Genealogical Magazine* 20–21 (1919–1920), various issues. For Gabriel Manigault's import-export business, see Maurice A. Crouse, "Gabriel Manigault: Charleston Merchant," *South Carolina Historical Magazine* 68 (October 1967): 220–231. For male-female friendships in early America, see Cassandra A. Good, *Founding Friendships: Friendships between Men and Women in the Early American Republic* (New York: Oxford University Press, 2015).
13. The city was home to more than two thousand coffeehouses. Every profession and trade claimed its own coffeehouse. Brian Cowan, *The Social Life of Coffee: The Emergence of the British Coffeehouse* (New Haven: Yale University Press, 2005); Peter Ackroyd, *London: The Biography* (New York: Anchor, 2003), 314–317; Flavell, *When London Was Capital of America*, 25, 124–125. For wealthy Carolinians' zeal to experience London and perform their Englishness, see Flavell, *When London Was Capital of America*, 9–11, 18–21. For Peter Manigault's connections through the Carolina Coffeehouse, see Peter Manigault to Anne Ashby Manigault, 9 April 1752, *South Carolina Historical and Genealogical Magazine* 32 (January 1931), 50–51.
14. Eliza Lucas Pinckney to Anne Ashby Manigault, c. February/March 1754, DE. Alexander Garden traveled to London to intercede with John. Fred E. Witzig, *Sanctifying Slavery and Politics in South Carolina: The Life of Reverend Alexander Garden, 1685–1756* (Columbia: University of South Carolina Press, 2018), 174–175. For Newgate, see Ackroyd, *London*, chapter 24.
15. The princess's residence, White House/Kew Palace, was demolished in 1802. The Dutch House is intact and now known as Kew Palace.
16. For the grounds and buildings, see *Discover Kew Palace* (Surry: Historic Royal Palaces, 2016).
17. The following paragraphs rely on Eliza Lucas Pinckney to unknown, c. 1753, DE. For interpretations of the visit, see also Bullock, *Tea Sets and Tyranny*, chapter 6; Susan Scott Parrish, *American Curiosity: Cultures of Natural History in the Colonial British Atlantic World* (Chapel Hill: University of North Carolina Press, 2006), 205–208. For Augusta, see Joanna Marschner et al., eds., *Enlightened Princesses: Caroline, Augusta, Charlotte, and the Shaping of the Modern World* (New Haven: Yale University Press, 2017); http://britishart.yale.edu/exhibitions/enlightened-princesses-caroline-augusta-charlotte-and-shaping-modern-world.

18. For a similar reaction, see George Fenwick Jones, ed., "John Martin Boltzius' Trip to Charleston, October 1742," *South Carolina Historical Magazine* 82 (April 1981), 104. For breastfeeding in the eighteenth century, see Nora Doyle, *Maternal Bodies: Redefining Motherhood in Early America* (Chapel Hill: University of North Carolina Press, 2018), chapters 3–4. For the early nineteenth century, see Stephanie E. Jones-Rogers, *They Were Her Property: White Women as Slave Owners in the Antebellum South* (New Haven: Yale University Press, 2019), chapter 5.
19. See, for example, Peter Manigault to Anne Ashby Manigault, 8 December 1753, *South Carolina Historical and Genealogical Magazine* 32 (October 1931), 270.
20. Eliza Lucas Pinckney to Anne Ashby Manigault, c. February/March 1754, DE.
21. Eliza Lucas Pinckney to Katherine Martin Carew, c. 1753, DE.
22. Eliza Lucas Pinckney to Anne Ashby Manigault, c. February/March 1754, DE. See also Constance B. Schulz, "Eliza Lucas Pinckney and Harriott Pinckney Horry: A South Carolina Revolutionary-Era Mother and Daughter," in *South Carolina Women: Their Lives and Times,* vol. 1, ed. Marjorie Julian Spruill, Valinda W. Littlefield, and Joan Marie Johnson (Athens: University of Georgia Press, 2009), 92.
23. Harriott Horry Ravenel, *Eliza Pinckney* (New York: Charles Scribner's Sons, 1896), 159.
24. Charles Pinckney, Rent Roll, 24 January 1753, Benjamin H. Rutledge Family Papers, SCHS.
25. Charles Pinckney, Rent Roll, 24 January 1753, Benjamin H. Rutledge Family Papers, SCHS.
26. Charles Pinckney, Rent Roll, 24 January 1753, Benjamin H. Rutledge Family Papers, SCHS.
27. Henry Laurens to Elias Ball, 1 April 1765, *The Papers of Henry Laurens,* 16 vols., ed. David R. Chesnutt et al. (Columbia: University of South Carolina Press, 1968–2003), 4: 595; Advertisement by Charles Pinckney, *South Carolina Gazette*, 5 February 1753. Regarding colonial-era enslaved families, the foremost authority on this subject explained, "the interplay between black desire for emotional sustenance and white desire for economic sustenance remains largely unreadable." Jennifer L. Morgan, *Laboring Women: Reproduction and Gender in New World Slavery* (Philadelphia: University of Pennsylvania Press, 2004), 102. See also Morgan, *Laboring Women*, chapter 4; Robert Olwell, *Masters, Slaves, and Subjects: The Culture of Power in the South Carolina Low Country, 1740–1790* (Ithaca, NY: Cornell University Press, 1998), 200–211.
28. *South Carolina Gazette*, 3 July 1755. See also *South Carolina Gazette*, 23 April 1753, 7 May 1753, 14 May 1753.
29. Eliza Lucas Pinckney to Anne Ashby Manigault, c. February/March 1754, DE.
30. Eliza Lucas Pinckney to Anne Ashby Manigault, c. February/March 1754, DE.

9. *"A HOME AFTER HER OWN HEART"*

1. Peter Manigault to Anne Ashby Manigault, 24 June 1753, *South Carolina Historical and Genealogical Magazine* 32 (July 1931), 179. For marriages in the southern colonies, see Kathleen M. Brown, *Good Wives, Nasty Wenches, and Anxious Patriarchs: Gender, Race, and Power in Colonial Virginia* (Chapel Hill: University of North Carolina

Press, 1996), especially 334–342; Lorri Glover, *All Our Relations: Blood Ties and Emotional Bonds among the Early South Carolina Gentry* (Baltimore: Johns Hopkins University Press, 2000), especially 67–70; Mary Beth Norton, *Liberty's Daughters: The Revolutionary Experience of American Women, 1750–1800* (New York: Little, Brown, 1980), chapter 2; Daniel Blake Smith, *Inside the Great House: Planter Family Life in Eighteenth-Century Chesapeake Society* (Ithaca, NY: Cornell University Press, 1980), chapter 4.

2. Peter Manigault to Anne Ashby Manigault, 26 February 1754, *South Carolina Historical and Genealogical Magazine* 32 (October 1931), 277–278. For Eliza bridging England and South Carolina, see also Sam S. Baskett, "Eliza Lucas Pinckney: Portrait of an Eighteenth-Century American," *South Carolina Historical Magazine* 72 (October 1971), 213–214; Kacy Dowd Tillman, "Eliza Lucas Pinckney as Cultural Broker: Reconsidering a South Carolina Legacy," *Southern Studies* 18 (Fall–Winter 2011): 49–66; Darcy R. Fryer, "The Mind of Eliza Pinckney: An Eighteenth-Century Woman's Construction of Self," *South Carolina Historical Magazine* 99 (July 1998), 225; Barbara L. Bellows, "Eliza Lucas Pinckney: The Evolution of an Icon," *South Carolina Historical Magazine* 106 (April–July 2005), 151.
3. Eliza Lucas Pinckney to Anne Ashby Manigault, c. February/March 1754, DE; Peter Manigault to Anne Ashby Manigault, 8 December 1753, *South Carolina Historical and Genealogical Magazine* 32 (October 1931), 270.
4. Eliza Lucas Pinckney to Frances Stuart Chatfield, undated, DE; *South Carolina Gazette*, 26 March 1753; *South Carolina Gazette*, 12 April 1753.
5. Eliza Lucas Pinckney to Frances Stuart Chatfield, undated, DE; Charles Pinckney to Peter Manigault, 8 April 1756, DE. For the political turmoil, see also Andrew Rutledge to Peter Manigault, c. 1753, DE. Members of the Board of Trade did not appear to care about Charles's title. In the commissioners' records, he appeared regularly between 1754 and 1758, sometimes described as "agent for the Governor and Council of South Carolina" and sometimes as "one of the Council of South Carolina." *Journal of the Commissioners for Trade and Plantations, from January 1754 to December 1758*, vol. 14 (London: His Majesty's Stationery Office, 1933), 279 (agent), 54 (council), 34 (council).
6. Eliza Lucas Pinckney to Frances Stuart Chatfield, undated, DE.
7. For South Carolinians' gentry lifestyle, see Cara Anzilotti, *In the Affairs of the World: Women, Patriarchy, and Power in Colonial South Carolina* (Westport, CT: Greenwood, 2002), chapter 2; Emma Hart, *Building Charleston: Town and Society in the Eighteenth-Century British Atlantic World* (Charlottesville: University of Virginia Press, 2010), especially 130–141; Cynthia M. Kennedy, *Braided Relations, Entwined Lives: The Women of Charleston's Urban Slave Society* (Bloomington: Indiana University Press, 2005), chapter 8, especially 159. For Virginia, see Brown, *Good Wives*, chapter 8; Michal Jan Rozbicki, *The Complete Colonial Gentleman: Cultural Legitimacy in Plantation America* (Charlottesville: University of Virginia Press, 1998). For women across the southern provinces, see Cynthia A. Kierner, *Beyond the Household: Women's Place in the Early South, 1700–1835* (Ithaca, NY: Cornell University Press, 1998), 25–48. For refinement generally, see Richard L. Bushman, *The Refinement of America: Persons, Houses, Cities* (New York: Knopf, 1992).

8. Eliza Lucas Pinckney to Mrs. Figg, c. December 1753/January 1754, DE; Peter Manigault to Anne Ashby Manigault, 8 December 1753, *South Carolina Historical and Genealogical Magazine* 32 (October 1931), 270.
9. Harriott Horry Ravenel, *Eliza Pinckney* (New York: Charles Scribner's Sons, 1896), 159.
10. The estate was lost to creditors in the mid-nineteenth century. Today, Carew Manor is a school for special-needs children.
11. Eliza Lucas Pinckney to Anne Ashby Manigault, c. February/March 1754, DE. See also Eliza Lucas Pinckney to Katherine Martin Carew, miscellaneous correspondence 1754–1755, *The Letterbook of Eliza Lucas Pinckney, 1739–1762,* ed. Elise Pinckney (Columbia: University of South Carolina Press, 1997), 82–86 (hereinafter *Letterbook*).
12. Charles Pinckney account, 1 July 1754, DE. For garden glassware, see Joan Thirsk, ed., *Agricultural Change: Policy and Practice, 1500–1750*, vol. 3, *Chapters from the Agricultural History of England and Wales* (New York: Cambridge University Press, 1990), 243. The story of the tree is an oral tradition maintained in Ripley. For Eliza asserting her English identity, see also Tillman, "Eliza Lucas Pinckney as Cultural Broker"; Baskett, "Eliza Lucas Pinckney," 209–213; Fryer, "The Mind of Eliza Pinckney," 215.
13. Advertisement by Charles Pinckney, *South Carolina Gazette*, 19 February 1753; Charles Pinckney account, 1 July 1753 and 1 July 1754, DE.
14. Charles Pinckney account, 1 July 1754, DE. For the centrality of consumption to colonial Americans' sense of identity, see T. H. Breen, *The Marketplace of Revolution: How Consumer Politics Shaped American Independence* (New York: Oxford University Press, 2004), especially chapter 1; T. H. Breen, "An Empire of Goods: The Anglicization of Colonial America, 1690–1776," *Journal of British Studies* 25 (October 1986): 467–499; Cary Carson, *Face Value: The Consumer Revolution and the Colonizing of America* (Charlottesville: University of Virginia Press, 2017); Hart, *Building Charleston*, 130–141; David S. Shields, ed., *Material Culture in Anglo-America: Regional Identity and Urbanity in the Tidewater, Lowcountry, and Caribbean* (Columbia: University of South Carolina Press, 2009). For material goods providing entry into new communities, see Carson, *Face Value*, 15, 63.
15. "For, even, afar-gone Consumption," Eliza Lucas Pinckney recipe book, DE. For the blurring of medicine and food in women's recipe books, see also Kathleen M. Brown, *Foul Bodies: Cleanliness of Early America* (New Haven: Yale University Press, 2009), 213–215. For women's medical knowledge, see Susan Hanket Brandt, "Marketing Medicine: Apothecary Elizabeth Weed's Economic Independence during the American Revolution," in *Women in the American Revolution: Gender, Politics, and the Domestic World,* ed. Barbara B. Oberg (Charlottesville: University of Virginia Press, 2019), 60–65.
16. For skin whitening and cosmetics, see Brown, *Foul Bodies*, 132–133; Jennifer Van Horn, *The Power of Objects in Eighteenth-Century British America* (Chapel Hill: University of North Carolina Press, 2017), 282–294, 312–320. For scientific knowledge, see Susan Scott Parrish, *American Curiosity: Cultures of Natural History in the Colonial British Atlantic World* (Chapel Hill: University of North Carolina Press, 2006).
17. "Memorandum," Eliza Lucas Pinckney recipe book, DE.

18. Marvin R. Zahniser, *Charles Cotesworth Pinckney, Founding Father* (Chapel Hill: University of North Carolina Press, 1967), 9. For overviews of motherhood, see Nora Doyle, *Maternal Bodies: Redefining Motherhood in Early America* (Chapel Hill: University of North Carolina Press, 2018); Norton, *Liberty's Daughters*, chapter 1; Smith, *Inside the Great House*, especially 46–52; Katy Simpson Smith, *We Have Raised All of You: Motherhood in the South, 1750–1835* (Baton Rouge: Louisiana State University Press, 2013), part 2.
19. Eliza Lucas Pinckney to unknown, c. 1753, DE (quotations); Zahniser, *Charles Cotesworth Pinckney*, 11.
20. Eliza Lucas Pinckney to George Mackenzie, c. 1760, DE. For mothers educating children, see also Kierner, *Beyond the Household*, 59–67; Smith, *We Have Raised All of You*, chapter 9.
21. Eliza Lucas Pinckney to Katherine Martin Carew, c. 1755, DE (quotation); Eliza Lucas Pinckney to Katherine Martin Carew, c. 1754, *Letterbook*, 82.
22. Eliza Lucas Pinckney to Mary (Polly) Lucas Atkinson, c. 1756, DE; miscellaneous correspondence, *Letterbook*, 75–77. For the importance of letters linking families across the Atlantic, see Sarah M. S. Pearsall, *Atlantic Families: Lives and Letters in the Later Eighteenth Century* (New York: Oxford University Press, 2008), especially 5–11 and chapter 1. For another divided family, see Susan Clair Imbarrato, *Sarah Gray Cary, from Boston to Grenada: Shifting Fortunes of an American Family, 1764–1826* (Baltimore: Johns Hopkins University Press, 2018).
23. *South Carolina Gazette*, 10 April 1755.
24. Zara Anishanslin, *Portrait of a Woman in Silk: Hidden Histories of the British Atlantic World* (New Haven: Yale University Press, 2016), 25–26, 96–97, 157–158. For London neighborhoods and trades, see Peter Ackroyd, *London: The Biography* (New York: Anchor, 2003), chapter 11.
25. The salmon dress is at the Charleston Museum, the yellow one at the National Museum of American History, Smithsonian Institution. The third dress disappeared. The report in the *South Carolina Gazette* comports with family stories recounted by Charles Cotesworth Pinckney (Thomas Pinckney's grandson) in *Life of General Thomas Pinckney* (1895; Memphis: General Books, 2012), 5. For sericulture, see Anishanslin, *Portrait of a Woman in Silk*, chapter 7; Ben Marsh, *Georgia's Frontier Women: Female Fortunes in a Southern Colony* (Athens: University of Georgia Press, 2007), 53–61.
26. Harriott Pinckney Rutledge Holbrook to Caroline Seabrook, 21 December 1843, DE (quotation); Pinckney, *Life of General Thomas Pinckney*, 5. Special thanks to Constance B. Schulz for this understanding of Eliza's dresses—among many insights.
27. Fred Anderson, *The War That Made America: A Short History of the French and Indian War* (New York: Viking, 2005), 56 (quotation). See also Fred Anderson, *Crucible of War: The Seven Years' War and the Fate of Empire in British North America, 1754–1766* (New York: Knopf, 2000), and the bibliographic essay in *The War That Made America*, 267–275, for sources and interpretations.
28. Anderson, *The War That Made America*, 71.
29. Eliza Lucas Pinckney to Katherine Martin Carew, c. 1755, DE.

30. Anderson, *The War That Made America,* 101–102.
31. Charles Pinckney to Peter Manigault, 8 April 1756, DE; Eliza Lucas Pinckney to Katherine Martin Carew, 7 February 1757, *Letterbook*, 87.
32. Eliza Lucas Pinckney to Katherine Martin Carew, 7 February 1757, *Letterbook*, 87. See also Frances Leigh Williams, *A Founding Family: The Pinckneys of South Carolina* (New York: Harcourt Brace Jovanovich, 1978), 15.
33. Eliza Lucas Pinckney to Katherine Martin Carew, 7 February 1757, *Letterbook*, 87–88.
34. Eliza Lucas Pinckney to Katherine Martin Carew, 7 February 1757, *Letterbook*, 88–89.
35. Eliza Lucas Pinckney to Katherine Martin Carew, 7 February 1757, *Letterbook*, 87–88. For parents separated from children, see Pearsall, *Atlantic Families*, especially 5–13.
36. Eliza Lucas Pinckney to Katherine Martin Carew, 7 February 1757, *Letterbook*, 88.
37. Keith Krawczynski, *William Henry Drayton: South Carolina Revolutionary Patriot* (Baton Rouge: Louisiana State University Press, 2001), 13–14. Eliza maintained her connection to the Draytons as they grew up.
38. Anderson, *The War That Made America*, 121–125, 130–131; Charles Pinckney, promissory note, 14 February 1758, DE.
39. Harriott H. Ravenel to Mrs. Rose, 10 March n.y., Smythe Family Papers, SCHS; Anishanslin, *Portrait of a Woman in Silk*, 310.
40. Eliza Lucas Pinckney's great-great-granddaughter, Harriott Ravenel, insisted that no painting was ever done, based on assurances of her grandmother, Eliza's granddaughter. Harriott H. Ravenel to Mrs. Rose, 10 March n.y., Smythe Family Papers, SCHS. Perhaps Eliza thought a painter would not capture her. A well-known portraitist, Jeremiah Theüs, painted several Charles Town women to look remarkably similar and wearing nearly identical dresses. Carson, *Face Value*, 156–157. See also Van Horn, *The Power of Objects*, 16–18; Maurizio Valsania, *Jefferson's Body: A Corporeal Biography* (Charlottesville: University of Virginia Press, 2017), 45–48.
41. Harriott Pinckney to Charles Cotesworth and Thomas Pinckney, March 1764, Smythe Family Papers, SCHS.

10. *"OPPRESSED WITH BITTER ANGUISH"*

1. T. P. Harrison, ed., "Journal of a Voyage to Charlestown in So. Carolina by Pelatiah Webster in 1765," *Publications of the South Carolina Historical Society* (Charleston, 1898), 16 (first quotation); Thomas J. Tobias, ed., "Charles Town in 1764 (Moses Lopez)," *South Carolina Historical Magazine* 67 (April 1966), 66 (second quotation). St. Michael's and the Statehouse were completed in 1760. George C. Rogers, Jr., *Charleston in the Age of the Pinckneys* (1969; Columbia: University of South Carolina Press, 1980), 58; Robert Olwell, *Masters, Slaves, and Subjects: The Culture of Power in the South Carolina Low Country, 1740–1790* (Ithaca, NY: Cornell University Press, 1998), 18–19.
2. Eliza Lucas Pinckney to Vigerous Edwards, February 1759, *The Letterbook of Eliza Lucas Pinckney, 1739–1762,* ed. Elise Pinckney (Columbia: University of South Carolina Press, 1997), 107 (hereinafter *Letterbook*). See also Eliza Lucas Pinckney to Rebecca Evance, c. 1759, *Letterbook*, 104.

3. Eliza Lucas Pinckney to George Morley, 14 March 1760, *Letterbook*, 144.
4. Eliza Lucas Pinckney recipe book, DE; Eliza Lucas Pinckney to Mary Mackenzie Drayton, c. July 1758, DE. For eighteenth-century women's recipe books, see Kathleen M. Brown, *Foul Bodies: Cleanliness of Early America* (New Haven: Yale University Press, 2009), 213–215. For malaria, see Randall M. Packard, *The Making of a Tropical Disease: A Short History of Malaria* (Baltimore: Johns Hopkins University Press, 2007); J. R. McNeill, *Mosquito Empires: Ecology and War in the Greater Caribbean, 1620–1914* (New York: Cambridge University Press, 2010); H. Roy Merrens and George D. Terry, "Dying in Paradise: Malaria, Mortality, and the Perceptual Environment in Colonial South Carolina," *Journal of Southern History* 50 (November 1984): 533–550.
5. Eliza Lucas Pinckney, "Days sett apart to be rememberd," DE; Eliza Lucas Pinckney to Rebecca Evance, c. 1759, *Letterbook*, 104.
6. Eliza Lucas Pinckney to Katherine Martin Carew, May 1759, *Letterbook*, 115.
7. Eliza Lucas Pinckney to Rebecca Evance, c. 1759, *Letterbook*, 104 (first quotation); Eliza Lucas Pinckney to Rebecca Evance, August 1758, *Letterbook*, 99–100 (second quotation). See also Eliza Lucas Pinckney to Ann Mildrum Lucas, 25 September 1758, *Letterbook*, 101.
8. Eliza Lucas Pinckney to Mary (Polly) Lucas Atkinson, 3 October 1758, DE. See also Eliza Lucas Pinckney to Ann Mildrum Lucas, 25 September 1758, *Letterbook*, 100–102.
9. Eliza Lucas Pinckney to Charles Cotesworth and Thomas Pinckney, August 1758, *Letterbook*, 94; Eliza Lucas Pinckney to Ann Mildrum Lucas, 25 September 1758, *Letterbook*, 100.
10. Eliza Lucas Pinckney to Mr. Gerrard, August 1758, *Letterbook*, 96.
11. Eliza Lucas Pinckney to Charles Cotesworth and Thomas Pinckney, August 1758, *Letterbook*, 94.
12. Eliza Lucas Pinckney to Charles Cotesworth and Thomas Pinckney, August 1758, *Letterbook*, 94. Eliza's emphasis on family duty, achievement, and family legacy matched the values of elite men raising sons. See Kathleen M. Brown, *Good Wives, Nasty Wenches, and Anxious Patriarchs: Gender, Race, and Power in Colonial Virginia* (Chapel Hill: University of North Carolina Press, 1996), 342–347.
13. Eliza Lucas Pinckney to Charles Cotesworth and Thomas Pinckney, August 1758, *Letterbook*, 95.
14. Eliza Lucas Pinckney to Mr. Gerrard, August 1758, *Letterbook*, 96. Gerrard was headmaster at the Camberwell school the boys attended.
15. Eliza Lucas Pinckney to George Morley, August 1758, *Letterbook*, 97; Eliza Lucas Pinckney to Rebecca Evance, c. 1759, *Letterbook*, 105.
16. Miscellaneous correspondence, *Letterbook*, 100–136. See also Harriott Horry Ravenel, *Eliza Pinckney* (New York: Charles Scribner's Sons, 1896), 169–170. For male-female friendships in early America, see Cassandra A. Good, *Founding Friendships: Friendships between Men and Women in the Early American Republic* (New York: Oxford University Press, 2015).
17. Eliza Lucas Pinckney to Ann Mildrum Lucas, 25 September 1758, *Letterbook*, 100–101; Eliza Lucas Pinckney to Rebecca Evance, August 1758, *Letterbook*, 99.

18. Eliza Lucas Pinckney to Vigerous Edwards, February 1759, *Letterbook*, 108. For the conflict between South Carolinians and Cherokees, see Daniel J. Tortora, *Carolina In Crisis: Cherokees, Colonists, and Slaves in the American Southeast, 1756–1763* (Chapel Hill: University of North Carolina Press, 2015); Tom Hatley, *The Dividing Paths: Cherokees and South Carolinians through the Revolutionary Era* (New York: Oxford University Press, 1995), chapters 9–10.
19. Eliza Lucas Pinckney to James Kirkpatrick, February 1760, *Letterbook*, 131 (quotation); Eliza Lucas Pinckney to Ann Mildrum Lucas, 25 September 1758, *Letterbook*, 100–102; Eliza Lucas Pinckney to Vigerous Edwards, 12 March 1760, *Letterbook*, 140.
20. Eliza Lucas Pinckney to Rebecca Evance, c. 1759, *Letterbook*, 106.
21. Eliza Lucas Pinckney to Ann Mildrum Lucas, 25 September 1758, *Letterbook*, 100–102.
22. Eliza Lucas Pinckney to Charles Cotesworth and Thomas Pinckney, August 1758, *Letterbook*, 95.
23. Eliza Lucas Pinckney to Mr. Gerrard, August 1758, *Letterbook*, 96 (quotation). For her English friends anticipating her return, see Eliza Lucas Pinckney to James Kirkpatrick, February 1760, *Letterbook*, 133; Eliza Lucas Pinckney to Wilhelmina-Catharine King, May 1759, *Letterbook*, 118.
24. Eliza Lucas Pinckney to Wilhelmina-Catharine King, May 1759, *Letterbook*, 119.
25. Eliza Lucas Pinckney to James Kirkpatrick, February 1760, *Letterbook*, 133 (quotation); Eliza Lucas Pinckney to Ann Mildrum Lucas, 25 September 1758, *Letterbook*, 102. A similar interpretation was offered in Sam S. Baskett, "Eliza Lucas Pinckney: Portrait of an Eighteenth-Century American," *South Carolina Historical Magazine* 72 (October 1971), 214–215.
26. Charles Pinckney Will, DE. For the plantations Eliza managed after Charles's death, see also Merrill G. Christophersen, *Biography of an Island: General Charles Cotesworth Pinckney's Sea Island Plantation* (Fennimore, WI: Westburg Associates, 1976).
27. For widows in South Carolina, see Cara Anzilotti, *In the Affairs of the World: Women, Patriarchy, and Power in Colonial South Carolina* (Westport, CT: Greenwood, 2002), especially 96–99, 118–122, 152–154; Cara Anzilotti, "Autonomy and the Female Planter in Colonial South Carolina," *Journal of Southern History* 63 (May 1997): 239–268; Lorri Glover, *All Our Relations: Blood Ties and Emotional Bonds among the Early South Carolina Gentry* (Baltimore: Johns Hopkins University Press, 2000), 8–9, 99; Cynthia A. Kierner, *Beyond the Household: Women's Place in the Early South, 1700–1835* (Ithaca, NY: Cornell University Press, 1998), 11–12. Anzilotti found in the surviving records of colonial South Carolina six hundred women who owned or managed property. For free black women, see Amrita Chakrabarti Myers, *Forging Freedom: Black Women and the Pursuit of Liberty in Antebellum Charleston* (Chapel Hill: University of North Carolina Press, 2011), chapter 3. For other economically powerful and/or independent women in this era, see Susan Hanket Brandt, "Marketing Medicine: Apothecary Elizabeth Weed's Economic Independence during the American Revolution," in *Women in the American Revolution: Gender, Politics, and the Domestic World*, ed. Barbara B. Oberg (Charlottesville: University of Virginia Press, 2019), 60–79; Kit Candlin and Cassandra Pybus, *Enterprising Women: Gender, Race, and Power in the*

Revolutionary Atlantic (Athens: University of Georgia Press, 2015); Patricia Cleary, *Elizabeth Murray: A Woman's Pursuit of Independence in Eighteenth-Century America* (Amherst: University of Massachusetts Press, 2000); Linda Colley, *The Ordeal of Elizabeth Marsh: A Woman in World History* (New York: Random House, 2007); Ellen Hartigan-O'Connor, *The Ties That Buy: Women and Commerce in Revolutionary America* (Philadelphia: University of Pennsylvania Press, 2009); Susan Clair Imbarrato, *Sarah Gray Cary, from Boston to Grenada: Shifting Fortunes of an American Family, 1764–1826* (Baltimore: Johns Hopkins University Press, 2018); G. Winston Lane, Jr., "Economic Power among Eighteenth-Century Women of the Carolina Lowcountry," in *Money, Trade, and Power: The Evolution of Colonial South Carolina's Plantation Society*, ed. Jack P. Greene, Rosemary Brana-Shute, and Randy J. Sparks (Columbia: University of South Carolina Press, 2001), 322–343; Ami Pflugrad-Jackisch, " 'What Am I but an American?': Mary Willing Byrd and Westover Plantation during the American Revolution," in Oberg, *Women in the American Revolution*, 171–191; Kaylan M. Stevenson, " 'Until Liberty of Importation Is Allowed': Milliners and Mantuamakers in the Chesapeake on the Eve of the Revolution," in Oberg, *Women in the American Revolution*, 39–59.

28. For widows in colonial America, see Vivian Bruce Conger, *The Widows' Might: Widowhood and Gender in Early British America* (New York: New York University Press, 2009). For slaveholding widows, see Kirsten E. Wood, *Masterful Women: Slaveholding Widows from the American Revolution through the Civil War* (Chapel Hill: University of North Carolina Press, 2004), chapter 2. For conservatism among white women planters, see Anzilotti, *In the Affairs of the World*, 2–3, 118–120; Catherine Kerrison, *Claiming the Pen: Women and Intellectual Life in the Early American South* (Ithaca, NY: Cornell University Press, 2006), 20, 189. For a New England woman who bridged gender roles and retained her family focus, see Cleary, *Elizabeth Murray*, especially 4–6, 52.

29. Charles Pinckney Will, DE; Thomas Smith Will, quoted in Anzilotti, *In the Affairs of the World*, 136. Anzilotti found that 75 percent of colonial South Carolina planters left property to their wives. According to a codicil to his will, Charles left Eliza the Ripley estate. When Charles Cotesworth reached age twenty-one, Eliza was to sign the property over to him. Charles Cotesworth proved the will in England, in March 1769, in anticipation of his return to North America. Between 1758 and 1769, Eliza rented out the Ripley estate. John Slatford, "An Eighteenth-Century American Family in Ripley, Part 2," in *Send and Ripley History Society Newsletters* 111 (July–August 1993), 7, lent to the author, from the research collection of Constance B. Schulz.

30. Eliza Lucas Pinckney to George Morley, 14 March 1760, *Letterbook*, 144. For wives as executors, see Kierner, *Beyond the Household*, 11–12; Wood, *Masterful Women*, 31; Anzilotti, *In the Affairs of the World*, 138.

31. Henry Laurens to Messieurs and Madame Laurence, 25 February 1774, *The Papers of Henry Laurens*, 16 vols., ed. David R. Chesnutt et al. (Columbia: University of South Carolina Press, 1968–2003), 9: 311; Eliza Lucas Pinckney to Wilhelmina-Catharine King, 27 February 1762, DE. For widows' decisions about remarrying, see Conger, *The Widows' Might*, especially 26–45; Elizabeth M. Purden, "Investing Widows:

Autonomy in a Nascent Capitalist Society," in *Money, Trade, and Power: The Evolution of Colonial South Carolina's Plantation Society,* ed. Jack P. Greene, Rosemary Brana-Shute, and Randy J. Sparks (Columbia: University of South Carolina Press, 2001), 344–362; Wood, *Masterful Women*, 149–157.

32. Eliza Lucas Pinckney to Wilhelmina-Catharine King, 27 February 1762, DE.
33. Charles Pinckney to Peter Manigault, 8 April 1756, DE; Eliza Lucas Pinckney to George Morley, February 1759, DE; Eliza Lucas Pinckney to William Henry Lyttelton, December 1759, DE. For Lyttelton's role in the war, see Hatley, *The Dividing Paths*, 108–115, chapter 10. Manuscripts related to his administration are in William Henry Lyttelton Papers, William L. Clements Library, University of Michigan.
34. Eliza Lucas Pinckney to George Morley, 14 March 1760, *Letterbook*, 144.
35. Samuel Martin, *Essay upon Plantership* (London: T. Smith, 1750), quoted in Justin Roberts, *Slavery and the Enlightenment in the British Atlantic, 1750–1807* (New York: Cambridge University Press, 2013), 34. For context, see Roberts, *Slavery and the Enlightenment in the British Atlantic*, chapter 1, especially 27, 68–69; Caitlin Rosenthal, *Accounting for Slavery: Masters and Management* (Cambridge: Harvard University Press, 2018).
36. Eliza Lucas Pinckney to George Morley, 14 March 1760, *Letterbook*, 144.
37. Eliza Lucas Pinckney to Mr. Gerrard, c. February 1760, *Letterbook*, 135; Eliza Lucas Pinckney to Katherine Martin Carew, July 1760, *Letterbook*, 178–179. For the illness, see also Harriott Pinckney to Wilhelmina-Catharine King, c. 1761, Smythe Family Papers, SCHS.
38. See, for example, Eliza Lucas Pinckney to Wilhelmina-Catharine King, May 1759, *Letterbook*, 118; Eliza Lucas Pinckney to George Morley, 8 February 1761, *Letterbook*, 160; Eliza Lucas Pinckney to unknown, February 1762, *Letterbook*, 179; Eliza Lucas Pinckney to Vigerous Edwards, 12 March 1760, *Letterbook*, 140.
39. Eliza Lucas Pinckney to Rebecca Evance, 19 June 1760, *Letterbook*, 152.
40. Charles Pinckney Will, DE; "Journal of a Voyage to Charlestown in So. Carolina by Pelatiah Webster in 1765," 5. For black communities and culture in colonial South Carolina, see Philip D. Morgan, *Slave Counterpoint: Black Culture in the Eighteenth-Century Chesapeake and Low Country* (Chapel Hill: University of North Carolina Press, 1998). For African American women in early South Carolina, see Myers, *Forging Freedom*; Cynthia M. Kennedy, *Braided Relations, Entwined Lives: The Women of Charleston's Urban Slave Society* (Bloomington: Indiana University Press, 2005). For research into enslaved women's lives, see Marisa J. Fuentes, *Dispossessed Lives: Enslaved Women, Violence, and the Archive* (Philadelphia: University of Pennsylvania Press, 2016).
41. Charles Pinckney Will, DE.
42. Eliza Lucas Pinckney to Jane Onslow, 27 February 1762, *Letterbook*, 185.
43. Eliza Lucas Pinckney to George Morley, 11 June 1761, *Letterbook*, 171.
44. Eliza Lucas Pinckney to Harriott Pinckney Horry, undated, DE. For urban slavery and colonial Charles Town, see Myers, *Forging Freedom*, especially 28–31. For white women and slaveholding, see Thavolia Glymph, *Out of the House of Bondage: The Transformation of the Plantation Household* (New York: Cambridge University Press,

2008), chapter 1; Stephanie E. Jones-Rogers, *They Were Her Property: White Women as Slave Owners in the Antebellum South* (New Haven: Yale University Press, 2019).

45. Eliza Lucas Pinckney to Rebecca Evance, 15 March 1760, *Letterbook*, 148 (first quotation); Eliza Lucas Pinckney to Rebecca Evance, 19 June 1760, *Letterbook*, 153 (second quotation). For the 1760 outbreak, see Tortora, *Carolina in Crisis*, chapter 5; Suzanne Krebsbach, "The Great Charlestown Smallpox Epidemic of 1760," *South Carolina Historical Magazine* 97 (January 1996): 30–37.
46. Eliza Lucas Pinckney to Wilhelmina-Catharine King, 27 February 1762, DE. For the French and Indian War after the fall of Montreal, see Fred Anderson, *The War That Made America: A Short History of the French and Indian War* (New York: Viking, 2005), chapter 23. For the Cherokee conflict, see Hatley, *The Dividing Paths*, chapter 10; Tortora, *Carolina in Crisis*, chapters 9 and 10; Kinloch Bull, Jr., *The Oligarchs in Colonial and Revolutionary Charleston: Lieutenant Governor William Bull II and His Family* (Columbia: University of South Carolina Press, 1991), chapters 3 and 4. For Eliza's attitude toward Indians, see Eliza Lucas Pinckney to George Morley, 27 February 1762, *Letterbook*, 173; Eliza Lucas Pinckney to Rebecca Evance, 15 March 1760, *Letterbook*, 147.

11. *CULTIVATING A LEGACY*

1. Eliza Lucas Pinckney to James Kirkpatrick, February 1760, *The Letterbook of Eliza Lucas Pinckney, 1739–1762*, ed. Elise Pinckney (Columbia: University of South Carolina Press, 1997), 131 (hereinafter *Letterbook*).
2. The death dates are unknown, but Antiguan sources recorded the burial dates for Thomas Lucas (11 August 1756), Ann Mildrum Lucas (25 October 1759), and George Lucas, Jr. (14 January 1760). Vere Langford Oliver, *The History of the Island of Antigua*, 3 vols. (London: Mitchell and Hughes, 1894–1899), 2: 199, 202. See also Carol Walter Ramagosa, "Eliza Lucas Pinckney's Family in Antigua, 1668–1747," *South Carolina Historical Magazine* 99 (July 1998), 258.
3. For gender roles in elite childrearing, see Kathleen M. Brown, *Good Wives, Nasty Wenches, and Anxious Patriarchs: Gender, Race, and Power in Colonial Virginia* (Chapel Hill: University of North Carolina Press, 1996), 342–348; Daniel Blake Smith, *Inside the Great House: Planter Family Life in Eighteenth-Century Chesapeake Society* (Ithaca, NY: Cornell University Press, 1980), chapters 2–3. For female planters focusing on family, see Cara Anzilotti, *In the Affairs of the World: Women, Patriarchy, and Power in Colonial South Carolina* (Westport, CT: Greenwood, 2002).
4. Eliza Lucas Pinckney to Wilhelmina-Catharine King, 27 February 1762, DE; Eliza Lucas Pinckney to Jane Onslow, 27 February 1762, *Letterbook*, 182–183 (second quotation); Eliza Lucas Pinckney to Mr. Longmore, 11 April 1761, *Letterbook*, 164 (third quotation).
5. Eliza Lucas Pinckney to Charles Cotesworth Pinckney, 7 February 1761, *Letterbook*, 159.
6. Eliza Lucas Pinckney to Wilhelmina-Catharine King, 19 July 1760, DE.
7. Eliza Lucas Pinckney to George Morley, 31 August 1760, *Letterbook*, 158; Eliza Lucas Pinckney to Rebecca Evance, 16 July 1759, *Letterbook*, 121 (quotation).

8. The fabric, shoes, and pin are at the Charleston Museum. For conspicuous consumption in Charles Town, see Emma Hart, *Building Charleston: Town and Society in the Eighteenth-Century British Atlantic World* (Charlottesville: University of Virginia Press, 2010), especially 130–141; David S. Shields, ed., *Material Culture in Anglo-America: Regional Identity and Urbanity in the Tidewater, Lowcountry, and Caribbean* (Columbia: University of South Carolina Press, 2009).
9. Eliza Lucas Pinckney to Charles Cotesworth and Thomas Pinckney, March 1760, *Letterbook*, 143 (first quotation); Eliza Lucas Pinckney to Charles Cotesworth Pinckney, 15 April 1761, *Letterbook*, 167 (second quotation). For the intersection of religion, education, and refinement, see Louis P. Nelson, *The Beauty of Holiness: Anglicanism and Architecture in Colonial South Carolina* (Chapel Hill: University of North Carolina Press, 2008), chapters 2–4.
10. Harriott Pinckney to Wilhelmina-Catharine King, c. 1761, Smythe Family Papers, SCHS.
11. Harriott Pinckney to Wilhelmina-Catharine King, c. 1761, Smythe Family Papers, SCHS. For Eliza and Harriott's relationship, see also Constance B. Schulz, "Eliza Lucas Pinckney and Harriott Pinckney Horry: A South Carolina Revolutionary-Era Mother and Daughter," in *South Carolina Women: Their Lives and Times,* vol. 1, ed. Marjorie Julian Spruill, Valinda W. Littlefield, and Joan Marie Johnson (Athens: University of Georgia Press, 2009), 79–108.
12. Eliza Lucas Pinckney to George Mackenzie, c. 1760, DE (first quotation); Eliza Lucas Pinckney to George Keate, February 1762, *Letterbook*, 181.
13. Harriott Pinckney to Wilhelmina-Catharine King, c. fall 1760, Smythe Family Papers, SCHS; Harriott Pinckney to Mrs. Favell, March 1763, Smythe Family Papers, SCHS.
14. Eliza Lucas Pinckney to George Keate, February 1762, *Letterbook*, 181–182; Harriott Pinckney to Charles Cotesworth Pinckney, May 1764, Smythe Family Papers, SCHS. For women's education in the early South, see Cynthia A. Kierner, *Beyond the Household: Women's Place in the Early South, 1700–1835* (Ithaca, NY: Cornell University Press, 1998), 59–67; Catherine Kerrison, *Claiming the Pen: Women and Intellectual Life in the Early American South* (Ithaca, NY: Cornell University Press, 2006); Katy Simpson Smith, *We Have Raised All of You: Motherhood in the South, 1750–1835* (Baton Rouge: Louisiana State University Press, 2013), especially chapter 9.
15. Harriott Pinckney to Miss R., April 1766, DE; Harriott Pinckney Horry, Description of Silk, c. 1829, DE. American producers of silk fought the stereotype that their product was inferior to France's. Zara Anishanslin, *Portrait of a Woman in Silk: Hidden Histories of the British Atlantic World* (New Haven: Yale University Press, 2016), 143. For Harriott managing the dairy, see Eliza Lucas Pinckney to Daniel Huger Horry, Jr., 9 March 1768, DE.
16. See, for example, Eliza Lucas Pinckney to Daniel Huger Horry, Jr., 9 March 1768, DE.
17. Harriott Pinckney to Charles Cotesworth Pinckney, January 1766, Smythe Family Papers, SHCS; Harriott Pinckney Horry to unknown, June 1769, Smythe Family Papers, SCHS. Harriott's cookbook is published: Richard J. Hooker, ed., *A Colonial*

Plantation Cookbook: The Receipt Book of Harriott Pinckney Horry, 1770 (Columbia: University of South Carolina Press, 1984).

18. Harriott Horry Ravenel, *Eliza Pinckney* (New York: Charles Scribner's Sons, 1896), 230–231.
19. Harriott Pinckney to Dorothy Golightly Drayton, 20 July 1763, DE; Harriott Pinckney to Charles Cotesworth Pinckney, 19 May 1766, Smythe Family Papers, SCHS. For context, see Jennifer Van Horn, *The Power of Objects in Eighteenth-Century British America* (Chapel Hill: University of North Carolina Press, 2017), chapter 4.
20. Ravenel, *Eliza Pinckney*, 240–242; Glossary, DE.
21. Harriott Pinckney to Miss R., April 1766, DE.
22. *South Carolina Gazette,* 19 February 1768.
23. Sarah M. S. Pearsall demonstrated the prevalence of children living outside their family of origin and the centrality of such separations to the colonial economy in *Atlantic Families: Lives and Letters in the Later Eighteenth Century* (New York: Oxford University Press, 2008), especially 13, 29–33. For the importance of letters, see William Merrell Decker, *Epistolary Practices: Letter Writing in America before Telecommunications* (Chapel Hill: University of North Carolina Press, 1998); Konstantin Dierks, *In My Power: Letter Writing and Communications in Early America* (Philadelphia: University of Pennsylvania Press, 2009); Pearsall, *Atlantic Families*; Steven M. Stowe, "The Rhetoric of Authority: The Making of Social Values in Planter Family Correspondence," *Journal of American History* 73 (March 1987): 919–933; Tamara Plakins Thornton, *Handwriting in America: A Cultural History* (New Haven: Yale University Press, 1996); Michael Zuckerman, "Penmanship Exercises for Saucy Sons: Some Thoughts on the Colonial Southern Family," *South Carolina Historical Magazine* 84 (July 1983): 152–166. For conduct literature, see C. Dallett Hemphill, *Bowing to Necessities: A History of Manners in America, 1620–1860* (New York: Oxford University Press, 1999); Sarah E. Newton, *Learning to Behave: A Guide to American Conduct Books before 1900* (Westport, CT: Greenwood, 1994); Richard L. Bushman, *The Refinement of America: Persons, Houses, Cities* (New York: Knopf, 1992). The most widely read advisory letters of the age included R. K. Root, ed., *Lord Chesterfield's Letters to His Son* (London: J. M. Dent and Sons, 1929).
24. Eliza Lucas Pinckney to Mr. Longmore, 31 August 1760, *Letterbook*, 157. For widows acting as both mother and father, see also Vivian Bruce Conger, *The Widows' Might: Widowhood and Gender in Early British America* (New York: New York University Press, 2009), chapter 3.
25. For mentioning Charles, see, for example, Eliza Lucas Pinckney to Rebecca Evance, c. 1759, *Letterbook*, 105.
26. Charles Cotesworth Pinckney to Harriott Pinckney, 6 April 1759, DE.
27. Ravenel, *Eliza Pinckney*, 168; Marvin R. Zahniser, *Charles Cotesworth Pinckney, Founding Father* (Chapel Hill: University of North Carolina Press, 1967), 268.
28. Charles Pinckney Will, DE; Eliza Lucas Pinckney to Charles Cotesworth Pinckney, 15 April 1761, *Letterbook*, 167.
29. For health fears, see Eliza Lucas Pinckney to Charles Cotesworth Pinckney, c. 1768, DE. Charles Cotesworth finished his studies on 27 January 1769.

30. Eliza Lucas Pinckney to unknown, c. 1760, DE; Eliza Lucas Pinckney to Charles Cotesworth Pinckney, 15 April 1761, *Letterbook*, 168.
31. John Drayton to James Glen, 5 April 1768 and 24 December 1769, James Glen Papers, SCL; Eliza Lucas Pinckney to Charles Cotesworth Pinckney, c. 1768, DE.
32. Charles Pinckney Will, DE; Charles Cotesworth Pinckney, *Life of General Thomas Pinckney* (1895; Memphis: General Books, 2012), 6. For youth culture at English schools, see Julie Flavell, *When London Was Capital of America* (New Haven: Yale University Press, 2010), chapter 4.
33. Harriott Pinckney to Charles Cotesworth Pinckney, January 1766, Smythe Family Papers, SCHS.
34. Harriott Pinckney to Charles Cotesworth Pinckney, May 1764, Smythe Family Papers, SCHS; Thomas Pinckney quoted in Ravenel, *Eliza Pinckney*, 209.
35. Harriott Pinckney to Rebecca Izard, 10 December 1766, DE; Thomas Pinckney to Harriott Pinckney, 24 November 1759, DE.
36. Harriott Pinckney to Charles Cotesworth Pinckney, January 1766, Smythe Family Papers, SCHS. For local and financially advantageous marriages, see Lorri Glover, *All Our Relations: Blood Ties and Emotional Bonds among the Early South Carolina Gentry* (Baltimore: Johns Hopkins University Press, 2000), 47–49, 95–101.
37. Eliza Lucas Pinckney to George Keate, February 1762, *Letterbook*, 180–181 (first quotation); Eliza Lucas Pinckney to Jane Onslow, 27 February 1762, *Letterbook*, 182 (second quotation); Eliza Lucas Pinckney to Wilhelmina-Catharine King, May 1759, *Letterbook*, 118 (third quotation). For the centrality of family rather than country to Eliza's identity, see Darcy R. Fryer, "The Mind of Eliza Pinckney: An Eighteenth-Century Woman's Construction of Self," *South Carolina Historical Magazine* 99 (July 1998): 215–237.
38. Eliza Lucas Pinckney to Wilhelmina-Catharine King, 27 February 1762, DE.
39. Eliza Lucas Pinckney to George Keate, February 1762, *Letterbook*, 180–181.
40. Assembly quotation in Walter J. Fraser, Jr., *Patriots, Pistols, and Petticoats: "Poor Sinful Charles Town" during the American Revolution*, 2nd ed. (Columbia: University of South Carolina Press, 1993), 38. See also Matthew Mulcahy, *Hubs of Empire: The Southeastern Lowcountry and British Caribbean* (Baltimore: Johns Hopkins University Press, 2014), 206–208.
41. Harriott Pinckney to unknown, 13 February 1768, Smythe Family Papers, SCHS; Eliza Lucas Pinckney to George Keate, February 1762, *Letterbook*, 181. For the South Carolina Regulator movement, see Rachel N. Klein, *Unification of a Slave State: The Rise of the Planter Class in the South Carolina Backcountry, 1760–1808* (Chapel Hill: University of North Carolina Press, 1990), chapters 1–2.
42. See also Zahniser, *Charles Cotesworth Pinckney*, 15–20.
43. Harriott Pinckney to Charles Cotesworth Pinckney, 3 March 1767, Smythe Family Papers, SCHS; Ravenel, *Eliza Pinckney*, 247. The will was proved 18 March 1769.
44. George C. Rogers, Jr., *Charleston in the Age of the Pinckneys* (1969; Columbia: University of South Carolina Press, 1980), 123; Zahniser, *Charles Cotesworth Pinckney*, 14; Ravenel, *Eliza Pinckney*, 247.
45. Edward McCrady, *The History of South Carolina under the Royal Government, 1719–1776* (New York, 1899), 659–660.

46. Harriott Pinckney Horry to Elizabeth Izard Blake, 27 November 1769, DE (quotation); Harriott Pinckney Horry to unknown, c. 1769, Smythe Family Papers, SCHS; Schulz, "Eliza Lucas Pinckney and Harriott Pinckney Horry," 95.
47. For her continued longing for Charles, see, for example, Eliza Lucas Pinckney to George Keate, 2 April 1786, DE.
48. Harriott Pinckney Horry to Thomas Pinckney, c. 1771, Smythe Family Papers, SCHS. Harriott Jr. is an author designation intended to avoid confusion for readers. She was not called Harriott Jr. in the family.
49. Harriott Pinckney Horry to Elizabeth Izard Blake, c. fall 1771, DE; Pinckney, *Life of General Thomas Pinckney*, 50; Maria Henrietta Pinckney, *A Notice of the Pinckneys* (Charleston: Evans and Cogswell, 1860), 16.
50. Quotation in Robert Olwell, *Masters, Slaves, and Subjects: The Culture of Power in the South Carolina Low Country, 1740–1790* (Ithaca, NY: Cornell University Press, 1998), 33.
51. Mulcahy, *Hubs of Empire*, 210–211.
52. Harriott Pinckney Horry to Thomas Pinckney, 12 March 1773, DE; Thomas Pinckney to Charles Cotesworth Pinckney, 16 April 1774, DE. Thomas completed his studies at Middle Temple on 25 November 1774 and returned to South Carolina around December 1774.
53. Josiah Quincy, Jr. Journal, 28 February–21 March 1773, in *The Travelers' Charleston: Accounts of Charleston and Lowcountry, South Carolina, 1666–1861*, ed. Jennie Holton Fant (Columbia: University of South Carolina Press, 2016), 36 (quotation). For Charles Cotesworth on the legal circuit, see Eliza Lucas Pinckney to Thomas Pinckney, 8 April 1773, DE. For colonial South Carolina political culture, see Robert M. Weir, " 'The Harmony We Were Famous For': An Interpretation of Pre-Revolutionary South Carolina Politics," *William and Mary Quarterly* 26 (October 1969): 473–501. For context, see Jack P. Greene, *The Quest for Power: The Lower Houses of Assembly in the Southern Royal Colonies, 1689–1776* (Chapel Hill: University of North Carolina Press, 1963).
54. Elizabeth Chalmers Huger to Eliza Lucas Pinckney, 1775, DE; Eliza Lucas Pinckney to Harriott Pinckney Horry, 1 March 1775, DE; Thomas Pinckney to Harriott Pinckney Horry, 23 May 1778, in Jack Cross, ed., "Letters of Thomas Pinckney, 1775–1780," *South Carolina Historical Magazine* 58 (1957), 151. Thomas's letters run through the four issues of the 1957 edition of the *South Carolina Historical Magazine*. He wrote this letter during the Revolutionary War but was reflecting on happier times in his family, before the conflict started.
55. Fraser, *Patriots, Pistols, and Petticoats*, 7–8, 23; Olwell, *Masters, Slaves, and Subjects*, 32; Nicholas Michael Butler, *Votaries of Apollo: The St. Cecilia Society and the Patronage of Concert Music in Charleston, South Carolina, 1766–1820* (Columbia: University of South Carolina Press, 2007). For Anglicization, see T. H. Breen, "An Empire of Goods: The Anglicization of Colonial America, 1690–1776," *Journal of British Studies* 25 (October 1986): 467–499.
56. Eliza Lucas Pinckney to Harriott Pinckney Horry, 20 February 1775, DE.
57. Eliza Lucas Pinckney to Harriott Pinckney Horry, c. May 1774, DE (first quotation); Eliza Lucas Pinckney to Harriott Pinckney Horry, 5 May 1774, DE (second quotation).

58. Eliza Lucas Pinckney to Thomas Pinckney, 8 April 1773, DE; Eliza Lucas Pinckney to Harriott Pinckney Horry, 5 May 1774, DE.
59. Eliza Lucas Pinckney to Harriott Pinckney Horry, c. May 1774, DE.

12. *A GATHERING STORM*

1. Walter J. Fraser, Jr., *Patriots, Pistols, and Petticoats: "Poor Sinful Charles Town" during the American Revolution,* 2nd ed. (Columbia: University of South Carolina Press, 1993), 49–65; Jim Piecuch, *Three Peoples, One King: Loyalists, Indians, and Slaves in the Revolutionary South, 1775–1782* (Columbia: University of South Carolina Press, 2008), 14–18; Kinloch Bull, Jr., *The Oligarchs in Colonial and Revolutionary Charleston: Lieutenant Governor William Bull II and His Family* (Columbia: University of South Carolina Press, 1991), 196–203; William R. Ryan, *The World of Thomas Jeremiah: Charles Town on the Eve of the American Revolution* (New York: Oxford University Press, 2010), 39–43, 137–139. Ryan provides a thorough overview of Charles Town in 1774–1776. William Bull II served as acting governor between Montagu and Campbell.
2. Thomas Pinckney to Harriott Pinckney Horry, c. February 1775, DE.
3. Eliza Lucas Pinckney to Harriott Pinckney Horry, 12 February 1775, DE.
4. Eliza Lucas Pinckney to Harriott Pinckney Horry, 12 February 1775, DE. See also Thomas Pinckney to Harriott Pinckney Horry, 20 February 1775, DE.
5. Eliza Lucas Pinckney to Harriott Pinckney Horry, 1 March 1775, DE; Thomas Pinckney to Harriott Pinckney Horry, c. February 1775, DE.
6. "Unanimously agreed to in the Provincial Congress of South Carolina, on Saturday the 3rd of June, 1775," reprinted in *Proceedings of the Massachusetts Historical Society,* vol. 13, *1871–1873* (Boston, 1873), 158. For fears about Indians (and slave insurrections), see Robert G. Parkinson, *The Common Cause: Creating Race and Nation in the American Revolution* (Chapel Hill: University of North Carolina Press, 2016), especially 20–21, 187. See also Matthew Mulcahy, *Hubs of Empire: The Southeastern Lowcountry and British Caribbean* (Baltimore: Johns Hopkins University Press, 2014), 211–213.
7. Charles Cotesworth Pinckney, *Life of General Thomas Pinckney* (1895; Memphis: General Books, 2012), 7; George C. Rogers, Jr., *Charleston in the Age of the Pinckneys* (1969; Columbia: University of South Carolina Press, 1980), 123; Bull, *Oligarchs,* 217; Fraser, *Patriots, Pistols, and Petticoats,* 71. For the brothers' military service, see also "Fighting the Revolutionary War," in *The Papers of the Revolutionary Era Pinckney Statesmen: Digital Edition,* ed. Constance B. Schulz (Charlottesville: University of Virginia Press, Rotunda, 2016), https://rotunda.upress.virginia.edu/founders/default.xqy?keys=PNKY-print-01–01–02&mode=TOC (hereinafter RSDE).
8. Eliza Lucas Pinckney to unknown, c. 1753, DE; Harriott Pinckney to Charles Cotesworth Pinckney, March 1763, Smythe Family Papers, SCHS.
9. For the 1775 trials, see Edward B. Rugemer, *Slave Law and the Politics of Resistance in the Early Atlantic World* (Cambridge: Harvard University Press, 2018), 189. For Dunmore and reactions, see Parkinson, *The Common Cause,* 153–159, 167–176. For explanations of the transformation toward independence, see Bernard Bailyn, *The*

Ideological Origins of the American Revolution (Cambridge: Harvard University Press, 1967); T. H. Breen, *The Marketplace of Revolution: How Consumer Politics Shaped American Independence* (New York: Oxford University Press, 2004); Pauline Maier, *From Resistance to Revolution: Colonial Radicals and the Development of American Opposition to Britain, 1765–1775* (New York: Knopf, 1972); Pauline Maier, *American Scripture: Making the Declaration of Independence* (New York: Knopf, 1997).

10. Harriott Pinckney Horry to Elizabeth Trapier, 28 November 1775, DE. For Eliza and Harriott during the war, see also Cokie Roberts, *Founding Mothers: The Women Who Raised Our Nation* (New York: Perennial, 2004), 1–11; Constance B. Schulz, "Eliza Lucas Pinckney and Harriott Pinckney Horry: A South Carolina Revolutionary-Era Mother and Daughter," in *South Carolina Women: Their Lives and Times,* vol. 1, ed. Marjorie Julian Spruill, Valinda W. Littlefield, and Joan Marie Johnson (Athens: University of Georgia Press, 2009), 79–108, especially 97–98. For wartime disruptions in other women's lives, see Patricia Brady, *Martha Washington: An American Life* (New York: Viking, 2005), chapters 6–7; Elaine Forman Crane, ed., *The Diary of Elizabeth Drinker: The Life Cycle of an Eighteenth-Century Woman,* abridged ed. (Philadelphia: University of Pennsylvania Press, 2010), 55–94; Ami Pflugrad-Jackisch, " 'What Am I but an American?': Mary Willing Byrd and Westover Plantation during the American Revolution," in *Women in the American Revolution: Gender, Politics, and the Domestic World,* ed. Barbara B. Oberg (Charlottesville: University of Virginia Press, 2019), 171–191; Woody Holton, *Abigail Adams, A Life* (New York: Free Press, 2009), especially chapters 8–13; Shelia L. Skemp, *First Lady of Letters: Judith Sargent Murray and the Struggle for Female Independence* (Philadelphia: University of Pennsylvania Press, 2009), chapter 3; Rosemarie Zagarri, *A Woman's Dilemma: Mercy Otis Warren and the American Revolution,* 2nd ed. (Malden, MA: Wiley Blackwell, 2015), chapter 4.

11. Elizabeth Trapier to Harriott Pinckney Horry, 2 August 1775, DE; Eliza Lucas Pinckney to Harriott Pinckney Horry, c. 1776, Phoebe Caroline Pinckney Seabrook, SCHS. Megan Hatfield likewise links Eliza's views to family. Megan Hatfield, "A Family upon the Deep Blue Sea: The Atlantic Life of Eliza Lucas Pinckney," Ph.D. diss., University of Miami, 2015. Barbara L. Bellows interprets Eliza as slower to support the patriots. Barbara L. Bellows, "Eliza Lucas Pinckney: The Evolution of an Icon," *South Carolina Historical Magazine* 106 (April–July 2005), 159–161. For women's primary focus on family, see also Patricia Cleary, *Elizabeth Murray: A Woman's Pursuit of Independence in Eighteenth-Century America* (Amherst: University of Massachusetts Press, 2000), chapter 5; Holton, *Abigail Adams*; Schulz, "Eliza Lucas Pinckney and Harriott Pinckney Horry"; Mary Beth Norton, *Liberty's Daughters: The Revolutionary Experience of American Women, 1750–1800* (Boston: Little, Brown, 1980), chapter 1; Roberts, *Founding Mothers*. For women's growing political consciousness in the Revolutionary era, see Linda K. Kerber, *Women of the Republic: Intellect and Ideology in Revolutionary America* (Chapel Hill: University of North Carolina Press, 1980), chapter 3; Norton, *Liberty's Daughters*, chapter 6; Cynthia A. Kierner, *Beyond the Household: Women's Place in the Early South* (Ithaca, NY: Cornell University Press, 1998), chapter 3; Carol Berkin, *Revolutionary Mothers: Women in the Struggle for*

American Independence (New York: Knopf, 2005), chapter 2. For the early Republic, see Rosemarie Zagarri, *Revolutionary Backlash: Women and Politics in the Early American Republic* (Philadelphia: University of Pennsylvania Press, 2007).

12. William Moultrie Memoir, excerpt in Harriott Horry Ravenel, *Eliza Pinckney* (New York: Charles Scribner's Sons, 1896), 262. See also S. Charles Bolton, *Southern Anglicanism: The Church of England in Colonial South Carolina* (Westport, CT: Greenwood, 1982), especially xi.
13. Charles Cotesworth Pinckney quoted in Fraser, *Patriots, Pistols, and Petticoats*, 75; Charles Cotesworth Pinckney Will, 14 December 1778, RSDE.
14. Thomas Pinckney to Harriott Pinckney Horry, 10 October 1775, in Jack Cross, ed., "Letters of Thomas Pinckney, 1775–1780," *South Carolina Historical Magazine* 58 (1957), 20–21 (first quotation); Thomas Pinckney to Harriott Pinckney Horry, 20 June 1776, "Letters of Thomas Pinckney," 72 (second quotation). See also Thomas Pinckney to Harriott Pinckney Horry, 18 June 1778, "Letters of Thomas Pinckney," 155; Thomas Pinckney to Harriott Pinckney Horry, 16 January 1779, "Letters of Thomas Pinckney," 224; Thomas Pinckney to Harriott Pinckney Horry, 24 December 1775, DE. The extant letters from this era are mostly from Thomas to Harriott and from Charles Cotesworth to Eliza. This appears to have been partly a strategy to divide writing duties, but other letters have not survived.
15. For siblings and egalitarian gender roles, see Lorri Glover, *All Our Relations: Blood Ties and Emotional Bonds among the Early South Carolina Gentry* (Baltimore: Johns Hopkins University Press, 2000).
16. Thomas Pinckney to Harriott Pinckney Horry, 7 October 1777, "Letters of Thomas Pinckney," 146 (first quotation); Thomas Pinckney to Harriott Pinckney Horry, 7 January 1779, "Letters of Thomas Pinckney," 162 (second quotation); Thomas Pinckney to Harriott Pinckney Horry, 7 May 1777, DE (last quotation). See also Thomas Pinckney to Harriott Pinckney Horry, 30 March 1776, "Letters of Thomas Pinckney," 30; Thomas Pinckney to Harriott Pinckney Horry, 17 July 1776, "Letters of Thomas Pinckney," 72; Thomas Pinckney to Harriott Pinckney Horry, 6 June 1777, "Letters of Thomas Pinckney," 81.
17. "Unanimously agreed to in the Provincial Congress of South Carolina"; Cynthia A. Kierner, *Southern Women in Revolution, 1776–1800: Personal and Political Narratives* (Columbia: University of South Carolina Press, 1998), 7; Piecuch, *Three Peoples, One King*, 45, 95–96.
18. Robert Olwell, *Masters, Slaves, and Subjects: The Culture of Power in the South Carolina Low Country, 1740–1790* (Ithaca, NY: Cornell University Press, 1998), 236–242; Fraser, *Patriots, Pistols, and Petticoats*, 78–79. For the loyalist exodus, see Maya Jasanoff, *Liberty's Exiles: American Loyalists in the Revolutionary World* (New York: Knopf, 2011); Mary Beth Norton, *The British-Americans: The Loyalist Exiles in England, 1774–1789* (Boston: Little, Brown, 1972); Rebecca Brannon, *From Revolution to Reunion: The Reintegration of the South Carolina Loyalists* (Columbia: University of South Carolina Press, 2016).
19. For the flight of families, see Kierner, *Southern Women in Revolution*, 95; Edward McCrady, *The History of South Carolina under the Royal Government, 1719–1776* (New

York: Macmillan, 1899), 557–558. South Carolinians passed even stricter prohibitions in 1778. See Piecuch, *Three Peoples, One King*, 96. For loyalist families, see also Cynthia M. Kennedy, *Braided Relations, Entwined Lives: The Women of Charleston's Urban Slave Society* (Bloomington: Indiana University Press, 2005), chapter 2; Brannon, *From Revolution to Reunion*, 5–22.

20. Harriott Pinckney Horry to Elizabeth Trapier, 28 November 1775, DE.
21. Charles Cotesworth Pinckney to Eliza Lucas Pinckney, 15 June 1776, DE. For context, see Benjamin L. Carp, "Changing Our Habitation: Henry Laurens, Rattray Green, and the Revolutionary Movement in Charleston's Domestic Spaces," in *Material Culture in Anglo-America: Regional Identity and Urbanity in the Tidewater, Lowcountry, and Caribbean*, ed. David S. Shields (Columbia: University of South Carolina Press, 2009), 285–309.
22. Charles Cotesworth Pinckney to Eliza Lucas Pinckney, 7 July 1776, DE; Thomas Pinckney to Harriott Pinckney Horry, 11 June 1776, "Letters of Thomas Pinckney," 69.
23. Thomas Pinckney to Harriott Pinckney Horry, 11 June 1776, "Letters of Thomas Pinckney," 69; Charles Cotesworth Pinckney to Eliza Lucas Pinckney, 5 June 1776, DE. Eliza's nephew Charles wrote her, too. See, for example, Charles Pinckney to Eliza Lucas Pinckney, 24 February 1779 and 28 March 1779, DE.
24. For a vivid description, see Ryan, *The World of Thomas Jeremiah*, 146–151. The palmetto tree was added to the flag in 1861.
25. Charles Cotesworth Pinckney to Eliza Lucas Pinckney, 29 June 1776, DE; Thomas Pinckney to Harriott Pinckney Horry, 29 June 1776, DE.
26. Declaration of Independence; Fraser, *Patriots, Pistols, and Petticoats*, 94–95.
27. "Unanimously agreed to in the Provincial Congress of South Carolina." For population, see Ryan, *The World of Thomas Jeremiah*, 111. See also Gregory E. O'Malley, *Final Passages: The Intercolonial Slave Trade of British America, 1619–1807* (Chapel Hill: University of North Carolina Press, 2014), 323–324; Parkinson, *The Common Cause*; Rugemer, *Slave Law and the Politics of Resistance*, chapter 5.
28. For enslaved laborers building infrastructure, see Ryan A. Quintana, *Making a Slave State: Political Development in Early South Carolina* (Chapel Hill: University of North Carolina Press, 2018), chapter 2. The connections between slavery and freedom are forcefully demonstrated in Edmund S. Morgan, *American Slavery, American Freedom: The Ordeal of Colonial Virginia* (New York: Norton, 1975).
29. Eliza Lucas Pinckney to Harriott Pinckney Horry, c. February 1775, DE. For power and violence of slaveholding women, see Thavolia Glymph, *Out of the House of Bondage: The Transformation of the Plantation Household* (New York: Cambridge University Press, 2008), chapters 1–2; Stephanie E. Jones-Rogers, *They Were Her Property: White Women as Slave Owners in the Antebellum South* (New Haven: Yale University Press, 2019). For enslaved couriers, see, for example, Charles Cotesworth Pinckney to Harriott Pinckney Horry, 24 September 1780, Smythe Family Papers, SCHS.

13. *THE HASTENING WAR*

1. Charles Cotesworth Pinckney to Eliza Lucas Pinckney, 7 July 1776, DE. See also Harriott Pinckney Horry to Eliza Lucas Pinckney, 30 December 1778, DE.

2. Thomas Pinckney to Harriott Pinckney Horry, 28 March 1777, in Jack Cross, ed., "Letters of Thomas Pinckney, 1775–1780," *South Carolina Historical Magazine* 58 (1957), 79 (first quotation); Thomas Pinckney to Harriott Pinckney Horry, 7 April 1778, "Letters of Thomas Pinckney," 148 (second quotation). See also Thomas Pinckney to Harriott Pinckney Horry, 31 January 1777, "Letters of Thomas Pinckney," 77; Charles Cotesworth Pinckney, *Life of General Thomas Pinckney* (1895; Memphis: General Books, 2012), 12; Thomas Pinckney to Harriott Pinckney Horry, 16 January 1779, "Letters of Thomas Pinckney," 224.
3. John Rutledge to George Washington, 5 July 1777, *The Papers of the Revolutionary Era Pinckney Statesmen: Digital Edition*, ed. Constance B. Schulz (Charlottesville: University of Virginia Press, Rotunda, 2016), https://rotunda.upress.virginia.edu/founders/default.xqy?keys=PNKY-print-01–01–02&mode=TOC (hereinafter RSDE); Thomas Lynch to George Washington, 5 July 1777, RSDE; Christopher Gadsden to George Washington, 4 July 1777, *The Papers of George Washington,* Revolutionary War Series, 20 vols., ed. Philander D. Chase et al. (Charlottesville: University Press of Virginia/University of Virginia Press, 1985–present), 10: 188 [hereinafter *PGW (RW)*]; Charles Cotesworth Pinckney to Daniel Huger Horry, Jr., 17 November 1777, RSDE; George Washington to John Hancock, 21 August 1777, *PGW (RW)* 11: 26; Pinckney, *Life of General Thomas Pinckney*, 13; Charles Cotesworth Pinckney to Eliza Lucas Pinckney, 24 February 1779, DE; editorial note, *PGW (RW)* 9: 629. See also "Fighting the Revolutionary War," RSDE.
4. Charles Pinckney to Eliza Lucas Pinckney, 24 February 1779, DE. For Eliza's and Harriott's concerns about crops, markets, and taxes, see Eliza Lucas Pinckney to Harriott Pinckney Horry, 28 May 1778, DE; Thomas Pinckney to Harriott Pinckney Horry, 23 May 1779, "Letters of Thomas Pinckney," 234.
5. Thomas Pinckney to Harriott Pinckney Horry, 21 November 1778, "Letters of Thomas Pinckney," 160; Charles Cotesworth Pinckney to William Moultrie, 24 May 1778, RSDE.
6. Eliza Lucas Pinckney to Harriott Pinckney Horry, 8 June 1778, DE (first quotation); Eliza Lucas Pinckney to Harriott Pinckney Horry, 28 May 1778, DE (second quotation). See also Eliza Lucas Pinckney to Harriott Pinckney Horry, 12 May 1778, DE.
7. Charles Pinckney to Eliza Lucas Pinckney, 28 March 1779, DE; Thomas Pinckney to Harriott Pinckney Horry, 3 June 1779, "Letters of Thomas Pinckney," 234.
8. For the brutality of the war, see Holger Hoock, *Scars of Independence: America's Violent Birth* (New York: Crown, 2017); Robert G. Parkinson, *The Common Cause: Creating Race and Nation in the American Revolution* (Chapel Hill: University of North Carolina Press, 2016); Jim Piecuch, *Three Peoples, One King: Loyalists, Indians, and Slaves in the Revolutionary South, 1775–1782* (Columbia: University of South Carolina Press, 2008). For women evacuating, see Margaret Manigault to Gabriel Manigault, 6 June 1775, Manigault Family Papers, SCL; Eliza Lucas Pinckney to Thomas Pinckney, 17 May 1779, DE; Cara Anzilotti, *In the Affairs of the World: Women, Patriarchy, and Power in Colonial South Carolina* (Westport, CT: Greenwood, 2002), 179–180.
9. Thomas Pinckney to Eliza Lucas Pinckney, 17 May 1779, DE; Harriott Horry Ravenel, *Eliza Pinckney* (New York: Charles Scribner's Sons, 1896), 168; Marvin R. Zahniser,

Charles Cotesworth Pinckney, Founding Father (Chapel Hill: University of North Carolina Press, 1967), 58. For the flight of enslaved people, see Piecuch, *Three Peoples, One King*, 158–172, 214–227; Cynthia M. Kennedy, *Braided Relations, Entwined Lives: The Women of Charleston's Urban Slave Society* (Bloomington: Indiana University Press, 2005), chapter 2; William R. Ryan, *The World of Thomas Jeremiah: Charles Town on the Eve of the American Revolution* (New York: Oxford University Press, 2010).

10. Parkinson, *The Common Cause*, 463; Hoock, *Scars of Independence*, 300–306; Lauren Duval, "Mastering Charleston: Property and Patriarchy in British-Occupied Charleston, 1780–82," *William and Mary Quarterly* 75 (October 2018): 589–622, especially 612–616.
11. Advertisement by Thomas Pinckney, 1 December 1779, RSDE. For context, see Erica Armstrong Dunbar, *Never Caught: The Washingtons' Relentless Pursuit of Their Runaway Slave, Ona Judge* (New York: Atria, 2017); Daina Ramey Berry, *The Price for Their Pound of Flesh: The Value of the Enslaved, from Womb to Grave, in the Building of a Nation* (Boston: Beacon, 2017).
12. Eliza Lucas Pinckney to Thomas Pinckney, 17 May 1779, DE. See also Zahniser, *Charles Cotesworth Pinckney*, 58–59.
13. Eliza Lucas Pinckney to Thomas Pinckney, 17 May 1779, DE; William Carher and John McCall, South Carolina Commissioners of the Treasury, Audits of Claims, 8 October 1779, DE.
14. Thomas Pinckney to Harriott Pinckney Horry, 23 May 1778, DE. For family genealogy, see Mabel L. Webber, "The Thomas Pinckney Family of South Carolina," *South Carolina Historical and Genealogical Magazine* 39 (January 1938): 15–35, especially 21, 25, 27.
15. Edward McCrady, *The History of South Carolina in the Revolution, 1775–1800* (New York: Macmillan, 1902), 184; Alexia Jones Helsley, "Rebecca Brewton Motte: Revolutionary South Carolinian," in *South Carolina Women: Their Lives and Times*, vol. 1, ed. Marjorie Julian Spruill, Valinda W. Littlefield, and Joan Marie Johnson (Athens: University of Georgia Press, 2009), 109–117.
16. Clinton quoted in Walter J. Fraser, Jr., *Patriots, Pistols, and Petticoats: "Poor Sinful Charles Town" during the American Revolution,* 2nd ed. (Columbia: University of South Carolina Press, 1993), 114; Zahniser, *Charles Cotesworth Pinckney*, 63; Fraser, *Patriots, Pistols, and Petticoats*, 129; Carl P. Borick, *Relieve Us of This Burthen: American Prisoners of War in the Revolutionary South, 1780–1782* (Columbia: University of South Carolina Press, 2012), 4. For overviews of the war in South Carolina, see Robert Olwell, *Masters, Slaves, and Subjects: The Culture of Power in the South Carolina Low Country, 1740–1790* (Ithaca, NY: Cornell University Press, 1998), 221–270; Jack Kelly, *Band of Giants: The Amateur Soldiers Who Won America's Independence* (New York: St. Martin's, 2014), 171–194, 211–212; Rebecca Brannon, *From Revolution to Reunion: The Reintegration of the South Carolina Loyalists* (Columbia: University of South Carolina Press, 2016), 3–33; Cynthia A. Kierner, *Southern Women in Revolution, 1776–1800: Personal and Political Narratives* (Columbia: University of South Carolina Press, 1998), 11–20; Fraser, *Patriots, Pistols, and Petticoats*, chapters 3 and 4; Hoock, *Scars of Independence*, 299–321.

17. Zahniser, *Charles Cotesworth Pinckney,* 63.
18. William Moultrie, *Memoirs of the American Revolution,* 2 vols. (New York: David Longworth, 1802), 2: 96–97; Johann Ewald, *Diary of the American War: A Hessian Journal,* ed. and trans. Joseph P. Tustin (New Haven: Yale University Press, 1979), 238–239. For the destruction of Charles Town, see also Emma Hart, *Building Charleston: Town and Society in the Eighteenth-Century British Atlantic World* (Charlottesville: University of Virginia Press, 2010), 186–188. Estimates of soldiers captured vary. See Borick, *Relieve Us of This Burthen,* xi, 46; Kelly, *Band of Giants,* 174; Andrew Jackson O'Shaughnessy, *The Men Who Lost America: British Leadership, the American Revolution, and the Fate of the Empire* (New Haven: Yale University Press, 2013), 230–231; Fraser, *Patriots, Pistols, and Petticoats,* 131. The initial surrender took place May 11. A final surrender was negotiated May 12.
19. Helsley, "Rebecca Brewton Motte," 116. The house remains in the Brewton family today and is considered one of the finest examples of Georgian architecture in America. See Cary Carson, *Face Value: The Consumer Revolution and the Colonizing of America* (Charlottesville: University of Virginia Press, 2017), 136–137. The British did not expect a long-term occupation and assumed loyalists would rally. O'Shaughnessy, *The Men Who Lost America*; Piecuch, *Three Peoples, One King*; Duval, "Mastering Charleston."
20. George Washington to Jonathan Trumbull, 11 June 1780, *Writings of George Washington from the Original Manuscript Sources, 1745–1799,* 39 vols., ed. John C. Fitzpatrick (Washington, DC: U.S. Government Printing Office, 1931–1944), 18: 509–510.
21. John Adams to Hezekiah Niles, 13 February 1818, Founders Online, https://founders.archives.gov/. For this perspective, see Gordon S. Wood, *The Radicalism of the American Revolution* (New York: Vintage, 1991). For alternative perspectives, see Carol Berkin, *Revolutionary Mothers: Women in the Struggle for American Independence* (New York: Knopf, 2005); Colin G. Calloway, *The Indian World of George Washington: The First President, the First Americans, and the Birth of the Nation* (New York: Oxford University Press, 2018); Hoock, *Scars of Independence*; Parkinson, *The Common Cause*; Justin Roberts, *Slavery and the Enlightenment in the British Atlantic, 1750–1807* (New York: Cambridge University Press, 2013).

14. *"SHATTER'D AND RUIN'D"*

1. Eliza Lucas Pinckney to Alexander Garden, 14 May 1782, DE (first quotation); Eliza Lucas Pinckney to Daniel (Charles Lucas Pinckney) Horry, 7 August 1783, DE (subsequent quotations). For the occupation, see Jim Piecuch, *Three Peoples, One King: Loyalists, Indians, and Slaves in the Revolutionary South, 1775–1782* (Columbia: University of South Carolina Press, 2008), chapter 5. For another South Carolina family's experiences, see Joanna Bowen Gillespie, *The Life and Times of Martha Laurens Ramsay, 1759–1811* (Columbia: University of South Carolina Press, 2001). For women in other locales, see Catherine A. Brekus, *Sarah Osborn's World: The Rise of Evangelical Christianity in Early America* (New Haven: Yale University Press, 2013), chapter 10; Elaine Forman Crane, "Religion and Rebellion: Women of Faith in the

American War for Independence," in *Religion in a Revolutionary Age,* ed. Ronald Hoffman and Peter J. Albert (Charlottesville: University Press of Virginia, 1994), 52–86; Elaine Forman Crane, ed., *The Diary of Elizabeth Drinker: The Life Cycle of an Eighteenth-Century Woman,* abridged ed. (Philadelphia: University of Pennsylvania Press, 2010), 55–94; Patricia Cleary, *Elizabeth Murray: A Woman's Pursuit of Independence in Eighteenth-Century America* (Amherst: University of Massachusetts Press, 2000), chapter 5; Martha J. King, " 'A Lady of New Jersey': Annis Boudinot Stockton, Patriot and Poet in an Age of Revolution," in *Women in the American Revolution: Gender, Politics, and the Domestic World,* ed. Barbara B. Oberg (Charlottesville: University of Virginia Press, 2019), 103–127; Ami Pflugrad-Jackisch, " 'What Am I but an American?': Mary Willing Byrd and Westover Plantation during the American Revolution," in Oberg, *Women in the American Revolution,* 171–191.

2. British soldier quoted in Rebecca Brannon, *From Revolution to Reunion: The Reintegration of the South Carolina Loyalists* (Columbia: University of South Carolina Press, 2016), 33; George Washington Greene, *The Life of Nathanael Greene, Major-General in the Army of the Revolution,* 3 vols. (New York: Hurd and Houghton, 1871), 3: 226; William Moultrie, *Memoirs of the American Revolution,* 2 vols. (New York: David Longworth, 1802), 2: 354–355; Holger Hoock, *Scars of Independence: America's Violent Birth* (New York: Crown, 2017), 304, 309, 317. See also Robert G. Parkinson, *The Common Cause: Creating Race and Nation in the American Revolution* (Chapel Hill: University of North Carolina Press, 2016); Piecuch, *Three Peoples, One King.*

3. For the Revolution as a civil war and women's involvement, see Carol Berkin, *Revolutionary Mothers: Women in the Struggle for American Independence* (New York: Knopf, 2005), chapter 3; Linda K. Kerber, *Women of the Republic: Intellect and Ideology in Revolutionary America* (Chapel Hill: University of North Carolina Press, 1980), chapter 2; Cynthia A. Kierner, *Beyond the Household: Women's Place in the Early South* (Ithaca, NY: Cornell University Press, 1998), chapter 3; Mary Beth Norton, *Liberty's Daughters: The Revolutionary Experience of American Women, 1750–1800* (Boston: Little, Brown, 1980), chapter 7; Cokie Roberts, *Founding Mothers: The Women Who Raised Our Nation* (New York: Perennial, 2004), chapters 3–4. For tumultuous effects of the war, see also Benjamin L. Carp, "Changing Our Habitation: Henry Laurens, Rattray Green, and the Revolutionary Movement in Charleston's Domestic Spaces," in *Material Culture in Anglo-America: Regional Identity and Urbanity in the Tidewater, Lowcountry, and Caribbean,* ed. David S. Shields (Columbia: University of South Carolina Press, 2009), 285–309; Lorri Glover, *Founders as Fathers: The Private Lives and Politics of the American Revolutionaries* (New Haven: Yale University Press, 2015), chapter 3; Phillip Hamilton, *The Making and Unmaking of a Revolutionary Family: The Tuckers of Virginia, 1752–1830* (Charlottesville: University of Virginia Press, 2003). Ami Pflugrad-Jackisch, studying Mary Willing Byrd, and Charlene M. Boyer Lewis, researching Peggy Shippen Arnold, are reorienting the narrative of the Revolution to center women.

4. Caroline Gilman, ed., *Letters of Eliza Wilkinson, During the Invasion and Possession of Charlestown, S.C. by the British in the Revolutionary War* (New York: Samuel Colman, 1839), 28–29, 105.

5. Hoock, *Scars of Independence*, 312; A. S. Salley, ed., *Col. William Hill's Memoir of the Revolution* (Columbia: Historical Commission of South Carolina, 1921), 9. For anarchy, see Cynthia M. Kennedy, *Braided Relations, Entwined Lives: The Women of Charleston's Urban Slave Society* (Bloomington: Indiana University Press, 2005), 30. For intentional shortages, see Berkin, *Revolutionary Mothers*, 27. For deprivations and dangers women endured, see also Lauren Duval, "Mastering Charleston: Property and Patriarchy in British-Occupied Charleston, 1780–82," *William and Mary Quarterly* 75 (October 2018), 591, 606–607; Kennedy, *Braided Relations,* chapter 2; Roberts, *Founding Mothers*, 83–84; Piecuch, *Three Peoples, One King*, chapters 6–7.
6. Gilman, *Letters of Eliza Wilkinson*, 46. For rape, see Berkin, *Revolutionary Mothers*, 39–41; Lauren Duval, " 'A shocking thing to tell of': Female Civilians, Violence, and Rape under British Military Rule," conference paper in author's possession; Hoock, *Scars of Independence*, 163–174, 312; Kerber, *Women of the Republic*, 46–47; Norton, *Liberty's Daughters*, 208–209.
7. For hiding valuables, see Elizabeth Motte Pinckney to Eliza Lucas Pinckney, 17 July 1780, DE; Charles Cotesworth Pinckney to Thomas Pinckney, 9 June 1780, DE. Duval, "Mastering Charleston," 595; Kennedy, *Braided Relations,* 30–31; Kerber, *Women of the Republic*, 120–121, 147–149; Norton, *Liberty's Daughters*, 195–224; Berkin, *Revolutionary Mothers*, 11, 149; Woody Holton, *Abigail Adams, A Life* (New York: Free Press, 2009), 143, 155, 178, 185.
8. See also Anne Firor Scott, "Self-Portraits: Three Women," in *Uprooted Americans: Essays to Honor Oscar Handlin,* ed. Richard L. Bushman et al. (Boston: Little, Brown, 1979), 70–72.
9. George C. Rogers, Jr., *Charleston in the Age of the Pinckneys* (1969; Columbia: University of South Carolina Press, 1980), 124; Eliza Lucas Pinckney to Thomas Pinckney, 4 December 1780, Phoebe Caroline Pinckney Seabrook, SCHS; Marty D. Matthews, *Forgotten Founder: The Life and Times of Charles Pinckney* (Columbia: University of South Carolina Press, 2004), 18–19.
10. Charles Cotesworth Pinckney to Harriott Pinckney Horry, 8 October 1780, Smythe Family Papers, SCHS; Marvin R. Zahniser, *Charles Cotesworth Pinckney, Founding Father* (Chapel Hill: University of North Carolina Press, 1967), 65; Rogers, *Charleston in the Age of the Pinckneys*, 124. For confiscated estates, see Maya Jasanoff, *Liberty's Exiles: American Loyalists in the Revolutionary World* (New York: Knopf, 2011), 74.
11. Charles Cotesworth Pinckney to Eliza Lucas Pinckney, 22 October 1780, DE (first quotation); Charles Cotesworth Pinckney to Eliza Lucas Pinckney, 16 October 1780, DE (second quotation). See also Charles Cotesworth Pinckney to Eliza Lucas Pinckney, 10 November 1780, 5:00 p.m., 10 November 1780, 10:00 p.m., 13 November 1780, 15 November 1780, 25 November 1780, 28 November 1780, all in DE. The death date is unknown.
12. Charles Cotesworth Pinckney to John Money, 30 June 1780, *The Papers of the Revolutionary Era Pinckney Statesmen: Digital Edition*, ed. Constance B. Schulz (Charlottesville: University of Virginia Press, Rotunda, 2016), https://rotunda.upress.virginia.edu/founders/default.xqy?keys=PNKY-print-01-01-02&mode=TOC (hereinafter RSDE).

13. Charles Cotesworth Pinckney to Edward Rutledge, [after 12 May 1780], RSDE; Thomas Pinckney to Eliza Lucas Pinckney, 11 June 1780, DE. For context, see Donald F. Johnson, "Ambiguous Allegiances: Urban Loyalties during the American Revolution," *Journal of American History* 104 (December 2017): 610–631, especially 614, 620–621. For other couples' dividing allegiances, see Cleary, *Elizabeth Murray*, especially 183–184; King, " 'A Lady of New Jersey,' " 103–110, 119–120; Charlene M. Boyer Lewis, "Most Troublesome Female Loyalist: Peggy Shippen Arnold and the Treason at West Point," conference paper in author's possession.
14. Mabel L. Webber, ed., "Josiah Smith's Diary, 1780–1781," *South Carolina Historical and Genealogical Magazine* 34 (April 1933), 78. See also Johnson, "Ambiguous Allegiances," 610, 627–628.
15. Harriott Pinckney Horry to unknown, c. 1782, DE; Edward Rutledge to Arthur Middleton, 26 February 1782, DE. South Carolinians called those fines "amercements." For a list of estates confiscated or amerced, see Mabel L. Webber, ed., "Josiah Smith's Diary, 1780–1781," *South Carolina Historical and Genealogical Magazine* 34 (October 1933), 194–199. For the process, see Cynthia A. Kierner, *Southern Women in Revolution, 1776–1800: Personal and Political Narratives* (Columbia: University of South Carolina Press, 1998), especially 95–98; Brannon, *From Revolution to Reunion*, especially 8, 49–51, 67–72.
16. Thomas Pinckney to Harriott Pinckney Horry, 11 June 1780, "Letters of Thomas Pinckney," 239; Elizabeth Motte Pinckney to Eliza Lucas Pinckney, 17 July 1780, DE.
17. "Letters of Thomas Pinckney," 240, fn. 49; Hoock, *Scars of Independence*, 197; Thomas Pinckney to Horatio Gates, 24 August 1780, in *The State Records of North Carolina*, 26 vols., ed. Walter D. Clark (Goldsboro, NC: Nash Brothers, 1886–1907), 14: 575 (quotation). For the Battle of Camden, see Andrew Jackson O'Shaughnessy, *The Men Who Lost America: British Leadership, the American Revolution, and the Fate of the Empire* (New Haven: Yale University Press, 2013), 257–259; Jack Kelly, *Band of Giants: The Amateur Soldiers Who Won America's Independence* (New York: St. Martin's, 2014), 175–180.
18. Thomas Pinckney to Harriott Pinckney Horry, 26 September 1780, "Letters of Thomas Pinckney," 242; Thomas Pinckney to Horatio Gates, 18 August 1780, *The State Records of North Carolina*, 14: 560 (second quotation).
19. Thomas Pinckney to Daniel (Charles Lucas Pinckney) Horry, 26 October 1780, DE; Charles Cotesworth Pinckney, *Life of General Thomas Pinckney* (1895; Memphis: General Books, 2012), 20.
20. Thomas Pinckney to Daniel (Charles Lucas Pinckney) Horry, 26 October 1780, DE. For the women-centered household at Mount Joseph, see Eliza Lucas Pinckney to Thomas Pinckney, 4 October 1780, DE. The details of Thomas's travels are unclear. Some family memories report Betsey going to Camden to care for him, and others say Betsey sent a cousin to transport Thomas to her mother's house. Harriott Horry Ravenel, *Eliza Pinckney* (New York: Charles Scribner's Sons, 1896), 295; Pinckney, *Life of General Thomas Pinckney*, 20.
21. Eliza Lucas Pinckney to Thomas Pinckney, August 1780, in Elise Pinckney, ed., "Letters of Eliza Lucas Pinckney, 1768–1782," *South Carolina Historical Magazine* 76 (July

1975), 159 (first quotation); Eliza Lucas Pinckney to Thomas Pinckney, 13 September 1780, DE; Eliza Lucas Pinckney to Elizabeth Motte Pinckney, 18 June 1780, DE.

22. Eliza Lucas Pinckney to Thomas Pinckney, 28 November 1780, Phoebe Caroline Pinckney Seabrook, SCHS; Charles Cotesworth Pinckney to Eliza Lucas Pinckney, 1 December 1780, DE.
23. Mabel L. Webber, ed., "Josiah Smith's Diary, 1780–1781," *South Carolina Historical and Genealogical Magazine* 34 (April 1933), 78. For a list of Carolinians in Philadelphia, see 78–83.
24. Charles Cotesworth Pinckney to Eliza Lucas Pinckney, 23 November 1780, DE (quotation); Charles Cotesworth Pinckney to Harriott Pinckney Horry, 8 October 1780, Smythe Family Papers, SCHS; Charles Cotesworth Pinckney to Daniel (Charles Lucas Pinckney) Horry, 4 October 1780, DE; Charles Cotesworth Pinckney to Daniel (Charles Lucas Pinckney) Horry, 16 October 1780, DE; Charles Cotesworth Pinckney to Harriott Pinckney Horry, 24 September 1780, Smythe Family Papers, SCHS. For prisoners of war, see Hoock, *Scars of Independence*, 188–197; Carl P. Borick, *Relieve Us of This Burthen: American Prisoners of War in the Revolutionary South, 1780–1782* (Columbia: University of South Carolina Press, 2012).
25. Charles Cotesworth Pinckney to Eliza Lucas Pinckney, 25 July 1781, DE; Thomas Pinckney to Eliza Lucas Pinckney, 26 July 1781, DE; "Fighting the Revolutionary War," RSDE; Zahniser, *Charles Cotesworth Pinckney*, 69.
26. Eliza Lucas Pinckney to Rebecca Evance, 25 September 1780, DE; Harriott Pinckney Horry to Elizabeth Blake Izard, 16 April 1782, DE; O'Shaughnessy, *The Men Who Lost America*, 247.
27. Ravenel, *Eliza Pinckney*, 286.
28. Ravenel, *Eliza Pinckney*, 286; Roberts, *Founding Mothers*, 111–112.
29. The house did not burn down. For a fascinating unraveling of the Rebecca Brewton Motte legend, see Steven D. Smith et al., *"Obstinate and Strong": The History and Archaeology of the Siege of Fort Motte* (Columbia: University of South Carolina–South Carolina Institute of Archaeology and Anthropology, 2007), 21–28, 34, https://scholarcommons.sc.edu/cgi/viewcontent.cgi?article=1052&context=anth_facpub. For Motte's life, see Alexia Jones Helsley, "Rebecca Brewton Motte: Revolutionary South Carolinian," in *South Carolina Women: Their Lives and Times,* vol. 1, ed. Marjorie Julian Spruill, Valinda W. Littlefield, and Joan Marie Johnson (Athens: University of Georgia Press, 2009), 109–126.
30. Eliza Lucas Pinckney to Elizabeth Motte Pinckney, 18 June 1780, DE (first quotation); Eliza Lucas Pinckney to Alexander Garden, 14 May 1782, DE (second and third quotations); Eliza Lucas Pinckney to Thomas Pinckney, 4 December 1780, Phoebe Caroline Pinckney Seabrook, SCHS (last quotation).
31. Eliza Lucas Pinckney to Rebecca Evance, 25 September 1780, DE. Mary Willing Byrd of Virginia had the same attitude. Pflugrad-Jackisch, " 'What Am I but an American?' "
32. Edward Rutledge to Arthur Middleton, 16 March 1782, DE; loyalist solider quoted in Piecuch, *Three Peoples, One King*, 290. For the loyalist exodus, see Jasanoff, *Liberty's Exiles*; Mary Beth Norton, *The British-Americans: The Loyalist Exiles in England,*

1774–1789 (Boston: Little, Brown, 1972); Brannon, *From Revolution to Reunion.* Between five thousand and seven thousand of the South Carolina evacuees were formerly enslaved people or free people of color. See Jasanoff, *Liberty's Exiles,* 77; Robert Olwell, *Masters, Slaves, and Subjects: The Culture of Power in the South Carolina Low Country, 1740–1790* (Ithaca, NY: Cornell University Press, 1998), 269; Piecuch, *Three Peoples, One King,* 287–291; Edward B. Rugemer, *Slave Law and the Politics of Resistance in the Early Atlantic World* (Cambridge: Harvard University Press, 2018), 209.

33. Eliza Lucas Pinckney to Charles Cotesworth Pinckney, 16 July 1782, Phoebe Caroline Pinckney Seabrook, SCHS.
34. Charles Cotesworth Pinckney to Harriott Pinckney Horry, 23 October 1782, DE.
35. Johann Ewald, *Diary of the American War: A Hessian Journal,* ed. and trans. Joseph P. Tustin (New Haven: Yale University Press, 1979), 305; Moultrie, *Memoirs of the American Revolution,* 2: 352; Jasanoff, *Liberty's Exiles,* 75; Kennedy, *Braided Relations,* 35; Olwell, *Masters, Slaves, and Subjects,* 269–270.
36. Moultrie, *Memoirs of the American Revolution,* 2: 359–360; Gilman, *Letters of Eliza Wilkinson,* 21; Edward Rutledge to Arthur Middleton, 16 March 1782, DE.
37. Thomas Pinckney to Harriott Pinckney Horry, 26 February 1783, DE.
38. Eliza Lucas Pinckney to Daniel (Charles Lucas Pinckney) Horry, 7 August 1783, DE (all subsequent quotations).

15. *HAPPY UNDER HER OWN VINE AND FIG TREE*

1. Alice DeLancey Izard to Ralph Izard, 11 December 1784, Ralph Izard Papers, SCL; Constance B. Schulz, "Eliza Lucas Pinckney and Harriott Pinckney Horry: A South Carolina Revolutionary-Era Mother and Daughter," in *South Carolina Women: Their Lives and Times,* vol. 1, ed. Marjorie Julian Spruill, Valinda W. Littlefield, and Joan Marie Johnson (Athens: University of Georgia Press, 2009), 100.
2. Harriott Pinckney Horry to Eliza Lucas Pinckney, 7–8 November 1785, DE; Charles Cotesworth Pinckney to Eliza Lucas Pinckney, 10 November 1785, Smythe Family Papers, SCHS.
3. Harriott Pinckney Horry to Daniel (Charles Lucas Pinckney) Horry, 28 February 1786, DE.
4. Eliza Lucas Pinckney to Daniel (Charles Lucas Pinckney) Horry, 16 April 1782, DE; Thomas Pinckney to Harriott Pinckney Horry and Maria Henrietta Pinckney, 29 June 1790, DE.
5. Advertisement by Charles Cotesworth and Thomas Pinckney, 26 January 1786, *The Papers of the Revolutionary Era Pinckney Statesmen: Digital Edition,* ed. Constance B. Schulz (Charlottesville: University of Virginia Press, Rotunda, 2016), https://rotunda.upress.virginia.edu/founders/default.xqy?keys=PNKY-print-01–01–02&mode=TOC (hereinafter RSDE).
6. Eliza Lucas Pinckney to George Keate, 2 April 1786, DE. Some aging women experienced a hurtful loss of status. See Elaine Forman Crane, ed., *The Diary of Elizabeth Drinker: The Life Cycle of an Eighteenth-Century Woman,* abridged ed. (Philadelphia: University of Pennsylvania Press, 2010), 123–124; Ann M. Little, *The Many Captivities of Esther Wheelwright* (New Haven: Yale University Press, 2016), 176–177; Laurel

Thatcher Ulrich, *A Midwife's Tale: The Life of Martha Ballard, Based on Her Diary, 1785–1812* (New York: Knopf, 1990), 262–352. For aging men's declining status, see Lisa Wilson, *Ye Heart of a Man: The Domestic Life of Men in Colonial New England* (New Haven: Yale University Press, 1999), chapter 7. Eliza had more in common with Mercy Otis Warren; see Rosemarie Zagarri, *A Woman's Dilemma: Mercy Otis Warren and the American Revolution*, 2nd ed. (Malden, MA: Wiley Blackwell, 2015), 158. See also Paula A. Scott, *Growing Old in the Early Republic: Spiritual, Social, and Economic Issues, 1790–1830* (New York: Routledge, 1997).

7. Eliza Lucas Pinckney to George Keate, 2 April 1786, DE.
8. Eliza Lucas Pinckney to George Keate, 2 April 1786, DE.
9. Maria Henrietta Pinckney, *A Notice of the Pinckneys* (Charleston: Evans and Cogswell, 1860), 11 (quotation); Eliza Lucas Pinckney to Daniel (Charles Lucas Pinckney) Horry, 7 August 1783, DE.
10. Pinckney, *A Notice of the Pinckneys*, 18; Charles Cotesworth Pinckney, *Life of General Thomas Pinckney* (1895; Memphis: General Books, 2012), 54.
11. For his later career, see Marvin R. Zahniser, *Charles Cotesworth Pinckney, Founding Father* (Chapel Hill: University of North Carolina Press, 1967).
12. Pinckney, *Life of General Thomas Pinckney*, 50 (quotation); Charles Cotesworth Pinckney to Eliza Lucas Pinckney, 22 February 1787, DE. For the brothers' renown at their deaths, see *Eulogy on Gen. Chs. Cotesworth Pinckney, President-General of the Society of the Cincinnati, Delivered by Appointment of the Society of the Cincinnati of South Carolina, on Tuesday, the 1st of November, 1825, at St. Philip's Church. By Alexander Garden, Vice-President of the State Society* (Charleston: A. E. Miller, 1825); *A Sermon Preached at St. Philip's Church, August 21, 1825, By Christopher Gadsden, On the Occasion of the Decease of Gen. Charles Cotesworth Pinckney. Published by the Vestry* (Charleston: A. E. Miller, 1825); Thomas Pinckney obituary, *Niles Weekly Register*, 15 November 1828, American Antiquarian Society Periodicals Collection.
13. Harriott Pinckney Horry to Elizabeth Trapier Martin, May 1786, DE.
14. Daniel Huger Horry, Jr. Estate Inventory, 16 January 1786, DE; 1790 Census, Department of Commerce and Labor, Bureau of the Census, *Heads of Families at the First Census on the United States Taken in the Year 1790, South Carolina* (Washington, DC: Government Printing Office, 1908). There were two hundred female heads of household in Charleston according to the 1790 census; see Ellen Hartigan-O'Connor, *The Ties That Buy: Women and Commerce in Revolutionary America* (Philadelphia: University of Pennsylvania Press, 2009), 23.
15. Thomas Pinckney to Harriott Pinckney Horry, 7 February 1785, DE; William Frazer to Harriott Pinckney Horry, 20 August 1792, DE; William Frazer to Harriott Pinckney Horry, 8 October 1792, DE. See also Charles Cotesworth Pinckney to Harriott Pinckney Horry, 14 May 1787; Charles Cotesworth Pinckney to Harriott Pinckney Horry, 30 May 1787; Thomas Pinckney to Harriott Pinckney Horry, 19 August 1789; Thomas Pinckney to Harriott Pinckney Horry, 30 September 1791; Gadsden and Hall to Thomas Pinckney, 6 May 1793, all in DE.
16. Thomas Pinckney to Harriott Pinckney Horry, c. 1790, DE. For other examples, see the correspondences of Jacob Read and Ann Edgar, Read Family Papers, SCL; Joseph

Manigault and Margaret Izard Manigault, Manigault Family Papers, SCL. For analysis, see Cara Anzilotti, *In the Affairs of the World: Women, Patriarchy, and Power in Colonial South Carolina* (Westport, CT: Greenwood, 2002), 125–129; Lorri Glover, *All Our Relations: Blood Ties and Emotional Bonds among the Early South Carolina Gentry* (Baltimore: Johns Hopkins University Press, 2000), chapter 3.

17. For republican motherhood and women's narrowing roles, see Linda K. Kerber, *Women in the Republic: Intellect and Ideology in Revolutionary America* (Chapel Hill: University of North Carolina Press, 1980); Mary Beth Norton, *Liberty's Daughters: The Revolutionary Experience of American Women, 1750–1800* (New York: Little, Brown, 1980); Rosemarie Zagarri, *Revolutionary Backlash: Women and Politics in the Early American Republic* (Philadelphia: University of Pennsylvania Press, 2007). For southern women, see Cynthia A. Kierner, *Beyond the Household: Women's Place in the Early South, 1700–1835* (Ithaca, NY: Cornell University Press, 1998); Ben Marsh, *Georgia's Frontier Women: Female Fortunes in a Southern Colony* (Athens: University of Georgia Press, 2007); Kirsten E. Wood, *Masterful Women: Slaveholding Widows from the American Revolution through the Civil War* (Chapel Hill: University of North Carolina Press, 2004). For other powerful Lowcountry women, see G. Winston Lane, Jr., "Economic Power among Eighteenth-Century Women of the Carolina Lowcountry," in *Money, Trade, and Power: The Evolution of Colonial South Carolina's Plantation Society*, ed. Jack P. Greene, Rosemary Brana-Shute, and Randy J. Sparks (Columbia: University of South Carolina Press, 2001), 322–343; Alexia Jones Helsley, "Rebecca Brewton Motte: Revolutionary South Carolinian," in *South Carolina Women: Their Lives and Times*, vol. 1, ed. Marjorie Julian Spruill, Valinda W. Littlefield, and Joan Marie Johnson (Athens: University of Georgia Press, 2009), 109–126. For a Virginian, see Ami Pflugrad-Jackisch, " 'What Am I but an American?': Mary Willing Byrd and Westover Plantation during the American Revolution," in *Women in the American Revolution: Gender, Politics, and the Domestic World*, ed. Barbara B. Oberg (Charlottesville: University of Virginia Press, 2019), 171–191.

18. Pinckney, *A Notice of the Pinckneys*, 8.

19. Johann David Schoepf, *Travels in the Confederation*, ed. and trans., Alfred J. Morrison (New York: Burt Franklin, 1911), rpt. in *The Travelers' Charleston: Accounts of Charleston and Lowcountry, South Carolina, 1666–1861*, ed. Jennie Holton Fant (Columbia: University of South Carolina Press, 2016), 52, 42–43; Joseph W. Barnwell, ed., "Diary of Timothy Ford, 1785–1786," *South Carolina Historical and Genealogical Magazine* 13 (July 1912), 143; Joseph W. Barnwell, ed., "Diary of Timothy Ford, 1785–1786," *South Carolina Historical and Genealogical Magazine* 13 (October 1912), 204, 188.

20. 1790 Census; Pinckney, *Life of General Thomas Pinckney*, 23–24. For Pinckney Island, see Merrill G. Christophersen, *Biography of an Island: General Charles Cotesworth Pinckney's Sea Island Plantation* (Fennimore, WI: Westburg Associates, 1976).

21. Important analyses include Edmund S. Morgan, *American Slavery, American Freedom: The Ordeal of Colonial Virginia* (New York: Norton, 1975); Justin Roberts, *Slavery and the Enlightenment in the British Atlantic, 1750–1807* (New York: Cambridge University Press, 2013).

22. Essay of 1785 quoted in Ryan A. Quintana, *Making a Slave State: Political Development in Early South Carolina* (Chapel Hill: University of North Carolina Press, 2018), 48; Charles Cotesworth Pinckney to Harriott Pinckney Horry, 30 May 1787, DE.
23. James Madison, *Journal of the Federal Convention*, ed. E. H. Scott (Chicago: Albert, Scott, 1893), 335. See also "Drafting and Ratifying the Constitution," RSDE; Marty D. Matthews, *Forgotten Founder: The Life and Times of Charles Pinckney* (Columbia: University of South Carolina Press, 2004), chapter 3; Edward B. Rugemer, *Slave Law and the Politics of Resistance in the Early Atlantic World* (Cambridge: Harvard University Press, 2018), 225–233; Zahniser, *Charles Cotesworth Pinckney*, 87–96.
24. Thomas Jefferson, *Notes on the State of Virginia* (London: John Stockdale, 1787), 271; Patrick Henry, 18 January 1773, in William Wirt Henry, *Patrick Henry: Life, Correspondence, and Speeches*, 3 vols. (New York: Charles Scribner's Sons, 1891), 1: 152–153. For the Hemingses, see Annette Gordon-Reed, *The Hemingses of Monticello: An American Family* (New York: Norton, 2008).
25. Pinckney, *Life of General Thomas Pinckney*, 23 (quotation). For the reintegration of loyalists, see Rebecca Brannon, *From Revolution to Reunion: The Reintegration of the South Carolina Loyalists* (Columbia: University of South Carolina Press, 2016), especially 6–10, 125–126, 133–134. For South Carolinians' cultural conservatism, see Robert M. Weir, " 'The Harmony We Were Famous For': An Interpretation of Pre-Revolutionary South Carolina Politics," *William and Mary Quarterly* 26 (October 1969): 473–501. Unequal representation in the legislature ensured that South Carolina ratified the U.S. Constitution. See Rachel N. Klein, *Unification of a Slave State: The Rise of the Planter Class in the South Carolina Backcountry, 1760–1808* (Chapel Hill: University of North Carolina Press, 1990), especially 167. See also Peter N. Moore, *World of Toil and Strife: Community Transformation in Backcountry South Carolina, 1750–1805* (Columbia: University of South Carolina Press, 2007); Manisha Sinha, *The Counterrevolution of Slavery: Politics and Ideology in Antebellum South Carolina* (Chapel Hill: University of North Carolina Press, 2000).
26. *State Gazette of South Carolina*, 23 June 1785; Edward Rutledge to Eliza Lucas Pinckney, c. June 1785, DE; "Duelling," *Evening Fire-Side, or Weekly Intelligence in the Civil, Natural, Moral, Literary and Religions Worlds*, 5 January 1805, 31–32 (quotation). See also Mabel L. Webber, "The Thomas Pinckney Family of South Carolina," *South Carolina Historical and Genealogical Magazine* 39 (January 1938), 24; *South Carolina Gazette and Public Advertiser*, 22 June 1785. For Huger's reputation, see Margaret Middleton Rivers Eastman et al., *The Huguenot Church in Charleston* (Charleston: History Press, 2018), 153.
27. Harriott Pinckney Horry to Elizabeth Izard Blake, 16 April 1782, DE. See also Charles Cotesworth Pinckney to Harriott Pinckney Horry, 3 July 1787, DE; Thomas Pinckney to Harriott Pinckney Horry, 6 February 1788, DE. For expenses, see Daniel (Charles Lucas Pinckney) Horry account, 25 December 1784 to 24 June 1785, DE.
28. Eliza Lucas Pinckney to Daniel (Charles Lucas Pinckney) Horry, 16 April 1782, DE (first quotation); Eliza Lucas Pinckney to Daniel (Charles Lucas Pinckney) Horry, 18 February 1787, DE (second quotation).

29. Edward Rutledge to George Washington, 24 January 1790, *The Papers of George Washington*, Presidential Series, 16 vols., ed. Dorothy Twohig et al. (Charlottesville: University Press of Virginia/University of Virginia Press, 1987–present), 5: 58 [hereinafter *PGW (P)*]; George Washington to Lafayette, 26 April 1790, *PGW (P)* 5: 60, fn. 3. For his life, see G. Melvin Herndon, "Pinckney Horry, 1769–1828: Rebel without a Cause," *Georgia Historical Quarterly* 70 (Summer 1986): 232–253.
30. Harriott Pinckney Horry to Miss A, c. 1786, DE; Harriott Pinckney Horry, Jr. to Eliza Lucas Pinckney, 25 December 1780, DE; Pinckney, *A Notice of the Pinckneys*, 7–8 (quotation, 8).
31. Thomas Pinckney to Eliza Lucas Pinckney, 29–30 August 1786; Thomas Pinckney to Eliza Lucas Pinckney, 16 September 1786; Thomas Pinckney to Harriott Pinckney Horry, 19 August 1789; Eliza Lucas Pinckney to George Keate, 2 April 1786, all in DE.
32. Harriott Pinckney Horry to Lady Augusta Mackenzie Murray, 8 January 1790, DE. See also Harriott Horry Ravenel, *Eliza Pinckney* (New York: Charles Scribner's Sons, 1896), 312.
33. Charles Cotesworth Pinckney to Harriott Pinckney Horry, 17 April 1790, DE.
34. Harriott Pinckney Horry to Lady Augusta Mackenzie Murray, 8 January 1790, DE. See also Schulz, "Eliza Lucas Pinckney and Harriott Pinckney Horry."
35. Archibald Henderson, *Washington's Southern Tour, 1791* (Boston: Houghton Mifflin, 1923), 138; Zara Anishanslin, *Portrait of a Woman in Silk: Hidden Histories of the British Atlantic World* (New Haven: Yale University Press, 2016), 310; *PGW (P)* 8: 99.
36. Harriott Pinckney Horry to George Washington, 14 April 1791, DE; *PGW (P)* 8: 99. See also Anzilotti, *In the Affairs of the World*, 163–164; T. H. Breen, *George Washington's Journey: The President Forges a New Nation* (New York: Simon and Schuster, 2016), 10–11.
37. For housewares, see Daniel Huger Horry, Jr. Estate Inventory, 16 January 1786, DE.
38. George Washington to Charles Pinckney, 11 January 1790, *PGW (P)* 4: 562. For the tours, see Breen, *George Washington's Journey*.
39. John Rutledge, Jr. to Thomas Pinckney, 28 April 1791, DE; Breen, *George Washington's Journey*, 73.
40. Ravenel, *Eliza Pinckney*, 311.
41. Henderson, *Washington's Southern Tour*, 138.
42. Breen, *George Washington's Journey*, 11; Henderson, *Washington's Southern Tour*, 139–140.
43. Quoted in Henderson, *Washington's Southern Tour*, 152.
44. Charles Pinckney to George Washington, 26 April 1791, *PGW (P)* 8: 138; Matthews, *Forgotten Founder*, 70–74.
45. Donald Jackson and Dorothy Twohig, eds., *The Diaries of George Washington*, 6 vols. (Charlottesville: University Press of Virginia, 1976–1979), 6: 126–128.
46. *Diaries of George Washington*, 6: 132.
47. Henderson, *Washington's Southern Tour*, 178, 182.
48. Washington asked Charles Cotesworth and his brother-in-law in the same letter. Both men declined. George Washington to Charles Cotesworth Pinckney and

Edward Rutledge, 24 May 1792, Founders Online, https://founders.archives.gov/; Matthews, *Forgotten Founder*, 76.

49. Eliza Lucas Pinckney to Daniel (Charles Lucas Pinckney) Horry, 7 August 1783, DE.

16. *ONE LAST JOURNEY*

1. Thomas Pinckney to Thomas Jefferson, 7 August 1792, Founders Online, https://founders.archives.gov/; *The Papers of George Washington*, Presidential Series, 16 vols., ed. Dorothy Twohig et al. (Charlottesville: University Press of Virginia/University of Virginia Press, 1987–present), 10: 467, fn. 13 [hereinafter *PGW (P)*]; Charles Cotesworth Pinckney, *Life of General Thomas Pinckney* (1895; Memphis: General Books, 2012), 25; Thomas Pinckney to George Washington, 29 November 1791, *PGW (P)* 9: 142, fn. 2 (first quotation); Thomas Pinckney to Thomas Jefferson, 13 December 1792, *The Papers of Thomas Jefferson*, vol. 24, ed. John Catanzariti (Princeton: Princeton University Press, 1990), 736 (second quotation).
2. Charles Cotesworth Pinckney to Thomas Pinckney, 25 May 1792, DE.
3. Charles Cotesworth Pinckney to Thomas Pinckney, 27 August 1792, DE.
4. Charles Cotesworth Pinckney to Thomas Pinckney, 27 August 1792, DE.
5. Charles Cotesworth Pinckney to Thomas Pinckney, 16 April 1793, DE; George Washington to Thomas Pinckney, 25 February 1795, *PGW (P)* 17: 580. George Washington wrote this after he developed a skin cancer. See also www.mountvernon.org/george-washington/cancer. For Philadelphia as a center of medical innovation, see Daniel Kilbride, *An American Aristocracy: Southern Planters in Antebellum Philadelphia* (Columbia: University of South Carolina Press, 2006), chapter 4.
6. Recounted in Steven Johnson, *The Ghost Map: The Story of London's Most Terrifying Epidemic and How It Changed Science, Cities, and the Modern World* (New York: Riverhead Books, 2006), 63. Elizabeth Marsh had a mastectomy in Calcutta in 1785; see Linda Colley, *The Ordeal of Elizabeth Marsh: A Woman in World History* (New York: Random House, 2007), 288–290.
7. Abigail Adams to John Quincy Adams, 17 November 1811, in *Abigail Adams: Letters,* ed. Edith Gelles (New York: Library of America, 2016), 846–850 (quotation 849); Benjamin Rush to John Adams, 20 September 1811, in *Letters of Benjamin Rush,* 2 vols., ed. L. H. Butterfield (Princeton: Princeton University Press for American Philosophical Society, 1951), 2: 1104. See also Edith B. Gelles, *Portia: The World of Abigail Adams* (Bloomington: Indiana University Press, 1992), 159–167; Woody Holton, *Abigail Adams, A Life* (New York: Free Press, 2009), 367–371.
8. Charles Cotesworth Pinckney to Thomas Pinckney, 16 April 1793, DE.
9. Charles Cotesworth Pinckney to Thomas Pinckney, 16 April 1793, DE.
10. Charles Cotesworth Pinckney to Thomas Pinckney, 16 April 1793, DE; "Journal of Josiah Quincy, Jr.," *Proceedings of the Massachusetts Historical Society* 49 (October 1915–June 1916), 434–435.
11. Charles Cotesworth Pinckney to Thomas Pinckney, 16 April 1793, DE.
12. Gadsden and Hall to Thomas Pinckney, 6 May 1793, DE.
13. Harriott Pinckney Horry, 1793 Travel Journal, April–December 1793, DE.

14. Harriott Pinckney Horry to Elizabeth Brewton Pinckney, 10 May 1796, DE; Harriott Pinckney Horry Will, 29 March 1828, DE.
15. For their plan and one woman's escape, see Erica Armstrong Dunbar, *Never Caught: The Washingtons' Relentless Pursuit of Their Runaway Slave, Ona Judge* (New York: Atria, 2017).
16. For context, see Cynthia M. Kennedy, *Braided Relations, Entwined Lives: The Women of Charleston's Urban Slave Society* (Bloomington: Indiana University Press, 2005), chapter 10.
17. Kilbride, *An American Aristocracy,* 5.
18. Harriott Pinckney Horry, 1793 Travel Journal, April–December 1793, DE.
19. Roger Parker Saunders to Thomas Pinckney, 23 April 1793, DE.
20. Charles Pinckney to George Washington, 20 September 1791, Founders Online. For an overview, see Laurent Dubois, *Avengers of the New World: The Story of the Haitian Revolution* (Cambridge: Harvard University Press, 2004). For effects in America, see James Alexander Dun, *Dangerous Neighbors: Making the Haitian Revolution in Early America* (Philadelphia: University of Pennsylvania Press, 2016). For South Carolinians' reactions, see Rachel N. Klein, *Unification of a Slave State: The Rise of the Planter Class in the South Carolina Backcountry, 1760–1808* (Chapel Hill: University of North Carolina Press, 1990), 210–211, 234–235; Marty D. Matthews, *Forgotten Founder: The Life and Times of Charles Pinckney* (Columbia: University of South Carolina Press, 2004), 77–79, 88; Edward B. Rugemer, *Slave Law and the Politics of Resistance in the Early Atlantic World* (Cambridge: Harvard University Press, 2018), 233–242.
21. Harriott Pinckney Horry, 1793 Travel Journal, 10–13 April 1793, DE.
22. Harriott Pinckney Horry, 1793 Travel Journal, 16–18 April 1793, DE (quotation 16 April).
23. Harriott Pinckney Horry, 1793 Travel Journal, 19–20 April 1793, DE.
24. Harriott Pinckney Horry, 1793 Travel Journal, 20 April 1793, DE. Eliza Lucas Pinckney (Eliza's granddaughter) married Ralph DeLancey Izard (Alice's son) in 1808.
25. Harriott Pinckney Horry, 1793 Travel Journal, 20–21 April 1793, DE.
26. Harriott Pinckney Horry, 1793 Travel Journal, 21 April 1793, DE; George Washington to Samuel and Elizabeth Willing Powel, 24 April 1793, *PGW (P)* 12: 477; Patricia Brady, *Martha Washington: An American Life* (New York: Viking, 2005), 195; Harriott Pinckney Horry, 1793 Travel Journal, 7 May 1793, DE (quotation). For Adams's absence, see Holton, *Abigail Adams*, 283.
27. Charles Cotesworth Pinckney to Thomas Pinckney, 9 May 1793, DE.
28. Thomas Pinckney to Thomas Jefferson, 31 January 1793; Thomas Jefferson to Thomas Pinckney, 12 April 1793, both in Founders Online.
29. Thomas Pinckney to Harriott Pinckney Horry, 27 January 1793, DE.
30. Charles Cotesworth Pinckney to Thomas Pinckney, 21 May 1793, DE.
31. Charles Cotesworth Pinckney to Thomas Pinckney, 21 May 1793, DE.
32. William Ward Burrows to Thomas Pinckney, 27 April 1793, DE.
33. For a brief overview of Philadelphia, see Gordon S. Wood, *Empire of Liberty: A History of the Early Republic, 1789–1815* (New York: Oxford University Press, 2009), 142–143. For Ricketts's circus, see George Washington to Samuel and Elizabeth

Willing Powel, 24 April 1793, *PGW (P)* 12: 477. For Washington, DC, plans (including quotation), see *Pennsylvania Gazette*, 24 April 1793. For Genêt, see Carol Berkin, *A Sovereign People: The Crises of the 1790s and the Birth of American Nationalism* (New York: Basic, 2017), part 2.

34. Harriott Pinckney Horry, 1793 Travel Journal, 7–8 May 1793, DE.
35. Harriott Pinckney Horry, 1793 Travel Journal, 9 May 1793, DE.
36. Harriott Pinckney Horry, 1793 Travel Journal, 9 May 1793, DE.
37. Harriott Pinckney Horry, 1793 Travel Journal, 10 May 1793, DE.
38. Harriott Pinckney Horry, 1793 Travel Journal, 10 June 1793, DE.
39. William Ward Burrows to Thomas Pinckney, 27 May 1793, DE; Charles Cotesworth Pinckney to Thomas Pinckney, 17 July 1793, DE.
40. Thomas Pinckney to Harriott Pinckney Horry, 9 July 1793, DE; Harriott Pinckney Horry, 1793 Travel Journal, 5 July 1793, DE.
41. Brady, *Martha Washington*, 199; Cokie Roberts, *Founding Mothers: The Women Who Raised Our Nation* (New York: Perennial, 2004), 266; Billy G. Smith, *Ship of Death: A Voyage That Changed the Atlantic World* (New Haven: Yale University Press, 2013), 204–216 (quotation 216). For context, see Thomas A. Apel, *Feverish Bodies, Enlightened Minds: Science and the Yellow Fever Controversy in the Early American Republic* (Stanford: Stanford University Press, 2016); Kathleen M. Brown, *Foul Bodies: Cleanliness in Early America* (New Haven: Yale University Press, 2009), chapter 7; Elaine Forman Crane, ed., *The Diary of Elizabeth Drinker: The Life Cycle of an Eighteenth-Century Woman,* abridged ed. (Philadelphia: University of Pennsylvania Press, 2010), 111–121; J. H. Powell, *Bring Out Your Dead: The Great Plague of Yellow Fever in Philadelphia in 1793* (Philadelphia: University of Pennsylvania Press, 1949); Smith, *Ship of Death*, chapters 8–9.
42. Harriott Pinckney Horry to Alice DeLancey Izard, c. June 1793, DE.
43. Harriott Horry Ravenel, *Eliza Pinckney* (New York: Charles Scribner's Sons, 1896), 317; Eliza Lucas Pinckney, "Days sett apart to be rememberd," DE.
44. Eliza Lucas to Thomas Lucas, c. 1743, *The Letterbook of Eliza Lucas Pinckney, 1739–1762,* ed. Elise Pinckney (Columbia: University of South Carolina Press, 1997), 63 (hereinafter *Letterbook*).
45. Eliza Lucas Pinckney to Ann Mildrum Lucas, 25 September 1758, DE.
46. Eliza Lucas to Thomas Lucas, 22 May 1742, *Letterbook*, 40.

EPILOGUE

1. "Marriages and Death Notices from the City Gazette," *South Carolina Historical and Genealogical Magazine* 21 (October 1920), 159; Eliza Lucas to Thomas Lucas, c. 1743, *The Letterbook of Eliza Lucas Pinckney, 1739–1762,* ed. Elise Pinckney (Columbia: University of South Carolina Press, 1997), 71.
2. "Conservation Complete for the Eliza Lucas Pinckney Gown," The Charleston Museum, www.charlestonmuseum.org/news-events/conservation-complete-for-the-eliza-lucas-pinckney-gown/.
3. Special thanks to Anne and Bill Williams, current residents of Ripley House, who showed me the property in 2018. Regarding Eliza's other homes, Wappoo is a

residential subdivision, and Belmont is part of a U.S. naval site. Harriott's Hampton is a state historic site. Fanny and Thomas's George Street mansion is headquarters for the Charleston Spoleto Festival. One of Charles Cotesworth's homes is part of Charleston's famous "Rainbow Row."

4. Harriott Pinckney Horry to William Ward Burrows, c. 1796, DE; Billy G. Smith, *Ship of Death: A Voyage That Changed the Atlantic World* (New Haven: Yale University Press, 2013), 210.
5. Harriott Pinckney Horry to William Ward Burrows, c. 1796, DE; Harriott Pinckney Horry Will, 29 March 1828, DE. St. Peter's exhumation records are incomplete from this era and the church archives yield no clear answers. St. Peter's Church Archives, Philadelphia. Special thanks to Chris Phillips for this information.
6. Jane Franklin Mecom is likewise in an unknown grave. Jill Lepore, *Book of Ages: The Life and Opinions of Jane Franklin* (New York: Knopf, 2013), 247–249.
7. "Marriages and Death Notices from the City Gazette," 158–159; "To The Earl of Warwick, on the Death of Mr. Addison," *The Poetical Works of Thomas Tickell* (London: C. Cooke, 1796), 95.
8. "Marriages and Death Notices from the City Gazette," 159.
9. Marty D. Matthews, *Forgotten Founder: The Life and Times of Charles Pinckney* (Columbia: University of South Carolina, 2004), 135. For Sunday dinners, see Thomas Pinckney to Harriott Pinckney Horry, 26 January 1817, DE. For Eliza's image, see also Barbara L. Bellows, "Eliza Lucas Pinckney: The Evolution of an Icon," *South Carolina Historical Magazine* 106 (April–July 2005): 147–165.
10. William Gilmore Simms, "A Memoir of the Pinckney Family of South Carolina," in Henry B. Dawson, *The Historical Magazine, and Notes and Queries, Concerning the Antiquities, History and Biography of America,* vol. 2, 2nd series (New York: J. M. Bradstreet and Son, 1867), 136 (first quotation); Maria Henrietta Pinckney, *A Notice of the Pinckneys* (Charleston: Evans and Cogswell, 1860), 11; Charles Cotesworth Pinckney, *Life of General Thomas Pinckney* (1895; Memphis: General Books, 2012), 52; Harriott Horry Ravenel, *Eliza Pinckney* (New York: Charles Scribner's Sons, 1896), viii, 317, 320.
11. Eliza Lucas Pinckney to [Charles Cotesworth Pinckney], 10 September 1785, DE; David Ramsay, *The History of South Carolina, from Its First Settlement in 1670 to the Year 1808,* 2 vols. (Charleston, 1809), 2: 209–210; Bellows, "Eliza Lucas Pinckney," 150.
12. Harriott Pinckney Horry, c. 1829, DE; Harriott Pinckney Horry to Margaret Ann Glover, c. 1829, DE; Harriott Pinckney Rutledge Holbrook to Caroline Seabrook, 21 December 1843, DE; Ravenel, *Eliza Pinckney*, 286 (quotation).
13. Harriott Pinckney Holbrook, ed., *Journal and Letters of Eliza Lucas: Now First Printed* (privately printed, 1850); Pinckney, *A Notice of the Pinckneys*; Ravenel, *Eliza Pinckney.* Other family writings include Harriott Pinckney Horry Travel Journals, 1795 and 1815, DE; Richard J. Hooker, ed., *A Colonial Plantation Cookbook: The Receipt Book of Harriott Pinckney Horry, 1770* (Columbia: University of South Carolina Press, 1984); Maria Henrietta Pinckney, *The Quintessence of Long Speeches Arranged as a Catechism* (Charleston: A. E. Miller, 1830); Charles F. McCombs, ed., *Letterbook of Mary Stead Pinckney, November 14, 1796 to August 29, 1797* (New York: Grolier Club, 1946);

Pinckney, *Life of General Thomas Pinckney*; Anna Wells Rutledge, ed., "Letters from Thomas Pinckney, Jr. to Harriott Pinckney," *South Carolina Historical and Genealogical Magazine* 41 (July 1940): 99–116.

14. The University of South Carolina Press reissued Elise Pinckney's edition of the letterbook in 1997. The Papers of Eliza Lucas Pinckney and Harriott Pinckney Horry Digital Edition launched in 2012. Schulz and her team thereafter turned to Charles Cotesworth Pinckney, Thomas Pinckney, and Charles Pinckney (Eliza's grandnephew). That project, The Papers of the Revolutionary Era Pinckney Statesmen, launched in 2016.

15. For leading scholars' analyses of women's circumscribed roles in the early Republic, see Linda K. Kerber, *Women of the Republic: Intellect and Ideology in Revolutionary America* (Chapel Hill: University of North Carolina Press, 1980); Cynthia A. Kierner, *Beyond the Household: Women's Place in the Early South, 1700–1835* (Ithaca, NY: Cornell University Press, 1998); Mary Beth Norton, *Liberty's Daughters: The Revolutionary Experience of American Women, 1750–1800* (New York: Little, Brown, 1980); Rosemarie Zagarri, *Revolutionary Backlash: Women and Politics in the Early American Republic* (Philadelphia: University of Pennsylvania Press, 2007). For independent and powerful women, see Catherine Allgor, *Parlor Politics: In Which the Ladies of Washington Help Build a City and a Government* (Charlottesville: University Press of Virginia, 2000); Zara Anishanslin, *Portrait of a Woman in Silk: Hidden Histories of the British Atlantic World* (New Haven: Yale University Press, 2016); Patricia Cleary, *Elizabeth Murray: A Woman's Pursuit of Independence in Eighteenth-Century America* (Amherst: University of Massachusetts Press, 2000); Ellen Hartigan-O'Connor, *The Ties That Buy: Women and Commerce in Revolutionary America* (Philadelphia: University of Pennsylvania Press, 2009); Alexia Jones Helsley, "Rebecca Brewton Motte: Revolutionary South Carolinian," in *South Carolina Women: Their Lives and Times,* vol. 1, ed. Marjorie Julian Spruill, Valinda W. Littlefield, and Joan Marie Johnson (Athens: University of Georgia Press, 2009), 109–126; Woody Holton, *Abigail Adams, A Life* (New York: Free Press, 2009); Daniel Kilbride, *An American Aristocracy: Southern Planters in Antebellum Philadelphia* (Columbia: University of South Carolina Press, 2006), especially regarding Margaret Manigault; G. Winston Lane, Jr., "Economic Power among Eighteenth-Century Women of the Carolina Lowcountry," in *Money, Trade, and Power: The Evolution of Colonial South Carolina's Plantation Society,* ed. Jack P. Greene, Rosemary Brana-Shute, and Randy J. Sparks (Columbia: University of South Carolina Press, 2001), 322–343; Barbara B. Oberg, ed., *Women in the American Revolution: Gender, Politics, and the Domestic World* (Charlottesville: University of Virginia Press, 2019), especially essays by Ami Pflugrad-Jackisch, Susan Hanket Brandt, and Martha J. King; Shelia L. Skemp, *First Lady of Letters: Judith Sargent Murray and the Struggle for Female Independence* (Philadelphia: University of Pennsylvania Press, 2009); Rosemarie Zagarri, *A Woman's Dilemma: Mercy Otis Warren and the American Revolution,* 2nd ed. (Malden, MA: Wiley Blackwell, 2015). For examples beyond British North America, see Kit Candlin and Cassandra Pybus, *Enterprising Women: Gender, Race, and Power in the Revolutionary Atlantic* (Athens: University of Georgia Press, 2015); Linda Colley, *The Ordeal of Elizabeth Marsh: A Woman in World History* (New York: Random House, 2007); Ann M. Little, *The Many Captivities of Esther Wheelwright* (New Haven: Yale University Press, 2016).

Index

Illustrations and maps are indicated by italicized page numbers.